# Lives Across Cultures

## Cross-Cultural Human Development

### Sixth Edition

**Harry W. Gardiner**
*University of Wisconsin–La Crosse*

 Pearson

330 Hudson Street, NY NY 10013

**Portfolio Manager:** Priya Christopher
**Content Producer:** Allison Campbell
**Portfolio Manager Assistant:** Anna Austin
**Content Producer Manager:** Maureen Richardson
**Content Development Manager:** Gabrielle White
**Art/Designer:** iEnergizer Aptara®, Ltd
**Digital Studio Course Producer:** Elissa Senra-Sargent

**Full-Service Project Manager:** iEnergizer Aptara®, Ltd
**Compositor:** iEnergizer Aptara®, Ltd
**Printer/Binder:** LSC Communications Owensville
**Cover Printer:** Phoenix
**Cover Design:** Lumina Datamatics, Inc.
**Cover Art:** Cienpies Design/Shutterstock

Acknowledgements of third party content appear on pages 188–192, which constitute an extension of this copyright page.

**Library of Congress Cataloging-in-Publication Data**

Names: Gardiner, Harry W., author.
Title: Lives across cultures : cross-cultural human development/Harry W.
    Gardiner, University of Wisconsin, La Crosse.
Description: Sixth Edition. | Boston : Pearson Education, Inc. publishing as
    Allyn & Bacon, [2018] | Includes bibliographical references and index.
Identifiers: LCCN 2016052557 | ISBN 9780134629445 (alk. paper) |
    ISBN 0134629442 (alk. paper)
Subjects: LCSH: Ethnopsychology—Cross-cultural studies. |
    Socialization—Cross-cultural studies. | Cognition and
    culture—Cross-cultural studies. | Personality and culture—Cross-cultural
    studies. | Developmental psychology—Cross-cultural studies.
Classification: LCC GN502 .G37 2016 | DDC 155.8/2—dc23 LC record available at
    https://lccn.loc.gov/2016052557

1  16

**Books a la Carte**
ISBN-10:    0-13-462944-2
ISBN-13: 978-0-13-462944-5

# Contents

# Foreword

It is an honor, once again, to have been invited to write the foreword to this—the sixth—edition of *Lives Across Cultures*. As an ongoing project, these editions have occupied the thoughts and actions of its author, Harry W. Gardiner, for more than two decades and influenced thousands of students. Following in the footsteps of its five predecessors, both with and without coauthors who dropped by the wayside for various reasons, this edition is worthy of continued admiration and celebration. At the same time, and with the same drum roll of eager endorsement, it is also appropriate to use this occasion to celebrate Harry's life and career. Personally, I want to thank him for his kindness in inviting me to write a few words about this revision. Before you read these wonderful pages, I offer a little historical context to bolster these accolades.

The psychological study of culture (and the cultural study of psychology) has a very long past but a short history. One could delve into the dusty tomes of long ago and find many instances of scholarly interest in the influence of culture on a wide range of topics that address how humans, regardless of culture, develop and cope with all that they face in the cradle-to-grave saga of their lives. All aspects of academic and applied psychology have been investigated to some extent against the background of a plethora of cultures, with some going back more than 2,000 years. The breadth and depth of such research and study is especially true in the realm of developmental and social psychology. Moreover, the precursors of such efforts importantly laid the foundation for what many have called the "modern movement" in culture-oriented psychology.

The mid-1960s marked the beginning of an explosion of interest by rapidly increasing numbers of psychologists in culture and its proxies, including diversity and ethnicity. During about a ten-year period, important books were written, special small conferences were organized, journals were inaugurated, and departments of psychology in some colleges and universities began offering courses that focused on culture. From the perspective of cross-cultural psychology, the union bringing together the *Journal of Cross-Cultural Psychology* and the International Association for Cross-Cultural Psychology (IACCP) was pivotal. The former began publication in 1970, and the inaugural meeting of the IACCP took place in 1972. This marked the first time that a psychology journal and an international psychological association, both with an exclusive focus on culture, joined hands. At that meeting, which was held at the University of Hong Kong, 105 psychologists from eighteen countries met each other, most for the first time. Although very few women registered for that first conference, a shortage of women in the field is no longer an issue. Reflecting vast demographic changes in American psychology, as well as in international psychology as a discipline, the majority of IACCP members are women, and many of them are currently in leadership positions. Nevertheless, it was thrilling for those of us who attended to meet many people we knew about but had never seen. Forty-seven (45%) of the attendees were from the United States. I was one of them, and so was Harry. Both of us were junior faculty members with aspirations to make culture the centerpiece of our careers. The four-day program had an aura of uniqueness and excitement. We seemed to sense that this inaugural meeting was the start of something special. That seminal event helped catapult Harry into a career that was influential and inspirational, especially in the cultural dimensions of developmental psychology. Several years later, the multidisciplinary Society for Cross-Cultural Research was formed, and Harry served as its president for two years.

I assume that most people who read this book are doing so because it is part of an undergraduate course in developmental psychology. I further assume that most will find it to be one of the more informed and easy-to-read academic texts that they will have the pleasure of reading. Written in an informal, conversational style, it provides a broad and thoughtfully updated account of "growing up" from the perspective of psychological science. In the early chapters, Harry gives an overview of the ways in which psychologists approach the psychological study of culture. Believing that it is important to know about the atmosphere that surrounded Harry, me, and our aging cohorts during that period of early growth, I want to encourage readers to learn more about influential precursors in the development of what has become a much more culturally infused psychology. To do this, I recommend reading more complete details in "Chronological Benchmarks in Cross-Cultural Psychology. Foreword to the Encyclopedia of Cross-Cultural Psychology," which is easily accessible in Unit 1 of the *Online Readings in Psychology and Culture* (available at http://scholarworks.gvsu.edu/orpc/contents.html).

As indicated previously, prior to the mid-1960s, psychologists gave relatively little attention to culture. Introductory psychology texts in the United States barely mentioned culture, the tacit assumption being that the content of these texts was valid around the world. (See "The Introductory Psychology Text and Cross-Cultural

Psychology: Beyond Ekman, Whorf, and Biased I.Q. Tests," published in Unit 11 of the aforementioned *Online Readings in Psychology and Culture*; available at http://scholarworks. gvsu.edu/orpc/contents.html). There were *no* texts or psychology journals expressly dedicated to research and scholarship in psychology and culture, and organizations totally focusing on culture did not exist. The few scholars at U.S. colleges and universities, and a smattering of others elsewhere around the world who wanted to expand psychology's horizons, were often viewed as "lone wolves" in their departments. Some were chided for being part of a "lunatic fringe" of psychologists who had the audacity to challenge, as was often the case, the veracity and generalizability of what was considered universally valid research in "mainstream" psychology. Harry was one of these pioneers.

We have seen great strides in attention given to culture and ethnicity as critically important factors in the shaping of lives. In fact, the attention given to culture by increasing numbers of psychologists has been one of the most striking developments in psychology and allied disciplines in the past 50 years. The sparse coverage of culture half a century ago has been replaced by a phenomenal spread of interest. For instance, although it used to be a bit of a struggle to find culture-oriented articles in more than a small handful of journals, one can now easily find such articles in dozens of journals and books. Much of this enriched coverage has been enhanced by the Internet. When Harry began his career, correspondence with like-minded psychologists was slow and usually carried out by either "snail mail" or air mail for most foreign connections. It usually took at least a week to exchange letters or share data. There was no Internet, so e-mail belonged in the realm of science fiction. There were no iPhones or iPads; no Twitter, Facebook, Instagram, Snapchat, Skype, or You Tube; or anything else that has strikingly increased the speed of scholarly interaction. Back then, most letters were typed on real clickity-clacking typewriters with inked ribbons and what was

called "onion skin paper" to make carbon copies. Word processing programs simply did not exist. Now, the exchange and sharing of massive amounts of material takes place in seconds, even if the exchange is between one researcher doing work in Siberia and another living in a rural village in India.

Enough of a brief walk down memory lane. I mainly want to emphasize that Harry and a growing number of colleagues around the world have gone to lengthy efforts and shown great tenacity and dedication to increasing the attention given to culture and ethnicity in the field of psychology. Harry is admirably informed about the ways in which culture and ethnicity help paint a more complex and informed portrait of human development. We can all be thankful that Harry has completed this sixth edition of *Lives Across Cultures*. Nothing would satisfy the gentle and self-effacing Harry more than knowing he has helped a new wave of students appreciate the many rich and unique ways that culture shapes every fiber of our being.

Thanks, Harry, for all you have done in your half century of consistent academic excellence.

Walter J. Lonner
*Professor Emeritus*
*Western Washington University*
*Bellingham, Washington*
*October 2016*

Walter J. Lonner has been involved in cross-cultural psychological research for nearly forty years. He is Founding and Special Issues Editor of the *Journal of Cross-Cultural Psychology*, the flagship publication in this area of international scholarship. A charter member, past president, and Honorary Fellow of the International Association for Cross-Cultural Psychology, Lonner has been involved in various capacities with about forty books on cross-cultural psychological research and applications.

# Preface

Welcome to the sixth edition of *Lives Across Cultures*! When this book was "born" in 1998, it had three "parents"—Harry Gardiner, Jay Mutter, and Corinne Kosmitzki. Jay left in 2002, when the book was four years old and the second edition appeared. Corinne and I continued "raising" (or revising) the text through its early childhood (third edition) in 2005, when it turned seven years old; its later childhood (fourth edition) in 2008, when it turned ten years old; and into its early adolescence (fifth edition) in 2011, when it became thirteen years old. With this sixth edition, *Lives Across Cultures* celebrates its eighteenth birthday. Corinne has decided to move on, so I am now the book's "single parent," ready to bring it into adulthood. There have been many changes as the text has matured, and it has been very interesting to travel with it through these stages of development. If readers continue their interest in it, then there are certain to be more editions in the years ahead.

When the first edition appeared in 1998, the goal was to share with readers the discoveries of the exciting and ever-expanding world of cross-cultural human development. As with each of the previous editions, the sixth edition links basic principles to practical everyday events to help readers cultivate a global and multicultural perspective on behavior and gain an improved understanding of and appreciation for development as it takes place in diverse cultural settings around the world. This approach is even more important in today's world than it was when introduced in the groundbreaking first edition.

As a teacher and cross-cultural researcher with extensive experience in small college and large university settings in the United States and abroad, the author, in common with previous editions, focuses on connections between personal experiences and the more formal theories and research that make up this discipline. He attempts to present it all in way that is easy to understand, engaging, and informative to readers. The author still believes readers learn best by example—both the ones presented here and those they create from their own experiences.

## Organization of the Text

The presentation of cross-cultural material in this text continues to differ in numerous significant ways from other books. Most notable is the effort to integrate and synthesize viewpoints and perspectives from various disciplines, including psychology, anthropology, sociology, and the health sciences.

Development is viewed from a *cross-cultural perspective*, designed to expand awareness and sensitivity to global similarities and differences in behavior, while helping reduce any ethnocentric thinking (judgment of other cultures or people by one's own values and standards), whether conscious or not. Readers are presented with numerous opportunities to experience variations in behavior not normally found in their own societies. Most important, this approach encourages readers to look more closely at the interconnections among culture, development, and behavior in their *own* lives and in others.

As the table of contents indicates, selected topics (e.g., socialization, language, personality, gender, family, social behavior) for which a substantial amount of cross-cultural research exists are discussed chronologically, demonstrating how behavioral processes unfold and change as individuals in multiple cultures pass from infancy and childhood through adolescence and into adulthood and old age.

## New to this Edition

The sixth edition retains the basic emphases of previous editions, particularly those of the fifth edition, whereby each chapter is placed within an ecological context. The chapters also include opening vignettes, which are discussed within each chapter, for better understanding of concepts and content. In addition, at several points throughout each chapter, readers are asked several questions that allow them to pause and reflect on important issues and on how the information they are reading applies to their own lives and to others with whom they are in contact. These questions appear in italics for greater attention.

As expected, this edition has been updated with the the latest in research findings and references. The chapters contain new photographs and boxed text, including new Points to Ponder material, to encourage readers to more closely observe their own and others' behavior, and critically evaluate it against the concepts presented throughout the book. Each chapter also contains new Study Questions.

- Chapter 1 includes expanded clarification of the distinction between emic-etic and individualism-collectivism, as well as additional information on the

Human Genome Project, including a website readers can access for further study.

- In Chapter 2, major theories are given expanded coverage, along with discussions of the strengths and limitations of each. This chapter also contains real-life examples of new applications of Bronfenbrenner's approach and applications of the developmental niche model to policy planning and early childhood development programs.

- New information on socialization, sleep, malnutrition, breastfeeding, and female genital mutilation, as well as an expanded discussion of China's "one child" policy are presented in Chapter 3.

- Chapter 4 includes new material on cultural images of aging, gay/lesbian relationships, and mothering and fathering, and an expanded discussion of the changing context of families and grandparents. Sections on mate selection, marriage and long-term relationships, and the transition to parenthood receive additional attention.

- Chapter 5 presents new research on cross-cultural comparisons of second language learning, as well as results from studies of dyslexia that provide insights into the relationships between cognition and language. This chapter also contains new material on reasoning and decision making in adulthood, including controversies surrounding cognitive aging.

- Chapter 6 has new material on environmental and genetic influences on temperament and personality development, cultural influences on identity formation, and changes in personality during later adulthood, as well as expanded coverage of the "aging" self.

- Chapter 7 focuses greater attention on early social relationships within the ecological context; the expanding roles of individualism and collectivism; and the critical issues of bullying, peer relationships, and play.

- Chapter 8 is devoted to culture and issues of gender and sexuality, with an expanded discussion of changing gender culture around the world, with attention paid to current issues such as transgenderism and gender neutral parenting.

- Chapter 9 focuses on ecological influences on health issues, illness behavior across cultures, obesity, eating disorders, acculturation, Alzheimer's, and coping strategies and behaviors.

- The final chapter, Chapter 10, was updated to reflect some of the future trends in cross-cultural developmental research and applications, and discusses how to meet the needs of individuals in an era of increasing globalization.

- The References section provides the latest citations, including a large number of works published since the last edition in 2010.

# Special Features

Most of the special features appearing in recent editions have been retained, although some have been revised. These include numerous interesting and readable pedagogical aids to assist readers in learning, remembering, and making practical use of the material covered.

## Opening Vignettes

Most chapters open with vignettes about two individuals from different areas of the world who illustrate several of the behaviors described in the chapter. Because a major goal of the text is to familiarize readers with as many cultures as possible, stories of individuals living in more than fifteen different cultures around the world are depicted. The development of these individuals is integrated into the chapter in which they appear, and their lives are discussed in terms of the behaviors being presented.

## Recurring Themes

Throughout each chapter, the principal themes (e.g., ecological and contextual approaches, developmental niche, developmental and cross-cultural perspectives) are regularly interwoven into the narrative to provide a comprehensive and cohesive understanding of development.

## Key Ideas

Efforts were taken to make concepts easy to understand by placing them in bold type the first time they appear, immediately defining them, and providing examples to illustrate their cultural relevance. For a quick review (or preview), each chapter ends with a concise summary of important points.

## Points to Ponder

Within each chapter, readers are asked to consider several questions relevant to themselves and others, the answers to which will help them better understand the ways in which culture influences behavior. Readers are asked to observe, analyze, and apply this information to various situations and to think critically about the meaning of these situations so they will better remember major points. Among topics discussed are understanding one's own developmental niche, observing public parenting, finding one's identity, and learning language.

## Further Readings

An annotated list of recommendations for further reading is provided at the end of the text. The books and articles suggested were selected for their ability to expand on topics covered in each chapter, as well as for their interesting and often amusing writing styles. Multiple URL addresses are included so readers can easily access additional information.

## Developmental Analysis

Carried over from the last edition is a series of Developmental Analysis boxes appearing in Chapters 3 to 9. Written in the first person, they tell the life story of Matilda "Maddi" Skelton, who engagingly applies important concepts to her own development over the lifespan. This pedagogical feature again helps clarify the material and provide continuity across chapters. It also encourages readers to write their own developmental analysis for a better understanding of how each one of them became the person he or she is today.

# Note to Instructors

*Lives Across Cultures* can be used as a core text in a course focusing on cultural similarities and differences in human development, whether it is in psychology, anthropology, or sociology. It can also be used as a supplement to basic courses such as General Psychology, Child and Adolescent Development, Lifespan Development, Cross-Cultural Psychology, Social Psychology, Cultural Anthropology, Sociology of the Family, and similar courses in which the instructor might want to provide a cultural focus not represented in standard textbooks.

# Note to Readers

You, the reader, will live in the world of tomorrow, where understanding and interacting with people of diverse cultural backgrounds will be a common everyday event and a prerequisite for success in the family, school, workplace, and society. It is for you that this book has been written. It is hoped that it will help you develop an appreciation for and sensitivity to the cultural similarities and differences that characterize those of us who live on Earth today, including your parents and grandparents, and those who will call it home in future

generations, including your children and grandchildren. It is also hoped that you will find this book both enjoyable and informative.

# Available Instructor Resources

The following resources are available for instructors and can be downloaded at http://www.pearsonhighered.com/irc. Login is required.

- **Instructor's Manual:** The instructor's manual is a wonderful tool for classroom preparation and management. Each chapter includes chapter objectives, suggested lecture topics, student activities, audiovisual materials, and things to do and think about. There is also a helpful list of journals, Internet resources, and professional organizations.
- **Test Bank:** The test bank portion contains a set of multiple-choice and short answer essay questions for each chapter to help students prepare for exams.

# Acknowledgments

The completion of a book like this cannot be accomplished without the generous assistance of a great many people. A genuine debt of gratitude is owed to the many reviewers of this new edition who offered valuable and significant suggestions and revisions for its improvement, many of which have found their way into this text.

Thanks also go to the editorial, production, and marketing staff at Pearson Education who contributed their time and talent to making this new edition possible.

Finally, a heartfelt thanks to my family, who has made this journey possible and supported my efforts over nearly two decades, a journey individuals and their ancestors have taken in various ways throughout history. For example, here is a picture of the hands of one-month-old Charlie Lamont, Harry and Ormsin Gardiner's grandson, born September 10, 2009, representing the "Alpha," or beginning, of life.

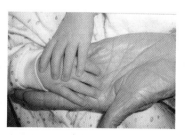

Charlie Lamont's hands

© Harry W. Gardiner

Next is a picture of the hands of 102-year-old Khun Mae Kasorn, the mother of Harry's Thai wife, representing the "Omega," or end, of a long and productive life. Khun Mae passed away on April 23, 2005.

Khun Mae Kasorn's hands

© Harry W. Gardiner

Separated by more than a century in age and by very different cultures thousands of miles apart, Charlie and his great grandmother symbolize but two unique examples of the ongoing development of the millions of "lives across cultures" to whom this book is dedicated.

Harry W. Gardiner
*Professor Emeritus*
*Psychology Department*
*University of Wisconsin–La Crosse*
*La Crosse, WI 54601*
*harry@gardiner.net*

# About the Author

**Harry Gardiner writing his first book**

© Harry W. Gardiner

I am Professor Emeritus at the University of Wisconsin–La Crosse, where I designed and taught courses in cross-cultural human development for more than twenty-five years. It was the inability to find a textbook for a course in cross-cultural human development that first led to the writing of this book. My undergraduate degree is from American International College, Springfield, Massachusetts, where I began my "international" quest so many years ago. My M.A. is from the University of Hawaii, where the real seeds of my interest in cross-cultural psychology were first planted. I completed my Ph.D. at Manchester University in England, where my personal journey into culture was forever changed when I met a young lady from Thailand, Ormsin Sornmoonpin, who was studying to be an electrical engineer.

I followed (or more accurately chased) her to Asia, where we were married in both Buddhist and Christian wedding ceremonies. I taught in the graduate program at Chulalongkorn University in Bangkok, Thailand, for two years before we moved to the United States. I "grew up" in an Asian American family, consisting of our two sons (Alan and Aldric) and two daughters (Alisa and Alexina), and now six grandchildren (Macinnes, Malinee, Sirina, Charlie, Eugene, and Eliza).

I was a charter member of the International Association for Cross-Cultural Psychology and have served as president of the Society for Cross-Cultural Research. I am currently a Consulting Editor for the *Journal of Cross-Cultural Psychology*. In addition to publishing articles in various journals and participating in national and international meetings, I have coauthored numerous chapters on cross-cultural topics for other books. I have engaged in training, teaching, and research in Europe, Asia, and the United States. In my "spare time," I enjoy writing for *Cobblestone*, a history magazine for young children, and have contributed interviews with Supreme Court Justice Sandra Day O'Connor; Muppet creator Jim Henson; Muriel Earhart

Morrissey, Amelia Earhart's sister; and Thomas Rockwell, son of Norman Rockwell, among others. Another great joy is watching the development of our six grandchildren as they navigate a much more culturally diversified world than I, or their parents, experienced at their ages.

**Harry and Ormsin's grandchildren: Mac, Malinee, Sirina, Charlie**

© Harry W. Gardiner

**Harry's children, Alisa, Alan, Alexina, and Aldric**

© Harry W. Gardiner

**Harry and Ormsin Gardiner at Machu Picchu, Peru**

© Harry W. Gardiner

# Chapter 1
# Introduction to Cross-Cultural Human Development

Books frequently begin by introducing their readers to the history of the field. This is certainly essential and, unfortunately, can sometimes be boring, but it will come later in this book (you can always skip it if you don't find it very interesting, *but* I highly recommended that you read it). Right now, I want to begin this text as I begin most of my classes—by relating a few of my own cross-cultural experiences in the hope you may find them not only interesting but also perhaps relevant in important ways to your own lives.

In the section About the Author, I mention that my wife, Ormsin, is from Thailand, and we have raised our four children in an Asian American family. My wife is the Asian, I am the American, and our children are the Asian Americans. I am the minority—the one with the blond hair and blue eyes. I don't like to admit it, but I'm also the shortest, making me a double minority! As you might imagine, raising children in a cross-cultural and bilingual home has resulted in many interesting and enlightening developmental experiences, some of which may help you better understand the processes involved in cross-cultural human development.

One experience concerns our eldest daughter, Alisa, and the way in which she became bilingual. Our cross-cultural family setting, similar to many others, provided a unique opportunity for this to occur. We were advised that the best approach to helping her become bilingual was to let her hear and speak both languages—Thai and English—without emphasizing that they *were* two languages. (Perhaps many of you have had similar experiences.) So, when she was an infant and young child, her mother spoke to her in Thai and I spoke to her in English. Then, one evening, when my daughter was about three years old, one of my Chinese students came to babysit. Alisa opened the front door, saw an Asian face, and began speaking Thai. The young lady patiently listened to her and then said, "I'm Chinese and I understand English, but I'll bet you were speaking to me in Thai, weren't you?" I watched as she thought about this and then turned to me and said, "I speak two languages, don't I? Daddy, I speak two languages!" I told her that indeed she did and asked, "What

did you think was happening all this time?" Alisa's reply, based on the experience of her unique developmental niche in a bilingual home, was, "I thought it was all one big language and Mommy understood some words and you understood others and . . . I understood them all!"

Throughout the chapters that follow, references are made to how important it is to understand culture, even one's own, and realize that not everyone has the same understanding of topics and events. Sometimes, when traveling, studying, or working in another culture, our experiences are frustrating, scary, or humorous. I had an opportunity to live in England for three years while completing my doctoral studies at the University of Manchester. During that time, there was one food craving I found nearly impossible to fulfill—*popcorn!* My roommate and I searched everywhere for it. The only place anything resembling it was available was at the cinema. The only problem—it was sticky, caramel-covered "goop," not the white, fluffy kernels sprinkled with salt and hot butter (and, in my case, garlic) with which we were familiar. Eventually, using the skills of Sherlock Holmes and Doctor Watson, we discovered small (tiny, actually) thirty-kernel bags of popping corn at the airport and bought the entire stock! A few days later, we visited a British family that had befriended us two "Yanks from across the pond" and took some with us. When we asked the husband if we could make some popcorn, he replied (much to our surprise), "No, that's impossible." When we asked why, he said, "Popcorn grows on bushes. You pick it and put caramel on it." We told him he might be confusing this with cotton, which grows on bushes but is not eaten! Nevertheless, he supplied us with a pot, and we put in some oil and threw in some kernels. When it began to make noise, we tried to explain that this was the corn popping. When it was done, we showed him. He took one look and immediately disappeared out the back door! A few minutes later, he returned with his neighbors, looked at us, and said, "Do it again!" For many years, I often thought I should open a stand on a street corner in London and surprise, amaze, and educate the British public with the wonders of popcorn! Now, if I could only get it to grow on bushes! The moral of this story: We all grow up in cultures where we understand what happens around us because the experiences are a shared familiar part of our environment and our daily lives. These experiences are not always easily understood by those living in different ecological settings, even within the same culture.

Harry Gardiner and his British friends making popcorn 30 years later.

(© Harry Gardiner)

More than three decades ago, the anthropologist Theodore Schwartz (1981), writing about the acquisition of culture, accurately declared that "anthropologists had ignored children in culture while developmental psychologists had ignored culture in children" (p. 4). Just two years later, John W. Berry (1983), a Canadian psychologist and pioneering researcher in cross-cultural psychology, noted that the discipline was "so culture-bound and culture-blind . . . [that] . . . it should not be employed as it is" (p. 449). Shortly thereafter, Gustav Jahoda (1986), a well-known European psychologist and early contributor to the developing discipline, was able to express a more optimistic view and point out that cross-cultural studies of human development had been steadily increasing in number. Yet, at the same time, he also criticized the field for being "too parochial in its orientation" (p. 418).

These were once considered serious criticisms of the newly emerging field. Fortunately, in, the years since, great strides have been made in our approaches to, and understanding of, cross-cultural human development. Throughout this book, the progress, excitement, and promise of this increasingly important and influencing area of study is described and discussed in detail.

In this first chapter, the foundation for the rest of the book is laid out by introducing some historical perspectives and expanding on some of the major concepts, themes, and issues briefly presented in the Preface. Let us begin by exploring the origins of cross-cultural human development.

## 1.1: What Is Cross-Cultural Human Development?

The field of cross-cultural psychology is remarkably diverse, and those who contribute to it bring with them a variety of viewpoints, including different definitions of the field itself. In Volume 1 of the revised *Handbook of Cross-Cultural Psychology*, Berry, Poortinga, and Pandey (1997) define **cross-cultural psychology** as *"the systematic study of relationships between the cultural context of human development and the behaviors that become established in the repertoire of individuals growing up in a particular culture"* (p. x). This definition clearly states that this is a *scientific* endeavor that shares with more familiar disciplines the use of theories, scientific methodologies, statistical procedures, and data analysis.

The term *human development* has also been defined in multiple ways. For the purpose of this text, **human development** is viewed as *changes in physical, psychological, and social behavior as experienced by individuals across the lifespan from conception to death.* Although this definition encompasses a wide range of experiences, the intention of this text is not to provide exhaustive and comprehensive coverage of all aspects of human development (Aren't you glad to hear that?). Instead, its goal is more limited, focusing on a number of representative topics that provide insight and understanding into how individuals develop and live their lives in different cultural settings. In doing this, examples from literally scores of societies throughout the world are presented. Considering the important dimensions just mentioned, and not finding the term **cross-cultural human development** adequately defined elsewhere, I recommend it be viewed as *cultural similarities and differences in developmental processes and their outcomes as expressed by behavior in individuals and groups.*

Because the term **culture** was just mentioned, it should be pointed out that most researchers agree that this is one of the most difficult and elusive social sciences terms to define. Almost everyone who studies culture has a different way of looking at it, reflecting, in part, different theories for understanding the concept and describing various forms of human behavior. E. B. Tylor (1871) was the first anthropologist to use the term in his two-volume work titled *Primitive Culture*. He defined culture as *"that complex whole which includes knowledge, belief, art, morals, laws, customs and any other capabilities and habits acquired by man as a member of society"* (p. 1). More than fifty years ago, two other anthropologists, Kroeber and Kluckhohn (1952) compiled a list of 164 definitions of the term!

In 2002, the United Nations Educational, Scientific and Cultural Organization (UNESCO) stated that culture is the *"set of distinctive spiritual, material, intellectual and emotional features of society or a social group, and that it encompasses, in addition to art and literature, lifestyles, ways of living together, value systems, traditions and beliefs"* (p. 1).

Azuma (2005) even proposed a new conceptualization of culture "beyond nationality, geography, class, and even ethnicity," which he tentatively calls "functional culture" (p. xii). It is his contention that "traditional culture" of past generations, uncontaminated and with distinct and static systems "envisioned by cultural anthropologists in the early 1900s[,] no longer exists" (p. xii). Rather, in the contemporary world, individuals come into contact with a variety of cultures as a result of the media, travel, reading, migration, and other activities, including, it might be added, such popular Internet social networks as Snapchat, Google+, Instagram, Pinterest, and YouTube.

## Points to Ponder

### Is Social Networking the New "Cultural Frontier"?

Today's widespread popularity of social networking helps create "an environment of connectedness," not always based in reality, among literally millions of individuals located around the world (often among individuals or in small groups). According to Brian Honigman (2012, November 29), who reported on social media statistics in *The Huffington Post*, Facebook has 850 million monthly users, with 43% being male and 57% female; the average user has 130 friends; and 21% of all users are from Asia. In 2012, there was a 41% growth in users from Brazil, India, Russia, South Korea, and Japan. On Twitter, 175 million tweets were sent each day during 2012, and the top three countries using Twitter are the United States with 107 million users, Brazil with 33 million, and Japan with nearly 30 million.

By 2015, of the 7.2 billion people on the planet, nearly 2.1 billion had social media accounts and 3.65 billion mobile users had access to the Internet using smartphones and tablets. Social networks in non–English-speaking countries, such as China and Russia, are growing at an even faster rate. The 1.4 billion Facebook users represented 47% of all Internet users. At last count, Twitter had 284 million users, 88% of whom accessed the application via mobile devices.

Social media has both advantages and disadvantages. On the positive side, individuals can connect with relatives, former friends, new friends, nurture relationships in a nonthreatening environment, and find and share information in real time. They can even find biological parents who gave them up for adoption. On the negative side, social media reduces or eliminates face-to-face socialization; diminishes the development of one's social skills, particularly among adolescents; and exposes individuals to harassment and/or bullying. It can also be huge waste of time. Whether social networks will be harmful to individuals, societies, or cultures is still unknown and will require more research. *What do you think? Which social media do you use? Which application is most important to you? How much time do you use each one? What do you see as the advantages and disadvantages for you personally?*

Returning to Azuma's (2005) comments on culture, "cultures interact with and influence each other," and traditions, which are part of functional culture, are "more fluid or fragmented" than they once were. In fact, cultures today import many of their features from other cultures and societies—features, which Azuma points out, "were quite foreign to people even a half century ago, and change and substitution of elements are constant" (p. xii). However, he goes on to emphasize that global culture does not become homogeneous because the way in which these features are distributed within cultures will differ as a result of "traditional emphasis, condition of industry and labor, natural resources, climate, or just by chance" (p. xii); and this will determine cultural specificity. He stresses that "such culture forms a developmental niche not as a loose collection of fragments but as a configuration that is structured yet inevitably fluid . . . [and] . . . Human development must be studied as embedded in a dynamically functioning group culture . . . [in which] . . . [m]ore lively understanding results from carefully analyzing how specific behaviors interact with cultural conditions that are always bound by time and place" (p. xii). As you will see later in this chapter and throughout the rest of this book, Azuma's contemporary view of culture fits very well with this text's definition and theoretical approach to understanding cross-cultural human development.

In the absence of an as yet widely agreed-on definition of **culture**, when the term is used in this text it will be referring to *the cluster of learned and shared beliefs, values (achievement, individualism, collectivism, etc.), practices (rituals and ceremonies), behaviors (roles, customs, traditions, etc.), symbols (institutions, language, ideas, objects, artifacts, etc.), and attitudes (moral, political, religious, etc.) that are characteristic of a particular group of people and that are communicated from one generation to another.*

A caveat regarding this definition may be in order before proceeding. Because there is no consensus regarding "the" definition of culture (and it is unlikely there ever will be), the definition presented here is a compilation of several previously published definitions combined with some original thoughts by the current author of what best constitutes this concept. As Shwalb (personal communication, 2005) has accurately pointed out, in most comparative studies, culture is "unfortunately equated with nationality, which is convenient for readers to understand . . . but not satisfying." He goes on to say that he would like to see culture "better distinguished conceptually from nationality, ethnicity, race, and religion." Many other social scientists, including the present author, would agree. However, as the reader might imagine, this effort, similar to defining culture, is a most difficult and complex task better left for another time.

As the field of cross-cultural psychology has evolved, concerns in the area of development have undergone a number of significant shifts. One hundred years ago, five major areas were of interest: emotional development, the biological basis of behavior, cognitive development, conscious and unconscious processes, and the role of self in development. During the 1950s and 1960s, the focus shifted to learning theory, the rise of experimental child psychology, interest in operant analysis of children's behavior, investigations of infant sensory and perceptual development, and the objective measurement of cognitive understanding among preverbal infants. In recent years, there has been revitalized interest in the emotional development and cognitive abilities of children, biological bases of behavior, and social relationships. More recently, advances in genetics, embryology, and developmental biology are transforming contemporary developmental and evolutionary theories that challenge once popular gene-centered explanations of human behavior. These points are illustrated numerous times throughout this book.

# 1.2: Cross-Cultural Human Development and the Other Social Sciences

In commenting on the central role that culture plays in our efforts to better understand behavior, Segall, Lonner, and Berry (1998) posed an interesting and critical question: "Can it still be necessary, as we approach the millennium (as measured on the Western, Christian calendar), to advocate that all social scientists, psychologists especially, take culture seriously into account when attempting to understand human behavior?" (p. 1101). At that time, the answer was (a qualified) "yes!" Fortunately, in the middle of the second decade of the twenty-first century, the situation has dramatically improved and only continues to get better with each passing year.

When discussing cross-cultural psychology and its subdiscipline of cross-cultural human development, it is obvious they share a long historical connection with general psychology. Although, as the well-known psychologist-anthropologist Otto Klineberg (1980) has pointed out, "There is no specific date that can be identified with the onset of interest in cross-cultural comparisons" (p. 34). Jahoda and Krewer (1997) have suggested that it might have been as early as the seventeenth century when the "dominant perspective of enlightenment philosophy was highly compatible with cross-cultural psychology's model of man" (p. 11). Since the 1960s, much of our psychological research—particularly that emphasizing the cross-cultural approach—has focused on the areas of abnormal, cognitive, social, and developmental psychology (Jahoda, 2009).

In terms of the other social sciences, the closest links are to anthropology and sociology with shared interests in specific approaches, methodological procedures, and research interests, including the socialization process and family influences on development. At the same time, this relationship has not always been a smooth one. For example, very few comparative studies of infant development in the past ever attempted to look at this topic within the characteristics of one's larger culture. At the same time, if researchers hoped to improve their studies in the future they would need to both gain greater ethnographic information about cultures as well as establish baselines of quantitative information for comparative purposes. As you will discover in reading this text, this is precisely the path that much of present-day, cross-cultural human development research has taken (Gardiner, 2001b; Matsumoto & van de Vijver, 2011).

In a lively and entertaining book titled *Psychology and Anthropology: A Psychological Perspective,* Gustav Jahoda (1982), a psychologist with a true appreciation and understanding of both psychology and anthropology, notes that "[a]nthropologists have always been concerned with psychology, even if unwittingly. . . . However, this interest has, in many respects, remained narrowly culture-bound, largely ignoring the wider perspectives provided by anthropology" (back cover).

It is hoped that future cross-cultural psychologists, in particular those interested in human development, will be able to forge a bond with other social scientists, notably anthropologists, and work as partners in laying a firm foundation for an empirically based understanding of human behavior that places a greater focus on developmental processes within cultural contexts. A welcome step in this direction has been made with several volumes that focus on emerging concepts and methods for measuring environment (or context) across the lifespan (Friedman & Wachs, 1999; Sternberg & Grigorenko, 2004) and childhood and family life (Abela & Walker, 2014; Georgas, Berry, van de Vijver, Kagitcibasi, & Pooringa, 2006; Weisner, 2002). Another important contribution is Pillemer and White's (2005) book, *Developmental Psychology and Social Change,* which discusses the historical evolution of developmental psychology, its goals, and its challenges. Specifically, the chapter by Charles Super on the globalization of developmental psychology is of particular value. Of even more recent interest is the presentation of a model describing how globalization affects adolescents' individual development and examining its effects on adolescents' family, peer context, school, and leisure activities (Tomasik & Silbereisen, 2011). Efforts such as these and others will greatly enrich our understanding of development and the vital role that culture plays in it.

# 1.3: Some Important Themes

This book differs in significant ways from most other volumes that focus on cross-cultural aspects of human behavior, most notably in its efforts to integrate a variety of important themes. Let us look at these in some detail and discover how they will weave their way through subsequent chapters.

## 1.3.1: A Cross-Cultural Perspective

Over the past two decades, social scientists have become increasingly aware of the contributions that cross-cultural research findings can make to our understanding of human development. Any attempt to include all or even a sizable number of these findings in a book of this length would be impossible. Therefore, I have decided to be selective and discuss representative areas of interest using a chronological-within-topics approach. For readers desiring a more comprehensive view of cross-cultural human development or those wanting to explore particular topics in greater depth, we refer you to the Further Readings and References sections at the end of this book. If you are eager to get started, you might consider looking at such classics as *Two Worlds of Childhood: U.S. and U.S.S.R.* by Urie Bronfenbrenner (1970) and a series of volumes on *Six Cultures* by Whiting (1963), Whiting and Whiting (1975), and Whiting and Edwards (1988). Edwards, Weisner, and others discuss the importance of these studies and the contributions of John and Beatrice Whiting in a special 2010 edition of the *Journal of Cross-Cultural Psychology*. The revised three-volume *Handbook of Cross-Cultural Psychology*, edited by John Berry and others (1997), contains several chapters relevant to the study of cross-cultural development and the role of cross-cultural theory and methodology. In addition, the eight volumes of the *Encyclopedia of Psychology* provide a definitive guide to the major areas of psychological theory, research, and practice (Kazdin, 2000), as does *The Corsini Encyclopedia of Psychology*, a four-volume update of the classic reference work (Weiner & Craighead, 2010). Also, the *Handbook of Culture and Psychology* presents a review of major areas and issues in cross-cultural psychology, including development (Matsumoto, 2001). Two additional recent volumes are the third edition of *Cross-Cultural Psychology: Research and Applications* (Berry, Poortinga, Breugelmans, Chasiotis, & Sam, 2011) and *Fundamental Questions in Cross-Cultural Psychology* (van de Vijver, Chasiotis, & Breugelmans, 2011). Finally, the informative three-volume set titled *The Encyclopedia of Cross-Cultural Psychology* contains brief overviews of hundreds of major concepts and biographical profiles of important contributors to cross-cultural psychology (Keith, 2013).

## 1.3.2: Goals for the Field

As to the nature and purpose of the cross-cultural method, Berry, Poortinga, Segall, and Dasen (2002), in a comprehensive overview of cross-cultural psychology, set forth three goals for the field. The first goal involves *testing or extending the generalizability of existing theories and findings.* In earlier writings, Berry and Dasen (1974) referred to this as the "transport and test goal" in which hypotheses and findings from one culture are transported to another so their validity can be tested in other cultural settings. For example, *are parental speech patterns in English-speaking families similar or dissimilar to those in Spanish-speaking families? Are the stages of cognitive development proposed by Jean Piaget specific to certain types of cultures, or are they universal?* The second goal focuses on *exploring other cultures to discover variations in behavior that may not be part of one's own cultural experience.*

In other words, if findings cannot be generalized, what are the reasons for this, and are the behaviors unique to these other cultures? A good example is a study by Jablensky and colleagues (1992), which demonstrates that although a number of symptoms characteristic of schizophrenia (a serious psychological disorder) exist in ten very different cultures, there is no single factor to explain differences in the formation or outcome of the disorder. At the same time, other psychological conditions appear to be "culture bound" and occur only among certain groups of people. One example is *pibloktoq*, found only among specific groups of Eskimos, in which individuals, with little or no warning, perform irrational acts—ripping off clothes, shouting obscenities, throwing objects, and running wildly into snowdrifts—lasting from a few minutes to as long as an hour (Kirmayer & Minas, 2000).

The third goal, which follows from the first two, is aimed at *integrating findings in such a way as to generate a more universal psychology applicable to a wider range of cultural settings and societies.* Examples of this include efforts by many cross-cultural researchers to refine and expand the usefulness of several theories, including the various ecological approaches cited in this text.

A fourth goal can be easily added to this list—*applying research findings across professional disciplines.* Some examples include preparing students to study, work, and travel abroad; improving minority children's academic and social success in school; assisting counselors, psychotherapists, social workers, and other professionals in helping immigrants better understand and adapt both psychologically and socially to a new culture. Additional examples consist of helping managers and employees in public, private, and government organizations meet the challenges of cultural diversity in the workplace, at home, and abroad, ultimately contributing to greater success in business practices and negotiations, and drawing attention to the basic human rights of people in all cultures.

At this point, you might be wondering, *"How can a cross-cultural perspective contribute to our understanding of human development?"* In answer to this question, I would point to several important benefits. First, looking at behavior from this perspective compels researchers to reflect seriously on the ways in which their cultural beliefs and values affect the development of their theories and research designs. Increased awareness of cross-cultural findings provides an opportunity to extend or restrict the implications of research conducted in a single cultural group, most notably the United States and similar Western societies. Nothing helps reduce ethnocentrism as quickly as looking at behavior as it occurs in other cultures. **Ethnocentrism** is defined as *the tendency to judge other people and cultures by the standards of one's own culture and to believe that the behavior, customs, norms, values, and other characteristics of one's own group are natural, valid, and correct while those of others are unnatural, invalid, and incorrect. If you have traveled to another culture, then it is likely you have experienced ethnocentrism first hand. Can you think of some examples? What were your reactions to these differences?*

Second, the number of independent and dependent variables to be investigated can be greatly increased in a cross-cultural design. Examples of studies in which this has been done include investigations of gender differences (Morinaga, Frieze, & Ferligoj, 1993), effects of parent–child relationships in diverse cultures (Gielen & Roopnarine, 2004), and individualism-collectivism and the attitudes toward school bullying of Japanese and Australian students (Nesdale & Naito, 2005). We generally think of an **independent variable (IV)** as *the condition introduced into or systematically manipulated in an experiment by the researcher*, and a **dependent variable (DV)** as *the subject's response or the behavior being measured in an experiment.* For example, you believe that watching violence in television cartoons makes young children more aggressive (your hypothesis). You show one group of children (matched for age, gender, socioeconomic background, etc.) violent cartoons and a similar group cartoons with no violence. You then measure the level of aggression shown by these children when in play situations. Your IV is the amount of cartoon violence to which children are exposed, and your DV is children's resulting levels of aggression when playing with others. *Try to think of a hypothesis of your own and identify the IV and the DV.*

Third, cross-cultural studies help us separate **emics**, or *culture-specific concepts*, from **etics**, or *universal or culture-general concepts.* McDonald's is a good example of an emic approach to cultural consumer behavior. The fast food restaurant successfully sells market-specific items in very different cultures, such as a Maharaja Mac (chicken burger) in India, McPalta (burger with avocado sauce) in Chile, and McBingsoo (shaved ice) in Korea. The etic approach is well illustrated by the coffee chain Starbucks, which provides a similar store structure in widely different cultures—strong coffee, soft lighting, and comfortable seating. *Can you think of some other examples?*

The **emic** (insider) **approach** focuses on a single culture, using criteria that are thought to be relative to it, and studies behavior from *within* the system itself, making no cross-cultural inferences with regard to the universality of any observations. An example is an anthropological field study in which a researcher lives with a group of people and tries to understand the culture through their eyes and experiences, avoiding the ethnocentrism of his or her own cultural background. The **etic** (outsider) **approach**, in contrast, looks at several cultures, comparing and contrasting them using criteria thought to be absolute or universal, and studies behavior from *outside* the system. An example that (happily) we don't see as often as we once did in cross-cultural psychology involves an investigator conducting what has been called "safari research." An illustration is a professor (not very familiar with the field) who goes on vacation to several countries, taking along a favorite questionnaire concerning _____ (you fill in the blank). He or she visits several universities, collects data from available students (who may or may not understand many of the colloquial English-language terms), returns home, and publishes the findings as "universal" attitudes of those living in cultures X, Y, and Z.

Separating emics from etics is better accomplished by testing theories or principles developed in one cultural context in another. The work of Freud, Piaget, and Kohlberg are examples. In some cases, findings lend support to the universality of behaviors in vastly different cultural settings (e.g., stages in language development and the sequence and timing of such behaviors as smiling, walking, stranger and separation anxiety, and pubertal development). However, results have sometimes suggested a need for modification of certain culture-bound concepts (e.g., intelligence, medical diagnosis, and, sometimes, gender behavior). For a comprehensive review of some of the significant findings of indigenous (or native) psychologists, see Kim, Yang, and Hwang (2006). Lori Lambert's (2014) book on indigenous research methodologies in the behavioral sciences will be useful to those planning work on native groups and tribes throughout the world.

One of the most frequently used approaches to describing, explaining, and understanding similarities and differences in multiple cultural contexts has been presented by Triandis (1989; 1995). This is the dimension of **individualism-collectivism**. A culture characterized as **individualist** is made up of *people who are responsible to themselves and their family and whose individual achievement is paramount.* Frequently mentioned examples of such cultures are the United States and most European societies. A **collectivist** culture, in contrast, is thought to consist of *people who consider the group to be most important, with an emphasis on traditions, cooperation, and a sharing of common goals and values.* Cultures so characterized include most of

Asia, Africa, and South America. However, in recent years, use of these characteristics has often been too limiting, and it has been recognized that components of each are found in most cultures and even within specific individuals (Green, Deschamps, & Paez, 2005; Triandis, 1995). Fischer and his colleagues (2009) have reported promising results on the development and validation of a research instrument for measuring the descriptive norms related to individualism-collectivism.

By focusing throughout this book on cross-cultural material, readers will be continually presented with opportunities to expand their awareness and sensitivity to global similarities and differences in human development and to reduce ethnocentric thinking. The cross-cultural perspective complements and extends the work of earlier researchers who successfully presented the more traditional, but often culture-specific, approach to understanding lifespan development by offering a broader worldview. By allowing readers to experience variations in behavior not normally found in their own societies (e.g., accelerated formal operational thought among some Asian populations, decreased susceptibility to visual illusions among certain African groups, and highly developed mathematical skills among Dutch children), this perspective contributes to our understanding of human adaptation. Perhaps, most important, it encourages a closer look at the interconnections among culture, development, and behavior—a major theme in contemporary developmental psychology.

Although this is certainly not the first effort to stress the importance of looking at cross-cultural data, it is given greater emphasis here because, as Segall (1979) so aptly stated, "It is to . . . theories of ecological, cultural, and socialization forces that we must turn for the most promising insights into why different peoples develop different . . . skills or develop the same skills at different rates" (p. 129).

The mention of socialization practices and the variety of ways in which we are influenced by ecological factors leads us to another major theme.

## 1.3.3: An Ecological Model

The importance of viewing behavior within its social setting was first recognized not by psychologists but by sociologists, who stressed the importance of the individual's subjective view. Among the early proponents of this view were C. H. Cooley (1902), W. I. Thomas and F. Znaniecki (1927), and G. H. Mead (1934). When psychologists became interested in the topic, they tended to ignore the social context in favor of cognitive processes. Such analysis was extended beyond the individual to the study of the environment with the introduction of the concepts of "psychological field" and "life space" by Kurt Lewin (1935). Explicit recognition of the need to study an individual's subjective view of social reality came with the pioneering work of MacLeod (1947) and has been extended by many others, including Triandis (2008).

One of the most important contributions to these evolving ideas, and one on which much of the presentation in this book is based, is the ecological model presented in the work of Urie Bronfenbrenner (1975, 1977, 1979, 1986, 1989, 1993, and 2005). In its original form, this model divided a child's environment into four nested and interrelated systems or contexts (one more was added later) and allowed us to see and understand (within a broad framework) how patterns of interaction within the family and the wider society are influenced by—and, in turn, influence—the connection between development and culture. Each system involves relationships defined by expected behaviors and roles. For example, a child behaves very differently at home, in school, or with playmates. *Take a moment and reflect on your own behavior as a child in these settings. Can you remember how your behavior differed in each setting?*

When relationships between systems are in harmony, development proceeds smoothly. Consider the relationship between home and school as an example. If expectations are much the same in both settings (e.g., try to do your best work, be careful and neat), then individuals are more likely to succeed and do well than if expectations differ significantly from one setting or environment to another. Bronfenbrenner's family-centered approach has allowed others to adapt and apply his model to

Can you find the Western anthropologist in this picture?

(Colaimages/Alamy Stock Photo)

contemporary issues and to develop applied programs involving parent education, counseling, disabilities, day care, and early childhood programs. This approach is presented and discussed in detail in Chapter 2.

Noted anthropologist, Dr. Dawn Chatty, discussing local problems with Harsous tribal member in Sahmah, Oman, in the Arabian Peninsula.

(Alberto Arzoz/Axiom/Design Pics Inc/Alamy Stock Photo)

## 1.3.4: The Developmental Niche

If Bronfenbrenner is correct in his view that culture and environment make significant contributions to one's development, then we might ask, *"How does this happen and how can we better understand the processes taking place?"*

One possible answer is provided by the cross-cultural developmental work of Harkness (2005), Parmar, Harkness, and Super (2004), and Super and Harkness (1986, 1994a, 1999, 2002, 2011). Based on an extensive series of studies among Kipsigis-speaking communities in Western Kenya, Super and Harkness, a psychologist–anthropologist, wife–husband research team, first presented a way of bringing together and integrating findings from the two disciplines. Called the **developmental niche**, it provides *a framework for understanding how various aspects of a culture guide the developmental process by focusing on the child as the unit of analysis within his or her sociocultural setting or context.* It is compatible, in many respects, with the ideas put forth by Bronfenbrenner and, in combination with it, comprises another major theme of this book. It, too, is presented and discussed in detail in Chapter 2.

## 1.3.5: A Developmental Orientation

It is well recognized that most of our behavior does not take place at isolated periods in our lives but rather evolves and continually develops throughout the lifespan. Although the growing body of cross-cultural research literature is significant, it frequently resembles "a confused mosaic of contradictory findings" (Gardiner, 1994). This may explain, in part, why none of the books that currently examine cross-cultural topics systematically present a developmental perspective as done here. Not all of the behaviors covered in this book will fit neatly into this orientation or be easily explained by some of the other themes or approaches. However, many do and, where appropriate, I will demonstrate how these behaviors evolve and change as individuals develop across the lifespan and across cultures.

To illustrate the importance of looking at behavior from a developmental orientation, let us briefly consider the development of memory and attention, or the increased ability to organize information. As children, we begin to think, attend, and store away memories. As adolescents and adults, we develop the ability to make inferences, understand reversibility, and make use of abstract thought. Information that may have been remembered in childhood as a list can now be recalled in adulthood as a total pattern. *What is your earliest memory? How old do you think you were? Why do you think this memory is so important?*

This brings us to another theme that will occur throughout this book—the chronological-within-topics approach.

## 1.3.6: A Chronological-Within-Topics Approach

In a book of this size, , it is impossible to do all things—that is, provide a comprehensive view of development in all the necessary detail and also focus on all the important cross-cultural findings. Recognizing this, the focus will be on selected topics for which a large and continually expanding literature of cross-cultural research exists, and these topics will be discussed chronologically—from the early beginnings of development through the last years of life.

Using this chronological-within-topics approach, I hope to effectively demonstrate how behavioral processes evolve and change as individuals pass from infancy and childhood through adolescence and into adulthood. As a result, it should become clear that our behavior is dynamic and involves change, which is at times orderly and predictable and at other times chaotic and unreliable; that both individual and cultural similarities and differences exist; and that specific cultural influences become important at different times and in different cultures. This approach includes basic concepts, principles, and theories that describe physical, psychological, cognitive, social, and personality changes that occur across the lifespan in a variety of cultural contexts.

## 1.3.7: Another Piece of the Developmental Puzzle: The Human Genome

In recent years, findings from the neurosciences have begun to significantly influence the study of human development. It is becoming increasingly necessary to take into account the role of genes and biological principles and their interaction with one's environment and psychological experiences. As Segalowitz and Schmidt (2003) point out, "While we see both cognitive and affective development—the mainstay of developmental psychology—as having interesting parameters being set by neurological factors, new discoveries in developmental neuroscience also highlight the plasticity and adaptability of the system. Patterns of development are both biologically rooted in our brains and heavily influenced by experience. And the biological influences are manifested through experience" (p. 65).

In addition, with the completion of the Human Genome Project (1990–2003), we have seen an explosion in the study of genetics and the discovery of a large number of specific genes that may be responsible for a variety of physical illnesses and psychological conditions, including cancer, diabetes, heart disease, multiple sclerosis, asthma, and depression. There are even those who believe this knowledge could lead to the ability to double the lifespan through a multitude of new treatments and therapies. For example, a group of Danish researchers have predicted that more than half of all babies born since the year 2000 in France, Italy, Germany, the United Kingdom, the United States, Japan, Canada, and other countries with long life expectancies will celebrate their hundredth birthdays (Christensen, Doblhammer, Rau, & Vaupel, 2009).

The Genome Project's goals of identifying the approximately 20,000 to 25,000 genes in human DNA, determining the sequences of the 3 billion chemical base pairs that make up human DNA, storing this information in databases, improving tools for data analysis, and transferring related technologies to the private sector have been accomplished. However, analysis of the data; its application to specific situations; and implications for the legal, ethical, and social issues arising from this project will last long into the future. For example, Justin Zook and his colleagues (2014) at the National Institute of Standards and Technology and a team from Harvard University and the Virginia Bioinformatics Institute of Virginia Tech have recently developed new methods for integrating data that produce a highly reliable set of genotypes that will serve as a benchmark for the sequencing of the human genome. Their methods make it possible to use an individual's genetic profile to assist in guiding medical decisions in the prevention, diagnosis, and treatment of a range of diseases. Their findings are available on the Genome Comparison and Analytics Testing (GCAT) website (www.bioplanet.com/gcat). These are exciting advances that, in many ways, will change the way individuals and their descendants across cultures will live their lives in the generations yet to come. The

Human Genome Organization holds a series of annual conferences around the world to present and discuss its latest research. The most recent meeting was in March 2015 with the theme "Transforming Human Genomics for a Sustainable Tomorrow."

Advances in genetic engineering and biotechnology raise serious questions in terms of culture and human development. For example, *what if you had a child who was born with a growth hormone deficiency? Would you (if you could afford it) pay large sums of money, perhaps as much as $1,500 to $2,500 or more, for a series of injections to increase the height of your child at critical stages of his or her development? Would you allow genetic engineering to increase the number of neurons in the brain during fetal development to have a potentially "smarter" baby?*

Carey (2003) points out that in the past, the greatest effect of culture on humans has been to alter the frequency of alleles (paired genes, alike or different, that affect a trait) and/or genotypes (the genetic makeup of an individual containing both expressed and unexpressed characteristics). Further advances in genetic engineering could allow scientists to create *new* alleles ". . . thus, changing mutations from a random phenomenon into a deliberate, scientifically guided enterprise" (p. 216). The result would be individuals with entirely new and unique genotypes that are not now part of the human genome. We can only imagine (and even that is difficult) what the effect might be on human development and culture. For example, it might soon be possible to create new alleles that could be used to help cure a genetic disease by neutralizing infected alleles.

Physical and cultural changes in human development have always been intertwined. For example, we can observe the many ways in which a culture's attitudes and beliefs about birth control, abortion, and related topics influence its members' social and religious attitudes, as well as its concern with the physical factors of reproductive fitness. A culture's attitudes toward marriage—who and who will not make appropriate partners—affect the ways in which dating and mating are structured. Advances in international travel (and Internet communication) have increased contact among cultures, sometimes resulting in an increased number of cross-cultural relationships, intermarriages, and bicultural children, with a subsequent reduction in "the reproductive isolation of human populations" (Carey, 2003, p. 215).

Only the future will determine how far the genetic revolution will take us. Although genes and their influences is not be one of the major topics on which I have much to say, I recognize the importance of this newly expanding research and urge the reader to learn more about it, as will I, when stories related to it appear in various media and professional journals.

# 1.4:  Practical Applications

It is my belief that a text emphasizing process, content, and skill (at understanding and interpreting cross-cultural behavior), but avoiding unnecessary jargon and seeking a broad perspective, provides a number of benefits to readers. Therefore, a large part of my focus is on the *everyday experiences* encountered by individuals of differing ethnic backgrounds within their own society, as well as between and among individuals of different cultural settings. It is further believed that if readers come to understand the processes involved, then they can begin to understand how to apply these principles for a deeper insight into the events and issues that touch their lives beyond the boundaries of their homes, neighborhoods, classrooms, communities, and nations. Throughout this book, the material is continually related to issues and concerns that are important and relevant to all of us. Efforts are made to encourage critical thinking that allows one to observe, examine, question, explore, analyze, and evaluate a variety of everyday situations within diverse cultural contexts.

There is an ancient Chinese proverb that states, "Tell me and I forget . . . teach me and I remember . . . engage me and I learn." Simply stated, this is another of this text's important themes—practical application. Many of today's texts are written for social science majors planning graduate study and frequently emphasize laboratory research—a shortcoming already recognized in my previous comments on the need for an ecological point of view. Although I believe a developmental text should be grounded in carefully researched theory, I also think that if it is to be maximally useful, it should avoid jargon and focus on readers' "real-life" experiences and, ultimately, assist them in relating more effectively with other individuals and in diverse environments. This is especially true today as the world, even at the local neighborhood level, becomes increasingly multicultural.

These goals are accomplished in several ways. In writing this book, topics have been selected that have meaning for one's daily living: socialization (Chapter 3), family (Chapter 4), cognition and language (Chapter 5), personality (Chapter 6), social behavior (Chapter 7), issues of gender and sexuality (Chapter 8), and health and illness issues (Chapter 9).

You aren't expected to accept what is presented without question. I believe in the Chinese proverb I just mentioned and try to practice what I preach by providing frequent opportunities for you to question, explore, and analyze the topics presented here. In doing this, you will arrive at a better understanding of your own behavior and that of others, modifying it where necessary and desirable, and developing and improving your cross-cultural interactions with others, now and in the future.

# 1.5:  Overview of the Book

Because the transition from theory to practice cannot be accomplished simply by reading about applications, every effort is made to present the material in each chapter in such a way that it explicitly encourages your active involvement.

First, as you notice, each chapter opens with vignettes focusing on issues and behaviors addressed in that chapter. This gives you an idea of what is covered and allows you to formulate your own ideas as you read the material. For example, *"What are the benefits of studying development cross culturally?" "What are the effects of culture on socialization?" "How does children's play differ from one culture to another?" "In what ways are adolescents similar or different throughout the world?" "How do cultures treat their elders or older adults?"*

Second, within the narrative, each new idea is defined, highlighted, and illustrated with cultural examples (many from the author's own experiences) that, hopefully, you will find both relevant and entertaining.

Third, real-life examples of cultural variations in childbirth, effects of culture on learning styles, growing old in different cultures, cultural variations in adolescent identity, and other important topics are presented and discussed.

Fourth, throughout the chapters, you are frequently asked to *stop* and consider what you have read, think about questions that are highlighted in italics, and apply ideas and concepts to your own life experiences. In addition, you are frequently asked to think critically about certain issues and topics. When you do this, you will have a better understanding and are more likely to remember information that is relevant to your life.

At the end of each chapter, you will find several study questions to help you focus on important points in each chapter.

# 1.6: Some Cross-Cultural Teasers

As this chapter comes to a close, here are a few "cross-cultural teasers," or questions, for which partial answers are provided. Each question receives further attention in future chapters.

- *Are there any universals in human development? If so, what are they?* One example of a universal is gender role assignment. Almost all societies appear to socialize boys and girls into gender roles (e.g., generally allowing more aggressive behavior among boys and encouraging more caring behavior among girls).

- *How can we explain cross-cultural differences in such behaviors as dependence and independence?* Part of the answer depends on where infants sleep after they are born. The United States is known as a culture that emphasizes individual achievement; parents generally place babies in their own cribs in their own rooms. Japan, a more collectivist culture, encourages dependence or interdependence; children are allowed to sleep with parents, often for many years. How does this affect development?

- Adolescents in many of the world's cultures confront the problem of identity by trying to answer the question, "Who am I?" For some, living in Nigeria, it is a relatively easy task. For others, growing up bicultural in New York City, it is more difficult.

- Eating disorders, such as anorexia and bulimia, are common in many Western societies. *Do young people throughout the world strive to attain the "ideal" body image?* You may be surprised by some of the answers found in Japan, Australia, and other countries.

- *How do different cultures view their elderly? Is grandparenting the same everywhere?* You will find some answers to these questions from China, Japan, the United States, and other countries.

- *How does family life differ from one culture to another?* In some societies, the roles of mothers and fathers may

surprise you. *Did you know children in some cultures become more closely attached to their fathers than to their mothers? Why would this be the case?* We'll find out later in this book.

- An increasingly common disorder among older adults today is Alzheimer's disease. *Did you know that people suffering from this disease are treated differently by their caregivers if both patient and caregiver are Hispanic, Native American, or Anglo?*

- *What's important in selecting a marriage partner—money, good looks, security, health?* You'll be surprised at some of the views expressed by men and women from cultures around the world. *How many chickens or cows do you think you're worth on the marriage market in another culture?*

Have I gotten your attention? Do you want to know the answers to these and other interesting cross-cultural questions? Would you like to know more about some of the similarities and differences in human behavior and how people live their "lives across cultures?" Then turn the page and read on.

## Summary: Introduction to Cross-Cultural Human Development

This chapter introduces the topic of cross-cultural human development and provides definitions of important terms and concepts. Discussion centers on several themes to be used in organizing developmental topics in a variety of cultural settings. These themes include a cross-cultural perspective, ecological model, developmental niche, developmental orientation, chronological-within-topics approach, and emphasis on practical applications. Suggestions are given for using the material in ways to help readers develop a greater understanding of, and sensitivity to, those of a different cultural background than their own, as well as to develop and improve any cross-cultural interactions they might experience.

## Study Questions

Explain what is meant by the term *cross-cultural human development.*

Demonstrate a familiarity with the important themes presented in this chapter, including the cross-cultural perspective, ecological model, developmental niche, developmental orientation, and chronological-within-topics approach.

Comment on the goals set forth for the field of cross-cultural psychology.

Distinguish between emic and etic approaches to the study of culture.

Explain the differences between individualism and collectivism, and provide clear examples.

Describe the Human Genome Project and its importance.

# Chapter 2
# Theories and Methodology

*Justin Tyme, an undergraduate major in psychology, has returned from a month in Thailand, where he attempted to collect data for his senior thesis. This was his first visit to a foreign country, and it was a memorable, but unsatisfying, experience. Why? Because Justin was not well prepared and made several serious (and avoidable) mistakes. First, he traveled to a culture he knew little about (because it sounded exotic). People spoke a language (Thai) he did not understand and that he found difficult to read, write, or speak in the brief time he was there because of its complexity (forty-four consonants, twenty-eight vowel forms, five tones, and written script). He found the weather too hot and humid, the food too spicy, and life in the village where he was doing his research "too slow." He had difficulty finding people to help translate his English-language, Western-designed, marital role preference scale so that it would have comparable meaning in Thai. He was upset because the few subjects he was able to get often didn't arrive on time (Asians, in general, are not as time conscious as Westerners, especially Americans), and when they did, they usually told him "Mai pen rai" (Don't worry). Finally, representative samples were difficult to obtain in a rural area that would match his samples back in Chicago, Illinois.*

*Dr. Kitty Litter, in contrast, an anthropologist from Cornell University, recently spent six months doing an ethnographic field study among a group of Indians in the highlands of Peru. Not only was she fluent in Spanish, the most widely spoken language in the country, but she also had a working knowledge of two native languages—Quechua and Aymara—from two previous trips to the country. She had read extensively about the customs of the tribal groups in this area and was very fond of the food. She especially enjoyed the tropical climate along the coast and the cooler temperatures in the mountains. She had spent considerable time designing the questions she was going to ask and had even prepared a Quechuan-language version of a psychological instrument she hoped to validate while there.*

Theories and methodology—sound exciting, don't they? Perhaps not, but these two topics are central to understanding what happens both in cross-cultural human development and in the chapters that follow. In this regard, there are two goals for this discussion of theories: (1) to provide a foundation for those who do not have a background in human development (or could benefit from a review of major concepts) to appreciate their contributions to our efforts to better understand behavior, and (2) to provide a framework for identifying complex human behavior and experience as it occurs within different cultural contexts and to explore possible reasons for the similarities and differences found in societies around the world. If research (cross-cultural or otherwise) is not carefully designed, conducted, analyzed, and understood, any findings that result are of little value. So, I shall try to make the discussion of these topics as simple, relevant, and interesting as possible.

## 2.1: Theories of Development

*Why do we study human development?* There are many reasons, but basically we do it to *understand, explain, predict,* and (in some instances) *control behavior.* To achieve these goals, we need to be familiar and comfortable with theories and their important concepts. As a graduate student in England, I was trying to select a topic for my doctoral dissertation when my major adviser asked me if there were any areas of psychology with which I was particularly uncomfortable. Without hesitation, I immediately replied, "Theories." (I shouldn't say this but, as an undergraduate student, I frequently skipped over theories because, as usually presented, I found them boring, confusing, and too abstract.) When it was suggested that I devote the next three years to the development of my own theory in order to decrease this discomfort (a form of "theoretical desensitization," I guess), I thought this was a "daft idea." Of course, I didn't tell this to my adviser! However, develop my own theory I did (Gardiner, 1966). Not only did I really enjoy doing my original doctoral research (on "newspapers as personalities"), but, when it was over, I was much less threatened by theoretical concepts and had a greater appreciation for the central role theories play in the social sciences. I hope you feel the same way when you reach the conclusion of this chapter (don't skip over them because they *are* important!).

## 2.1.1: What Is a Theory?

Simply stated, a **theory** is *a set of hypotheses or assumptions about behavior.* A theory consists of guesses or speculations that allow us to answer such questions as "Why does a particular behavior occur?" For example, *why do Chinese children generally appear calmer, less active, and easier to soothe when distressed than Western children? Why are ethnic customs and values of greater importance to some minority youths than others? What factors most influence the ways in which contemporary cultures treat their elderly?*

When we study human development, we can't look at all aspects of an individual's, a group's, or a culture's behavior. Theories help us organize our ideas and limit what we look at, and serve as a guide (or blueprint) in the collection of data. Sometimes, it seems as if there are as many theories as there are people. In a sense, there are, because each of us has our own informal, unscientific, unverified, and highly idiosyncratic theories that we use almost every day. Built up over years of personal observation and experience, these informal theories help us understand the behavior of those with whom we come into contact. For example, when we meet someone for the first time, our informal theory of personality helps us decide whether we like or dislike this person, whether we want to interact with this person again, and so on. However, we must go beyond these informal theories to truly understand and explain the complexity of human development. We need theories that are more formalized and rooted in scientific principles if we are to be able to compare and contrast behavior within and across cultures and draw conclusions about similarities and differences. In the pages that follow, six theories are discussed. Although you may (or may not) be familiar with some or all of them, it might be helpful, in terms of our discussion, to think of the theories of Piaget, Kohlberg, and Erikson as traditional or mainstream psychological theories that focus on the individual, with primary attention to internal cognitive processes (e.g., knowing and thinking, moral reasoning, and psychosocial development). In contrast, the theories of Bronfenbrenner, Super and Harkness, and Vygotsky can be viewed as interactionist theories because they focus on the interactions between the individual and his or her environment in specific psychological domains (e.g., ecology and the interrelationship of the developing individual and his or her changing physical and social environment; links between children's behavior and the developmental niche in which they are raised; and cultural influences on development of language, thinking, and guided participation).

Before looking at each theory, consider a comment made by Judith Rich Harris (2006) in her book *No Two Alike,* in which she proposes a new theory of personality but observes, "Someone who thinks up a new theory is the

last person who should be trusted with the job of testing it. A new theory should be tested by independent researchers who aren't cronies of the theorist . . . proposing theories and doing research to test them are jobs that should be carried out by different entities" (p. 265). This is wise advice, but in the case of the theories discussed here, this sometimes occurs and sometimes not.

## 2.1.2: Bronfenbrenner's Ecological Model

In Chapter 1, I briefly noted that one of the most important contributions to the study of human development within cultural contexts, and one on which much of this text's presentation is based, is the ecological model presented in the pioneering work of Urie Bronfenbrenner (1975, 1977, 1979, 1986, 1989, 1993, 2005). At the center of Bronfenbrenner's thinking is his contention that human development is a dynamic, interactive process in which humans create the environments in which they live and these, in turn, help shape their own development. In this regard, he was influenced by the work of Lev Vygotsky, whose sociocultural theory will be discussed later in this chapter.

Simply stated, this model views behavior and development as a *shared function* of the characteristics of the individual (biological or genetic factors and personality) and the environment (social, physical, and cultural aspects of one's present surroundings such as family, school, and neighborhood), along with the larger contemporary and historical contexts of which these are an integral part, including society and period of time in which one is born and lives his or her life.

Bronfenbrenner's (1999) original model has been "undergoing successively more complex reformulations to attain its present, still-evolving form" (p. 4). Later versions of this approach (Bronfenbrenner, 2005; Bronfenbrenner & Morris, 1998; Trudge, Mokrova, Hatfield, & Karnik, 2009) have been renamed the *bioecological model.* By doing so, it identifies a child's own biology as a critical environmental factor affecting development, while incorporating earlier concepts, along with new ideas, into a series of propositions that focus more directly on the role of environment and the concept of time. Those readers who want to know more about this evolving model, which remains more theoretical than practical at the moment, are directed to the references mentioned previously. Note: The Trudge et al. (2009) article evaluates the uses and misuses of this approach. Readers would benefit from reading this article.

In this text, I have chosen to focus primary attention on Bronfenbrenner's earlier model (without the recent propositions), which I believe continues to offer significant advantages for viewing and understanding the connection between culture and human development. Where appropriate, reference will be made to some of his more recent ideas and formulations.

The **ecology of human development**, as defined by Bronfenbrenner (2005), involves *"the scientific study of the progressive, mutual accommodation throughout the life course, between an active, growing human being and the changing properties of the immediate settings in which the developing person lives, as this process is affected by relations between these settings, and by the larger contexts in which the settings are embedded"* (p. 107). In short, an individual is seen *not* as a passive, static, and isolated entity on which the environment exerts great influence (much like a *tabula rasa,* or blank slate), but as a dynamic and evolving being that interacts with, and thereby restructures, the many environments with which he or she comes into contact. These interactions between individual and environment are viewed as two directional and characterized by reciprocity. For example, while a child's development is being influenced and molded by parents, family, school, and peers, he or she is, at the same time, influencing and molding the behavior of others. *Take a moment and try to think of examples from your own life where situations like this occurred in your family, at school, or among friends. Why were they important? How did you deal with them? What were some of the outcomes?*

Bronfenbrenner has suggested that an individual's perception of the environment is often more important than "objective reality," and that this perception influences one's expectations and activities. A recognition and acceptance of the critical role played by the cultural or environmental context seem particularly suited to the study of human behavior and development.

In his critique of traditional research carried out on children, Bronfenbrenner (1979) has stated, "Much of contemporary developmental psychology is the science of the strange behaviors of children in strange situations with strange adults for the briefest possible periods of time" (p. 513). In other words, in striving to achieve experimental rigor and control, we have often lost sight of the scientific and practical relevance of our findings by ignoring how the same phenomena might occur outside such artificial environments. One of the other major goals of this text is to stress the relevance and practicality of such findings. For example, although social workers and others have employed Bronfenbrenner's model since the 1970s, more recent studies demonstrate a deeper understanding and wider application of ecological principles in actual practice (Ungar, 2002). Bronfenbrenner's approach has become increasingly employed in studies of multiple risk factors among children and the adverse effects on their development (Dex & Sabates, 2015; Evans, Li, & Whipple, 2013; Sabates & Dex, 2013). For example, Dex and Sabates (2015) identified ten risk factors in parent–child interaction, family–child interaction, and home environment

(ecological factors) that contribute to developmental difficulties. These factors include having a physical disability, having an adolescent mother, living in overcrowded housing, having parents with financial problems, alcoholism, drug misuse, or domestic violence. Results indicate that early intervention contributes to improvement in children's behaviors and greater chances of successful development at later stages. Although not stated, such risk factors might be present in a variety of cultures and worthy of further investigation.

The ecological model allows us to go beyond the setting being immediately experienced—whether in a laboratory, a classroom, or a backyard—and permits the incorporation of indirect, but nevertheless very real, effects from other settings, as well as from the culture as a whole. Bronfenbrenner originally divided the ecological environment into four **nested systems**: *microsystem, mesosystem, exosystem, and macrosystem* (see Figure 2.1). Most of us have seen depictions of Russian matryoshka nesting dolls similar to the ones shown in the following photo. The set consists of wooden figures that separate to reveal a series of smaller ones finally showing the innermost one—a baby. These denote a relationship of object-within-similar-object. Because Bronfenbrenner was born in Russia, he probably purposely chose this easily understood metaphor for his theory of nested systems.

Russian matryoshka nesting dolls.

(© Harry Gardiner)

This conceptualization of the ecological environment has been retained in his more recent bioecological model and is given attention in discussions throughout this text. A fifth system, the *chronosystem*, with its focus on time and sociohistorical conditions, has been mentioned only occasionally in the literature, and seldom by Bronfenbrenner himself. However, as we shall soon see, the concept and importance of time has become a more significant part of the newly reformulated bioecological model and was so recognized in the last integrative book he wrote on his

**Figure 2.1** Bronfenbrenner's Ecological Model of Human Development

SOURCE: Alan Gardiner © 2016. Based on data from The Ecology of Human Development by Urie Bronfenbrenner.

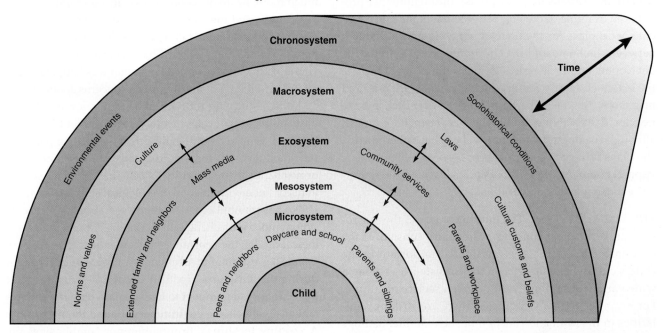

model before he died in 2005 (Bronfenbrenner, 2005). An example of the importance of time in this model might include a child's reactions to his or her parents' divorce. Young children frequently blame themselves for the divorce, and researchers have shown that the negative effects seem most crucial during the first year after the divorce, but within two years family relationships between parents and children improve and become more stable. An example of a sociohistorical condition affecting behavior would be the continued improvement and success of women selecting careers and entering the workforce.

**THE MICROSYSTEM** In Figure 2.1, the first level, the microsystem, is the layer closest to the child and contains those structures with which the child has direct contact, for example, family or preschool and resulting behaviors such as dependence, independence, cooperation, or competition. This is the most basic level, the one at which individuals engage in face-to-face interactions, and their behaviors frequently reflect social position. Bronfenbrenner expanded his original definition to include home, church, school, hospital, or day care center. Other factors include the effects of the physical environment on behavior, including background noise, crowding, and the number and types of toys available to a child. For a real-life example of the microsystem, consider Charlie, the youngest child in his family. He attends preschool while his mother and father are at work. It is here that he learns to play "nicely" with other children, share toys, obey the teacher, and develop basic social skills.

**THE MESOSYSTEM** The second level, the mesosystem, recognizes that the individual microsystems in which a child functions are not independent but are closely interrelated or connected and influence each other. This layer provides the connection between these structures. According to Bronfenbrenner's newly revised definition, the mesosystem is made up of two or more microsystems (e.g., home and day care, day care and school, or family and peer group). It is the mesosystem that links or ties together information, knowledge, and attitudes from one setting that help shape behavior or development in another setting. For example, while parents emphasize the importance of learning at home, preschool teachers provide stimulating activities at school that motivate a child to learn more. In this regard, Steinberg, Darling, and Fletcher (1995) looked at authoritative parenting and adolescent adjustment within the ecological setting and reported a number of benefits, including lower levels of delinquency and substance abuse among both male and female adolescents. Charlie's older sister, Sirina, is in second grade and is functioning in the mesosystem. For example, Siri's mother frequently meets with her daughter's teacher, Miss Santiago, to discuss her progress in school and seek advice on improving her study habits at home.

**THE EXOSYSTEM** Beyond the child's immediate environment are social settings of which he or she may not be a part but that, nevertheless, interact with one or more structures in the microsystem and influence his or her development in significant ways. These settings or institutions make up the third level—the exosystem. As defined by

Bronfenbrenner, the exosystem includes formal settings such as parents' place of work or community health and welfare institutions (e.g., hospitals). Bronfenbrenner provides an example of the link between the home and a parent's workplace for the developing child and of the link between the home and the children's peer group for the developing adult. Other less formal settings might include the extended family (aunts, uncles, cousins, friends, and neighbors). Malinee, Charlie and Siri's older sister, is experiencing daily activities within the exosystem; for example, although she doesn't know much about her father's work, she plays on a coed soccer team sponsored by his athletic apparel company after school and is learning the importance of team work and discipline.

THE MACROSYSTEM   The outermost circle, the macrosystem, is the most complex system and consists of the customs, values, and laws considered important in the child's culture. The focus is on the consistencies among a wide variety of settings within a given society or culture. For example, in many countries, there are striking similarities in the form and function of such familiar settings as school playgrounds, post offices, shopping malls, and even fast food restaurants. This system or level does not pertain to a specific context or environmental setting but is important because it has an effect on all previous systems. It determines acceptable versus unacceptable behavior. For example, Macinnes, the oldest child in the family we have been looking at, is in high school, and, as a result of his accumulated experiences in these previous systems, is considered to be a smart, well-behaved, conscientious, helpful, and law-abiding member of his community, as well as an example for his younger siblings, friends, and peers.

THE CHRONOSYSTEM.   In Bronfenbrenner's ecological model, the exact role of the chronosystem is somewhat difficult to describe because it has not received the same attention as the other four systems. In fact, the term does not always appear in the reformulated bioecological model, although the elements that characterize it—time and sociohistorical conditions—constitute a major part of the new model. In his final writing, Bronfenbrenner (2005) makes the point that ". . . the chronosystem is a methodological construct; the remaining four are theoretical but can also become substantive when put to empirical use" (p. 165). In general, this layer focuses on time as it relates to a child's various environments. For instance, it includes the physiological changes that occur as the child matures and his or her reactions to these changes, as well as the changed environment in which he or she now functions. Another example is the timing of the death of an important person in the child's life such as a parent, sibling, or grandparent. Each of the children mentioned previously was exposed to the severe economic difficulties of the year 2009 and beyond. However, due to their age differences, they

experienced events in unique ways, and the impact on their development varied. For example, Macinnes became much more aware of economic issues and moral behavior as they affected the country and his family; Malinee had to cut back on some of her activities due to a reduction in family income; and Siri and Charlie, because they were so young, didn't always understand what was happening but often heard their parents discussing concerns about money.

When studying individual behavior, a great deal of past and present developmental research either has tended to view it at a fixed point in time or, if over a long period of time (and if conducted longitudinally), has assumed little or no change in an individual's personal characteristics or in his or her environmental or ecological setting. As Muuss (1996) has pointed out, ". . . time used to be perceived as synonymous with changes in chronological age. In the ecological model, the constancy or change over time (of both E and P) is essential to assessing the nature of the changes during the life course" (p. 320). Bronfenbrenner has used this chronosystem model to help explain how time simultaneously affects the environment (E) and the person (P). According to Muuss, Bronfenbrenner "emphasizes the interacting nature of these changes, and it is the interacting nature of (E) and (P) that Lewin, and more explicitly, Bronfenbrenner, have brought to our attention" (p. 320).

In his later writings, Bronfenbrenner (2000), although not employing chronosystem terminology, placed increasing emphasis on "time and timing as they relate to features of the environment, as opposed to characteristics of the person" (p. 20)—what he has called "space through time: environment in the third dimension" (p. 20). Much of the progress in this area has emerged from researchers, primarily sociologists, using what Elder (2000) has called the "life course perspective." For a discussion of the basic principles of this perspective and recent research, see Elder and Giele (2009). For recent research efforts and application of the life course perspective to specific issues—for example, nutrition—see Herman et al. (2014).

Muuss (1996) provides an example of chronosystem research that might be conducted to investigate behavior among family members and the role time or timing might play in it. He points to the effect the arrival of a new baby might have on parents' interactions with each other and with other children. "By assessing the mother's interaction (with the older siblings) before, during, and after pregnancy, research suggests that the mother's interaction patterns change rather noticeably as a function of these pregnancy/child-bearing conditions" (p. 320). In addition, in several studies, Steinberg (1987, 1988) and Steinberg and his colleagues (1995) examined the relationship between the timing of puberty and its effects on family relationships and parent–adolescent distance.

The ecological model, with its emphasis on the analysis of specific behaviors in increasingly complex settings, nicely complements the other themes and provides one of the central focal points around which these themes cluster. In fact, such a multilevel approach significantly expands the possibilities for explaining a variety of behaviors, as does the next approach.

## 2.1.3: Super and Harkness' Developmental Niche

The concept of the *developmental niche* (at least the "niche" part) was originally borrowed from the field of biological ecology, where *niche* describes the combined features of a particular animal's environment or habitat. Super and Harkness (1994a) use the example of a robin and a pigeon, both of which might live in the same section of a city park but differ in where they build their nests, the kinds of materials they use, and the type of food they eat from the surrounding environment. The birds create a distinct niche for themselves based on each behavior. The fact that this concept of a niche can be employed in biology and in psychology demonstrates, as indicated previously, that there is some unity to scientific efforts. In fact, much of the usefulness of the developmental niche concept lies in its ability to serve as an integrative framework providing connections among culture, socialization, and ecology. In fact, the framework has been used by the authors and others in conducting research in a wide variety of areas, including cognitive, motor, and language development; temperament; sleep and arousal; emotional expression; literacy; and health. It has been used extensively in the study of **ethnotheories**, or *parents' cultural belief systems about the nature of children, the processes of development, and the meaning of behavior* (Harkness & Super, 1996), as well as, more recently, in intervention programs for inner-city children (Harkness, Hughes, Muller, & Super, 2005) and parents' beliefs about children's social and emotional development in cultural context (Harkness, Super, & Mavridis, 2011).

As Sara Harkness and her colleagues (2005) have pointed out, the developmental niche concept owes much to the theoretical thinking and research of several earlier pioneers. For example, there are the "culture and personality" studies of the anthropologists Ruth Benedict and Margaret Mead, as well as Beatrice Whiting's idea of parents as "providers of settings" in which children were able to explore a variety of social behaviors. The authors refer specifically to the approach ". . . interwoven in early anthropological accounts of parenting in other cultures, . . . [which] . . . has emerged more recently as a distinctive focus in the developmental, as well as anthropological, literature, drawing from psychological research on parents' ideas as a force in children's development and on the anthropological construct of 'cultural model'" (p. 338). Although each perspective resulted in critical contributions, Harkness et al. state that ". . . none of them accommodate sufficiently two core issues . . . the integration of various elements in the child's culturally structured environment and the endogenous aspects of individual development that alter the specifics of individual–environment interactions. The developmental niche is a theoretical framework that attempts to acknowledge and integrate this set of considerations" (p. 338).

In applying the term to psychology, Super and Harkness (1994a) originally state that "at the center of the developmental niche, therefore, is a particular child, of a certain age and sex, with certain temperamental and psychological dispositions. By virtue of these and other characteristics, this child will inhabit a different cultural 'world' than the worlds inhabited by other members of his family—and further, the child's world will also change as the child grows and changes" (pp. 96–97). In later writing, Harkness and her colleagues (2005) state that "the primary view is to take the place of the child and look outward to the everyday world" (p. 338).

Although the approach has been used to analyze the niche of single individuals, it has more often been used to compare and contrast cultures or societies that vary in geographic location and historical background. However, the framework has also shown its usefulness in studying variations within a single community and in demonstrating changes in child care that occur as a result of migration. See, for example, Eldering (1995).

Every child's developmental niche consists of three interrelated components (see Table 2.1). First, there are the

**Table 2.1** Components of the Developmental Niche

**1. Physical and Social Settings of Daily Life**

Size, shape, and location of living space

Objects, toys, reading materials

Ecological setting and climate

Nutritional status of children

Family structure (e.g., nuclear, extended, single parent, blended)

Presence of multiple generations (e.g., parents, grandparents, other relatives)

Presence or absence of mother or father

Presence of multiple caregivers

Role of siblings as caregivers

Presence and influence of peer group members

**2. Customs of Child Care and Child-Rearing**

Sleeping patterns (e.g., cosleeping vs. sleeping alone)

Dependence vs. independence training

Feeding and eating schedules

Handling and carrying practices

Play and work patterns

Initiation rites

Formal vs. informal learning

**3. Psychology of the Caregivers**

Parenting styles (e.g., authoritarian, authoritative, laissez-faire)

Value systems (e.g., dependence, independence, interdependence)

Parental cultural belief systems or ethnotheories

Developmental expectations

physical and social settings of daily life in which a child lives (e.g., nuclear family living typically found in many Western cultures versus extended family arrangements found in many Asian, South American, or African countries). Aspects of this component include (1) the kind of company a child keeps (e.g., in rural Kenya, families frequently consist of eight or more children who serve as ready-made playmates and caregivers); (2) the size and shape of one's living space (e.g., in a large North American home, children often have their own rooms compared with families living in overcrowded apartments in Tokyo, where small rooms sometimes serve as combined living, dining, and sleeping areas); and (3) presence or absence of multiple generations living together (e.g., children, parents, grandparents, and other relatives). The differences in these components are clearly observable in the case of Kamuzu (living with his mother, grandmother, and three siblings in a shack in Soweto) and Jeremy (living with his parents and sister in a wealthy neighborhood of Johannesburg, South Africa) described in the opening vignette of Chapter 3.

The second component of the developmental niche focuses on culturally regulated customs of child care and child-rearing practices. These include (1) informal versus formal learning (e.g., family teaching of important skills within most rural African tribal groups versus formal in-school learning characteristic of most Western societies), (2) independence versus dependence training (e.g., independence practiced by most Western parents versus dependence or even interdependence found among the majority of Asian parents), and (3) eating and sleeping schedules (e.g., in many North American and European homes, there are three meals a day at specified times versus the five to six small meals at unscheduled times customary in many Asian cultures). Again, consider and contrast the educational experiences of Jeremy (who attends an exclusive private school) and Kamuzu (who attends a poorly funded segregated school). Other examples include the customary use of playpens in Holland to keep infants happy and safe and the care of younger siblings by older ones in Kenya (Super & Harkness, 1994a).

Finally, the third component relates to the psychology of the caregivers or the psychological characteristics of a child's parents (e.g., developmental expectations, parental cultural belief systems, and types of parenting styles). According to Super and Harkness (1994a), this component "is an important channel for communicating general cultural belief systems to children, through very specific context-based customs and settings" (p. 98). These authors, like us, see a connection between the developmental niche and Bronfenbrenner's approach when they comment: "Drawing from ecological and systems theory, we suggest that the three components interact with each other as a system . . . to maintain consonance among them."

**Figure 2.2** Schematic Representation of the Developmental Niche

**SOURCE:** Handbook of Cross-Cultural Psychology Vol 2, 2e by John W. Berry, T. S. Saraswathi, Pierre R. Dasen. Copyright © 1997, by Allyn and Bacon. Reprinted by permission of John Berry.

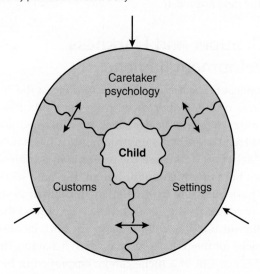

The niche is an 'open system,' however, in that each component interacts independently with elements in the larger culture" (Harkness & Super, 1995, p. 227).

Considering each component, *think about your family as you were growing up—what were the physical and social settings of your daily life; what kind of child-rearing practices or child care did your parents employ; and how would you describe their expectations, belief systems, and parenting styles?* By applying this to your own life, you will gain a greater understanding of this approach and some of the influences that made you the person you are today. *Do you notice differences between you and your siblings? What are they? Why do you think they occur? Do you think they will change with time?*

Super and Harkness (1994a) propose that these components interact and function as a dynamic but not always completely coordinated system in which the individual and the developmental niche adapt and are mutually influential (see Figure 2.2).

For example, although there is a conformity among certain elements of the niche (ecological settings consistent with parental beliefs), inconsistency can result from many factors, including external influences, limited resources, or historical change. Yet, these three subsystems tend to accurately represent the environment as constructed by the child's daily experiences. Thinking about it, this framework can be equally well applied to adult development by expanding the third component—the psychology of the caregivers—to include the psychology of others (e.g., mates and coworkers) who might affect the adult. For an interesting example and expansion of this idea, see a discussion of the developmental niche in Somalia in Box 2.1.

# Box 2.1  Childhood in Somalia: An Example of the Developmental Niche

In an extremely informative and detailed study, Norwegian psychologist Ragnhild Dybdahl explored childhood within the Somali sociocultural context and using the concept of the developmental niche. As part of her study, she conducted open-ended interviews in Mogadishu, Somalia, with twenty mothers, ranging in age from twenty-two to forty (mean age = thirty), and twenty-three children (mean age = ten). Most of the women lived with their husbands, and about one-fourth of them had been raised as nomads. The average number of family members was 7.5 and included various combinations of parents, children, grandparents, parents' siblings, and distant relatives staying as long-term guests. Topics of interest consisted of reasons for having children, normative child care, and the roles parents and children play in the Somali culture.

According to Dybdahl, the first component of the Somali developmental niche is characterized by the culture's economic and health problems; the nomadic way of life, with its emphasis on the extended family and clan; and the child's social and physical settings organized around school and Quranic school (based on the Koran or sacred teachings of Islam), play, work, and household chores, especially care of younger siblings. The second component is characterized by socialization practices in which the infant, initially spending all its time with its mother, is gradually cared for by someone else. Although formal schooling plays a role, informal education is far more important and is the means by which children are taught how to perform household chores and other activities. Quranic school serves as a mode of traditional education. The third component, based on interview comments from mothers, is characterized by mothers' focus on physical health, obedience, resourcefulness, helpfulness and hard work, with expectations differing according to a child's age.

Dybdahl reported on the emergence of several themes associated with Somali childhood: (1) a clear responsibility for family and relatives; (2) the importance of such values as pride, hard work, loyalty, and obedience; (3) a constant struggle for survival and good physical health; and (4) the emotional importance attached to children as sources of short- and long-term security.

As a result of her interviews and observations, Dybdahl argues that Somali society represents a combination of modernism and traditionalism along with collectivism and individualism. According to Dybdahl, her interviews with children provided a view of the niche from inside the culture. She points out that despite the difficult living conditions at the time of her study . . . [just before "Operation Restore Hope" in 1989] . . . with war developing and the existence of poor health conditions, people still believed in the future and in the possibility of change and improvement in one's life. She suggests that this may be due to a combination of fac-

tors, including the nomadic tradition of moving from one location to another and the belief that relatives and family will provide help if needed.

Dybdahl concludes that children must be studied within the context and culture in which they live. Because developmental outcomes in Western societies have often come to be the norm for many of the world's children, avoiding ethnocentrism and developing a global perspective have produced a greater need for cross-cultural research. Dybdahl is further convinced that to make what she calls the "person–setting interaction" the focus of investigation, anthropologists and psychologists need to combine their efforts, and the developmental niche could be a useful concept for doing this. For an updated report on this research, see Dybdahl and Hundeide (1998).

In follow-up studies, the author used some of her experiences from this study to design a successful psychological intervention program with young children and their mothers in the ecological context of war-torn Bosnia and Herzegovina. Findings revealed severe trauma with wide variations in displays of distress that were greatly helped and reduced by means of a simple and inexpensive intervention program adapted to their needs and to an understanding of the developmental niche in which they lived (Dybdahl, 2001, 2002, 2005).

SOURCE: From "The Child in Context: Exploring Childhood in Somalia," paper presented by Ragnhild Dybdahl at the Twenty-Sixth International Congress of Psychology, Montreal, August 1996. Reprinted by permission.

In an important extension of their pioneering approach to development, Super and Harkness (2012) look more closely at how one's environment serves as culture in developmental research. They discuss, in depth, two anthropological concepts of culture they believe are of critical importance to understanding behavior within context—the immediacy of culture and its integrating nature.

More recently, in reviewing contributions of African research on child development (specifically in Senegal), Super, Harkness, Barry, and Zeitlin (2011) have spoken of "thinking locally and acting globally." What they mean is that although developmental science is becoming more globalized because children's environments (ecological settings) are locally structured, indigenous knowledge is required to understand what is happening. They urge more local research because it has already made many key contributions to developmental processes such as cognition, motor development, and attachment.

As to the immediacy of culture, it is the position of Harkness and Super (1994a) (similar to our comments in Chapter 1) that psychologists (primarily in the past, but many even today) have tended to ignore culture when considering development or given it little attention. In this regard, they are critical of Bronfenbrenner's original model, which represents culture as the macrosystem located in the outer circle in his diagram (see Figure 2.1) because the developing child is standing at the center, isolated from the macrosystem by family, neighborhood, school, and other settings in the microsystem, mesosystem, and exosystem. I tend to agree with some of these criticisms and suggest modifications as you will see in the many examples presented throughout this book.

The integrating nature of culture is seen in the pioneering work of many anthropologists, including Margaret Mead, Ruth Benedict, and John and Beatrice Whiting, and in much of the research being done today. As Super and Harkness (1999) point out, these efforts suggest "a relatively new and promising agenda for interdisciplinary psychologists as they seek a more sophisticated understanding of behavior and development: Look for structures that integrate experience, and look for their immediacy in everyday life" (p. 283). This represents a promising direction for future research and study. For more on the ways in which culture serves as an integrating force in development and why the expanded cultural perspective on the environment represented in this text is becoming increasingly important, see Harkness et al. (2005).

In recent years, Harkness and Super (2015) have used the developmental niche approach to look at culture and early childhood development in terms of their implications for policy planning, improving program effectiveness, and assessing children's healthy development in cultural contexts. Some of their research methods and approaches will be discussed later in this chapter. In the meantime, for a sometimes lighthearted look at their ideas, see Day (2013) at http://www.slate.com/blogs/how_babies_work/2013/04/10/parental_ethnotheories_and_how_parents_in_america_differ_from_parents_everywhere.html.

## Points to Ponder

### Understanding Your Developmental Niche

After reading about the developmental niche, you will be better able to remember its components and understand the significance of each if you take the time to apply them to yourself. For example, think about the first component—*physical and social settings*. When you were growing up, what was the size, shape, and location of your bedroom? Did you have to share it with brothers/sisters? What kinds of toys did you play with (gender specific or gender neutral)? What were the kinds of reading materials to which you were exposed? Did you live in a house or an apartment? Where was it located? What was the climate? What kinds of food and meals did you eat? What was your family structure (nuclear, extended, single parent, blended)? Did you live with your parents, grandparents, or other relatives? Was one of your parents absent—mother or father—and, if so, for what reason? Did you have multiple caregivers? Did you have close

friends? What influences did they have on you? Consider the second components—*customs of child care and child-rearing*. Can you recall if you slept alone in your room, with brothers/sisters, or with your parents, and, if so, until what age? Do you think you have a personality that might be described as dependent or independent? Did you feed/eat on a schedule or whenever you were hungry? Were you held and carried a lot or seldom? What games did you play when you were young? Give some examples of your formal and informal learning experiences. Finally, consider the third component—*psychology of the caregivers*. How would you describe your parents' behavior raising you—authoritarian, authoritative, laissez-faire, or something else? Can you characterize their cultural belief system(s)? Did they agree or disagree on the ways in which you should be raised? Did they have any developmental expectations? What were they?

## 2.1.4: Piaget's Theory of Cognitive Development

Jean Piaget (1896–1980), the Swiss-born psychologist, first developed an interest in cognitive development while working with Alfred Binet on intelligence testing in Paris. Piaget became curious about children's thinking and problem solving and why children of the same age made similar mistakes when trying to solve problems. For years, he carefully recorded the cognitive changes he observed in his three children in their home in Geneva. From these and other observations, he theorized that individuals learn by actively constructing their own cognitive world. To Piaget, development is a dynamic process that results from an individual's ability to adapt thinking to meet the demands of an ever-changing environment and, as a result, to formulate new ideas.

According to Piaget's view, normal cognitive growth passes through four distinct periods: infancy, early childhood, middle childhood, and adolescence (see Table 2.2).

**Table 2.2** Piaget's Periods of Cognitive Development

| Period | Approximate Age | Description | Cognitive Milestones |
|---|---|---|---|
| Infancy | Birth to 2 years | Sensorimotor | Object permanence |
| Early childhood | 2 to 6 years | Preoperational | Egocentric thinking, use of symbols |
| Middle childhood | 6 to 12 years | Concrete operations | Conservation |
| Adolescence | 12 years and older | Formal operations | Abstract thinking |

Each period is highlighted by the development of age-typical cognitive skills. Although Piaget provided age ranges for these various developmental periods, he recognized that the exact age at which a particular individual enters a specified period could be significantly affected by that person's physical, cognitive, or cultural experience—what Bronfenbrenner has referred to as the *ecological setting.*

It was Piaget's belief that cognitive development occurs as a result of children's attempts to adapt to their environments and to make sense of the many experiences taking place around them. The ability to do this requires the systematic development of progressively more complex mechanisms or structures. At the center of this activity lies the scheme. A **scheme** is *an organized pattern of thought or action applied to persons, objects, or events in an effort to make sense of them.* In short, it is a mental picture of the world and the things in it. For example, infants develop a wide variety of schemes during the first few months, including schemes for mother, breast, bottle, and father's voice. Over the years, increased interactions with the environment result in these schemes becoming more sophisticated and better coordinated, so by the time an individual reaches formal operations, they are capable of thinking about behaviors and imagining their consequences.

According to Piaget, cognitive development and the ability to adapt to the environment depend on the processes of assimilation and accommodation. **Assimilation** is *the process by which new information and ideas are incorporated or fitted into existing knowledge or schemes.* **Accommodation** is *the process of adjusting or modifying existing schemes to account for new ideas and information.* Anyone who has traveled abroad and attempted to make sense of new surroundings or tried to explain new objects or words to a foreign visitor has engaged in assimilation and accommodation—sometimes with success, sometimes with failure, and sometimes with humor! For example, what happens when Hakon from Norway tries to explain the making of a snowman to Yang, who lives in Malaysia and has never seen or touched snow? In this situation, Yang must make use of accommodation and adjust an existing scheme with which Yang is familiar (perhaps shaved ice) or create a new scheme (snow) to explain this new idea of a snowman. *Can you recall a situation in which you have had to use assimilation and accommodation to explain an idea to someone else? What was it? Did you find it easy or difficult? Did the other person eventually understand?*

It is through active and open interaction with one's environment or surroundings that individuals learn to balance these twin processes of assimilation and accommodation. In terms of Bronfenbrenner's ecological systems approach, these cognitive processes can be said to begin in the family (microsystem); gradually extend to increasingly complex situations that arise in the neighborhood, at day care, or at school (mesosystem); and as the individual eventually moves into adolescence and adulthood, operate in the workplace (exosystem) and the culture at large (macrosystem).

Although there is no doubt that Piaget's theory has had a significant impact on the study and understanding of cognitive development in mainstream Western psychology, his ideas have been challenged on several points. First, some have criticized his emphasis on individual activity occurring apart from social interaction. Such a focus reflects a more individualistic cultural perspective such as that found in North America and Western Europe, and thereby fails to consider similarities or differences in cognitive development in more traditional collectivistic cultures (e.g., China, Japan, and the islands of the South Pacific). Second, some have suggested that Piaget may have overestimated the contribution of motor activity and underestimated the ages at which children are capable of learning and performing a variety of behaviors by themselves. Third, Piaget's claim that once a person moves to a new period of cognitive development, the competencies mastered at that level will be exhibited in other phases of that individual's thinking, does not appear to be fully supported by cross-cultural research findings. Although advances may be apparent in some domains of a person's thinking processes, this may not always be true in other domains. This could be a fertile area for future research.

In the beginning, when Piaget was developing his theory and conducting his early studies, he paid little attention to cultural factors and the effects differences might have on cognitive development. However, as Thomas (1999) has noted, "In later years, Piaget did admit some influence of variations in environments, but still considered genetically controlled maturation to be the primary force behind mental development" (p. 65). Whatever one's position is regarding Piaget's theory, it was the first to introduce cognition into developmental psychology and continues to have considerable influence on contemporary research and practice, most notably on social cognition, self-recognition, and attachment and, as we see in Chapter 5, has been applied to the study of cognitive development in many cultures throughout the world—with varying success.

Lourenco and Machado (1999) suggest that Piaget's theory primarily has been misunderstood and criticized because developmentalists have forgotten his original major goals—"to investigate ontogenetic emergence of new forms of thinking and the construction of necessary knowledge" (p. 158). Instead, they "persist in thinking developmental psychology is concerned with children, adolescents, and adults at specific ages rather than with how they development over time . . . . " (p. 158). For additional reviews and critiques of Piaget's theory, as well as others presented in this chapter, see Bergen (2007) and Green and Piel (2010).

## 2.1.5: Vygotsky's Sociocultural Theory of Development

As discussed, Piaget's position was that cognitive development is largely an individual accomplishment, directed and shaped, in part, by the environment (and, in part, by genetics). However, as indicated, he said little about the importance of the social context in learning. This view was challenged by the Soviet psychologist Lev Semyonovich Vygotsky (1896–1934).

Vygotsky was one of several children raised in an orthodox Jewish family in Russia. As a young man, he frequently wrote critically about Soviet government policies with which he did not agree. As a result, his scientific writings were banned, although his highly acclaimed and influential book *Thought and Language* (Vygotsky, 1934) was finally published in Russian the year he died of tuberculosis. The book is now available in English in a revised edition (Vygotsky, 1968). Many of his notebooks, archival writings, and unpublished materials between 1931 and 1934 have recently been discovered and may provide more insights into his ideas on higher emotions and consciousness (Zavershneva, 2010). (For an interesting, and generally ignored, view of how Vygotsky's Marxist orientation influenced the development of his psychological principles and also affected his life, see Gielen and Jeshmaridian, 1999; also Packer, 2008.)

Vygotsky suggested that development is the result of interaction between cultural and historical factors. He believed that the key feature of development lies in matching a child's demands with the requirements of his or her culture. Vygotsky suggested that there were three major components in this process: the role played by culture, the use of language, and the child's zone of proximal development. Briefly, the **zone of proximal** (nearby) **development (ZPD)** refers to *the distance between a child's actual developmental level and the higher-level potential* (Vygotsky, 1978). It is *the difference between what children can achieve independently and what their potential level of development might be if given help or guidance.* This concept of the ZPD emphasizes Vygotsky's view that social influences contribute significantly to children's development of cognitive abilities and that mentoring or guidance strengthens their growth.

To tie this into several of the major themes already discussed, let us consider the case of twelve-year-old Dabir, a young Saudi adolescent. We might say that the process of learning, which takes place through mentoring in a number of Dabir's diverse ecological settings (home, mosque, school), defines his developmental niche at a particular time in his life. As Vygotsky would view it, Dabir does not have his own ZPD but participates in a shared ZPD with those around him (e.g., siblings, parents, teachers, and peers). This is also true with regard to Deratu (introduced in the opening vignette in Chapter 5), who does not go to school but learns the important cultural and practical lessons necessary for living in rural Ethiopia from the daily guidance provided by her mother.

Although much of Vygotsky's work has been praised for its originality and usefulness, like the pioneering ideas of Piaget, it, too, has its critics. For example, some argue that the zone of proximal development is vague and cannot be adequately measured. Others believe that parts of Vygotsky's theory have been lost or misunderstood in translation and, therefore, are confusing and incomplete. Nevertheless, the theory still represents an increasingly important contribution to cross-cultural human development, with Vygotsky's zone of proximal development appearing more frequently in educators' teaching methods (Thomas, 1999). As an example, Thomas points out, "Rather than waiting for children to display a particular form of reasoning before attempting to teach skills and knowledge that depend on that form, teachers who follow Vygotsky's lead will attempt to teach the new learnings somewhat before the time children might exhibit their readiness spontaneously" (p. 48).

Interestingly, Bronfenbrenner (2005) points out that Vygotsky, along with others, ". . . served to redefine our conceptions of what a child is, what an environment is, what the nature of interaction is, and what development is—except that we have resisted any effort to think through and be explicit about exactly what these new conceptions are" (p. 63). He even goes as far as to point out that aspects of his model were foreshadowed by Vygotsky's theory and "With respect to the macrosystem, once again it was a Vygotskian concept that paved the way" (p. 100). Vygotsky's theory continues to offer opportunities for finding links between cognitive development within cultural and social contexts, particularly in multiethnic societies such as the United States, Malaysia, India, Canada, Australia, and Continental Europe, where children of different backgrounds approach school and cognitive tasks in a variety of ways. For a discussion of the distinction between the classical and nonclassical paradigms of Vygotsky and a comparative analysis of issues and solutions provided within the cultural-historical theory and such Western theories as psychoanalysis, cognitive psychology, and behaviorism, see Obukhova (2012).

## 2.1.6: Erikson's Psychosocial Theory

Erik Erikson, a German-born psychoanalyst and student of Sigmund Freud's daughter, Anna, was the first person to propose a developmental theory encompassing the entire lifespan. Beginning with Freud's stages of psychosexual development, Erikson, a student of anthropology, modified and expanded them to focus greater attention on the social context of development (psychosocial) and less attention on biological and sexual development (psychosexual).

**Table 2.3** Erikson's Stages of Psychosocial Development

| Stage | Crisis | Psychosocial Task |
|---|---|---|
| Infancy | Trust vs. mistrust | Develop first social relationship with primary caregiver(s); develop a fundamental trust in life and the world |
| Toddlerhood | Autonomy vs. shame and doubt | Explore the social environment outside the primary relationship; recognize self as an individual being |
| Early childhood | Initiative vs. guilt | Negotiate one's place within social relationships; learn about the impact of one's social behavior on others; develop a sense of power |
| Middle childhood | Industry vs. inferiority | Learn the importance of social norms and the personal consequences of conformity and nonconformity; develop a sense of competence |
| Adolescence | Identity vs. role confusion | Find social roles and social environments that correspond to one's identity and principles; form one's own identity |
| Young adulthood | Intimacy vs. isolation | Negotiate one's own identity within the context of intimate relationships |
| Middle adulthood | Generativity vs. stagnation | Make a contribution to the larger society; acquire a sense of accomplishment and a place in the world |
| Late adulthood | Integrity vs. despair | Become an integral and active part of one's family and community; come to terms with one's life and choices |

Unlike Freud, his emphasis was on the growth of normal or healthy (rather than abnormal or neurotic) personality development, and he was particularly interested in cultural similarities and differences in the socialization of children and the development of identity during adolescence.

Erikson's theory provides a useful framework for attempting to define and unravel some of the major changes in social behavior that take place at various points in the lifespan. As shown in Table 2.3, he proposed a sequence of eight stages ranging from infancy to later adulthood, each accompanied by a psychosocial crisis requiring resolution if one is to move successfully from one stage to the next. These crises or periods of increased vulnerability and heightened potential involve conflicts between newly developing competencies and a desire to maintain the status quo.

When applying Erikson's theory, as is done at different points throughout the book, there are several points to keep in mind. First, although he assigns an age range to each of his eight stages, these should be considered *only as a guide* because of differences among individuals. Second, successful resolution of a crisis will depend on how a particular culture views the crisis, the sequence in which a particular stage occurs, and the solution evolving from it. Third, although many of Erikson's original ideas were based on development in Western societies, I attempt to modify some of these to show their potential usefulness and increased applicability in other cultural and ecological settings.

## 2.1.7: Kohlberg's Theory of Moral Development

The study of moral development is closely identified with the work of Lawrence Kohlberg, who completed his first research as part of his doctoral dissertation. Responses to a series of **moral dilemmas** (*hypothetical incidents involving a conflict between an individual's desires or needs and the rules of society*) by seventy-two boys, ages ten, thirteen, and sixteen years, were analyzed to determine how moral reasoning developed. For each dilemma, subjects were asked to evaluate the morality of a specific act mentioned in the dilemma. On the basis of these findings, Kohlberg (1981) identified three levels of moral development with two stages in each level, representing a more sophisticated and complex orientation toward justice and normative moral principles (see Table 2.4).

Most children nine years of age or younger are considered to be in the preconventional level, but so are many adolescent offenders and adult criminals. Most adolescents and adults are in the conventional level. The postconventional level is not generally reached before the age of twenty, and then generally only by a minority of individuals.

One of the main assumptions underlying Kohlberg's theory is that these six stages are universal and are present in cultures throughout the world. However, Kohlberg concedes that the stage at which individuals complete their development and the time it takes to be completed may vary from one culture to another.

There have been several criticisms of Kohlberg's theory. First, it is *gender biased* because it was originally based on studies of male subjects (without the inclusion of any women) in one American city—Chicago. Second, his stages are *culturally biased* because they are largely dependent on Western philosophy, and efforts have been made to apply them to non-Western cultures, which may have very

**Table 2.4** Kohlberg's Stages of Moral Development

| Level | Stage | Behavior |
|---|---|---|
| I. Preconventional | 1. Punishment and obedience orientation | Obeys rules to avoid punishment |
| | 2. Instrumental orientation | Obeys rules to receive rewards |
| II. Conventional | 3. "Good child" orientation | Conforms to rules to avoid disapproval by others |
| | 4. Law and order orientation | Conforms to rules to maintain social order |
| III. Postconventional | 5. Morality of contract, individual rights, and democratically accepted law | Accepts and follows laws for the welfare of the larger community |
| | 6. Morality of individual principles and conscience | Believes in and follows self-chosen universal ethical principles |

different moral viewpoints. Nevertheless, his contribution to the understanding of the development of moral reasoning is important, and I shall attempt to modify some of his ideas to show how they might be made more relevant and applicable to other cultural and ecological settings.

As the study continues, we move through the rest of the chapters in this book, I refer back to these theories and show how they help explain various aspects of human development within a wide range of cultural settings and niches. From time to time, I also indicate how these theories might be expanded and modified to better understand and explain cross-cultural similarities and differences in behavior. Let us now look at some of the methodological issues and approaches related to the study of cross-cultural human development.

# 2.2: Methodology in Cross-Cultural Human Development

As noted in Chapter 1, there are many different definitions of culture; therefore, it should not be surprising that there are an almost infinite number of ways to approach and measure cultural differences and similarities. For example, psychologists generally tend to focus on individual behaviors, whereas anthropologists typically tend to look at the behavior of groups. Those doing cross-cultural research in human development frequently make an effort to look at both individual and group behaviors. This is not always easy because each culture and those who live within it, including parents, peers, teachers, and others, have their own ideas and beliefs about children and the ways in which they should develop.

Imagine you are a social scientist (e.g., psychologist, anthropologist, or sociologist) interested in studying the effects of child-rearing practices on children's personality development. Looking at your own culture, you find the range of behaviors limited. So, it seems like a good idea to seek out other cultures, which may have different practices such as swaddling (found among the Hopi Indians in the American Midwest and many Russian and Chinese families), severe independence training (characteristic of certain African tribal groups), or strict dependence or interdependence training (often noted in Japanese families). Taking this approach offers several benefits. First, you are able to increase both the range of independent variables (child-rearing practices) and their effects on the dependent variable (children's personality development). Second, this approach allows (perhaps) for a clearer distinction between biological and environmental influences. For example, if developmental sequences or processes are found to be similar across a variety of diverse cultures, then it might

suggest that genetic or biological factors are a significant contributor. If, however, there are wide differences among the cultures, it is more likely that environmental factors play a larger role. Finally, by conducting cross-cultural research in another culture, one becomes aware of his or her own ethnocentric biases that could influence the design, conduct, and interpretation of the results.

Carrying out a cross-cultural study may sound easy. However, here is the heart of the problem: Jumping on and off planes in far away and often exotic locations can be exciting, rewarding, and great fun, but it's not all beer and curry! Think about the young undergraduate student, Justin Tyme, in our opening vignette, and consider some other possible difficulties—getting required visas to visit certain countries is often difficult, time consuming, and expensive; you may not be allowed to conduct your research once you get there; you and the local food don't always agree; and you can become frustrated and lonely. In short, you have a great many challenges to meet and resolve. However, as Dr. Kitty Litter, the anthropologist in our other vignette, demonstrates, with careful preparation and training, an individual can survive the culture experience and return with important research data and a better and deeper understanding of a culture much different than, or in some cases similar to, one's own. As we see in the next section, although there may be problems in doing cross-cultural research, there are also solutions.

## 2.2.1: Studying Development Cross Culturally: Some Methods, Problems, and Solutions

The intent is not to cover all possible methods, problems, and solutions in this section—besides being impossible, much of this work has been done very well by others. Rather, the aim is twofold: (1) to familiarize you with some of the important information in this area so you gain an appreciation for what cross-cultural researchers have to deal with and (2) to prepare you to understand methods and findings you will encounter as you journey through the remainder of this text.

When conducting research in cross-cultural human development, researchers are interested in discovering principles that are universal to all (or most) cultures (etics), as well as principles that are unique or specific to certain cultures (emics)—a distinction made in Chapter 1. At the same time, they are concerned that the methods they employ are (1) **objective** (*unbiased and not influenced by a researcher's preconceived notions*), (2) **reliable** (*findings are observed consistently and accepted by independent observers*), (3) **valid** (*behaviors and findings are what the researcher claims them to be*), and (4) **replicable** (*other researchers using the same methods report the same or very similar results*).

In this regard, cross-cultural methods are firmly rooted in basic psychological methodology involving the use of experiments (experimental and control groups to test hypotheses), cross-sectional designs (one-time testing of separate age groups), longitudinal designs (repeated testing of same individuals over time), sequential designs (combination of longitudinal and cross-sectional designs), and correlational studies (measurement of relationships between and among variables).

Although cross-cultural psychology shares with its sister social sciences a number of similar needs in designing research (e.g., selecting subjects, defining variables, and choosing appropriate measures and methods), it has to deal with unique issues such as the complexity of culture, interdependence of culture and self, indigenous (or native) psychology versus universal psychology, communication across cultures, and interpretation of cultural findings. For detailed discussions of some of these issues and approaches to their resolution, see Berry, Poortinga, and Pandey (1997), Cole (1998), Lonner (2005), Matsumoto and Juang (2008), Smith (2004), and van de Vijver and Leung (2000). A more recent book by Matsumoto and van de Vijvir (2011) addresses some of the methodological problems unique to cross-cultural research that need to be resolved if research and findings are to be valid and reliable and, eventually, lead to real-world cultural applications. For more specific discussions of issues related to measurement in cross-cultural human development, see Friedman and Wachs (1999), Keller and Greenfield (2000), and Super and Harkness (2000). For information on conducting fieldwork studies, see Hobbs and Wright (2006).

Matsumoto (2000) has discussed some of the critical questions and issues in this area, and because many of these also apply to the conduct of cross-cultural human development research, they are summarized here: (1) *theories and hypotheses*—can the theories under investigation be appropriately applied to all cultures in the study, and do the hypotheses have the same meaning for all subjects independent of their cultural backgrounds? (2) *methods*—are the subjects representative of their culture and are they equivalent for comparative purposes, and are all measures (e.g., scales and items) reliable and valid in all cultures under investigation and do they have linguistic equivalence (determined through the method of back translation from original language to target language and back to original language until all meanings are equivalent)? (3) *data and analyses*—are there any unique cultural responses operating and have they been controlled? and (4) *interpretations and conclusions*—are findings and interpretations free of cultural bias and value judgments based on the researcher's own cultural background? These serious and complex questions must be carefully considered and adequately answered if research across cultures is to make

significant contributions to our knowledge about similarities and differences in human development.

Because of the seriousness of one of the issues mentioned previously—linguistic equivalence—additional comments regarding the translation and adaptation of instruments and materials from one culture to another deserve special attention. The International Test Commission, consisting of members from a number of international psychological organizations, has prepared a set of twenty-two specific guidelines for conducting multicultural studies that anyone interested in conducting cross-cultural research should take into account before designing and carrying out a particular study (see van de Vijver, 2001, for a complete listing of these guidelines). These are divided into four categories: (1) context guidelines focusing on general principles for test translations, (2) development guidelines for enhancing equivalence, (3) administrative guidelines for attaining comparability of administration in the use of different language versions, and (4) guidelines for documentation or score interpretations.

One technique widely used to achieve linguistic equivalence when a researcher is unfamiliar with or not fluent in one or more of the languages to be used in a project is **back translation**. This procedure involves *translating material (instruments, surveys, etc.) from a "source" language (e.g., English) to a "target" language (e.g., Arabic) by a bilingual translator fluent in both languages*. The target translation (Arabic) is then translated by another bilingual translator back to the source (English) language. This continues until there is agreement that the translations are linguistically equivalent. Because this technique often relies on literal translation of the material, ignoring such issues as comprehension and readability, a second procedure involving a group or committee with expertise in a variety of areas (language, culture, psychology, anthropology) carries out the translation process until there is agreement that all language versions are equivalent.

As for the use of specific methods, there are numerous ways in which these can be categorized. One approach is to consider four possible types of cross-cultural studies: (1) investigation of theories and concepts originally developed in Western countries as they may (or may not) apply in non-Western settings (e.g., Piaget's stages of cognitive development and Kohlberg's levels of moral development); (2) replication in one culture of studies previously conducted in another culture (e.g., children's acquisition of language skills, peer pressure during adolescence, and expression of emotion in toddlers); (3) collaborative research in which researchers from two or more cultures participate equally in the design and conduct of a study (e.g., assessment of personality in five cultures; a cross-national study of children's behavior with friends; and exploration of ethnic identity in Russia, Finland, and South Africa); and (4) administration of test materials designed and standardized in one culture but used in other cultures (e.g., tests of intelligence, personality, and socialization).

A popular approach among psychologists, as well as some sociologists, is **cross-cultural comparisons** in which *individuals from at least two different cultural groups are measured and compared on some aspect of behavior* (e.g., European and Asian attitudes toward the criminal justice system). As for individual methods, a technique widely used by anthropologists in their cultural studies is **ethnography**. Typically, a researcher lives for a time in a culture observing, interviewing, and sometimes testing its members, and produces *a detailed description of a society's way of life, including its attitudes, customs, and behaviors*. The early works of Margaret Mead, Ruth Benedict, and others are examples. Information contained in hundreds of these reports has been classified and indexed in the **Human Relations Area Files (HRAF)** and is frequently used in **hologeistic research**, *projects in which hypotheses about such topics as gender differences in aggression or preference for breastfeeding versus bottle-feeding can be tested on a worldwide sample of more than 340 societies.*

Another approach that has been around for quite a while but is receiving increased attention from researchers today is the **narrative method**, which, depending on the researcher, looks at multiple narrative materials, including stories (oral or written), diaries, letters, and their analyses. For a description and discussion of this approach, see the book *Narrative Methods* by Atkinson and Delamont (2006) and *The Psychology of Narrative Thought* by Beach (2010).

Matsumoto (2000) points out that "in recent years, there has been an interesting merging of research approaches across disciplines, with an increasing number of scientists adopting comparative techniques for use in single-culture immersion research, and comparative researchers adopting qualitative ethnographic methods to bolster their traditional quantitative approach" (p. 39). This can be seen as a positive sign that these social science disciplines, often at odds, may be showing signs of understanding and learning from each other, a point emphasized previously.

More recently, Matsumoto and Juang (2008) and Matsumoto and van de Vijver (2011) have cited ecological-level studies in which data are obtained from individuals in several different cultures, summarized or averaged, and used as descriptors for those cultures. Two of the most prominent ecological-level studies of culture are the work of Hofstede (2001), Hofstede and Hofstede (2004), and Hofstede, Hofstede, and Minkov (2010) on work-related values in multinational business organizations and Schwartz's (1995, 2011, 2012) value orientations, both of which are discussed later in this book.

Keller and Greenfield (2000) look more specifically at some of the contributions that developmentalists' research make to cross-cultural psychology—methodologically,

theoretically, and empirically. For example, in terms of methodology, they point to the use of "contextualized procedures, such as naturalistic observation, suitable for studying behavior in its cultural context" (p. 52). Theoretically, "developmentalists point to the fact that the culturally constructed behavior of adults can be viewed as an endpoint along a developmental pathway, and that adults provide cultural socialization to the next generation" (p. 52). Finally, empirically, they point out that "a developmental approach leads researchers to investigate the culture-specific shape of developmental stages" (p. 52).

For those who want to know more about cross-cultural research methodology from a primarily psychological viewpoint, including additional problems and solutions, the volumes by Segall, Dasen, Berry, and Poortinga (1999), Berry et al. (1997), and Keith (2013) are recommended. Cross-cultural research methodology, as practiced by anthropologists, is discussed in a volume by Ember and Ember (2000).

Let us now take a closer look at some of these issues and several of the research methodologies used in the cross-cultural study of human development, particularly those associated with our two major theoretical viewpoints—the ecological model and the developmental niche.

## 2.2.2: Methods for Assessing Components of the Developmental Niche

Super and Harkness (1999) have presented, in extensive detail, their suggestions for successfully measuring and assessing the components of the developmental niche. This section provides an overview of their methodology, which involves a combination of psychological and anthropological research techniques. Anyone with a serious interest in the developmental niche approach is advised to consult this important work that blends theory and methodology in a way seldom done in the study of cross-cultural human development. It stands as a model for others in the field and as an example of the effort to bring closer together anthropology and psychology that we hope to see more of in the future.

According to Super and Harkness, the first group of methods (participant observation and ethnographic interviewing) is indispensable for selecting and understanding important components or units of the developmental environment, and for providing the foundation for determining what should be measured and how to create hypotheses that will demonstrate how various components of the developmental niche are related to each other. They point out that **participant observation** (*a technique in which an investigator* *lives for a time with or near a group of people and observes its daily life, activities, and rituals*) and **ethnographic interviews** (*asking group members to describe their culture's typical behaviors, attitudes, beliefs, and values*), if carefully carried out, can help identify elements within each of the three developmental niche components (see Table 2.1). An example of their use in actual research is in a study by Levy (1996), in which he reports that differences in parental beliefs and practices about learners and teaching in Tahiti and Nepal may be a result of differences in the level of societal complexity in these two cultures.

Other techniques useful in identifying important aspects of all three components, but settings in particular, include spot observations and diaries. Results from **spot observations** (*a series of random unannounced observations of a group, sufficient in number to allow for statistical analysis*) and **diaries** (*written accounts of changes in daily activities kept by participants over varying periods of time such as a full twenty-four-hour day*) are useful for "describing the physical and social settings of daily life not only in terms of their particular qualities but also in terms of their empirical distributions . . . [and] . . . provide a basis for identifying regularities in settings and activities that may differ between groups, or that one wants to relate thematically to other elements in the niche, or to developmental trends" (Super & Harkness, 1999, p. 304).

Measuring customs (the second component of the developmental niche), according to Super and Harkness (1999), requires (1) a qualitative approach, in which behavioral consistencies are identified either through **direct observation** of a cultural group or by means of **ethnographic descriptions** of its everyday attitudes, beliefs, and behaviors, and (2) a quantitative approach producing "measures of individuals' views on the nature and importance of the custom or measures of the frequency of occurrence of the identified practice, or both" (p. 308). They assert that the ideal approach to assessing and measuring the customs component "demonstrates their existence, documents their occurrence, and explains their relationship to the settings of daily life and to the psychological theories that guide them" (p. 308).

Measuring caregiver psychology or parental beliefs and values (the third component of the niche) also requires a combination of qualitative and quantitative approaches. These may include **structured questioning** (frequently based on findings obtained from the methods previously discussed) and **formal methods** originally employed in the cognitive sciences (see Borgatti, 1992, for additional information).

Truly understanding culture and the critical role it plays in human development requires an appreciation of qualitative, as well as quantitative, findings. In the words of Super and Harkness (1999), "Findings in one domain suggest further exploration or reexamination in another,

and replication of patterns suggests salient cultural themes" (p. 312). Their unique organizational scheme provides answers to many questions about culture and development while setting forth even more challenges for the future.

## 2.2.3: Studying Ecological Systems

Unlike Super and Harkness, who constructed their approach to human development and conducted much of their own research in support of it, Bronfenbrenner has primarily been the developer of ideas and hypotheses, whereas others have conducted research to show the validity of his approach. To illustrate this, let us briefly look at some examples of representative research carried out on each of the four ecological systems.

First, Brown, Lohr, and Trujillo (1990), in an effort to show how the peer microsystem of adolescents becomes increasingly differentiated and influential in one's behavior, reported on the ways in which both positive (acceptance, friendship, status, and popularity) and negative (drinking, smoking, stealing, and cheating) behaviors are associated with different adolescent lifestyle decisions.

Second, Muuss (1996) has stated, "A mesosystem analysis examines the quality, the frequency, and the influence of such interactions as family experiences on school adjustment" (p. 325). An interesting example of this is Epstein's (1983) study of the longitudinal effects of family–school–person interactions on student outcomes, which, unexpectedly, reported that the interaction of family and school was of far greater importance and influence than the variables of race and socioeconomic status. Noted among the findings was a continuing influence of the family and school environments far beyond the early childhood years, lending support to the interaction effects among systems proposed by Bronfenbrenner. As an example, Epstein pointed out that students experiencing the greatest change in independence were those initially scoring low on this behavior (and whose families failed to emphasize decision making), but who attended schools that placed a strong emphasis on student participation.

Third, as you may remember from our original comments, Bronfenbrenner has asserted that decisions made in the exosystem (e.g., in parents' workplaces) can have an extremely important influence on the life of a child or adolescent (even though they are not part of that setting). Flanagan and Eccles (1993) effectively demonstrated this point in their two-year longitudinal study of changes in parents' work status and their effects on the adjustment of children before and after their transition to junior high school. Results indicated that of four family types identified (based on patterns of change or stability in parental work status), children in deprived and declining families were less competent than their peers in stable or recovery families. Although most of the subjects experienced some difficulty in school adjustment, the transition was shown to be especially difficult for those whose parents were simultaneously dealing with changes in their work status.

Fourth, although the macrosystem is in many ways removed from the daily life of an individual, it does consist of extremely important societal influences (political, religious, economic, and other values) that clearly affect human development. Bronfenbrenner (1967) demonstrated the influence of macrosystem values in an early comparison of peer group and adult pressures on children in the United States and the former Soviet Union. At that time, in the Soviet Union, a cohesive core of socially accepted and politically endorsed values left little room for differences in expectations between the adults or peers in one's environment. In the United States, in contrast, there were frequently unmistakable differences between these significant people, with the result that children and adolescents often found themselves being pulled in different directions. With the breakup of the former Soviet Union, the situation that once existed in the United States (and, to a large extent, still appears to) now is much more characteristic of the former Soviet Union as well.

In closing this discussion, it seems only fair to give Bronfenbrenner the last word on the challenge of operationally defining elements of his evolving bioecological model as well as on his efforts to scientifically measure them. As he states, "Thus far, I have accorded more attention to the conceptual rather than to the operational aspects of this challenge. I did so for a reason; namely, most of the research designs and methods of measurement currently in use in developmental science are not well-suited for what I have referred to elsewhere as 'science in the discovery mode' (Bronfenbrenner & Morris, 1998). To be more specific, these designs and methods are more appropriate for verifying already formulated hypotheses than for the far more critical and more difficult task of developing hypotheses of sufficient explanatory power and precision to warrant being subjected to empirical test . . . . In summary, most of the scientific journey still lies ahead" (Bronfenbrenner, 1999, p. 24). For those interested in reading more about these issues, see any of the several references mentioned in this discussion.

## Summary: Theories and Methodology

This chapter focuses on theories and methodologies used in the conduct of cross-cultural research in general and developmental research in particular. We began with reasons for studying human development—to *understand, explain, predict, and* (in some instances) *control behavior.* To successfully achieve these goals, we need to use theories or *sets of hypotheses or assumptions about behavior.* The chapter discussed, in detail, six approaches that will receive significant attention throughout this text—Bronfenbrenner's ecological model, Super and Harkness' developmental niche concept, Piaget's theory

of cognitive development, Vygotsky's sociocultural theory of development, Erikson's psychosocial theory, and Kohlberg's theory of moral development. We discussed some of the ways in which cross-cultural methods might be classified; distinguished between different types of cross-cultural researchers (natives and sojourners); and commented on specific techniques, including ethnographies, cross-cultural comparisons, and hologeistic studies. We concluded with a discussion of methods for assessing components of the developmental niche and ecological systems.

## Study Questions

Explain the purpose of theories in the study of human development.

Comment on the theory you believe best describes human development and give reasons and examples to support it.

Select a culture, other than your own, and describe the five systems of Bronfenbrenner's theory as they explain behavior within it.

Describe and discuss Bronfenbrenner's ecological model of human development.

Describe Harkness and Super's developmental niche model.

Compare and contrast the human development theories of Piaget and Vygotsky.

Select a human development topic you want to investigate and describe the theoretical and/or methodological approach you would use and your reasons.

# Developmental Analysis
## Introduction

Throughout the remainder of this book, you will have the opportunity to explore your own development. By finding ways to apply important concepts to your own life, you will not only better understand them but will also become more aware of whom you are and the various influences (cultural, familial, biological, and social) that have contributed to your unique development.

One difficulty with organizing the large amount of material in a book like this is that most research is not collected in a longitudinal manner. As you read through Chapters 3 to 9, you will become familiar with these seven areas of focus: socialization, family, language and cognition, self and personality, social behavior, issues of gender and sexuality, and health. As you explore each of these areas, it is recommended you take time to examine how each has contributed to your development and, in many cases, continues to play a role. Try to relate the many concepts to your own life by jotting down brief examples from your experiences.

To help you in this self-exploratory effort, you will find in each chapter a developmental box presenting the fictionalized life of "Maddi" Skelton, who will be followed throughout the book as she describes her life in terms of the material presented in each chapter. Her life will be described in the first person from infancy through the later adult years. This will help provide continuity among the various topics presented throughout the book.

These developmental boxes, beginning with socialization in Chapter 3, will serve as examples of how you might reflect on your own life. Begin by first describing your culture and the ecological system and developmental niche in which you grew up. Subdivide your notes into sections labeled Infancy, Childhood, Adolescence, and Adulthood. Within each section, describe your development in terms of culturally influenced behaviors such as sleep, feeding patterns, food preferences, attitudes toward caregivers (parents, teachers, siblings), early learning (formal and informal), rites of passage characteristic of your culture, family relations, and any other important aspects of the socialization process that had an effect on the person you are today. Be sure to use concrete examples from your own life. By the time you reach Chapter 9, not only will you understand these concepts better but you will also have authored your own autobiography—something you will likely treasure and add on to as you make your way through additional life stages.

Enjoy!

# Chapter 3
# Culture and Socialization

*Kamuzu Mathebula is fourteen years old and lives in Diepkloof, a section of Soweto, an all-black township outside Johannesburg, South Africa. He lives with his mother, grandmother, two brothers, and a sister in a shack made of discarded plastic sheeting and wood with a corrugated iron roof. There is no electricity or running water. Diarrhea and tuberculosis are common here. His mother, a widow, works as a maid for the Martins, an Afrikaner (white South African) family, five miles away. Kamuzu has attended poorly funded segregated schools most of his life. With the end of apartheid (the white government–enforced system of "separateness") in 1990, his future has been looking better. Rather than working long hours for meager wages in one of the local textile factories, Kamuzu hopes to attend the University of Witwatersrand in Johannesburg to become a doctor and help his people.*

*Hendrik and Patricia Martin, the Dutch-descended Afrikaner family that Kamuzu's mother works for, have a son named Jeremy who is also fourteen years old. He and his younger sister, Yvonne, live in a wealthy neighborhood of large, well-kept homes. Jeremy's father is the president of an import–export company started by his grandfather, and his mother teaches science at the exclusive private school that he and his sister attend. His goal, similar to Kamuzu's, is to attend the university in Johannesburg and study medicine.*

Two young South African boys—the same age, residing just a few miles apart near the tip of the African continent—supposedly live in the same society but have been raised in clearly different environments (*developmental niches*) by very different families, yet they both want to become doctors.

How can we account for the similarities and differences in the development of these two young adolescents? Although it is true that Kamuzu and Jeremy share a number of characteristics, in large measure they are a reflection of two distinct cultures—different social contexts, parental belief systems, societal values, and cultural perspectives. Every one of us, like each of them, is influenced by a unique combination of factors, including the genetic material inherited from our ancestors, the family in which we are raised and the style of

parenting to which we are exposed, the friends we make and the schools we attend, the historical period in which we are born, and (of pivotal importance) the culture and ecological contexts in which we live out our lives. As Sigel, McGillicuddy-DeLisi, and Goodnow (1992) have noted, "Since it is a culture which serves to define values, beliefs, and actions of families, it is imperative and in fact a virtual necessity for the applied developmental psychologist to develop a knowledge base of cultures" (Roopnarine & Carter, 1992, p. ix.).

Indeed, although this is essential, knowledge of cultures is not enough. To genuinely understand and explain cultural differences in development, we first need to look at the way in which a culture defines these values, beliefs, and actions, and this requires an understanding of the crucial process of socialization.

## 3.1: Ecological Context

As pointed out, the ecological approach looks at human development in terms of the individual within a number of changing environments where growth and development occur as a result of relationships between and among the individual and others surrounding him or her. A child is first studied in the context of the family followed by the community and then the expanded culture. We begin by considering the concept of socialization and its influence on various behaviors across the lifespan and across cultures.

### 3.1.1: What Is Socialization?

Similar to many concepts in developmental psychology, socialization can be variously defined. For our purposes, we will view **socialization** as *the process by which an individual becomes a member of a particular culture and takes on its values, beliefs, and other behaviors in order to function within it.* It is through the process of socialization that society teaches desirable behavior while inhibiting undesirable behavior, prepares individuals to become successfully functioning members in its principal institutional settings (family, school, community, and workplace), and guarantees that important traditions (although sometimes modified) will be passed to future members of the culture.

It is far from easy to describe or explain cultural socialization. Contemporary theories focus on the thousands of interactive exchanges between a child and family members over a long period of time during which each is influencing the behavior of the other, making it difficult to assess cause and effect. In addition, explanations have become more complex and multidimensional than those offered by earlier approaches (Grusec & Hastings, 2008).

Edwards (1996) has noted that socialization theories have also undergone substantial revision. For far too long, theories and their proponents were ethnocentric (e.g., proposing that explanations of behavior in one society applied equally well in others). As we frequently note throughout this book, such theories relied heavily on research and assumptions based in Western societies, with the result that theories were either nongeneralizable to other cultures or failed to take into account the richness of human diversity. In a sense, theorists were victims of their own socialization and were promoting a Westernized view of the world that they frequently imposed on the cultures they were studying, rather than letting indigenous behaviors emerge and be recognized. As evidence, Edwards (1989) cites some of her own earlier work in which Mayan children in Zinacantan, Mexico, learned toilet training and other self-care skills by means of imitation and thereby made a relatively easy transition from infancy to early childhood, compared with other cultures in which these activities are characterized by resistance and great difficulty. There would appear to be an entirely different cultural context operating in this Mayan culture than what we tend to see in North America and some cultures of Western Europe. Values important to the successful functioning of these Mayan children are being transmitted in a way that provides a foundation for the development of infants and toddlers, who closely observe and carefully imitate and respond to their elders and others, rather than expecting others to respond to them. A researcher who has made significant contributions to our understanding of socialization, particularly in the area of cognition, is Barbara Rogoff (2003). Her book *Apprenticeship in Thinking* (Rogoff, 1990) is recommended in Chapter 5 as a source for additional reading in this area. Rogoff's approach to this topic has been greatly influenced by the work of the Soviet psychologist Lev Vygotsky, whose work on culture and cognitive development is discussed in detail in the same chapter. Rogoff (personal communication, 2004) developed the concept of *guided participation* to expand on Vygotsky's concept of the *zone of proximal development* "in order to draw attention to the opportunity to

learn through participation in nonverbal and tacit forms of interaction as well as through societal arrangements, not just from instruction or scaffolding." Guided participation emphasizes the bidirectional, or two-way, nature of socialization and the fact that children are active participants in their own socialization. In describing this concept, Brislin (1993) provides an example familiar to those who have lived in or conducted research in many of the countries in South and Southeast Asia—namely, the cultural requirement that children learn that the right (clean) hand is for eating and the left (unclean) hand is to be used for personal hygiene. If children do not learn this behavior through participation in daily home activities, then parents, other adults, or even older siblings will guide the children in the appropriate way. For example, while eating, one of these "teachers" might be seen inhibiting use of the left hand while gently guiding the right toward the food. The point, Brislin says, is "that the children's behavior directs the teacher's behavior. If children learn through simple observation, there is no need for the more active intervention of holding down and guiding hands" (p. 130). Contrast this more directive approach with the observational approach of Mayan child training cited previously, as well as in Rogoff (2011) and Correa-Chavez, Mejia-Arauz, and Rogoff (2015).

Let us now consider how the socialization process relates to two of our major themes: the ecological model and the developmental niche.

## 3.1.2: Ecological Model and Developmental Niche

As already noted, socialization is a lifelong process occurring within the multiple environments or social contexts in which we live, influencing the activities in which we participate, and contributing significantly to our development across the lifespan.

In Chapter 2, we introduced two important themes that are interwoven throughout this book: Bronfenbrenner's **ecological model** and the concept of the **developmental niche**. The ecological model allows us to look at human development as it occurs in its real world settings or ecological context and comprises five categories of interrelated systems. It is within these interconnected contexts that socialization takes place and in which we begin to see the development of "lives across cultures."

The socialization process and the interaction between an individual and his or her environment in its various contexts (*microsystem, mesosystem, exosystem, macrosystem,* and *chronosystem*) are at the center of the ecological model. For example, if one were interested in comparing and contrasting the self-concepts of adolescents in Israel and Palestine, then it would be critical to consider their socialization experiences within their culture, home, school, and among peers, as well as their exposure to the media, child-rearing practices, parental attitudes and values, and other important influences. In this regard, *take a moment and think of your own self-concept. What were some of the socialization experiences that influenced you? Was one more important than another? In what ways? What do you see as your present self-concept? Are you satisfied or not satisfied with it?*

Likewise, socialization plays a major role in the three interrelated components of Super and Harkness' developmental niche. An interesting example is a study by McDade and Worthman (2004) focusing on "socialization ambiguity." The authors noted that nontraditional lifestyles such as globalization were presenting young people in the islands of Samoa with new socialization opportunities along with possibilities of "stress-inducing dissonance" (conflicts resulting from incompatible beliefs and attitudes held simultaneously). Their findings revealed socialization ambiguity to be a significant source of stress on two different islands, although the direction varied, possibly an indication of dissimilar socialization objectives on each island. *Can you think of any event or situation in your life when you experienced "socialization ambiguity"? Do you recall how it was resolved?*

To illustrate how the developmental niche and family context can interact in important ways to affect child behavior, we provide three brief examples that will receive detailed attention later. First, if a child is doing poorly in school, this can have an impact on behavior within the family and affect the parent–child relationship in several ways (e.g., neglect or abuse). A home situation involving neglect or abuse can have effects on a child's relationships with parents, peers, teachers, and other family members. In addition, a child's temperament within a particular cultural context (e.g., Brazil or Japan) may affect the way parents interact with that child and, in turn, influence the development of personality and self-concept. Finally, a sick, fussy, or light-sleeping child may keep parents awake at night, making them less effective at work or in their relationship with each other. (Variations in sleep patterns and their relationship to the approaches mentioned previously are discussed in the next section.)

With (hopefully) a clear understanding of the ecological model, the developmental niche, and the cross-cultural theme, we are now prepared to look at some cultural variations in socialized behavior.

## 3.1.3: Some Cultural Variations in the Socialization of Behavior

As pointed out in Chapter 1, in a book of this type, with its major focus on cultural similarities and differences, it is impossible to provide the same comprehensive view of human development as more traditional developmental texts. For a general overview of human development principles, we direct the reader to one of these texts. Our goal is to consider selected topics for which a large or growing body of cross-cultural research evidence exists and discuss these topics chronologically—from the early beginnings of infancy through the later years of adulthood. Another aspect, unique to this discussion, is the incorporation (and suggested modification) of Erik Erikson's psychosocial theory of development in an effort to place these behaviors within a cross-cultural perspective. (See Chapter 2 for a review of the major aspects of this theory.)

We begin our discussion of selected topics, which are followed in a similar fashion in subsequent chapters, with a consideration of some of the principal behaviors socialized by most parents across cultures. We turn first to socialization during pregnancy, prenatal development, and birth.

## 3.1.4: Pregnancy, Prenatal Development, and Birth

Joining a birth preparation class or exercise class during the early stages of pregnancy provides women with opportunities to interact with other mothers or soon-to-be mothers and become socialized into one of the most important experiences of their lives. They must be objective and extremely careful in assessing the information they receive because no two mothers have the same experience and theirs may be quite different from other mothers. However, especially for young first-time mothers, the experience may prove to be very beneficial.

In an interesting and creative approach, Kara Smith (2001), a language education professor, explored her use of "prebirth gender talk" for the initiation of gender socialization of her baby in the womb following a gender-identifying ultrasound. Findings showed that, in this particular case, gender socialization began in utero, and the labeling of the fetus predetermined the personality for her and also, knowing it was a male, allowed her tone of voice to become "sharper" and "stronger." Presented as a "case study in narrative," Smith documented the words spoken and feelings expressed to her second child beginning in the second trimester, in utero, in an effort to document engendered language and socialization. She concluded that knowledge of the baby's gender imposed social mores on her "interaction" with it, and she began nurturing specific male traits and stereotypes. To learn more and read a transcript of this mother's "prebirth talk," go to http://www.redorbit.com/news/health/158908/prebirth_gender_talk_a_case_study_in_prenatal_socialization/.

In terms of actual childbirth, women are likely to experience differences in length and difficulty of labor. Yet, in the United States, a socialization of birth procedures is often applied to large numbers of mothers-to-be during delivery: placed on their backs, attached to a fetal monitor and IV for delivery of medicine, injection of pain-relieving drugs, and administration of an episiotomy to widen the birth area. In some cultures, women hold on to a rope, lie in a hammock, relax in a pool or Jacuzzi, or even squat or kneel on the floor. Doctors and nurses are frequently replaced by midwives, female relatives, family, and friends. For a detailed discussion of the ecology of birth and the birth process across cultures, see Chapter 4.

# 3.2:  Infancy

When a newborn arrives in the world, independent of its particular culture, he or she has many basic needs that require immediate attention. How these needs are met and the manner in which infants are socialized varies considerably across cultures and often among ethnic groups *within a single society*. In fact, as we shall see frequently throughout this book, *there is often more variability in certain behaviors within cultures than between or among cultures.* [A very important point to remember.]

From the first hours of infancy, culture influences patterns of parenting (e.g., when and how parents care for infants, how much parents allow infants to explore their surroundings, how nurturing or restrictive parents might be, and which behaviors parents value and socialize). Bornstein (2002) expressed it succinctly when he says, "With the birth of a baby, a parent's life is forever altered. Those changes, in turn, shape the experiences of the infant and, with time, the person he or she becomes. Linked, parent and child chart that course together. Infancy is a starting point of life for both infant *and* parent" (p. 33).

Many skills and abilities are influenced by socialization in this early period—physical (sitting, crawling, walking, grasping), cognitive (language), social (emotional expression, attachment, temperament), and more. Many of these will be discussed later in this book. At this point, let us look at three of the most basic behaviors parents need to socialize.

## 3.2.1: Sleep

Although all babies require sleep, psychological, anthropological, and even pediatric literature reveals considerable variation in cultural sleeping arrangements and amount of sleep needed (McKenna, 2002, 2012; McKenna & Gettler, 2015). For example, infants generally require between sixteen and twenty hours of sleep per day, waking about

every two to three hours to feed. This changes around four months, when babies sleep between ten and twelve hours at night with one or two feedings. Changes continue as the child gets older.

According to Harkness and Super (1995), the way sleep is organized, including where and with whom, is an intriguing aspect of culture because, although it is a private rather than public behavior, it is highly structured by different societies and tends to be relatively resistant to change. As these researchers point out, "Parents play a primary role in the assignment of settings and routines for sleep, thus perpetuating a cycle of culture transmission within the privileged context of the family" (p. 227). For example, in an early study of Kipsigis farming families in the highlands of rural Kenya in East Africa, Harkness and Super noted that although the next-to-youngest child continues to sleep with its mother and other siblings after the birth of a younger child, it no longer sleeps at the mother's front but rather at her back. This change, along with the termination of breast feeding and back-carrying, results in a "fundamental shift in the child's physical and social settings of life" (p. 227).

Sleep management is one of the earliest culturally determined parent–child interactions and may provide a useful framework for interpreting cross-cultural differences in the varying emphases placed on such behaviors as autonomy and dependence. Others have made a similar argument with regard to the development of interdependence and sensitivity to the needs of other people.

In a somewhat related effort, aimed at studying development as adaptation, Chisholm (1983) conducted an extensive investigation among Navajo Indians in North America of their use of the cradleboard (a small wooden frame to which an infant is strapped) to determine whether it might cause disruption in mother–infant interaction. (See photo of a Hopi Indian cradleboard.) The Navajo cradleboard, or literally "baby diaper," has several purposes, such as infant transport, babysitting device, and regulator of infant states, including level of physiological responsiveness or arousal and sleep. According to Chisholm, a child is asleep most (as much as 85%) of the time he or she is on the cradleboard, but the numbers of hours on the board may vary from only a few to as many as twenty-three, with fifteen to eighteen being normal. Chisholm concludes that cradleboard use seems to have no lasting effect on a child's behavioral development, and any observed group differences between Navajo and Anglo children are likely a result of sociocultural differences within the infant's environment—what we would attribute to the child's ecological settings and the developmental niche.

Although it is a common practice among middle-class families in the United States and Canada to put

Native American children strapped to cradleboards during their first year walk at about the same time as other children.

(World History Archive/Alamy Stock Photo)

development of a feeling of *trust versus mistrust* (e.g., the world is good and comfortable—trust—or threatening and uncomfortable—mistrust). Whichever view develops will depend largely on the parent–infant relationship. For example, many infants learn to trust that if they cry because they are hungry, then someone will pick them up and feed them. Parents, in turn, learn to trust that their infants will be quieted and comforted when they are fed because the pattern of interaction is consistent.

Similar patterns develop near the end of infancy (during the second and third year) with regard to the second crisis of *autonomy versus shame and doubt*. For example, either children will begin to explore their surroundings on their own (sometimes getting into trouble) and decide for themselves what they want to wear, eat, or do, or they will obediently follow the demands of parents, develop doubts about their abilities, and feel incapable of making decisions and governing their own behavior.

young infants in their own room to sleep (in part, to give them an early start down the road to independence), many Mayan mothers (American Indian peoples of Mexico and Central America) view this custom as equivalent to child neglect. In contrast, interdependence—a prominent personality and cultural characteristic among Japanese—can be attributable, at least in some measure, to the fact that Japanese children (sometimes due to an overcrowded microsystem) frequently sleep with their parents until the age of six or even, in some cases, to the beginning of puberty, when independent sleeping marks a culturally recognized change in one's developmental niche. Similar findings have been found in China, where "all-night cosleeping" during infancy and early childhood is the norm, decreasing in prevalence with increasing age, and unusual after puberty. In urban China, the prevalence of regular bed sharing has been found to be 18.2% and as high as 55.8% in seven-year-olds (Liu et al., 2003), and in Korea, 73.5% of mothers approve of bed sharing between three and six years of age (Yang & Hahn, 2002).

The parent–child relationship and its effect on the development of dependence, independence, or interdependence can also be viewed within the framework of Erikson's psychosocial theory. According to Erikson's model, which, as we have cautioned, tends to present a predominantly Westernized perspective, social maturation during the first year of infancy is reflected in the

Japanese children often sleep with their parents for the first several years.

(Paylessimages/Fotolia)

If we look at trust and independence, as illustrated in the Kipsigis and Japanese examples, then the Western bias inherent in Erikson's theory becomes obvious. In these cultural contexts, social maturation is not associated with increased independence, but rather with increased interdependence within the family. In both cultures, infants first develop trust and attachment as a result of sleeping with parents. Some degree of autonomy in Kipsigi infants is achieved when breastfeeding ends, and the older child is moved from the mother's front to her back to accommodate the arrival of a new baby. In the Japanese culture, in which a mother sleeps with the child for an even longer period, interdependence would appear to be even stronger than in Kipsigi society. Consideration of these examples strongly suggests that we may need to make adaptations in Erikson's theory when attempting to apply it in another cultural context.

The practice of **cosleeping** (*a child sleeping with the parent*) is, in fact, routine in most of the world's cultures, and was the practice in the United States until shortly after the beginning of the twentieth century. Studies have suggested that the United States and other parts of North America are nearly alone in their expectation that children sleep in their own beds, in their own rooms, apart from their parents, at least for a time during the early months after birth (McKenna, 2012). The well-known pediatrician Benjamin Spock, to whom generations of American parents turned for advice on raising their children, stated that "it's a sensible rule not to take a child into the parents' bed for any reason" (Spock & Rothenberg, 1992, p. 213). Super and Harkness (1982), in contrast, have suggested that the expectation that infants will be able to sleep through the night without some contact or involvement with parents may be "pushing the limits of infants' adaptability" (p. 52). In a study of children in India, ages three to ten years, it was reported that 93% of them were cosleeping (Bharti, Malhi, & Kashyap, 2006). Again, we see the importance of cultural, as well as individual and familial differences, in the determination of a particular behavior such as sleep patterns. *Where did you sleep when you were an infant—in your parents' bed, in a nearby crib, or in a separate room? If you are married and have children of your own, where do they sleep?*

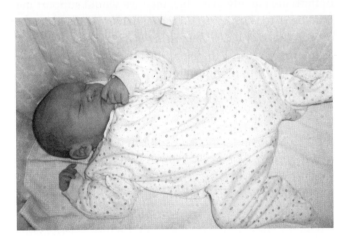

Western infants often begin to develop independence by sleeping alone.

(© Harry Gardiner)

When considering sleep practices among parents in different cultures, it may not be the specific practice itself but rather the cultural context and values that are the most important consideration. This view supports the ecological and developmental niche themes expressed throughout this text and leads us to another basic infant need requiring socialization—feeding.

## 3.2.2: Feeding

When infants are not sleeping, much of their time is spent eating. Just ask any new parent! How, what, and when to feed a child is another socialized behavior heavily influenced by the developmental niche, social context, parental beliefs, and values of one's culture.

Children need adequate nutrition, before birth as well as during infancy, if they are to grow properly and develop into healthy children and adults. The first two to three years are critical for physical development of the brain. The effects of nutritional deficiencies in infancy can be carried into adulthood and even affect another generation in terms of a mother's poor diet, inability to carry a baby to full term, or delivery of a low-birth-weight infant. According to figures released in *The State of the World's Children, 2009* (United Nations Children's Fund (UNICEF), 2009), more than 150 million children in developing countries younger than five years were malnourished. This malnutrition contributes to more than half of the nearly 12 million deaths in children younger than five occurring in developing countries each year. This number reflects both good and bad news in the fight against malnutrition. On the positive side, there were fewer malnourished children than the previous decade. However, progress varies significantly among cultural regions. For example, in Latin America and the Caribbean, percentages had declined and were less than 10%, whereas numbers actually increased in Africa. According to 2012 statistics, percentages for Latin American and the Caribbean have declined further to 3%, but they have continued to increase in various parts of Africa (http://www.childinfo.org). Harohalli R. Shashidhar (2014) indicates that malnutrition is responsible for 300,000 deaths per year in children younger than five years in developing countries and contributes indirectly to half of all deaths in children worldwide (http://emedicine.medscape.com/article/985140-overview).

Malnutrition can have an impact on an individual's resistance to disease and to the normal development of intellectual or cognitive abilities. In fact, Pollitt, Gorman, Engle, Martorell, and Rivera (1993), in a study conducted in Guatemala, report finding a link between inadequate nutrition in infancy and cognitive functioning in adolescence, notably among those living in poor socioeconomic circumstances. In a study among low-income Nicaraguan mothers, findings revealed a clear relationship between maternal beliefs about infant feeding and a child's nutritional level during the first year (Engle, Zeitlin, Medrano, & Garcia, 1996). These authors conclude their study by stating that "behavioral encouragement to eat as observed here did not reflect the sense of responsibility of the mother about feeding [and that] . . . further work is needed to determine the ways in which mothers translate their belief in helping children to eat into feeding behaviors" (p. 443). On the positive side, UNICEF (2009) reported that more than 300,000 children were saved from malnutrition in Niger in 2005, but that long-term programs were needed to address the issue. This is true in numerous other countries and regions of the world as well.

For a long time, mothers around the world have been told that breastfeeding is the ideal method for providing nourishment to babies. The reasons most frequently mentioned include the fact that breast milk is more easily digested than other types of milk (e.g., milk from goats or cows), it protects against disease by providing natural immunization, and it is (obviously) immediately available. In most non-Western cultures, it is the method most preferred by mothers and strongly encouraged by the World Alliance for Breastfeeding Action (WABA), a global network that sponsors World Breastfeeding Week each year and has a website containing a large number of resources (http://www.waba.org.my). WABA is part of the Millennium Development Goals project, supported by the United Nations and countries around the world, aimed at reducing the world's extreme poverty by half, halting the spread of HIV/AIDS, and providing universal primary education by 2015.

Recent findings suggest that long-term breastfeeding may have additional benefits for the mother as well (e.g., significantly reducing the risk of developing type 2 diabetes). Using data from two Nurses' Health Studies of more than 150,000 women who had given birth, Steube, Rich-Edwards, Willett, Manson, and Michels (2005) found a 15% decrease in risk for each year of breastfeeding in the first study and 14% decrease in the second. Although not able to explain precisely how breastfeeding may help to protect mothers against diabetes, they suggest it improves insulin sensitivity and glucose tolerance and may help maintain blood sugar balance.

As you might expect, cultural attitudes play a significant role in whether babies are breastfed or bottle fed. For example, in the United States, Hispanic women are reported to have the highest breastfeeding rate among all racial/ethnic groups. More than 80% of mothers begin breastfeeding immediately after birth and six months later 45% are continuing (Centers for Disease Control and Prevention (CDC), 2010). Yet, some cultures, many of them in the West, tend to make a woman feel embarrassed about engaging in this natural function in public. When mothers return to work shortly after their child's birth,

as many tend to do in North American and European countries, they may be unable to continue breastfeeding. Also, if bottle-feeding is the method of choice, then more fathers are able to participate in feeding and bonding with their infants. The United Nations estimates that improved breastfeeding practices could save the lives of almost 1.5 million children a year. Unfortunately, few of the 129 million infants born each year receive optimal breastfeeding (e.g., breast milk with no other foods or liquids for the first six months of life, followed by breast milk and solid or semisolid foods from about six months of age on, and continued breastfeeding for up to at least two years of age along with complementary foods), and some babies are not breastfed at all (UNICEF, 2001). In fact, in 2005, UNICEF stressed that the world had a major opportunity to reduce the toll of HIV/AIDS on infants by supporting exclusive breastfeeding. More recently, the World Health Organization (WHO) recommends exclusive breastfeeding for infants during the first six months to facilitate optimal growth, health, and development. In many parts of the world where there is no clean water, a scarcity of food, and formula is expensive, breastfeeding can make a major difference in the well-being, health, and life expectancy of children. However, less than 40% of infants under six months globally are exclusively breastfed (InCultureParent Staff, 2012). *Were you breastfed or bottle fed? Which would you prefer for your own children? Why?*

At this point, we want to emphasize that research findings have not yet *clearly* demonstrated that one method has long-term benefits over the other. If both options are equally available, then we would support the opinion of most experts and recommend breastfeeding for the reasons mentioned here. However, the method is not as important as what happens during the feeding process. The feeding situation provides an excellent opportunity, through socialization, for parents to establish an emotional connection with their infant (attachment or bonding) that has been shown to have important implications for interpersonal relationships throughout the remainder of the lifespan. (For an excellent overview of this topic, see Colin (1996).)

As one moves through the lifespan, these early cultural experiences with food strongly influence what, when, and how much an individual will eat. For example, *which would you rather eat right now—a hamburger with French fries, a salad with organic vegetables, a bowl of rice with spicy flavored beef, snake on crackers, octopus, grasshoppers, or (perhaps)—after hearing these choices—nothing?* Depending on your cultural training, the mention of any one of these meals might make you hungry or completely suppress your desire to eat. Although hunger and the feeding process begin biologically, they are individually socialized by cognition, learning, and experiential factors deeply rooted in the culture and often within the immediate family. As with other behaviors, eating preferences may show greater variability within families or within cultural subgroups than they do across cultures. For an interesting ethnographic perspective on cultural food practices in an increasingly globalized world, see Watson and Caldwell (2005).

### 3.2.3: Crying

All babies cry. But what does their crying mean, and is it responded to in the same or similar way in all cultures? Crying is the newborn's earliest form of communication with those in its immediate surroundings—the world of the micro- and mesosystems. Through crying, a baby lets others know that it is hungry, is not feeling well, has a wet diaper, wants attention, would like its older brother to stop annoying it, or conveys other information about its condition. In a sense, when newborns and infants cry, they are bringing their parents and others into their world and socializing them into understanding what their feelings are when they have no other way of expressing them. Although most parents in diverse cultures around the world can clearly differentiate these cries and distinguish one from another, it is almost impossible to teach this skill to others; experience seems to be the best teacher.

We have known for a long time that infants with various disorders (cystic fibrosis, Down syndrome, and others) cry differently than normal babies, and that individuals across cultures can recognize and differentiate among these various cries. We also know that mothers can discriminate different types of crying in low-birth-weight premature and full-term infants, and that crying among hearing-impaired infants differs from those with normal hearing abilities. In an important development, Green, Irwin, and Gustafson (2000) have started to synthesize findings from several approaches into a framework that one day could be used to relate crying to early health and development. We know that fathers and other males respond in as nurturing a way to an infant's crying as do mothers and other women.

*When and how often should a caregiver respond to a child's crying? If it is responded to frequently, will the child be spoiled? If crying is ignored, will insecurity be the result?* Do you know how your parents responded to your crying? If not, ask them. These are difficult questions, and not all experts agree on the answers. In general, crying should be responded to frequently, especially during the first year and will not result in spoiling, but rather will greatly assist in promoting secure attachment. In terms of Erikson's theory, frequent responding to crying appears to promote attachment and assist in resolving the crisis of trust versus mistrust mentioned previously.

## 3.3: Childhood

When we use the term **childhood**, we are referring to *the period extending from the end of infancy, about one and a half to two years of age, to just before the beginning of adolescence, typically about the age of eleven or twelve*, depending on the particular culture.

Some children experience difficulties and get "hung up" in the transition between childhood and adolescence.

(© Joe Oppedisano)

Edwards (1996), in a discussion of the parenting of toddlers, has outlined the developmental tasks she believes children are confronted with during their second and third years. We view each of these as an area of behavior in need of socialization and indicate, in parentheses, the chapters in this book in which they receive extensive discussion. These include, but are not limited to, learning to function independently or interdependently to become a functioning member of a society (discussed in this chapter), developing the beginnings of a self-concept (Chapter 6), understanding gender roles and establishing gender identity (Chapter 8), developing a moral conscience and the handling of aggressive behavior (Chapter 7), and taking a place in the larger family grouping (Chapter 4).

When older children enter elementary school, they come under the influence of two very different socialization agents—teachers and peers. In the school setting, the socialization process teaches children more about themselves (their personalities, abilities, and roles) and how to develop social relationships with adults who are not their relatives (teachers) and peers (other students), as well as ways to master some of the challenges of everyday life.

For the remainder of this section, let us consider the effects of socialization on formal and informal learning and on academic achievement in classroom settings.

## 3.3.1: Formal versus Informal Learning

Most of the socialization experiences of children in non-industrialized countries take place in informal settings (e.g., within the family or among peers and siblings) and are a fundamental part of one's daily activities. **Informal learning** is not characterized by a defined curriculum and is *generally picked up by means of observation and imitation.* According to Cushner (1990), "The responsibility for learning falls mainly on the learner, making it rather personal, with extended family members often playing a critical role in the act of instruction. . . . Change, discontinuity, and innovation are highly valued" (p. 100). For example, in certain African and South American tribal groups, young boys learn hunting and fishing skills, as well as methods for navigating their way through jungles and rivers by observing and imitating adult males in their culture. Girls learn cooking and child care techniques, not in school, but by helping their mothers, aunts, and other women in the daily activities of family and village life. Traditions change very little in some cultures; this is the way it has been for centuries and the way it is almost certain to be long into the future. Some of these skills are also informally taught to American children—how many of you have gone hunting or fishing with one of your parents or have helped prepare meals at home? (For a taxonomy of three types of informal learning—self-directed, incidental, and socialization—see Schugurensky, 2000.)

In other countries, as well as in the United States, the majority of children learn important cultural skills as part of their society's formal education system. As Cushner (1990) points out, **formal learning** is *"set apart from the context of everyday life and is typically carried out in the institution we know as school [and is characterized by] . . . an explicit and highly structured curriculum [in which] . . . material is learned from a book that may or may not be useful at a later time"* (p. 100). For a particularly insightful discussion of the failures of formal schooling in African societies, see Serpell's (1993) seminal work on Zambia.

The issue of formal versus informal schooling gives us another opportunity to look at the two crises Erikson says are characteristic of the stage of childhood. As shown in Table 2.3, these are *initiative versus guilt* and *industry versus inferiority.* To put these crises into perspective, let us consider the case of Tamiko and Alexina. Tamiko, aged ten, lives and goes to school in Akita, Japan. Similar to most children in her country, her success or failure depends more on her effort and character than on her innate ability. She is learning and working productively and harmoniously in mixed-ability groups similar to what she will encounter when she is an adult. Cooperation is seen as essential to the success of the group and the individual, and formal instruction occurs with this in mind. In this case, the developmental niche in which early learning takes place will share certain characteristics with the adult niche in which Tamiko will later live and work. The Japanese believe that parents and teachers must coordinate their efforts so there is a high level of contact between the school and the home throughout a child's formal schooling. For Tamiko and her parents, academic work comes before everything else and involves long hours of study. There is a Japanese expression—"Pass with four, fail with five"—referring to how many hours of sleep are needed to succeed.

Tamiko's education actually began prior to entering formal preschool when her mother taught her to read, write, and perform simple mathematics. She spends more hours in school each year than almost any other children anywhere else in the world. This includes her regular classes, followed by several hours in a "juku" (cram school), and finally studying and doing homework at home until the early morning hours. Although the latter is not formal in the strict sense of the word, it is nevertheless very serious and regimented.

Alexina, also ten years old, lives in Minnesota in the Midwestern part of the United States and is equally serious about her education. However, in her case, the focus is more on independence and self-expression. She has learned that autonomy and individual achievement are valued over group collaboration. Getting ahead is a personal goal, as characterized by Alexina's ability to take the initiative to complete assignments on her own. As with Tamiko, there will be a certain consistency between the values and behaviors present in the developmental niches of childhood and adulthood. However, unlike the Japanese, Americans believe that education is to be provided in the school, not in the home. This again points out the distinction between formal and informal schooling mentioned previously. If you think about the opening chapter vignettes, Kamuzu's educational experience, although not as rich in opportunities, would be similar in many ways to that of Tamiko (e.g., more cooperative or group learning and more informal home schooling). Jeremy, like Alexina, would be expected to show greater independence, autonomy, and self-expression. Again, in the case of Jeremy and Kamuzu, we observe more variability in their individual educational experiences within the South African culture than we do between the experiences of Jeremy in his culture and Alexina in the United States.

How might we apply Erikson's model and resolution of crises to these four children? In Tamiko's case, *initiative* and *industry* are achieved only after successfully recognizing the need for others to assist in the learning process. The same is somewhat less true in Kamuzu's situation because his school is underfunded and he had to learn more in the informal settings of his home and community. In Alexina's case, industry is achieved when she is able to take initiative independently and become a "self-starter." Her success in this area is reflected in her school report card, which has a category for "industriousness." In this respect, Jeremy behaves similarly to Alexina. In short, Alexina's culture and Jeremy's subculture view initiative and industry in independent terms, whereas Tamiko's culture and Kamuzu's subculture, to a lesser extent, look at these qualities in interdependent terms. Again, when applying Erikson's theory to non-Western cultures, it is of crucial importance to consider the relevance and cultural definitions of his concepts (e.g., independence and autonomy, initiative and industry). If this is not done, then a researcher is liable to make serious misinterpretations of cultural behavior.

Let us close this discussion with an interesting example of informal math learning among some of Brazil's more than 200,000 "Mennios de Rua" and Columbia's "Gamines" or "Chupagruesos"—street children. Many of these children survive by selling fruits, vegetables, and other items on street corners. Most of them dropped out of school by the time they were ten, before learning good math skills. Although they conduct scores of informal financial transactions each day without making a mistake, the majority of them are unable to complete a formal, written math problem requiring them to calculate change (not unlike what they do every day) without making numerous errors. Their school (ecological setting) is the street, and it is here that they have been socialized and have learned functional math skills that allow them to survive in the street culture of large Latin American cities where they live. For an interesting discussion of these different cultural practices and the advantages and disadvantages of each, see the book *Street Mathematics and School Mathematics* by Nunes, Schliemann, and Carraher (1993).

# 3.4: Adolescence

We know that *adolescence begins in biology*, when hormones that bring about physical changes and prepare the body for sexual reproduction are released into the bloodstream. However, *adolescent development ends in culture*, where one's status is defined by the new role played in society and the transition to adulthood begins. From an ecological or cultural contextual perspective, adolescence is seen as a developmental stage in some, but not all, cultures. According to Cole and Cole (1996), its distinctiveness as a stage depends in large measure on whether "young people reach biological maturity before they have acquired the knowledge and skills needed to ensure cultural

reproduction" (p. 629). For example, in the United States and Canada, there sometimes are young adolescents (ages twelve and older) with children of their own, and these parents, without a job or educational training, are totally incapable of providing for the welfare of their children or of themselves. Contrast this with the !Kung San people living in the Kalahari Desert in Botswana and parts of Namibia and South Africa. Even before reaching the years of adolescence, older children have learned through socialization to hunt animals and gather wild plants as part of their nomadic life. They, similar to their North American counterparts, are biologically capable of reproduction, but they already know their developmental niche and have the skills to economically support themselves and a family.

Adolescence provides another opportunity to dramatically illustrate how the major themes of this text can be used to describe and explain how cultures structure and teach the kinds of activities that Cole and Cole (1996) say need to be mastered to "carry out the full process of human reproduction [and how these] . . . shape the psychological characteristics that one develops at the end of childhood" (p. 629). It is at this point in the lifespan that we can again clearly observe the development of "lives across cultures." For example, compare two fourteen-year-old girls growing up in cultures separated by both time and space. Mankushai is a member of the Masai tribe and lives on a flat grassy plain in southern Kenya. Her days are spent in her husband's village working side by side with her mother-in-law cooking and taking care of her young daughter Consolata. Far away, in the United States, in California, Alisa spends her days in school studying chemistry, calculus, and world history so she will be able to attend college and prepare for a career as an economist. Each lives in a developmental niche within an ecological system, surrounded by family, peers, and teachers, learning her culture's values and being socialized into an adult role. But how different their lives are and how different they will continue to be as they move through the lifespan.

Before leaving this topic, let us consider the socialization process from the perspective of immigrants and how they sometimes give up many of the values and customs of their native culture and take on those of their adopted culture, and the effects this might have on their behavior. This can be seen in studies involving first- and second-generation American Chinese adolescents who were compared with Chinese adolescents from Hong Kong, others whose parents had immigrated to Australia, and European and Anglo Australian adolescents. For example, Chiu, Feldman, and Rosenthal (1992) found that first- and second-generation Chinese American adolescents, in terms of their adolescent problems and the severity of them, were similar to nonimmigrant adolescents. However, immigration appeared to result in reduced perceptions of parental control, which was unrelated to adolescents' views of their parents' warmth toward them. However, across generations, Chinese American adolescents were found to place less value on the family as a "residential unit," consistent with the values expressed by European and Anglo Australian adolescents, yet the authors indicated that they still differed from the other groups on this particular value.

The influx of millions of Syrian and other Middle Eastern immigrants and their families into European countries throughout 2015 and 2016 presents both unique problems and new opportunities for understanding the dynamics of successful or unsuccessful socialization. We are hopeful that social scientists will take this opportunity to analyze the problems of large-scale immigration and examine possible solutions for all involved, especially young children.

Much of an adolescent's time is again spent in the school setting where he or she comes under the influence of even more socialization agents, including involvement in school organizations, music activities, or sports endeavors. During this period, at least part of their development will be influenced by the presence or absence of rites of passage.

## 3.4.1: Rites of Passage

In many cultures, the transition from childhood to adolescence is marked by some sort of public recognition. Called **rites of passage,** these are *ceremonies or rituals that recognize or symbolize an individual's movement from one status to another.* These "coming-of-age" experiences vary significantly from one culture to another; however, according to an important and pioneering study by Schlegal and Barry (1991), they are found in most nonindustrialized societies, where nearly 80% of girls and close to 70% of boys go through some form of initiation.

In eastern Africa, ten- to twelve-year-old boys in the Kaguru tribe are led into the bush, stripped of all clothing, and ritually circumcised while being taught the sexual practices of adulthood by male members of the community. Later, they return to their village, are celebrated at a large feast, receive new names, and are expected to become responsible adult members of their society. Passage for a Kaguru girl is not as complex as for boys and occurs when she experiences first menstruation, and she is taught the ways of womanhood by her grandmother or older women in the tribe. She is fortunate in escaping the very painful and widespread practice of female genital surgery (called "circumcision" by some and "female genital mutilation" (FGM) by others) already experienced by an estimated 100 to 140 million girls and

women in twenty-eight countries in Africa, India, the Middle East, and Southeast Asia, a procedure that has no health benefits and is internationally recognized as a violation of human rights (WHO, 2008). In fact, WHO (2010) defines it as "all procedures that involve partial or total removal of the external female genitalia, or other injury to the female genital organs for non-medical reasons" (p. XX). Recent figures indicate FGM is still practiced in thirty countries in parts of the Middle East; Asia; and eastern, western, and northeastern Africa, as well as within some immigrant communities in Australia, Europe, and North America (UNICEF, 2012). The practice is legally outlawed in Belgium, Sweden, and the United Kingdom. In 2012, the United Nations General Assembly voted unanimously to make major efforts to end the practice. For more on the prevalence and effects of these practices, see Okedu, Rembe, and Anwo (2009) and Abdulcadira, Margairarazb, Boulvaina, and Irion (2011).

The transition from adolescence to adulthood in North America and many other Western countries is not marked by such clearly defined rituals. In fact, many would say there are no true rites of passage experienced by all members of these societies at this particular stage in the lifespan, and if there ever were, then they have likely been modified or have completely disappeared. Among certain ethnic groups within the larger society, some commonly experienced ceremonies such as the Bar or Bat Mitzvah for Jewish boys and girls may come close to being a rite of passage. Although not experienced by all adolescents at the same time, or by many at all, the following are sometimes mentioned as *possible* rites of passage in North American society: graduation from high school or college, passing a driver's test, marriage, or a first job. The lack of commonly accepted rites of passage in these societies may be attributed, in part, to a lack of conformity in developmental niches; for example, two families living next to each other may have significantly different backgrounds, cultural origins, ethnicity, values, and traditions than those found in more homogeneous societies.

Age certainly is not a very helpful marker in cultures such as the United States because there are several criteria by which individuals are considered adults (e.g., age sixteen for driving, eighteen for voting, and twenty-one for drinking). American adolescents, and their counterparts in many other countries, often linger in a "cultural limbo" between the ages of twelve to the early twenties when they may (or may not) one day be considered adults.

An exception to the preceding comments is the **vision quest**, an experience common to many of the more than 500 culturally diverse Native American tribes in North America. Performed primarily as a rite of passage for adolescent males, it begins with the taking of a boy, age fourteen or fifteen, into a "sweat lodge," where his body and spirit are purified by the heat given off by burning cedar. Sitting with the boy is a medicine man who advises him and assists him with ritual prayers. Later, he is taken to an isolated location and left alone to fast for four days. He prays, contemplates the words of the medicine man, and waits for a vision that will reveal to him his path in life as a member of his tribal culture (Delaney, 1995). As another example, Navajo girls at the time of menarche take part in a rite of passage that involves morning running and the baking of a ceremonial cake. For an interesting description of the Native American vision quest, see http://www.native-americans-online.com/native-american-vision.html.

It is clear from this discussion that various cultures treat their young people very differently. Some provide a clearly defined niche within the microsystem of the family where the parents, elders, and others initiate and prepare their young people to move into the wider realms of the mesosystem, exosystem, and macrosystem and to deal with the challenges and opportunities available to them as recognized adults. Other cultures, such as many Western societies, could do more to prepare their young people for the often difficult transition to adulthood.

In discussing rites of passage, it is important to keep in mind that each culture uses these as a way of helping its adolescents arrive at an understanding of their **identity**, or *self-definition as a separate individual in terms of roles, attitudes, beliefs, and values*. In the case of the Kaguru mentioned previously, adult male identity is achieved when young boys undergo circumcision, and adult female identity is attained when young girls experience their first menstruation. Identity and adulthood are defined and achieved in terms of tribal customs and beliefs. In North American societies, identity is achieved when adolescents demonstrate some measure of independence, initiative, and industriousness, although these qualities are not always clearly defined.

The differences between these cultures can be considered in terms of Erikson's fifth crisis—*identity versus role confusion*. Failure to achieve identity in these cultures results in what Erikson refers to as "role confusion." The difficulty in terms of this crisis lies in how each culture defines identity and marks the onset of adulthood. In many respects, achievement of identity is less ambiguous in traditional, nonindustrialized societies because rites of passage are clearly defined and adolescents know what is expected of them to become an adult. Conversely, in many industrialized societies, true rites of passage (which apply to all members of a given society) do not exist; consequently, there is ambiguity in how identity is defined and achieved. The result is that many adolescents do not know who they are or how they are supposed to behave as adults.

Some theorists and researchers imply that Erikson's theory also applies to preindustrial societies. However, when used to explain such behaviors as identity versus role confusion, the theory contains Western biases (e.g., viewing identity achievement as rooted in autonomous judgments). For an extended discussion of identity formation, see Chapter 6.

## Points to Ponder

### The Socialization Experience

If you are an immigrant or have a parent, grandparent or friend who is an immigrant, take some time to talk with her or him about the socialization experience. In what culture was the person born? To which culture did he or she emigrate? At what age? How difficult or easy was the process of adjustment or assimilation? What were the most difficult changes? What were the easiest adjustments to make? Did the person become bilingual? How easy/difficult was it to learn and use two or more languages? To which culture does the person feel most attached? Why?

# 3.5: Adulthood

Developmentalists have historically devoted most of their attention to the earlier part of the lifespan, particularly the years from birth through adolescence. As a result, there is a great deal of research; many findings; and a host of theories describing, explaining, and predicting the events that occur during the first two decades of life. A similar situation applies to cross-cultural human development—only recently have the last three quarters of the lifespan received serious attention. Even so, treatment of topics has been sparse and inconsistent. Cole and Cole (1993) explain it well: "Since psychologists are sharply divided over the relative roles of biology and culture in the process of development, it is only natural that they should be sharply divided on the question of whether development continues into adulthood and old age" (p. 656).

We know from casual observation that *the experience of adulthood varies dramatically across and even within cultures* and depends on many factors, including age, gender, socioeconomic status, occupation, family structure, and timing of life events (e.g., marriage, parenthood, grandparenthood, and retirement).

Many psychologists (whose research you will become familiar with in subsequent chapters) have paid little attention to developmental changes, including socialization, after adolescence. For example, G. Stanley Hall (1904,

1922), who wrote the first book on adolescence in 1904, believed that senescence (old age) began shortly after adolescence ended, generally when one reached the late thirties or early forties. Of course, he based this assumption partly on the fact that life expectancy was much shorter at that time. Jean Piaget, in his theory of cognitive development, proposed that individuals reached the final stage of formal operations during their late adolescence or early adulthood years. Only recently have attempts been made to explain cognitive changes in later adulthood through the establishment of a stage of postformal operations (see Chapter 5).

Two psychologists who did attribute significant developmental changes to the years of adulthood, and some of whose ideas have been subjected to cross-cultural examination, are Lev Vygotsky and Erik Erikson. Vygotsky, a Russian psychologist and one of the founders of the cultural-historical viewpoint, made some of the earliest contributions to our understanding of cognitive development within social settings, or cultures. (His ideas, many of which are similar to those expressed in our major themes, were introduced in Chapter 2.) Erikson, as we have previously noted, is one of a small number of theorists who emphasize cultural and social development across the entire lifespan, separating the years following adolescence into early, middle, and later adulthood. It is in this area that his views coincide most closely with those of the ecological, or cultural context, approach. Limited findings from anthropological, sociological, and cross-cultural studies, particularly those looking at adolescence, tend to support his theoretical assumptions but, as we emphasized, may have to be modified to explain cross-cultural differences.

During early adulthood (early twenties to mid-thirties), in cultures throughout the world, a majority of adults are dealing with the crisis of *intimacy versus isolation* (see Table 2.3. Decisions are made about establishing a close, intimate relationship with another person, or individuals go their way alone and fail to achieve an intimate relationship. Chapter 7 looks in detail at intimate relationships in a variety of cultures and at the impact of this crisis on one's life.

Lefrancois' (1996) comment that age ranges be used only as descriptive guidelines is relevant here in terms of the cultural example we provided in the section on adolescence. Confronting the crisis of intimacy versus isolation usually requires that the individual has achieved a sense of identity, probably is self-supporting, and is involved in a long-term and interdependent relationship. With this in mind, consider fourteen-year-old Mankushai of the Masai tribe in Kenya, East Africa, mentioned previously. Mankushai lives in her husband's village, cooks his meals, and takes care of their daughter Consolata. Except for her age, she would appear to be in the stage of early adulthood. What about other cultures such as those parts

of India where child marriages are common? In which stage do we put these individuals? Compared with earlier stages of development, there is less cross-cultural research on this stage and the crisis contained within it. This raises additional questions and problems about applying this theory beyond Western societies. We clearly need more critical analysis of ideas and concepts, as well as additional research, to extend the cross-cultural usefulness of such theories.

When one reaches middle adulthood (mid-thirties to mid-sixties), a new crisis appears that involves *generativity versus stagnation* (see Table 2.3). Middle-age adults make work and career decisions, raise children, and show concern by guiding the next generation, or they become stagnant, self-absorbed, and self-centered. Some of our previous comments regarding the role parents play in socialization would appear to be relevant here. It is through socialization within their ecological settings that individuals have the kinds of experiences that help them as adults find a balance between their self-interests and the interests of others. Unfortunately, as with some other areas, there is a lack of cross-cultural findings related to this stage of crisis; the need for additional theorizing and research is clear. For contemporary thinking and research on the psychological, social, and cultural aspects of generativity in the lives of adults, see de St. Aubin, McAdams, and Kim (2003).

Finally, looking once again at socialization, it is in this period of adulthood, as individuals move into the working world, that "globalization" and a clear understanding of cross-cultural differences in business practices become increasingly important. In certain occupations and careers, employees must be socialized to operate within a global organizational culture or they will not be successful. In addition, some people form relationships with, and often marry, mates from different cultures. In such situations, they encounter differences in the assumptions and values in their own socialization and confront decisions about how they will socialize and raise their own children in multicultural and multiethnic contexts. Discussion of this latter topic will also be expanded on in Chapter 4. For insight into the challenges and rewards of a multicultural childhood and its effects on personal identity, see *Third Culture Kids* by Pollock and Van Reken (2009) and *Belonging Everywhere and Nowhere* by Bushong (2013).

# 3.6: Late Adulthood

During the last period in the lifespan (midsixties and after), older adults find themselves dealing with the crisis of *integrity versus despair* (see Table 2.3). According to Erikson, when individuals reach this stage they tend to reflect on their lives. Either they find that they are generally happy and satisfied with their choices, having fulfilled many of their goals and having made their best efforts (integrity), or they find themselves filled with despair over missed opportunities or mistakes made, which leaves them unhappy and dissatisfied. *Think about your aging relatives—parents, grandparents, great grandparents (if you are fortunate to have them), aunts, uncles, and others, and even talk with them. How do they view these years of late adulthood? Are they happy or unhappy? What concerns do they have?*

## 3.6.1: Cultural Views of Aging

*What role does culture play in shaping the ecological setting in which we age and how we are socialized as older members of the society?* We hypothesize that the outcome of the integrity versus despair crisis of late adulthood might often be negative in some Western societies, which place great emphasis on economic and career success and in which nuclear families are the norm. In these cultures, parents or other relatives in their later years are sometimes seen as burdens to be moved from the microsystem of the family to rest homes in the mesosystem or exosystem. In societies in which young people enjoy the greatest status, the elderly are more often rejected. Contemporary North American society is currently such a society, but given rapid increases in its older population, the ecological setting will soon undergo dramatic changes.

Contrast this with many Asian, South American, or African cultures, in which intergenerational families are still the norm and older relatives are looked after by their family or by the village community. Family members look to them as wise and knowledgeable members of the society with much to offer. Rather than attempting to push back the aging process and appear young, many look forward to aging.

People are living longer than ever before, with many reaching 100 years of age and beyond. In 2012, the United Nations estimated the number of such individuals (centenarians) to be greater than 316,000; in 2015, it was 450,000. Although exact numbers are difficult to determine, this is one of the fastest growing parts of the population. In fact, several remote areas of China, Japan, and Brazil have become known for having large numbers of people who live unusually long lives. In parts of China, senescence is postponed well into late adulthood, and a disciplined, highly active lifestyle is routine. Some commonly cited reasons for longevity include diet (lots of fresh vegetables, little meat and fat), mutual interdependence, family and neighborhood cohesiveness, and regular exercise. The ecological system is set up to socialize aging individuals as functional members of society well into old age. What is important to remember is that each culture has its own beliefs about growing old and what roles older people play in society.

It is interesting to note that when Erikson reached the eighth decade of his life, he reviewed his theory and suggested that increases in life expectancy might require a rethinking of his ideas, especially those related to development during adulthood (Erikson, Erikson, & Kivnick, 1986). We encourage others to begin this careful rethinking and, in the process, attempt to apply these new ideas to cross-cultural human development.

# Summary: Culture and Socialization

It should be clear after reading this chapter that universally accepted generalizations about the complex relationships among family, culture, and socialization are sometimes difficult. Numerous variables contribute to cultural differences, including cultural contexts, societal beliefs and values, individual views of children and their place in society, rural versus urban living, family structure, and parenting styles, to mention only a few. However, cross-cultural research on human development also shows that we are gaining a much better understanding of the significant role culture plays in socialization at all levels, from birth through the last years of the lifespan. Traditional, primarily Western, theoretical explanations of human development are, in large part, obsolete and were never very accurate when transported to other cultures in an effort to describe, explain, and predict behavior for which they were never intended.

You are reading this at a time when many societies are undergoing dramatic changes in the way they and their family structures operate. For example, since 1979, China has had a formal family planning policy, popularly known as the "one child policy." In fact, this is a misnomer because, unknown to many, only about 36% were subject to it, and there were numerous exceptions in which families were allowed to have more than one child (e.g., rural families if the first child is disabled or a girl, ethnic minorities, and residents of Macau and Hong Kong). However, in November 2013, this policy received much attention when the government announced further relaxation of the policy by saying it would allow families to have two children if one of the parents is an only child. However, because of the high cost of raising children, many families will not take advantage of this change. In October 2015, China's ruling Communist Party announced that it will abolish the decades-old one child policy and allow all couples to have two children, although no date for when it would take effect was announced. There appear to be several reasons for this change, one being that China's working age population is dramatically shrinking (with a projected loss of 67 million workers between 2010 and 2030, its elderly population will likely increase from 110 million to 210 million by 2030, with senior citizens representing a quarter of the population). Another reason for the policy change is the variety of social problems brought about by decades of forced abortions and female sterilization. Although many Chinese families welcome the change, some think it comes too late for them, with others indicating they do not now want a second child, and still others finding they can't afford another child. We will have to wait to see what effect this change will have on Chinese families, their developmental niches, and their overall culture.

In the United States, high divorce and remarriage rates, single mothers, larger numbers of same-sex marriages, and increasingly larger numbers of working mothers are reshaping family relationships. In countries throughout the world, we have seen major changes in the roles played by children and their parents, and yet, as Roopnarine and Carter (1992) have pointed out, "Perceptions of children and how a culture manages to mesh those perceptions with children's own birthright and value to members of a society, its rituals, functions, and expectations, are not well understood" (p. 251). We have only started the journey toward understanding; much lies ahead of us.

---

## Study Questions

Define the term *socialization,* and explain its importance to understanding cross-cultural human development.

Discuss the components of the developmental niche, and give examples from your own experience.

Explain what is meant by *rites of passage* and the role they play in adolescent identity.

Compare and contrast formal and informal learning, and give examples of each.

Describe and explain each of the adulthood crises described by Erikson, and explain their effects on behavior during adulthood and later adulthood. Be able to provide clear examples.

Compare and contrast cultural views of aging.

---

## Developmental Analysis
### Socialization

My name is Matilda Skelton, but everyone—thankfully—calls me "Maddi." I was named for my great grandmother, who immigrated to the United States from England in 1847. I was born on September 17, 1938, in Elfville, Pennsylvania, a small farming community settled by Irish immigrants (population 1,734). The town consisted of a feed and grain store, post office, small grocery store, Catholic Church, school, railroad depot, barber shop, gas station—and not much else! The person I am today was very much influenced by my early socialization experiences in Elfville and with my family. Let me explain.

In terms of my developmental niche, I lived in a rural setting, in a nuclear family, consisting of my two parents, a younger sister, and a younger brother. I spent my early years establishing relationships with members of my family and playmates. I learned to deal with feelings of dependence, independence, cooperation, and competition. My early caregivers were my parents, relatives, or other mothers in town. We didn't have a day care center or preschool when I was young—it was typical of the era for mothers to stay at home while raising their children.

As an infant, I slept in a crib in my parents' room for a couple of months and was then moved to my own room. I was breastfed for nine months. When I cried, my parents picked me up and comforted me. Like most American children, I was part of a formal school system. My siblings, friends, and I walked to a small school consisting of kindergarten through eighth grade, with most classes taught in the same room by the same teacher. My parents and teachers worked together to ensure that I had a good education. I did chores on the farm and enjoyed learning about the animals. When I was fourteen, I began traveling eight miles by bus to attend high school; my ecological system was expanding. In terms of informal learning, my mother taught me to cook and take care of my siblings, and my father taught me to drive a tractor and play a guitar. My parents were Catholic, although my mother took religion more seriously than my dad.

As I was entering adolescence during the 1950s, America was characterized by malt shops, rock 'n' roll music, the hula hoop, and "hot" cars. Television was just arriving. At the same time, the nation was plagued by racial injustice, anti-Communist paranoia, and the fear of nuclear war. The closest event to a rite of passage for me was getting my driver's license at the age of sixteen. Like most of my friends, I struggled to establish an identity and often felt confused. After high school graduation in 1956, most of my girlfriends decided to be secretaries, teachers, or nurses.

I decided to go to college and chose an unusual major for girls at the time—business. My first contact with another culture was during my junior year, when I spent a semester in Italy. I was the first in my family to travel abroad or even outside Pennsylvania. It was a wonderful experience and really opened my eyes to the world. In 1962, I traveled to England for graduate work in economics. It was there that I met my future husband—Giorgio Carlo Conte—a student from Italy. He asked me to go out with him seven times before I finally accepted! Socialization can work in surprising (and wonderful) ways.

Giorgio and I were married on March 9, 1968, at my grandparents' home in Coudersport, Pennsylvania. We combined American and Italian traditions. We moved to Minnesota, where I was an economics professor at a wonderful liberal arts college. Giorgio worked at an international bank. Our daughter, Elizabeth Lucia, was born in 1969, and our son, Alexander Donato, was born in 1970. When they were young, we frequently traveled to Italy so they could spend time with their grandparents and relatives.

I have many fond memories from my childhood, adolescence, and adulthood. I can recall our 1940 Chevrolet sedan, my dad serving in World War II, riding my bicycle to the grocery store, our icebox, a large Philco radio around which we would gather to listen to radio programs, and visiting grandparents. I also remember going to the movie theatre on Saturdays to see two films, two cartoons, news, and previews of coming attractions—for 25 cents, you got all of this, a candy bar, and a bag of popcorn! Each of these experiences had a socializing effect on me in one way or another. I am now seventy-seven years old and continue to go through socialization changes. I'll tell you more about this and other events in my life in the next chapter. Ciao for now!

# Chapter 4
# The Family in Cultural Context

*The sun is just beginning to rise in Boslanti, along the Saramacca River in central Suriname, the smallest country in South America. Sindy Sowidagkijm, twenty-four, and her husband David, twenty-six, surrounded by a midwife and several female relatives, including two grandmothers, are nearing the birth of their third child. The two older children, on the other side of the small wooden house, are lulled to sleep by the rhythmic sound of light rain on the corrugated iron roof. Suddenly, a baby's cry fills the room, and little Jacob makes his arrival known to all. Sindy, exhausted but happy, will breastfeed her newborn and take a deserved rest. David will dream of the day when his new son will join him and his uncles on the family fishing boat. The others will proudly spread the word about the newest citizen in Boslanti.*

*At Mt. Sinai Hospital, in downtown New York City, John and Ruth Hazelton have just entered the brightly lit delivery room on the eighth floor. At thirty-eight, this is Ruth's first pregnancy, and it has been unusually difficult. She is lightly sedated with an intravenous needle pumping a labor-inducing drug into her arm. Two hours later, following an emergency Cesarean section performed by two doctors and two nurses, she is sleeping quietly in the recovery room, having not yet seen her new daughter. Just down the hall, relaxing in a rocking chair in a birthing room and talking with her husband Walter, five-year-old daughter Sarah, other family members, and two close friends is Patricia Mezzanotti. In a half hour, she will give birth to a son in a quiet homelike atmosphere and begin the bonding process by immediately holding and feeding her newborn.*

## 4.1: Ecological Context

The family is central to the ecological approach, serving as the source for an individual's development, linking contexts and development, and transmitting this from generation to generation. This approach allows us to view the many ways in which development and behavior adapt to various cultural and biological contexts. It recognizes that cultures share processes that, in many circumstances, can be considered universal. At the same time, it recognizes that some cultures display significant differences that emerge from their unique cultural contexts.

What is a family? What defines its structure? Is it nuclear—husband, wife, and children? Is it extended, including grandparents, aunts, uncles, and other relatives? Does it consist of two parents of different genders, the same gender, a single parent of either gender, married or unmarried individuals, with children or without children? Is there one woman with multiple husbands, one husband with multiple wives, multiple men and women living together, with children or without? Can a family be any or all of these? These are issues considered in this chapter.

## 4.2: Cultural Variations in the Family Life Cycle

In the words of William F. Kenkel (1985), "*Families have a beginning, they grow in numbers, their membership next declines, and eventually the original family exists no longer. The individual is born, grows, enters a period of decline, and inevitably passes from the scene. The striking parallel between the life pattern of a normal individual and the history of a typical family gave rise to the concept* **family life cycle**" (p. 375). Although not a literal analogy, this concept provides a framework that allows us to consider the shifting attributes that affect individual behaviors and interactions within the family, community, and cultural context. This chapter looks at the family life cycle in terms of developmental stages and relating these to real-life examples of families living in a wide variety of ecological settings throughout the world. I begin with the selection of a mate and the process of marriage.

### 4.2.1: Mate Selection

Buss (1994b) begins his classic and pioneering study of mate preferences in thirty-seven cultures with a statement that cannot be disputed: "Every person is alive because of a successful mating. People in the past who failed to mate are not our ancestors" (p. 197). Considering how much of a person's life might be spent with a partner and the impact this relationship has on one's social, emotional, and psychological development (as well as on one's children), selection of a mate is one of our most important decisions. "*How do we select a marriage partner?" "What characteristics do we consider important?" "Are there cultural differences in selecting a mate?"*

In an effort to answer these questions, Buss (1994b) (with the help of fifty other researchers) conducted an extensive study of more than 10,000 individuals living in thirty-seven cultures. The approach involved asking subjects to indicate how important each of eighteen characteristics was in selecting a mate and then to rank thirteen of these in terms of their desirability. Findings revealed that, across cultures, men and women looked for mates who were kind and understanding, intelligent, had an exciting personality, and were healthy. [For a recent discussion of this research and a deeper explanation, see Buss' (2015) book on evolutionary psychology and its applications.]

Buss (1994b) originally indicated that he and his team of researchers were surprised by some of the results, particularly cultural variations concerning the most variable characteristic—chastity or the lack of previous sexual experience. It would be surprising if cultures did not vary in the value placed on chastity because other sources on sexuality usually note cross-cultural variation in practices, values, and expectations (Hamon & Ingoldsby, 2003; Hatfield & Rapson, 2005). Such variation was indeed shown in Buss' study. Although chastity was considered irrelevant or unimportant in a prospective mate by both men and women in the Netherlands, Sweden, and Norway, it was viewed as indispensable in China and scored very highly by those from India, Taiwan, and Iran. Among those who viewed chastity as only moderately desirable were those living in Colombia, Estonia, Japan, Nigeria, Poland, South Africa, and Zambia. Yet, in an overwhelming majority of countries (two-thirds), chastity was desired in a marriage partner more by men than by women. (See Figure 4.1.) [In a study of 1,100 undergraduates at three American universities, using the same scale and characteristics, the top three "essential characteristics" for both men and women were mutual attraction and love, dependable character, and emotional stability; chastity was placed last by both men and women (University of Iowa Health Sciences, 2009). Although the results are interesting, a word of caution is in order—these are results from simply one Western culture whose sexual practices and beliefs have been evolving over a number of years.]

Other categories in the Buss (1994b) study showing large cultural differences in response were "*good housekeeper* (highly valued in Estonia and China, little valued in Western Europe and North America); *refinement/neatness* (highly valued in Nigeria and Iran, less valued in Great Britain, Ireland, and Australia); and *religious* (highly valued in Iran, moderately valued in India, little valued in Western Europe and North America)" (p. 199). Buss cautions that although these differences are important, there is undoubtedly much variability across individuals within these cultures. This once again reinforces our point made previously that *there are often greater differences within cultures than between or among cultures.*

Looking more specifically at what each of the genders wanted in a mate, Buss (1994b) found some interesting differences. As for women: "From the Zulu tribe in South Africa to coastal-dwelling Australians to city-dwelling Brazilians, women place a premium on good earning capacity, financial prospects, ambition, industriousness, and social status more than men—characteristics that all provide resources" (p. 199). Men were found to prefer women who are younger than they are—how much younger depends on the culture. For example, in those cultures where men often have more than one wife (e.g., Zambia and Nigeria), men prefer brides who are younger by as much as seven or eight years. In cultures where only one wife is permitted (e.g., Germany, Spain, and France), the preference was for brides only slightly younger. In all cultures, women had a preference for older men since men tend to mature later than women and also tend to have greater access to more financial resources than do younger men. Finally, "in *all* known cultures worldwide, from the inner-continental tribal societies of Africa and South America to the big cities of Madrid, London, and Paris, men place a premium on the physical appearance of a potential mate" (p. 200). According to Buss, there is a good reason for men to favor youthfulness and physical appearance, even though they may not be fully aware that "these qualities provide the best signals . . . that the woman is fertile and has good reproductive capacity" (p. 200).

Hamon and Ingoldsby (2003) also have explored the processes of mate

**Figure 4.1**  Cross-Cultural Differences in the Importance of Chastity

**SOURCE:** Love and Sex: Crosscultural Perspectives by Elaine Hatfield and Richard L. Rapson, Copyright © 2005 by University Press of America. Reprinted by permission of Rowman & Littlefield Publishing Group.

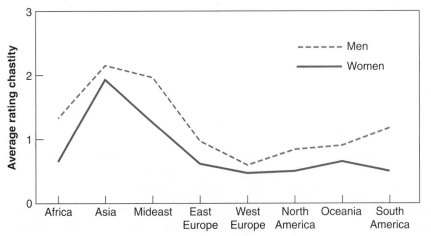

selection in a variety of cultures, including those in North America, the Caribbean and South America, Africa, the Middle East, Asia, and Europe. With contributions from twenty authors, using a common set of guidelines and formats, it is easy for readers to make comparisons between and among more than sixteen cultures spread throughout the world. For this reason, the book appears in the Further Readings section at the end of this book. For a unique and comparative analysis of family trends in Asia, see Quah (2008); to understand how the function of the family has changed and how these changes affect family roles in cultures across the world, see Georgas, Berry, van de Vijver, Kagitcibasi, and Pooringa (2006); and for a global perspective on contemporary issues in family studies, see Abela and Walker (2014).

More recently, Ayachi (2014) examined the criteria for mate selection in Maghreb, the eastern region of North Africa consisting of the following countries—Mauritania, Morocco, Libya, Algeria, and Tunisia. Rapid economic, political, social, and religious changes have affected the mate selection process of the younger generation. However, as the authors point out, "While the process . . . has changed considerably, young people often make compromises to take account of their families' wishes and selection criteria to gain approval" (p. 319). Although there are new and more liberating processes guiding mate selection, Ayachi states that ". . . some young people fall back on more traditional methods, consulting with a range of other people before getting engaged" (p. 319). Even so, significant changes are taking place. For example, there is much greater respect for "the dignity and aspirations of women within marriage . . . mutual support between spouses within the home" . . . and encouragement of . . . "shared responsibility for child rearing." In addition, "The more traditional religious expectations of husbands having absolute authority in the home are diminishing in favour of a more enlightened religiosity" (p. 319).

The most comprehensive study of mate selection appears to be that of Schwarz and Hassebrauck (2012), focusing on more than 21,000 subjects (recruited from an online dating service) ranging in age from eighteen to sixty-five, and using a scale of eight-two mate selection criteria. Like other studies, results showed large gender differences (e.g., women are more demanding than men and more criteria are important for them). Men, as in previous studies, indicate a preference for younger, physically attractive, and creative women. Age and education level showed little variation, suggesting to the authors that mate selection preferences remain very stable over a lifetime. They conclude that although mate selection has been studied for more than seventy years, there remains more for future study.

*Do men and women actually act on their preferences?* Perhaps we'll get some answers when we look at the next topic—marriage.

## 4.2.2: Marriage and Other Long-Term Relationships

Children generally benefit from a stable system of primary caregivers, commonly including, but not limited to, the biological parents. Thus, heterosexual long-term relationships are facilitated, sanctioned, and protected in most societies, although a variety of different relationships are becoming more common and will be discussed within this chapter. The motivation for marriage is to provide a stable environment for children. In fact, the cultural definition of "family" (which is undergoing some contemporary changes) influences the ecological system on many levels. For example, it shapes the microsystem by ensuring (in many cases) that two parents (of different genders or the same gender) are present and regulates the macrosystem because it views this form of "family" as an important element of societal structure. It also affects all three components of the developmental niche by determining family structure, presence or absence of parents and other relatives, customs of child care, parenting styles, values, belief systems, and developmental expectations. For an in-depth discussion of issues facing marriages and families today, see Schwartz and Scott (2010) and Abela and Walker (2014).

In addition to (hopefully) providing a good and healthy environment for children, individuals commit themselves to long-term relationships for other reasons. Marriage may also be a means to gain or maintain status in one's society. In most cultures, simply being married gives married men and women a higher status than their unmarried counterparts. In some cases, unmarried adults may be stigmatized and even denied full adult status. Along with social status, marriage may result in higher economic status. The pooling of resources of two families or a dowry paid by the family of the bride can mean considerable financial gain for both spouses. In August 2009, a thirty-nine-year-old Kenyan man offered forty goats and twenty cows to visiting Secretary of State Hillary Clinton for the hand of her daughter, Chelsea, in marriage. In response, Mrs. Clinton said her daughter was very independent, "So I will convey this very kind offer." If accepted, Chelsea would be his second wife because polygamy is legal in Kenya and his wife ". . . has no problem with this." Finally, and certainly not to be forgotten, individuals may be motivated to share their lives out of a desire for love and companionship.

Anthropologists have demonstrated that marriage takes many forms in cultures around the world. These include **monogamy**, in which *one man is married to one woman;* **polygyny** or **polygamy**, in which *one man is married to several women;* **polyandry**, in which *one woman is married to several men;* and **cenogamy** or **group marriage**, in which *all the women and men in a group are married* *simultaneously to each other.* Polygyny is found on every continent. It is common in many Islamic countries, African societies, and parts of Asia, and it is also found in North America. An abundance of wives of different ages not only represents wealth and power but it also ensures the reproductive success of the man. A verse from the *Qur'an (4:3)* helps explain the practice in Islam: *"Marry women of your choice, two or three or four; but if you fear that you shall not be able to deal justly with them, then only one or one that your right hands possess. That will be more suitable, to prevent you from doing injustice"* (Emerick, 2000). Although some Muslim majority countries still retain traditional Islamic Law permitting polygyny, some movements within Islam challenge its acceptability.

Polyandry is much less common. In some regions of Tibet and Nepal, brothers may share the same wife. However, in most cultures in which polyandry is accepted, husbands do not share blood relations. In general, polyandry is associated with greater economic power of women. Men in polyandrous societies have to be more considerate of women's needs to prevent them from switching their attention to more generous and caring husbands. Thus, wives can rely on generous shares of their husbands' wealth or income and may acquire considerable wealth themselves. Only a few societies, found in some regions of Western Africa, allow both women and men to be married to multiple spouses.

A number of cultures permit sexual relations of some sort between individuals of the same gender. The very few studies that address the subject in a cultural context mainly focus on gay or homosexual relationships between men. Because such studies are still limited in number, it is difficult to know with certainty what percentage of societies accept, tolerate, or even support same-gender relationships. Nonetheless, Bolton (1994) concludes from a review of anthropological studies that male homosexual relations are common in 41% to 64% of societies studied. By comparison, data on lesbian relationships are not as readily available, but Bolton argues that "societies, which are tolerant of homosexuality, are consistent in expressing that tolerance across age and gender categories" (p. 162).

A recent survey by the Pew Research Center (2013) of 37,653 respondents in thirty-nine countries finds broad acceptance of homosexuality (or gay or lesbian relationships) in North America, the European Union, and much of Latin America, as well as equally widespread rejection in predominantly Muslin nations, Africa, and parts of Asia and Russia. Opinions regarding acceptability are divided in Bolivia, Israel, and Poland. According to the survey, in some countries, age appears to be a contributing factor ". . . with younger respondents offering far more tolerant views than older ones. And while gender differences are not prevalent, in those countries where they are, women are consistently more accepting of homosexuality than men" (p. 2).

The presence or absence of gay or lesbian relationships in a given society once again illustrates the concept of the developmental niche, namely, how certain behaviors may develop or be inhibited in response to cultural conditions. In societies that tolerate or even support relationships between people of the same gender, there are a greater number of gay and lesbian relationships. In contrast, societies that strictly prohibit homosexual relations report fewer instances of homosexuality. These differences do not occur as a result of a higher or lower percentage of gays and lesbians in the population, but as a result of differential opportunities to develop a certain preference and behavior within one's ecological surroundings and to express it as part of one's developmental niche.

There has been a slow and limited acceptance of gay and lesbian families during the early years of the twenty-first century. For example, in 2001, the Netherlands became the first society to legalize same-gender marriages, followed by Belgium in 2003, Canada and Spain in 2005, South Africa in 2006, Norway and Sweden in 2009, and Portugal and Iceland in 2010. Other countries, although not permitting marriages, have approved same-gender civil unions. In a landmark decision, a divided U.S. Supreme Court (5-4) ruled on June 26, 2015, that states cannot ban same-gender marriages. The United States becomes the twenty-first country to legalize same-gender marriage nationwide. Such couples now have the same benefits and legal rights as married heterosexual couples and are legally recognized on birth and death certificates. Interestingly, same-gender partners are generally older when getting married than opposite-gender ones, and the risk of divorce seems higher among female couples than male or heterosexual couples (Andersson & Noack, 2011). It has been suggested that as same-gender couples begin to have children, the risk of divorce could be reduced. However, this remains a hypothesis and will need to be further investigated.

How and why individuals are attracted to each other varies significantly across cultures. Another distinction might be referred to as the "Eastern versus Western ideal." In many Western cultures, perhaps best represented by the United States, marriage is often viewed as the culmination of *romantic love.* The belief is that each person has an "ideal" mate that he or she is destined to meet, fall in love with, marry, and live with "happily ever after." Your author recalls a student telling him how her parents, living in Yugoslavia, met and married. One day, her father climbed a hill next to his village and watched a young woman washing clothes in the river below. He returned the next day and watched her again. On the third day, he walked down to the river, told her he had been watching her for three days and had fallen in love with her and wanted to marry her. She said, "Yes." They were now celebrating their twenty-fifth wedding anniversary! However, there are other people who find "true love" several times and have the marriage certificates to prove it.

The "Eastern ideal" continues to characterize many of the arranged marriages in Asia, Africa, and some other parts of the world. This ideal is based on the premise that each person has several possible mates with whom they could develop a successful marriage. Frequently, as in India, families will discuss a possible future liaison between their infant children. Sometimes, the children are aware of this arrangement; sometimes, they are not. They are expected to marry (or bring shame and embarrassment to their families); if they are lucky, they may one day fall in love with each other. A female Indian graduate student, speaking in one of the author's cross-cultural courses, related that she was returning home to Bombay to get married. When asked by a student what her future husband did, she replied, "I don't know because I've never met him." The liberated young American women in class told her that she shouldn't marry someone she didn't know. Her reply, which makes an interesting cultural point, was that she trusted her parents to make a wise decision regarding a future husband because they knew her and him and his family. In the meantime, she could concentrate on her studies while they (the American women in class) would have to search for their own husbands, go through the trials and errors of dating, and hope that in the end it would all work out. In reality, arranged marriages tend to be quite stable. *Do you know anyone in such a marriage? How would you react if your parents suggested such an arrangement?*

Many of those who live in collectivist cultures view marriage as the coming together or blending of two families. For example, in northern Kenya, the creation of a new house is a significant part of the marriage ceremony. Once the wedding date is established, based on lunar calculations, the groom's family literally disassembles the new house, moves it to the bride's village, and rebuilds it. Prior to the wedding ceremony, the bride is taken through a rite of passage during which she is initiated into womanhood by the village's female elders and is taught what to expect from married life. Among the Mande, another African group, girls between ages twelve and eighteen attend clitoridectomy schools, where they have their clitorises removed and are formally taught how to be wives. They learn secret languages and codes that allow them to communicate with other married women. In Africa, as well as other parts of the world, many wedding customs are currently undergoing change and reflect a mixture of the traditional and the modern.

Harry and Ormsin Gardiner's Thai wedding ceremony.

(© Harry Gardiner)

The same might be said of contemporary Japan, where love marriages are increasingly replacing the earlier practice of arranged marriages. Whichever practice is followed, certain traditional customs frequently remain. For example, a *yuinou*, or ceremonial betrothal gift (often in the form of money), is first presented by the bridegroom-to-be through a go-between to the bride-to-be's household. In anthropological terms, this represents the bride's price. The bride's parents are then expected to spend several times the value of the *yuinou* on a new home for the couple. Most wedding ceremonies in Japan are performed according to Shinto customs, followed by the drinking of sake (rice wine) as confirmation of the marriage and later by a celebration party.

# 4.3: The Birth Process Across Cultures

The vignettes that opened this chapter, Sindy and David Sowidagkijm in Suriname, as well as Patricia and Walter Mezzanotti and John and Ruth Hazelton in New York City, illustrate that although newborns arrive every day in cultures around the world, the birth experience depends very much on cultural traditions and is deeply embedded within an ecological setting influenced by family, community, and culture.

In some societies, having a baby is just another normal event in one's life and takes little preparation. This is illustrated in the following example taken from the !Kung in the Kalahari Desert of Africa: "The first labor pains came at night and stayed . . . until dawn. That morning, everyone went gathering. Mother and I stayed behind. We sat together for a while, then I went and played with the other children. Later, I came back and ate the nuts she had cracked for me. She got up and started to get ready. . . . We walked a short way, then she sat down by the base of a large nehn tree, leaned back against it, and little Kumsa was born" (Shostak, 1981, pp. 53–54). Similarly, in rural Thailand, pregnancy does not significantly change a woman's behavior, and she "generally carries on with her household chores until the time of birth—even, in some cases, up to the last few minutes before delivery. Rural children are usually born at home with the mother resting on a mat or mattress on the floor assisted by a non-medically trained midwife and older relatives or neighbors" (Gardiner & Gardiner, 1991, p. 183). In many cases, a few hours later, the new mother is often up and actively participating in family activities.

Whether it is at home or in a hospital, in many parts of North America, including the United States, fathers-to-be are typically present during labor and encouraged to actively participate in the delivery of their child. Not so in some parts of South America or in East Africa, where an expectant Ngoni mother is assisted by other women, while husbands and other men are completely excluded.

Clearly, not every culture approaches childbirth in the same way. In the next section, we look at the birth process in more detail and consider its variations across cultures.

## 4.3.1: The Ecology of Birth

Individual feelings about pregnancy and childbirth may differ, yet the vast majority of families across the world have at least one child. How those children are conceived in today's world, with advances in medical technology, may vary widely. For example, it may be in the "the old fashioned way" through sexual intercourse when a male sperm penetrates a female ovum resulting in a zygote or fertilized egg. Conception may also occur outside a woman's body by means of in vitro fertilization (artificial insemination in which sperm from a husband, anonymous donor, or other person is injected into a woman's vagina at an appropriate time), embryo transplant, or use of a surrogate (substitute mother) who gives birth for another woman—in some cases, this has been a stranger, a sister, or even a woman's own mother, resulting in a woman giving birth to her own grandchild!

For a long time, what we knew about childbirth practices came from a Western, largely American, perspective that viewed the procedure as a medical event. Interestingly, this was not always the case. In fact, childbirth in Canada and the United States, like most other countries, was handled exclusively by women until the mid-nineteenth century, when physicians, almost all of whom were men, began delivering babies and made it a medical rather than a social event.

In the original edition of her now classic cross-cultural investigation of childbirth in four cultures, Brigitte Jordan (1978) anticipated the approach taken here when she noted that, in the past, little attention had been given to social, ecological, or cultural aspects of childbirth. In the Preface to the fourth edition of this book, Jordan and Davis-Floyd (1993) state that "an anthropology of birth must focus on the study of birthing *systems* and not the comparison of individual and isolated practices. We know that birth is everywhere a socially marked crisis event that is consensually shaped and socially patterned [consisting of] . . . practices that make sense from the inside out, though not necessarily from the outside in" (pp. 11–12).

In a section of her book titled, "The Ecology of Birth," Jordan (1978) discusses the particular locations in which babies are born (e.g., the United States, the Yucatan, Holland, and Sweden) and how these locations reflect culture-specific patterns (or ecological settings, as we would view them) with which individuals' lives are forever entwined. She also comments on the cultural implications of these specific arrangements.

**YUCATAN**   Of the four cultures presented by Jordan and Davis-Floyd (1993), the Yucatan imposes the least changes in the expectant mother's surroundings, maintaining its familiar and reassuring qualities by encouraging the Mayan woman to lie in the same hammock in which she sleeps each night "whose strengths and tautness she knows to exploit for maximum support and comfort [thereby providing] . . . the kind of security that marks the event as a normal part of family life" (p. 68).

In the Yucatan, there is a clear expectation that the father-to-be will be present during labor and birth, not only to take an active role but also to observe "how a woman suffers." Frequently, if a child is stillborn, it is blamed on an absent father. In addition, the pregnant woman's mother should be present, often in the company of others from the family microsystem, including sisters, sisters-in-law, mothers-in-law, godmothers, and sometimes neighbors and close friends. According to Jordan (1978), all of these people make a contribution to a successful birth, and the intensity of their emotional and physical involvement is "mirrored in the strain on their faces and in the signs of fatigue that become evident in them as well as in the mother" (p. 38).

Immediately following birth, it is believed that the mother and her child are susceptible to the influence of evil spirits from the bush and must remain inside the house for one week before returning to normal activity. An infant girl will have her ears pierced within the first hour after birth and sometime within the next three days will receive her first earrings, often a family heirloom. Nearly all newborns are breastfed, with nursing beginning a few minutes after birth and continuing whenever the infant appears hungry or anxious.

**HOLLAND AND SWEDEN**   In Holland, similar to the Yucatan, women generally give birth at home, assisted by a midwife or physician, and the country continues to maintain one of the lowest infant mortality rates in the world—3.66 deaths per 1,000 live births (Central Intelligence Agency (CIA), 2013). In Sweden, often cited as the one of the countries with the lowest infant mortality (2.60 deaths per 1,000 live births), almost all babies are delivered in hospitals with the help of highly trained midwives (CIA, 2013). [As of 2016, the country with the lowest infant mortality rate is Monaco with 1.81 deaths per 1,000 live births.] What Holland and Sweden have in common is a program of government-sponsored prenatal care for every woman and the availability of abortion on demand with the result that pregnancies tend to be wanted pregnancies and all babies are wanted babies.

**UNITED STATES** In the United States, ranking 168 in the world in infant mortality (6.16 deaths per 1,000 live births) in 2013, the majority of births (approximately 98%) continue to be in hospital settings under the control of medical specialists. However, unlike the three countries mentioned previously, there is a wider range of options available. For example, although some families prefer to have their babies delivered at home with the assistance of a midwife, increasing numbers, similar to the Mezzanotti family in our opening vignette, are taking advantage of birthing rooms located in hospitals, where technology is available in a homelike atmosphere.

In this regard, an experimental project cited by Jordan (1978) is of historical (and perhaps even contemporary) interest. During a period of three years in the early 1970s, two nurse-midwives conducted the majority of normal deliveries in a California hospital. During this period, there was a dramatic drop in the number of stillbirths, fetal deaths, premature births, and neonatal deaths. When physicians once again took charge, these types of incidents increased, with the prematurity rate going up nearly 50% and neonatal mortality more than tripling (Levy, Wilkinson, & Marine, 1971). These findings suggest that this topic should receive more research attention. In the years since this experimental project, several other small-scale studies have confirmed the success rate of nurse-midwife–assisted deliveries. MacDorman and Singh (1998) reported findings from the first large-scale study to examine the infant mortality risks for *all* single, vaginal births at thirty-five to forty-three weeks gestation delivered by nurse-midwives in the United States during the year 1991 (182,461 births or about 4.4% of all births that year). After controlling for a variety of social and medical risk factors, the authors compared the data for midwives with a random sample of 25% of physician-attended births in 1991. Results indicated that infant deaths were 19% lower for births attended by nurse-midwives, the risk of neonatal mortality (death during the first twenty-eight weeks of life) was 33% lower, and

the risk of delivering a low-birth-weight infant was 31% lower. Differences in these birth outcomes may be explained, in part, by the differences in prenatal, labor, and delivery care practices demonstrated by nurse-midwives, including more time spent with patients during prenatal visits; greater emphasis on counseling and education; and provision of emotional support before, during, and after delivery. Such findings lend support to Jordan's (1978) earlier contention that who is allowed to be present during birth significantly influences not only the birth experience but also the outcome of the birth process itself. More than fifteen years prior to the 2009 debate over the cost of health care in the United States, it was estimated that the use of midwifery care for 75% of the births in the United States would produce a savings of more than $8.5 billion per year (Madrona & Madrona, 1993). For more current information on the state of midwifery, see Hoope-Bender, Campbell, Fauveau, and Matthews (2011).

Writing nearly forty years ago, Jordan (1978) concluded her original birth study with the following statement: "What we need to keep in mind here is that birthing systems themselves are part of a larger cultural system . . . within an economic and political structure, via the socialization of birth participants" (p. 73). This point is even more relevant today, especially in light of our recurring themes, which focus on the cultural context in which development takes place.

In a sense, if you know a society's approach to childbirth, you will understand a great deal about the values and beliefs that are at the heart of its ecocultural system, how it socializes its members, and how it conducts its interpersonal relationships.

# 4.4: The Transition to Parenthood

Following the birth of a child, parents have to take on new identities—those of mother and father—perhaps the most difficult roles they will ever be required to perform. Kenkel (1985) puts the transition to parenthood in perspective when he states that "one of the significant features with regard to the parent role is a general lack of preparation for it. . . . Related to [this] . . . is the fact that the transition . . . is abrupt [and] . . . largely irrevocable" (pp. 455–456).

Becoming a parent results in major life changes that affect not only the parents and their infant, but also many others within the ecological setting in which this event occurs. For example, Heinicke (1995) writes that within a family system, "the personality characteristics of the parents as well as their relationship support systems (partner and extended family) to a significant extent define future parenting transactions with their child" (p. 277). We might ask, "What about other niche influences such as the social and physical environment and customs of child care?" These surely play an equally important role and are worthy of future research on the part of those interested in cross-cultural human development.

In this regard, Belsky (1985) hypothesizes that "supportive developmental experiences give rise to a mature healthy personality, that is then capable of providing sensitive parental care which fosters optimal child development" (p. 86). This again points to the importance of the ecological setting and the transmission from one generation to another of successful parental belief systems learned within a healthy family environment. In fact, Vondra and Belsky (1993), in a later study of the developmental origins of parenting, state that "by assuming an ecological perspective . . . and by adopting a longitudinal design, research has begun to provide a more adequate test of developmental and clinical theory on the origins of parenting" (p. 25). In a volume devoted to the transition to adulthood and family relationships, Scabini, Marta, and Lanz (2006) analyze family relationships by gender and generation and offer new research questions.

In addition, a significant contribution to understanding the complexities and importance of the transition to parenthood has recently been made by Walker (2014). She states that, "The growing number of divorces in the early years of marriage, often when couples have young children, has put renewed focus on how couples manage the transition to parenthood" (p. 125). Qualitative research involving more than 1,000 individuals in England who had been or were in a committed couple relationship shows the importance of four distinct factors in this transition: "the decision to have children, problems associated with pregnancy and the postnatal period, changes in roles and responsibilities, and the pressures associated with becoming a parent and their impact on the couple relationship" (p. 126). Following a detailed discussion of each factor, the author points out that parenting interventions developed in Australia and the United States (advice about the impact of parenthood, health professional training, peer group discussions, and online services such as websites and help lines) have been found effective in very different cultural settings (e.g., Hong Kong, New Zealand, Iran, and many European countries) (Knerr, Gardner, & Culver, 2011). She concludes that "Enhancing our understanding about how couples experience the transition to parenthood, the choices they make and the responsibilities they face can enable policymakers and practitioners to develop services that facilitate smoother transitions and reduce stressors within couple relationships" (p. 133) and, in the end, ensure more positive and healthy outcomes for children's development.

# 4.5: Infancy and Childhood

Each day throughout the world, approximately 750,000 individuals become new parents (CIA, 2009). Contrary to what many of these parents may think, a newborn is not always the pretty, smiling, curly-haired cherub they have imagined or seen in pictures or television commercials. Rather, a newborn is frequently an unattractive little creature—sometimes very small (or very big), often bald, toothless, hungry, and complaining—that has come to live with the new family for many years into the future. During the first few days and weeks, most new couples wonder if they are capable of nurturing this new person and attending to its needs. Fortunately, the majority of parents *are* capable and, with later additions to the family, often get even better at it.

On arrival, most **newborns** (the *term applied to babies from birth through the first two weeks,* after which the term *infant* is used) are well equipped to deal with their new environment. For the most part, their senses work well, and they have a large repertoire of reflexes to help them adjust to the world beyond the womb. So effective are these reflexes, and so resilient are newborns, that following the devastating earthquake in Mexico City in September 1985, babies were found alive in the ruins of one hospital nursery six days later. In Sichuan, China, following the May 2008 earthquake, a four-month-old baby girl was found in her dead mother's arms alive and still breastfeeding. In the January 2010 earthquake in Haiti, a five-year-old child survived eight days buried in the rubble of her home. Four days after the disastrous Japanese tsunami in 2011, a four-month-old baby girl was found alive under a pile of debris, and a five-month-old girl was found alive in the rubble of the 2015 Nepal earthquake.

In the initial days and months following birth, parents devote much attention and concern to satisfying their child's basic needs for sleep, hunger, and elimination (see Chapter 3). As Bornstein (1995) observes, "Infants forever alter the sleeping, eating, and working habits of their parents; they change who parents are and how parents define themselves. . . . Parenting an infant is a 168-hour-a-week job" (p. 3). As children get older and move into the years of early, middle, and later childhood, development keeps pace. At the center of all this activity, largely determining the nature of the parent–child relationship, are parental belief systems.

## 4.5.1: Parental Belief Systems

In every culture, parents tend to develop shared ideas about the nature of children, their developmental processes, and the meaning of their behaviors. Strongly influenced by the cultural context, these ideas are entwined with other aspects of life, including time and place, meaning of self, family, and parenthood (see Box 4.1).

# Box 4.1 Parenting Among African Pygmies

There are about 150,000 Pygmies living in parts of several African countries, including Rwanda, Cameroon, Gabon, Congo, Burundi, and Zaire. The majority range in height from 4 feet to 4 feet, 8 inches (1.2 meters to 1.42 meters). Although no one is sure why they are so small, research studies suggest it may be a combination of factors, including a growth hormone deficiency and an evolutionary adaptation to their ecological setting that allows them to move quickly and silently through the forest.

An Efe mother braids the hair of a child in the Ituri forest in the Congo.

(Friedrich von Hörsten / Alamy Stock Photo)

One group, the Efe (who prefer to be known by their tribal name rather than the often derogatory term emphasizing short stature), are hunters and gatherers living in the Northeastern region of the Ituri forest in the Congo, formerly Zaire. They are believed to be the oldest pure ethnic group in the world with a culture, language, and tradition at least 10,000 years old. They live in small, extended family groups (about twenty to thirty people) consisting of brothers and their wives, children, unmarried sisters, and perhaps parents. They live in temporary camps composed of leaf huts used for sleeping, food storage, and protection from the weather. These huts, moved when the food supply runs low, are arranged in a semicircle, creating a shared communal space where most day-to-day activities take place.

Sharing and cooperation among the Efe in terms of food, work, and child care are essential to their survival. The workload is high, and many activities such as foraging are engaged in by both men and women, although only men hunt.

There is a strong belief among Efe that the mother *should not* be the first person to hold a newborn baby. This belief not only prevents an Efe woman from going off to give birth on her own, but it also introduces a child to multiple caregivers early. In fact, infants are frequently nursed by women other than their own mothers.

Fathers have an early presence in the child's life. For example, it is common practice for them to view the birth from the doorway of the hut. When not hunting, they and other men are often present in camp and often watch and hold the children (theirs and others), although most child care is the responsibility of mothers.

The developmental niche of the Efe is intensely social. The continuous presence of others, along with early multiple care, helps prepare Efe children for their social world, while protecting them from common dangers in the physical environment.

**SOURCE:** "Infusing Culture into Parenting Issues: A Supplement for Psychology Instructors" from unpublished manuscript, St. Louis Community College by Vicki Ritts. Copyright © 2001 by Vicki Ritts. Reprinted by permission of Vicki Ritts.

As Harkness and Super (1996) point out in an important contribution to the literature of culture and human development, these cultural understandings are organized into categories referred to as **parents' cultural belief systems** and "relate in *systematic ways to action—including . . . styles of talking to children, methods of discipline, or seeking advice from experts.* Ultimately [these belief systems] . . . exert a powerful influence on the health and development of children, and they are a key component in the development of parents themselves" (pp. 2–3). Parental beliefs represent one component of the developmental niche—the psychology of the caregiver.

Developing a philosophy of child-rearing is one of the major tasks faced by new parents (Francis-Connally, 2000; Kenkel, 1985). In a particularly interesting application of this idea, Richman and others (1988) observed mother–child interactions in five cultures (three industrial and two agrarian) and reported several prominent differences. Among the more interesting was the finding that Gusii mothers of Kenya hold their nine- to ten-month-old infants and engage in soothing physical contact more than do middle-class mothers in Boston, Massachusetts, but, at the same time, look at and talk to them less often. Why? According to Richman and her colleagues, there are several reasons for this behavior, all of which make perfect sense once you understand the ecology of the cultures involved. For example, among the Gusii, (1) infant mortality rates are high, and holding and soothing provide a greater chance of survival; (2) there is a belief that language is not understood by children until about the age of two; and (3) the culture teaches that one should avoid making direct eye contact with others. In American culture, there is a belief that (1) language learning should begin early and (2) placing infants in playpens where they can play by themselves begins the process of independence so highly valued in American society.

Ever since Sigel (1985) edited one of the first volumes discussing this concept, interest in parental belief systems as an approach to understanding cultural similarities and differences has grown rapidly (Sigel & McGillicuddy-DeLisi, 2002). This concept has been fostered by the emergence of parallel trends in social anthropology, psychology, and new interdisciplinary approaches to culture and human development (Dasen, 2003; Harkness & Super, 1996, 2003).

Also contributing to this unifying concept are some of the approaches serving as major themes for this book. For example, the ecological model of Bronfenbrenner provides a dynamic, interactive paradigm of parent–child interactions as they occur within a continually expanding cultural context that shapes the development of effective parental beliefs and practices. The developmental niche framework proposed by Super and Harkness assists in "conceptualizing relationships among parental belief systems, customs, and practices of childrearing and the organization of physical and social settings for children's daily lives" (Harkness & Super, 1996, p. 5).

After reviewing these and similar studies, it becomes apparent that the following questions have not been adequately answered by the research literature: *"In general, are there relationships between specific parenting beliefs and parenting behaviors?" "Are there universals, as well as variations, in what we might call 'good parenting'?" "Do certain kinds of parenting lead to certain kinds of outcomes for children both cross-culturally and within cultures?" "What form do parental cultural belief systems take in cultures where relatives other than parents (e.g., uncles, aunts, grandparents, and in-laws) play critically important roles?"* These questions are offered in the hope that those who might pursue future studies in these areas will help extend our understanding of human development within the context of culture.

Throughout the remainder of this chapter, we will learn how parents' cultural belief systems influence the manner in which lives develop across cultures, beginning with mothering and fathering behaviors. [See Newland et al. (2013) for an extended discussion of some of the unique and complimentary ways in which fathers and mothers support their children's development within ecocultural niches impacted by the socioeconomic and cultural context.]

### 4.5.2: Mothering

In their research on mothering, Barnard and Martell (1995) note that cultures consider this behavior extremely important, especially since mothers are the primary day-to-day teachers of culture. The authors also point out that opportunities to view similarities and differences in the mothering role have been limited because mothering generally takes place in the privacy of the family. Although these researchers do not use Bronfenbrenner's ecological model terminology, their thinking sounds similar. For example, they state that "the role [of mothering] . . . develops in relation to the family system wherein roles of father,

siblings, and other extended family members are enacted as well. . . . Each person's role is connected with all others in the family system and because that is true there are always variations within cultures. [For example] . . . as the position of women changes, aspects of the mothering role will be assumed by others in the family or in the society" (p. 3).

According to Harkness and Super (1995), mothering has historically been associated with women because in most cultures women have provided primary care for children. In this regard, and in light of our discussion of Japanese families in this chapter, it is interesting to consider Barnard and Martell's (1995) analysis of the Japanese words for *woman, mother, man,* and *father:* "The character for woman is a stick figure with a protuberance, resembling a pregnant abdomen, whereas the character for mother resembles the chest with two breasts. The symbol for man, on the other hand, is the rice field illustrating work. The character for father is a stone axe symbolizing power" (p. 4). More accurately, the symbol for man is a combination of two characters, one representing a rice field and the other representing power, which symbolizes hard work (Gardiner, 1996). *Parenting* is represented by three characters literally translated as "to stand," "a tree," and "to watch," which, when combined, can be interpreted as "watching over a growing child" (Gardiner, 1996). For a visual representation of these characters, see Figure 4.2.

Barnard and Martell (1995) also point out that these Japanese characters came from the original Chinese language and represent ethnic and intergenerational thinking about these roles within both cultures. These character distinctions raise several intriguing questions: *"Are mothering, fathering, and parenting distinct roles?" "Are birthing and nurturing unique characteristics of the mother's role, whereas support and family control are assigned to the father's role?" "Is parenting different than mothering and fathering?"*

In a review of research on mothering, Barnard and Solchany (2002) discuss the concept of allomothering (or "shared mothering"), a term coined by Hrdy (2009), which includes those people who help care for a child, "including (but not limited to) the mother's mate, extended family, peers, and neighbors" (p. 21). These are all individuals we find interacting with and influencing a child's development as he or she moves among the micro-, meso-, and

**Figure 4.2** Japanese Characters Related to Parenting

Man      Woman      Father      Mother      Parenting

exosystems of his or her unique ecological environment. Examples of allomothering can be found in many African tribal villages, Israeli kibbutz, and even American day care or child care settings, in which the safety, nurturance, and responsibility for children's well-being is shared by a number of people. The authors also discuss the meaning of motherhood in the context of becoming a woman, preparation for motherhood, important functions of mothering (e.g., expected nurturing, monitoring and surveillance, and caregiving–social partner role), and the challenges of mothering.

In the presentation of an interesting and enlightening series of ethnographic studies, Barlow and Chapin (2010) analyze mothering in the widely differing cultural contexts of the United States, Sri Lanka, Papua New Guinea, China, and Ecuador, providing views of mothers as socializers with insights into questions related to socialization and enculturation, cultural patterning, and contemporary change. Among the points they make are that ". . . discipline and childrearing are situated within a larger community of important others. These others, acting as witnesses, coaches, and judges, are actively involved in shaping children's and mother's behavior. Together, these efforts to shape children's behaviors and influence the kinds of persons they become communicate important cultural messages about mother, child, family, and community to each participant" (pp. 332–333).

Amy Chua's (2011) controversial book, *Battle Hymn of the Tiger Mother*, presented one mother's "Chinese way" of a strict authoritarian parenting style that suggested it produced high achievement children, unlike easygoing Western parenting, and ignited a global debate over the topic of mothering. Subsequent research demonstrated that children raised this way generally had lower grades, were more depressed, and were more alienated from their parents (Kim, Wang, Orozco-Lapray, Shen, & Murtuza, 2013). Results demonstrated that supportive and easygoing parents show better developmental outcomes than tiger parents, who showed the worst outcomes. [Readers can view the film—*The Joy Luck Club* (Tan, Stone, et al. (Producers) & Wang (Director), 1993)—depicting older Chinese mothers and their Chinese American daughters and the clash of Chinese and American cultures that shaped their lives, including some harsh child-rearing practices and overly high academic expectations.]

## 4.5.3: Fathering

Research on the role of fathers is of relatively recent origin (Doucet, 2006; Parke, 2002), and research on cross-cultural comparisons is still comparatively rare (Aldous, Mulligan, & Bjarnason, 1998; Gardiner, 1994; Lamb, 1987, 2004; Lykken, 2000; Yang, 1999). In fact, cross culturally, only a minority of child care is carried out by men. However, it is

promising to note that when fathering is studied, it is being increasingly observed from both the ecological model and contextual approach (Day & Lamb, 2004; Parke, 2002; Sullivan, 2004), as well as from the lifespan perspective (Elder, Modell, & Parke, 1993; Parke, 2000). A major contribution to understanding the role of fathers in a wide range of cultural settings is the recent book—*Fathers in Cultural Context*—by Shwalb, Shwalb, and Lamb (2013). It contains chapters on Japan, China, Malaysia, Central and East Africa, Brazil, the United States, and other countries.

Also of interest is a study by Marsiglio and Cohan (2000) clarifying the basic features of a sociological perspective as it relates to the study of fathers' involvement with, and influence on, their children. The authors focus on the social, organizational, and cultural contexts of fathering, with particular emphasis on the interplay between social structures and processes at the macro, meso, and micro levels, along with social psychological issues.

In this regard, Parke (2002) stresses "the importance of examining developmental changes in the adult because parents continue to change and develop during adult years" (p. 28). He points out that the age at which an individual becomes a parent can significantly affect the ways in which men and women carry out their paternal and maternal roles, and that education, self-identity, and career tasks are related to the demands of being a parent. For example, the average age of marriage in Egypt and the Sudan is twenty-five to thirty-five years for men and twenty to thirty years for women in urban areas, twenty to twenty-five for men and sixteen to eighteen for women in rural areas.

In Nigeria, among the Muslim Hausa, a boy usually enters his first marriage around the age of twenty, often to a girl of thirteen or fourteen who has just reached puberty. For a Yoruba male, marriage typically takes place when the man is in his mid- to late twenties and the girl is about sixteen to eighteen years of age. Among the Southeast Asian Hmong, large numbers of whom have migrated to the United States, it is common for men in their twenties to thirties to marry young girls in their early to middle adolescent years. Although many of these young people may be adequately prepared, as part of their developmental niche, to assume parental responsibilities at these relatively young ages, others are not; and, recently being children themselves, they will find married life and child-rearing difficult.

As Shwalb, Nakazawa, Yamamoto, and Hyun (2003) have noted, in a review of research on Chinese, Japanese, and Korean cultures, fathering is affected by many contexts, including history, changing families, work roles, and marital relationships. For example, although China has promoted gender equality at work and encourages both women and men to be active in child-rearing, Japanese and Korean fathers have often reduced their involvement in family matters to provide financially for their families. Chinese fathers appear to blend a combination of warmth, control, and authoritativeness in their parenting style. Korean fathers, who historically focused greater attention on their sons, now spend more time with each child because of the drastic reduction in family size. The authors suggest that more research is needed not only on fathers' direct influence on their children but also on how they influence children indirectly through the husband–wife relationship. (See also Shwalb, Shwalb, & Lamb, 2013).

In a review of research on fathers and families, Parke (2002) notes that substantial progress has been made in understanding the paternal role and its impact on fathers themselves, as well as on their children and others within and outside the family. Among his conclusions are that (1) although mothers still have the greater responsibility in raising children, the level of father involvement has continued to increase; (2) fathers can and do show qualities of competent caregiving; (3) cross-cultural findings point to the importance of cultural and environmental contexts, as well as the possible importance of biological factors, in determining and shaping differences in play styles between mothers and fathers; (4) fathering roles show greater variability across cultures than do mothering roles; and (5) men's marital relationships and their "sense of self" are significantly affected by fathering activities. *Think about your relationships with your parents as you were growing up. What kinds of activities did you engage in with each of them? Did your interactions change as you got older? Was one parent more actively involved in your development than the other? What lasting effects, positive or negative, did their involvement have on you?*

Finally, Parke (2002) points out that the study of father–child relationships is now "a more fully contextualized issue. Fathers in the context of their social relationships both within and beyond the family are increasingly the appropriate point of entry for understanding the issue of both parental roles and their impact on themselves and others" (pp. 62–63).

This approach and the need for meeting the needs of fathers within an ecological perspective have been effectively presented in the work of Meyers (1993). To provide maximum benefits for fathers (and mothers), he proposes that parent education programs address issues such as the enhancement of child and marital communication skills, provide social support for parents, increase their involvement in child-rearing, and provide authoritative child care knowledge, while acknowledging diversity among parents in terms of their differing social and cultural backgrounds, including parents who are single, adolescent, low income, or minority. As mentioned previously, Newland and her colleagues (2013) discuss many of these same issues within contemporary ecocultural niches.

One last effort of note is a book by Flouri (2005) reviewing the effects of differing fathering styles on children's mental health, academic achievement, socioeconomic status, adolescent relationships, and delinquency. The research is based on more than twenty studies she conducted in the United Kingdom using data sources collected over a period of more than forty years. Among her findings are those showing that father involvement protected against the experience of homelessness in adult sons, but not in daughters, from low, but not high, socioeconomic groups, and was associated with low risk for delinquency in sons, but not in daughters. In addition, a father's interest in child education was related to a daughter's, but not a son's, educational attainment in adult life.

## Points to Ponder

### Observations of Public Parenting

We all go to grocery stores. This is one of the best and most ecological environments in which to observe different styles of parenting. On one of your next shopping trips, take time (10–15 minutes or so) to casually watch parents, their child(ren), and their interactions and conversations with each other. Note whether both parents are present or only the mother or father. What would you guess are the ages of the parents? How many children are there? What are their genders? How old would you estimate them to be? What kind of conversations take place? How do the parent(s) discipline the child(ren) if there is "misbehavior," and what is (are) the misbehavior(s)? Would you evaluate the parental style as "easy" or "strict"? Why? If there are several children (perhaps brothers/sisters), do they get along well or do they argue with each other or the parents? If you have the opportunity to observe more than one set of parents (or perhaps children with grandparents), look for diversity in the family background and compare/contrast behaviors. What can you conclude from these observations? How do these experiences compare with what you have read in this chapter or what you experienced as a child?

# 4.6: Adolescence

As a child makes the transition from childhood into adolescence, accompanied by a variety of developmental changes (e.g., physical, social, and cognitive), seeking to find a balance between dependence and independence, as well as trying to establish an identity, parent–child relationships frequently undergo significant change, more in some cultures than others. Coleman (2014) points out, ". . . change is gradual and, contrary to popular belief, does not bring with it a complete breakdown of relationships . . . [and research] . . . has emphasized continuity as much as change, and there has been a greater emphasis recently on the positive role that parents can play during this stage of child development" (pp. 203–204).

Parenting of adolescents has only recently become a major topic of concern in the research literature. In fact, just over three decades ago, one author found so little information on family relationships during the adolescent years that it was impossible to write a very lengthy review of the topic (Adelson, 1985). Although a significant body of relevant literature and several useful reviews have since appeared (Coleman, 2014; Lerner, Brennan, & Noh, 1998; Steinberg & Silk, 2002), relatively little detailed attention has been given to the study of adolescence in many cultures other than the United States and a few scattered societies around the world (Arnett, 2006; Ferguson, Maurer, Matthews, & Peng, 2013; Lansford, 2012; Noller & Atkin, 2010; Sorkhabi, 2012).

The lack of cross-cultural, parent–adolescent research from the standpoint of cultural context may be the result of several factors. First, many theories of adolescent development place greater emphasis on biological than on social or cultural factors as primary determinants of psychological characteristics. Second, there is continuing disagreement within the field as to whether adolescence represents a universal period of development. Although theorists take the viewpoint that it does, others argue that adolescence may be a developmental stage in some cultural settings, but not in others.

Among those specifically interested in studying adolescence from the ecological perspective are Garbarino (1985, 2000), Muuss (1988), and Muuss and Porton (1998). In the words of Muuss (1988), a strong adherent of this approach: "An ecological model goes far beyond what is presently known, opening up new perspectives and generating new hypotheses that are bound to move developmental research from the clearly defined, easily controllable research laboratory into the ecological field" (p. 300).

Crosnoe and Johnson (2011), in a review of adolescent research in the twenty-first century, give credit to methodological advances that permit better empirical research related to theoretical models. For example, they focus on adolescents' physical, interpersonal, psychological, and institutional "pathways" and how these connect with ecological contexts and patterns of societal stratification and historical change. This represents a significant contribution to contemporary adolescent research.

## 4.6.1: The Ecological Model and Adolescence

Employing the ecological model, let us look at the structures that influence the development of adolescents, irrespective of the cultures in which they live. First, various **microsystems** are involved, including the primary one of the family (parents, siblings, extended family members); the system involving friends, peers, and school; and perhaps other systems made up of neighbors and other social groups. Microsystems are continually undergoing change, as are the individuals who move in and out of them. As Muuss (1996) points out, a healthy microsystem is one based on reciprocity, especially in the relationships between parents and adolescents: "If a microsystem is rich in information, it enhances learning and development by providing opportunities in which questions are asked and answered, exploration and experimentation encouraged, and guidance provided [and it] . . . will foster opportunities for success in later life" (p. 324).

Next, there is the **mesosystem**, which links the adolescent's various microsystems (e.g., family, school, and peers). In many cultures, conflicts exist between the parents' values and peer group values. This lack of agreement can result in family conflict, regardless of culture. White (1993) provides the following quote from a Japanese adolescent (which could just as easily have been made by a North American, European, or Latin American young woman): "When I'm with my best friend I feel safe. Talking to her gives me peace. She never gets angry, or tries to get me to change. And she never embarrasses me in public the way my mother does" (p. 144). *Most of us can think of a time when one of our parents embarrassed us in public. What events do you recall? How did you feel, and what did you do?*

Although an adolescent may not actively participate in the next ecological level, the **exosystem**, much of what goes on there (e.g., at local government meetings, in parents' workplaces, or in the mass media) may indirectly affect him or her. For example, the school board in Salto, Uruguay, may determine that school enrollment will be down next year and be unable to hire fourteen-year-old Manuel Sacco's mother, Graciela, to teach for them. This will lower the family income and mean that Manuel and his brother and sister will have fewer new clothes and less food and may have to transfer to other schools.

Finally, there is the adolescent's **macrosystem**. Although of considerable importance, this is probably the least studied of all ecological systems; except for anthropological research, it almost never receives systematic investigation. As Muuss (1996) points out, "Although the macrosystem does not impinge directly on the life of the individual adolescent . . . it contains an overarching societal ground plan for the ecology of human development. [This includes] . . . a core of general cultural, political, social, legal, religious, economic, and educational values and, most important, public policy. As such, a macrosystem may be thought of as a societal blueprint" (p. 330).

American children, 3% of Hispanic American children, and 2$ of European American children live with their grandparents.

Having active and vital grandparents can provide grandchildren with positive role models for old age, as illustrated by the following quote from a young girl named Patty, who said with great admiration about her grandmother, "She is a dynamo. A speedball. When my mom was in the hospital, she came over and cleaned the house and did the cooking. I helped her; we did it together. We dance, and I get tired before she does. She even chops wood. I hope I am like that. She says I am" (Kornhaber, 1996, p. 113). (For more about grandparenting in the United States, we recommend the book by Kornhaber in the Further Readings section of the end of this book.)

Harry and Ormsin Gardiner with their grandchildren—Charlie, Mac, Malinee, and Sirina.

(© Harry Gardiner)

## 4.7.2: Caring for the Elderly

For generations, respect for those who have reached their later years has been higher in Japan, China, and many other countries than it has in the United States. Although this may still be true, in the case of the Japanese, the image may be overly idealized. As pointed out previously in this chapter, fewer elderly Japanese today are living with their children, and more are returning to low-paying jobs to support themselves.

Just as Japan is changing, so too is China, another of the world's oldest cultures. In China, the elderly were once revered, and the extended family was the primary unit of care for the elderly. Although the family is still a central focus, it is facing problems and its role is changing. For example, with increased industrialization, many rural farmers are moving to the cities, leaving their aging relatives behind. Those families that remain in rural areas often develop a reciprocal arrangement in which a married son

provides for his elderly parents and, in return, receives help from them with child care, housework, and even gardening. Those who are elderly and have no children may be eligible to move into one of the country's new homes for the elderly. To do so, one must meet four criteria: (1) have no living children nearby to provide care, (2) not be bedridden or require constant medical care, (3) be willing to enter the home, and (4) qualify for local welfare assistance (Olson, 1994). In addition to the difficulties already mentioned, elder abuse, inadequate housing, and insufficient retirement programs are becoming serious problems.

In Germany, community-based services are also increasing, but they are unable to meet the growing numbers of elderly, 75% of whom need help with daily activities and 10% of whom are bedridden.

In the United States, and many other countries, as individuals live longer, it is becoming increasingly common that adult children in middle adulthood are required to provide care for aging relatives, particularly parents, as well as for their own children. Finding themselves caught between the needs of two generations, these individuals are often referred to as the *sandwich generation*. Up to 70% of this caregiving is currently provided by women, most often adult daughters, wives, and daughters-in-law. In the United States, families provide about 80% of all long-term care for the elderly. For a view of how Koreans, Latinos, Africans, and Arabs treat their elderly, see Box 4.2.

## Box 4.2  Cultural Views and Treatment of the Elderly

As individuals grow older, they experience changes in physical, cognitive, and social abilities. Here, we highlight some of the ways in which elderly are viewed and treated across cultures.

### Korean Elderly

Historically, Korean society has been strongly influenced by Chinese culture and, in particular, Confucianism, which provides guidelines governing relationships between father and son, minister and ruler, husband and wife, elder and younger brothers, and friends. Broadly speaking, Korea is a collectivist or "relationship culture" in which the group is placed above the individual, resulting in pressure to conform to cultural norms and group demands.

The *Book of Rites* states that Koreans must respect parents, take good care of them, and bring no dishonor to them or family. Filial responsibility is the obligation of an adult child, and elderly parents typically live with their first married son who, with help from siblings, provides financial support and health care. The family remains of utmost importance in Korea today, although the proportion of elderly living apart from their children has been on the rise. Growing concern over rapid industrialization, urbanization, and changes in filial care by the younger generation has resulted in recent welfare laws and an increase in the provision of social and health services for the elderly.

## Latino Elderly

Although Latinos or Hispanics come from many different countries, they are united by a common language, and although differences exist across cultures, some generalizations are possible. For example, certain attitudes and values are common in Latino cultures. One of these is *familialism*, emphasizing sharing and cooperation over competition. A sense of family pride and loyalty and extended family support is the norm. Families remain the traditional support system despite urbanization and modernization. Other cultural values include *simpatia*, stressing loyalty, dignity, friendliness, politeness, affection, and respect for others; *personalismo*, emphasizing the importance of personal goodness and getting along with others over individual ability and individual success; and *respecto*, valuing and acknowledging hierarchies that define an individual's proper place in society on the basis of age, gender, race, and class. These values play a major role in beliefs about care of the elderly, as does the Catholic religion with its emphasis on charity as a virtue. The result is that Latinos often do not behave assertively; instead, they believe problems or events are meant to be and cannot be altered.

In Latino cultures, the elderly are thought to have an inner strength that can be a resource for the younger generation. They see themselves as important members of the family because they are links to the past; they do not feel useless or like a burden, and they are not ashamed to ask for help. They occupy a central role in the family and are treated with respect (*respecto*), status (*su lugar*), and authority (*su experiencia y sabiduria*).

Children, particularly daughters, play a major role in caring for the elderly and providing assistance, although not all elderly necessarily live with their children. Interestingly, if daughters do not care for their mothers, complaints are more hostile than if they are neglected by their sons. Daughters are also expected to visit and phone more frequently than sons. When a parent's condition severely deteriorates, formal services may be used by the family, although institutionalization is rare.

## African Elderly

Black African societies vary in their views and treatment of the elderly. At times, older individuals are held in esteem as vast storehouses of knowledge and power. At other times, their legitimacy to knowledge and power is questioned.

In a majority of African societies, old age is viewed as a sign of divine blessing. In fact, in several African languages the elder is the "big person" (Diop, 1989). Many African women who reach middle age experience the removal of restrictions in an often gender-typed society, and their status and power is approximately the same as men. However, not all views and treatment of the elderly are positive. In many societies, young people no longer fear the influence or ancestral powers of elders, and, as poverty increases, there is less support for the elderly.

## Arab Elderly

Arabs have many traits in common, but generalizing about Arab culture is difficult because of major regional differences. Nevertheless, some generalizations help in understanding how elderly are treated in Arab cultures.

Muslim ideology, as presented in the *Qur'an*, provides a sociological and legal framework of life containing the doctrines that guide Muslims to "correct" behaviors. The word "Islam" means "submission to the will of God," and a Muslim is "one who submits." Thus, religion guides and affects an Arab's entire way of life and thinking.

The extended family has always been highly valued in Arab cultures. Typically, fathers provide for the family; discipline the children; and maintain the cohesiveness, order, honor, and social standing of the family, while mothers are responsible for the care and nurturance of the children. An elderly person's status commands authority in an Arab Muslim household and increases with age. Honor and respect for the elderly is contained in the *Qur'an*, and it is assumed that families will look after the elderly. Traditionally, elderly parents live with the oldest son.

**SOURCE:** "Culture and Aging" from unpublished manuscript, St. Louis Community College by Vicki Ritts. Copyright © 2001 by Vicki Ritts. Reprinted by permission of Vicki Ritts.

# 4.8: The Changing Context of Families

Before bringing this chapter to a close, it should be recognized that the ecological settings of families throughout the world have been changing during the past several decades. Even though especially true in the United States, it is happening globally as well. The stereotype of the "all-American family," consisting of two children (a girl and a boy) living in a single-family home in a middle-class neighborhood with the father working and the mother staying at home to provide child care, is no longer the norm—if it ever were.

World War II brought significant changes in the American family. For example, in the years between 1940 and 1946, three million more Americans entered marriages than expected—many because they didn't think they'd see their loved ones again. With large numbers of husbands and fathers away in the service, mothers and other women took over their jobs in factories and other businesses. When the war ended and fathers and other men returned, they were confronted by women, wives, and children who had become independent, enjoyed their new lives, and resented the idea that they should go back to the way things were before. Divorce rates skyrocketed as they often do after such events, and many women then had to continue working to support their families.

Today, less than 10% of mothers in two-parent homes stay with children while their spouses go to work. Families are more likely to consist of single parents, parents who are not married but living together, or gay parents; blended families made up of stepparents and stepchildren; or families in which grandparents are responsible for raising minor-age children. According to 2013 figures from the *Statistical Abstracts of the United States*, 30% of homes with children younger than eighteen were headed by a single parent—23.7% by a mother and 6.3% by a father (ProQuest, 2013). In addition, the number of children being raised by gay or lesbian parents may be as high as 9 million, but it is difficult to estimate because many of these parents keep their sexual orientation secret to avoid harassment. In addition to these changing demographics, efforts to understand the ecology of families and the developmental niche of children within them are complicated by the fact that some children are born into an intact family, spend time in a single-parent family following a divorce, move into one of thirty-two different types of blended family environments when the custodial parent remarries, and may even be cared for by grandparents at some point (United States Census Bureau, 2000). Although the challenges may be great, the need to understand how families throughout the world raise their children and the influence culture has on this process is even greater.

Since 1979, China has had what has been called a "one child policy." What was not well known to everyone was that it applied to only about 30% of the population, allowing minority families, some rural families, and others to have more than one child. In recent years, it was further relaxed, allowing certain families such as those in which parents who were single children with no siblings and those with a disabled child to have another child. On October 29, 2015, the Communist Party announced the abolishment of this thirty-five-year-old policy, indicating that all couples will be allowed to have two children. However, no date was given for the changes to take effect, and it was expected to occur over several years. There appear to be several reasons for this change, including a shrinking working-age population (projected to decline from 853 million in 2015 to 650 million by 2050) and an increasing elderly population (expected to climb from 131 million currently to 243 million by 2030). The policy has led to abortions and forced female sterilizations that skewed the gender ratio to 118 boys born to every 100 girls, meaning China no longer (and for many years has not) had enough child-bearing women to stabilize its population. However, many families believe it is too late to have another child, the costs involved are too high, and some families don't want to have any children. We will have to see what effects this has on the developmental niches of Chinese families and the culture overall.

## Summary: The Family in Cultural Context

This chapter opens with a description of the family life cycle and is followed by a discussion of mate selection and marriage rites in a variety of cultures throughout the world, stressing the influence of one's ecological setting in determining the important influences on each of these events. In an exploration of the birth process, the focus is on the ecology of birth and similarities and differences in cultural practices, most notably in the Yucatan, Holland, Sweden, and the United States. With the transition to parenthood, cultural belief systems begin to play a major role in family decision making, as illustrated in mothering and fathering behavior during the years of infancy and childhood. Next, adolescence is viewed from the standpoint of the ecological model, and the importance of peer relationships is discussed from a cross-cultural perspective. For many, the years of adulthood frequently consist of the raising of adolescent children (and even adult children), as well as caring for elderly parents. Finally, the transition to becoming a grandparent in Japan, China, and the United States receives considerable attention, as does the recognition that family ecology is undergoing dramatic change.

## Study Questions

Discuss cultural variations in mate selection and marriage.

Define and give examples of parental belief systems from different cultures.

Consider adolescence from the ecological model point of view.

Discuss the changing context of families, and comment on cultural approaches to grandparenting and care for the elderly.

# Developmental Analysis
## The Family in Cultural Context

When I was growing up, the most common family structure included two married parents, with the father providing financial security and the mother acting as the family nurturer and caregiver. My own family seemed to fit this model quite well. While my father was frequently working outside on the farm, my mother was at home, raising three children and keeping the house in order. My father believed it was his responsibility to provide a roof over our heads and food on the table, as well as to be a loving caregiver for his children. My mother and father seemed to balance their roles and were both equally involved in teaching us the values they lived by. With clean clothes in the drawers, hearty food to eat, and periodic visits to grandparents, our home life felt very comfortable.

Outside the home, I spent time with a rather large group of friends that included boys and girls. Most of us remained platonic friends throughout high school, with occasional thoughts of romance or finding a future mate. As I entered college, I began to think about the possibilities in the next phases of my life, including college, marriage, and children. My parents met while still in high school and married shortly thereafter. I went against this model by first going to college, continuing on to graduate school, and not marrying until I was almost thirty years old. I am also two years older than my husband, something quite rare in each of our cultures.

I will always remember when I first met Giorgio Carlo Conte, a fellow student from Italy. I was studying economics in England as a Ph.D. candidate; he was completing his studies in international relations. Giorgio sat across from me at the table in the library and struck up a conversation about football (a game that I knew in the United States as "soccer"). He shared his passion for the game and grew very animated as he described the techniques of various players. Over the next several weeks, Giorgio continued to come to the library, settle into the seat across me, and strike up a conversation. We enjoyed casual talk and learning more about one another, until one day he asked me out. I initially refused, explaining the need to focus on my studies and thanked him for his kindness. I figured that was the end of that. Seven requests later (he was persistent!), I eventually accepted his invitation to tea. We soon discovered that we had many of the same goals and ambitions in life. For example, it was very important for me to find a mate that would provide a healthy environment for children and who would respect my devotion to education and a career. I quickly found that these things were also very important to Giorgio. We were married four years later.

The births of each of our children were significant moments in our life together. Both of our children were born in a sanitized, brightly lit hospital room. I was not sedated, nor did I receive any type of anesthesia or pain reliever during delivery. My husband was unable to be present in the hospital room while I delivered our children because it was not permitted at the time. These days, fathers are often in the birthing room serving as coaches to the mother. When our daughter gave birth to her first child, she opted for a midwife and labored at home for several hours. In fact, when she arrived at the hospital she was just fifteen minutes away from giving birth! She tells me that although she would have liked to experience the entire birth at home, she appreciated having access to modern medicine in the hospital.

Because both Giorgio and I had full-time careers, we shared in the parenting of our two children. We came to rely on our parents more as the children grew, and Giorgio's parents eventually came to live with us in the United States. I think the transition was difficult for them, but the benefit of time with their grandchildren was worth it. Giorgio's parents have both passed away, and our children feel blessed to have such wonderful memories of their grandparents.

We are grandparents ourselves now and thoroughly enjoy our roles. It is wonderful to see our own children as parents and quite flattering when they ask us for parenting advice! I frequently feel the need to balance my roles as mother, wife, grandmother, and daughter. I try to spend as much time with my grandchildren as possible while also caring for my aging mother, who is living in an assisted living home. I'm a living example of the "sandwich generation."

# Chapter 5
# Culture, Language, and Cognition

*Deratu lives in one of the oldest nations in Africa—Ethiopia, a Greek word meaning "sunburned faces." Like almost 80% of the people in this nation in northeastern Africa, she lives in a rural village where her family grows sugarcane and raises goats and chickens. Deratu, similar to more than half the children in the country, does not attend school, nor does she have many toys. What she needs to know, she learns in an informal manner from the work she has been assigned according to her age and gender because this is the way new members of each generation learn what is expected of them. At five years of age, she helped her mother fetch water and gather wood for the fire. Now, at eleven, she helps with the cooking and cares for her younger brothers and sisters. In just a few years, at about fifteen, she will start a family of her own. Deratu's learning is very much a social activity guided by her mother, who teaches her the important cultural and practical lessons she will need to survive in her rural Ethiopian village.*

*Maria, two weeks away from her twelfth birthday, lives in Brazil, in São Paulo, the seventh most populated city in the world. Brazil is the largest country in South America, occupying almost half the continent. She has attended the country's free public schools since she was six years old. Maria's parents and teachers have always described her as a naturally curious and inquisitive child. Learning how to read and write came easily to her. As a newly emerging adolescent, she is beginning to look more abstractly at the world and is using more logical problem-solving skills than she would have been able to use just two years ago. Now, Maria spends much time with her elderly grandmother. Although the girl sometimes gets impatient with the grandmother's deliberate speech, she enjoys the stories of the "old days" and admires her grandmother's excellent memory of even small details.*

Deratu and Maria live worlds apart, both physically and psychologically. This chapter looks at culture, cognition, and language and their effects on development. It considers two opposing theoretical viewpoints and some of the cross-cultural evidence that supports or refutes these views. As you progress through this chapter, you will be better able to understand and explain the cognitive and linguistic behavior of these two young women, using key concepts from these theories.

First, let me explain what I mean when using the terms *cognition* and *language*. **Cognition** can be thought of as *the act or process of obtaining knowledge, including perceiving, recognizing, reasoning, and judging* (Gander & Gardiner, 1981). Cognition involves thinking, knowing, remembering, categorizing, and problem solving. **Language** refers to *a system of symbols used to communicate information and knowledge. How does thinking affect language? How does language affect thinking? How do they influence each other?*

Later in this chapter, I discuss the links between cognition and language as they occur throughout life. Two of the major theoretical frameworks discussed in Chapter 2 will guide us in this discussion: Piaget's cognitive developmental theory and Vygotsky's concept of the "zone of proximal development." [For a comparison and critical evaluation of these two theories, especially Vygotsky, see McLeod (2014).]

## 5.1: Ecological Context

*Is cognition dependent on language or vice versa? Do people who speak different languages think about and experience the world differently? How do different cultures teach their children language? How easy is it to become bilingual, trilingual, or quadrilingual? How important is the ecological context in learning language?*

According to *Ethnologue* (Lewis, Simons, & Fennig, 2013), a comprehensive reference book, there are currently about 7,105 known "living" (or used) languages in the world. When infants arrive in the world, they are unable to speak because they do not have language; it must be learned. Although they appear to be biologically designed to learn language, which language or languages they will eventually speak depends on their social and cultural environment or ecological setting. It becomes a truly fascinating journey of discovery for parents and children.

Today, most linguists believe that language influences a number of cognitive processes, while other processes can be viewed as a result of universal factors. In addition, contemporary researchers tend to focus more on looking at the manner and extent to which language influences thought.

Some researchers have begun to focus on how bilingual speakers learn languages. For example, Basseti and

Cook (2011) attempt to separate the effects of culture from the effects of language regarding such cognitive activities as perceptions of emotions, colors, space, time, and motivation. More recently, experimental research has begun to suggest that linguistic influence on thought may not have lasting effects, but rather decreases with time as speakers of one language are immersed in another language (Bross & Pfaller, 2012). Other researchers have even begun to look at the ways in which mobile technology plays a role in the learning of second languages. For example, in a study of Chinese and Swedish students, Viberg and Gronlund (2013) show that technology is the most important "culture shaping factor, more important than age or culture inherited from the physical environment."

Many contemporary researchers believe that thinking is not entirely determined by the language we speak. Rather, *how* we talk about people, objects, or events may make us pay more or less attention to certain aspects of these events, people, or objects. In different languages, we find different linguistic elements that make it easier to communicate about certain events or objects. For example, English has a progressive form that allows English speakers to distinguish between ongoing events and events that have concluded ("I worked all afternoon" vs. "I have been working all afternoon"). Some languages (e.g., German and Hebrew) do not have a progressive form. Speakers of these languages are still able to communicate about the temporal sequence and duration of events, but they have to make a greater effort to do so. Some researchers may argue that distinguishing between the duration of events may not be as important in German- and Hebrew-speaking cultures as it is in English-speaking cultures. In other words, if something is encoded in a culture's language, it must be important.

*What is Vygotsky's position on these issues?* He claimed that cultural influence, mental processes, and language are dynamic processes that occur simultaneously. This means that constant social interaction with those around us helps shape the quality of mental abilities and language at various ages. With this theoretical perspective in mind, Vygotsky (1978) coined the expression, *"talking to learn."* By this, he meant that as children verbally interact with others, they internalize language and use it to organize their thoughts.

Other researchers go even further and suggest that as parents interact with their children, the children learn language and become socialized into a particular set of cultural values and beliefs (Budwig, Wertsch, & Uzgiris, 2000). For example, in her extensive studies of language acquisition in a Samoan village, Ochs (1988) showed the presence of two major ways of speaking the language: "good speech" and "bad speech." The latter contains fewer consonants and is mainly spoken in informal contexts. Good speech is used when speaking to strangers or in formal settings, such as schools, church services, and when talking to a person of high status. Along with learning both "good speech" and "bad speech," Samoan children learn about the social contexts in which using each "language" is appropriate.

Consequently, as children pass through Vygotsky's zone of proximal development in their language learning, they also acquire specific cognitive skills and become enculturated into a way of life. [See Chapter 2 for a definition and brief discussion of the zone of proximal development (i.e., the difference between what children can achieve independently and what they can achieve with help or guidance).] An effective method for achieving this is **scaffolding**, which refers to *the temporary support or guidance provided to a child by parents, older siblings, peers, or other adults in the process of solving a problem.* In construction, scaffolding is placed around a building to provide temporary support. Once completed, the scaffolding is removed, and the building is left to stand on its own. Similarly, the amount of scaffolding a child may need, in the form of guidance and support, depends on his or her ability to solve a problem alone. When the problem has been solved, the parent or others can remove the temporary scaffold (guidance) until help is again needed.

Here, a mother is shown mentoring her young son as he learns shapes of objects and how to place them in the right arrangement. As with reciprocal socialization, parents carefully observe their children's behavior to determine how much help they may need in completing a task or activity. As the activity continues, parents become increasingly sensitive to their children's needs, with the result that children do better on subsequent tasks.

A mother using scaffolding to help her child learn a new skill.

(© Harry Gardiner)

In conclusion, the original question—*"Is cognition dependent on language or vice versa?"*—has lost some of its relevance. In shifting from studying language(s) to studying language and culture, researchers acknowledge that both language and cognition are cultural phenomena. Consequently, language and culture are both part of a person's ecological system, where they contribute jointly to an individual's experience. Look back at Deratu and Maria in the opening vignettes to observe these connections.

# 5.2: Infancy

## 5.2.1: Early Cognitive Development in Cultural Contexts

Piaget's and Vygotsky's interest in children's intellectual development as a focus for understanding how ideas change over time has drawn attention to several important issues related to the study of cultural differences. For thirty years, hundreds of researchers throughout the world have subjected these theories to careful scrutiny. The result is that the cross-cultural literature is immense, and this text cannot begin to give it the full attention it deserves. However, there are a number of excellent reviews for those who want to pursue the topic further. These include the work of Rogoff and Chavajay (1995), Bronfenbrenner (1993), and Segall, Dasen, Berry, and Poortinga (1999).

Of all Piaget's periods, the sensorimotor (occurring during infancy) has been the least studied from a cross-cultural perspective. A major reason is that observation methods and data-collecting techniques based on Piagetian concepts have only relatively recently been standardized. One of the first cross-cultural studies of sensorimotor intelligence, using a scale developed by Corman and Escalona (1969), was conducted in Zambia (Goldberg, 1972). In general, although minor differences in behavior were noted (a slight advance for African infants over American at six months and a slight lag at nine and twelve months), Goldberg's findings tend to support Piaget's observations. Later studies, conducted by Dasen and his colleagues (1978; Dasen, 1984) on the Ivory Coast, suggested that African infants are advanced in their development of object permanency and other object-related cognitive behaviors. In yet another African study, this one conducted in Nigeria, Mundy-Castle and Okonji (1976) reported that although early manipulation of objects is similar for English and Igbo infants, important differences emerge in later interactions. Their observations lend support to our emphasis on the importance of looking at cognitive behavior from an ecological point of view. For example, European and American infants spent considerable time handling objects (often by themselves), whereas their African counterparts were receiving more emotional support and social stimulation from those around them. It

may be that these differences in stimulation were responsible for the emergence of varying patterns in cognitive development (e.g., more socially oriented intelligence in Africans and more technologically oriented intelligence in Westerners). Although the developmental niche was not one of their concerns, we would suggest that the microsystem (family) and macrosystem (cultural values) may well have had an important effect on the development of these differential cognitive behaviors.

In an early review of the cross-cultural literature, Dasen and Heron (1981) recognized that differences in the ages at which the substages of this period are attained do occur. However, they go on to stress that "in emphasizing these cultural differences, we may overlook the amazing commonality reported by all these studies: in fact, the qualitative characteristics of sensorimotor development remain nearly identical in all infants studied so far, despite vast differences in their cultural environments" (p. 305). Werner (1979) concluded that "even in the first stage of cognitive development, that of sensorimotor intelligence, culture seems to influence the rate of development to some extent, although, admittedly, the similarity of structure and process is more striking than the differences. Content seems to have little relevance to the activation of sensorimotor schemata" (p. 216).

## 5.2.2: Language Acquisition

Along with these astounding cognitive developments, infancy is also marked by the first attempts to produce speech and language. Prominent linguist Noam Chomsky believes that language ability is "hardwired" into the human brain. When born, infants have the entire range of human language possibilities available to them. Which language(s) they acquire depends on the languages to which they are exposed on a regular basis. Observations show that the babbling sounds of infants show remarkably similar patterns across many languages. This means that all infants produce basic sounds such as "ma," "da," "fa," "ba," and so on. At this point, parents and others in the child's social environment begin to play a crucial role in language development. When the infant produces a sound that is part of the language spoken in his or her environment, the sound is acknowledged and celebrated as an attempt to communicate (those of you with children or young siblings can remember the excitement surrounding the first utterance of "Dada" or "Mama"). In contrast, any sound that is not part of the language environment is dismissed as babbling. Soon, due to lack of encouragement, the infant stops producing these nonrelevant sounds and focuses on combining relevant sounds into meaningful words. This account of language acquisition demonstrates Vygotsky's concept of scaffolding, as well as the developmental niche. The caregivers, with their specific language characteristics, gently guide the child in developing the tools for communication within a specific cultural environment. Once the child has learned language to communicate, the basis for facilitating further cognitive and language development through social interaction is set.

Cross-cultural studies of language development show that the acquisition of certain linguistic elements, such as nouns, verbs, and grammatical structure, may vary. A variety of studies examining the child's understanding and use of these language markers in Mandarin, Italian, and English showed the following general results: an overall bias in infancy to use nouns; no differences among children in these cultures in the time they begin to use nouns; and as the use of verbs varies across languages, so does the complexity of grammar and vocabulary.

These studies clearly demonstrate Vygotsky's claim that culture plays an active role in directing cognitive activity, even in infancy. Uzgiris and Raeff (1995), in a study of parent–child play interactions, stated that the variety of activities involved in play (e.g., talking, touching, and interacting) help children learn skills that will enable them to be active participants in later cultural interactions. You can probably see how these ideas fit into and support our major themes. For example, it is within the family context (mesosystem) that early parent–child interactions take place, and it is here that infants are introduced to the activities (e.g., play and the use of language) that help prepare them for successful participation in the broader cultural contexts of the workplace (exosystem) and for understanding important values and attitudes (macrosystem).

As Tamis-LeMonda, Baumwell, and Cabrera (2014) have recently pointed out, from a cultural perspective, "Parent–child interactions are influenced by the beliefs and values of cultural communities, and by culturally prescribed linguistic conventions that are part of a child's socialization" (p. 146). This supports the previous attention we have given to children's socialization and the ecological environment in which they have been raised, especially as it concerns language development.

Along similar lines, Bornstein and his colleagues (1992; Bornstein, 2000) looked at the various ways in which young infants in Argentina, France, Japan, and the United States were engaged in conversation by their mothers. In each culture, mothers were more conversant with older children (thirteen-month-olds) than they were with younger children (five-month-olds), and exhibited multiple cultural differences in interactions and speech patterns when talking with them. For example, expressive speech was employed more often by Japanese mothers than it was by Argentinean, French, or American mothers. Japanese mothers were also more responsive to their children when they were engaged in play with them, whereas American mothers responded more quickly and favorably to their children when they were playing with physical objects.

This behavior on the part of Japanese mothers is compatible with their culture's stress on interdependence as an important value. (You may recall the discussion in Chapter 3 of interdependence and Japanese child-rearing practices, the second component of the developmental niche, as they relate to socialization.)

Argentinean, French, and American mothers, in contrast, gave greater attention to speech that communicated information to their infant or child. This is consistent with other findings in cultures characterized by individualistic behavior, such as the three Western societies represented in this study. Still, not all of these mothers communicated the same kind of information to their children. For example, American mothers asked lots of questions, reflecting, in part, the view within American society that children are active participants in the learning process and often (as we saw in the previous theoretical discussion) construct their own knowledge. In contrast, French mothers provided their infants and children with less stimulation but greater emotional support. Finally, Argentinean mothers appeared to be the most direct in their interactions with their children, which is indicative of a more authoritarian approach to dealing with children (Bornstein et al., 1992). It should be noted that little research attention has focused on the important role played by fathers in language development, and this remains a fertile area for future research.

## 5.2.3: Early Second-Language Acquisition and Bilingualism

Contact between individuals who do not share the same language has become commonplace in today's world. For example, immigrants may share neighborhoods with natives, international business people may spend months abroad, and refugees may seek an escape from war in their own countries (e.g., Syrians fleeing their country in 2015 and 2016). The need to communicate in a new ecological system often makes it necessary to acquire a second language—to become bilingual. I raise this discussion on bilingualism in this chapter because it illustrates the dynamics of the language–cognition–culture link within a developmental framework. Questions such as *Do children learn a second language faster or better than adults?* or *Does the age at which a person learns the language affect how the language is learned?* have been at the center of bilingualism research for many years.

**DEVELOPMENTAL FACTORS**   A popular view claims that before a certain age, children learn a language naturally and easily. This supports the idea of a "critical period" for second-language acquisition. Werker and Hensch (2015) review the critical period literature and present a model and examples based on advances in neurobiology that show there is no longer a question of whether there *is* a critical period in language acquisition, rather there is a question of what processes are responsible for opening these periods, keeping them open, closing them, and allowing them to be reopened.

The "critical period" appears to last a specific number of years during which a second language can be learned as easily and as well as the first language. However, after this critical period, a language learner will have greater difficulty being able to acquire a second language to the same extent he or she did with the native language.

The age at which this critical period is supposed to occur is one of several points debated by those interested in language. Some set the first ten years of life as the critical years for language acquisition. Others suggest that no distinctions in language learning can be found until after puberty. However, more recent studies contradict the "critical period" assumption entirely. In particular, Birdsong and Molis (2001) found that postpubescent learners were not always less proficient than younger learners; in fact, some late learners spoke the language as well as native speakers. This should not be the case if a true "critical period" for language acquisition exists. Hakuta, Bialystok, and Wiley (2003) report similar results in their analysis of data from more than 2 million Spanish and Chinese immigrants. They observed a decline in second-language proficiency among older immigrants, but the decline was not as steep as might be expected outside a "critical period."

A mother reading to her two children.

(© Harry Gardiner)

Although research does not completely support the claim that second-language acquisition is limited by a "critical period" of development, we can reliably assume that "younger is better" when it comes to learning a second language. After a thorough review of existing research, Ellis (1994) concludes that (1) children learn a second language faster than adults in the long run, and (2) early second-language learners are more likely to have a nativelike pronunciation and proficiency than late learners. In addition, findings about brain development in infancy favor second-language acquisition at a very young age. Kuhl and her colleagues (2008) argue that the brain is "primed" for the sounds of a particular language by about the eleventh month of life. If infants are exposed to only one language, then their brain will not process sounds associated with another language. In contrast, a child that grows up in a bilingual environment will learn two languages in the same manner as if it were one language. The brain has not learned to distinguish the two and is flexible enough to process both. For a good introduction to and discussion of second-language learning theories and research, see Mitchell, Myles, and Marsden (2013). *Does this mean that taking language classes in high school or at the university are useless because students cannot expect to become proficient in a second language? What has been your experience? Have you studied in a foreign country?* I now turn to the ecological model for additional insights on bilingualism.

**ECOLOGICAL FACTORS**   An easily identifiable ecological factor that influences second-language acquisition is the learning context itself. Sociolinguists distinguish two types of situations in which a second language can be learned, including (1) natural settings and (2) educational settings.

Examples of *natural settings* might include learning a second language as a native language while living in a country—a setting familiar to most immigrants. A natural setting is also present when learning a second language that serves as the "official language" of a country. For example, India maintains English as one of two "official" languages (Hindi being the other), which makes it necessary for many Indians to learn English as their second language. "Official" languages other than the native languages can also be found in Zaire (French) and Nigeria (English). Yet, even in "natural bilingual settings," the ecological system may shape the mastery and fluency a child can achieve in both languages. Recall the story from the introduction of this book in which Harry Gardiner's three-year-old daughter, Alisa, becomes aware of speaking two languages. She explains: "I thought it was all one big language and Mommy understood some words and you understood others and I understood them all!" Clearly, the parents provided Alisa with an environment that fostered bilingualism. Kasuya (2002) agrees when stating, ". . . there are some socialization circumstances which almost always produce bilingual children, and other socialization circumstances that produce monolingual children. . . ." (p. 295). For example, such circumstances include how many family members communicate regularly in one or both languages and how accepted both languages are in the larger community. *Is more than one language spoken in your home? If so, can you use both of them? Is your ability about equal in each? Can you read and write both languages?*

*Educational settings* are those in which formal second-language instruction takes place. The traditional "foreign language classroom," a common high school or college experience for many readers, comes to mind. In addition, other educational settings might include bilingual education programs, such as for immigrant students in the United States, or the education of ethnic minority children in mainstream classrooms, as is common in Britain, Germany, and the United States. *Have you studied another language in school? How well do you speak or read this language? Do you think you could learn a second or third language?*

A widespread assumption is that a second language is learned differently in various settings but that the patterns are somewhat unclear. We do know that it is not always the natural setting that leads to the mastery of a second language. In fact, it is more likely that educational settings provide better opportunities to learn a second language, but only if they involve immersion in both the native and the second language (e.g., bilingual programs). Speaking in "ecological terms," being immersed in a second language means language is used within multiple levels of the ecological model (e.g., school, workplace, sports club, grocery store, and the media).

Related to these settings are important social and psychological factors. For example, there is general agreement among researchers that attitudes toward the target language and culture, as well as motivation to learn the language, have an enormous influence on second-language learning. In an illustrative study, Scully (2002) collected data from Filipinas (who married into Japanese households) about their attitudes toward Japanese culture and their success in learning Japanese. The author found that immersion in the culture and family life and positive attitudes toward Japanese culture predicted the mastery of Japanese. See Table 5.1 for a depiction of the relationship of attitudes, motivation, and potential language learning outcome.

**Table 5.1** Attitudes toward Native and Target Culture and Potential Outcomes of Second-Language Learning

| Attitudes Toward | | |
| --- | --- | --- |
| Native Culture | Culture Target | Potential Learning Outcome |
| + | + | Strong motivation and high proficiency in both languages |
| − | + | Strong motivation to learn target language, losing competence in the native language |
| + | − | Failure to acquire the second language, maintaining native language only |
| − | − | Failure to learn second language, losing native language competence |

+ Positive attitudes.
− Negative attitudes.

**SOURCE:** Based on material from The Study of Second-Language Acquisition by R. Ellis, 1994. Oxford, U.K.: Oxford University Press, © Harry Gardiner.

# 5.3: Childhood

As we move from the infancy and early childhood periods to the school-age period, the majority of cross-cultural Piagetian studies have focused on the transition from the preoperational period to the concrete operational period and the attainment of conservation (Gardiner, 1994). These studies show great variability in their findings (Rogoff, 1990). Fishbein (1984) points out that the research literature on these topics, published during the 1960s and early 1970s, reports consistently more advanced development in children from Westernized cultures when compared with children from developing cultures. However, Kamara and Easley (1977) have drawn attention to what they believe are three serious faults with the majority of this work. They express the following criticisms: (1) the study of thinking in both of these periods depends heavily on the use of language, yet most of the researchers who conducted these early studies had little knowledge of either the culture or the language of their subjects; (2) although Piaget favored the use of clinical interviews for gathering information about children's thinking processes, many of these investigators attempted to employ various types of standardized measures that required little use of language; and (3) accurate birth dates of subjects were not always available, and attempts to approximate ages were frequently off by as much as two years. These are serious criticisms still deserving of further attention on the part of cross-cultural researchers. Better designed studies, taking into account these criticisms, are likely to provide more reliable results and more insight into learning and behavior during these transitional periods.

## 5.3.1: Stages of Knowing and Learning

In an extremely interesting and creative cross-cultural study, Nyiti (1982) attempted to avoid the pitfalls mentioned by Kamara by varying the languages used and employing three of Piaget's well-known conservation tasks for substance, weight, and volume. Subjects consisted of ten- to eleven-year-old Micmac Indian children from Cape Breton Island in Canada and white English-speaking European Canadians. The European Canadian children were interviewed in English by an English-speaking European, whereas the Indian children were divided into two groups. In the first group, children were initially interviewed in English by an English-speaking European and later in Micmac by a Micmac-speaking Indian. In the second group, the order of interviewing was reversed. When the white European Canadians and Micmac Indian children were tested in their native languages, their performances on conservation tasks were nearly identical and were comparable to those of other European, Canadian, and American children. However, when tested in English, Micmac Indian children performed at a significantly lower level than the other two groups. More important, the results indicated that nearly twice as many children at both age levels, when interviewed in their native language, were more capable of solving each of the three conservation tasks than were the Micmac Indian children interviewed in English. Nyiti concludes his study by stating that "it appears that cognitive structures described by Piaget are universal and represent a necessary condition for any successful acculturation [and] . . . while children in different cultures may have to deal with different realities, they all apply the same operations or processes of thought" (p. 165).

In an important and exhaustive early review of cross-cultural findings on conservation task performance, Dasen (1972) sorted results into four types, each supported by several studies. These included (1) cultural groups in which conservation appears at about the same time as it does in American and European children (i.e., Nigerians, Zambians, Hong Kong Chinese, Iranians, and Australian Aborigines); (2) groups in which conservation generally develops earlier (i.e., Asians); (3) cultures in which conservation appears as much as two to six years later (i.e., African and lower-socioeconomic-status Americans and Europeans); and (4) groups in which some individuals fail to engage in concrete operations even when they reach adolescence (i.e., Algerians, Nepalese, Amazon Indians, and Senegalese). What can we conclude from this vast amount of cross-cultural data? First, support for the universality of the structures or operations underlying the preoperational period is highly convincing. Second, whether these structures become functional and the rate at which this might take place appear strongly influenced by factors within one's culture—further validation of the importance of looking at cognitive development from the ecological systems approach.

Finally, it appears that although the rate and level of performance at which children move through Piaget's concrete operational period depend on cultural experience, children in diverse societies still proceed in the same sequence he predicted (Mwamwenda, 1992; Segall et al., 1999). An early study by Price-Williams, Gordon, and Ramirez (1969) also supports this view. For example, in one of their studies, conservation tasks were administered to two groups of Zinacantean children—half from pottery-making families and half from non–pottery-making families. Those children who had helped their families by working with clay showed signs of conservation at earlier ages than those without such experience.

This young Zinacantean girl takes great pleasure in making traditional pottery.

(J Marshall - Tribaleye Images / Alamy Stock Photo)

## 5.3.2: Language Skills and Language Socialization

Jean Piaget's theory of cognitive development also provides clues as to how cognition and language might be related; that is, the ability to understand and use symbols requires certain cognitive skills. According to Piaget, a child first demonstrates the cognitive skills necessary for language use in the preoperational stage of cognitive development. The child needs to understand that different sounds and gestures do not simply stand alone but can serve as symbols for actual objects. Once grasping the concept of "symbols," he or she has acquired the necessary cognitive tools to use language as a form of communication about actual objects.

Suzuki (1998) gives another specific example of a particular cognitive skill and language competence. According to Piaget, one of the characteristics of preoperational thought is the inability to take another person's perspective. Instead, the child's thinking is guided only by how the world relates to him or her; for example, a child might answer the question "Why should you not hit your brother?" by saying "So that I won't get in trouble" instead of "Because he might get hurt." Suzuki argues that the ability to use passive construction in Japanese is closely related to a child's ability to go beyond preoperational egocentric thought. The results show that children in this study, ranging in age from 3.4 years to 6.9 years, interpreted passive sentence construction very differently, depending on their age and on their ability to adopt nonegocentric worldviews.

Childhood is the age in which socialization through language is most prominent. A good example of language socialization is a linguistic study by Brooks, Jia, Braine, and Da Graca Dias (1998). These researchers examined the ages at which Portuguese-, English-, and

Mandarin-speaking children learn to distinguish between quantifiers such as "all" and "each" in their respective languages. The study shows that Portuguese and Mandarin-Chinese speakers had learned to distinguish between "all" and "each" conceptually and linguistically by the time they were five years old. English speakers, in contrast, were much less discriminating in their use of these quantifiers.

Once again, it is important to keep in mind the larger ecological systems in which languages are embedded. For example, China and Portugal can be considered as cultures with more collectivist belief systems (macrosystem) than the United States. The words "all" and "each" refer to objects or activities that are either collectively shared or not shared. Children in these cultures may learn words and concepts representing a relationship between "individual" and "collective" earlier than children in more individualistic societies. Eventually, through learning language and using language in social interaction, Portuguese and Chinese children also learn about social relationships that are considered important in their collectivist societies. Although certainly a simplified explanation, it may clarify the idea of language as a contributing influence to both cognitive development and socialization.

Another cognitive and linguistic challenge faced by many children between the ages of three and ten is learning how to read and write. If we consider the vast array of languages and how they are expressed in oral and written form, we can guess that the difficulties confronting children in their quest to become literate also vary greatly. For example, many European languages are phonetically based, meaning that a symbol primarily represents a sound rather than a meaningful word. Words are combinations of symbols and, therefore, sounds. Individually, the symbols and sounds d-e-s-e-r-t are not meaningful. However, when combined, they obtain meaning. This specific attribute of language allows the novice reader who knows the symbol and each sound associated with it, to find the meaning of the word by "sounding" out each symbol. This is difficult to do in languages such as Chinese, which uses a combination of phonetic symbols and logographic symbols. Logographs are symbols that primarily represent a meaning; their sound is secondary. Novice readers have to know the meaning of the symbol to understand it. Good examples of logographs in European language use are Roman numerals. The symbol "X" has a specific meaning, namely, the number "ten." Sounding out "X," no matter in what language, will not help find the meaning.

Considering all this, it should not be surprising to learn that many studies of early literacy show that learning how to read and write are affected by the characteristics of a child's language. For example, a comparison between American and Chinese first graders revealed a different pattern of literacy (Stevenson & Stigler, 1992).

English students had learned to break down words into sounds. This enabled them to figure out words they had not yet been taught. Students who did not have this skill were often unable to read even the words they had already been taught. In contrast, Chinese first graders were able to read almost all the words they had been taught, but very few of the words not yet taught.

The study of dyslexia provides more insight into the relationship between cognition and language. Do the characteristics of a language also influence the underlying cognitive abilities necessary for mastering reading and writing? Dyslexia, broadly defined as *deficits in reading and writing*, leads to difficulties in word recognition, spelling, and reading fluency. Dyslexia seems to be more common in English-speaking children than in speakers of other languages (Caravolas, 2005). English-language learners have to master a language that is not very consistent in how letters are associated with sounds, making it more difficult to learn phonetically. For example, the sound /i/ in the words "beef," "chief," and "leaf" is represented by three different letter combinations. Languages such as Finnish or Turkish are much more consistent in how letters are pronounced. Learning these languages requires the awareness of sounds and the ability to distinguish them. It is the lack of phonetic awareness that may lead to symptoms described as "dyslexia." In contrast, learning Chinese requires memorization of picturelike characters that represent whole words. Lack of phonetic awareness will likely not impact reading and writing as much because Chinese-language learners rely more on their visual processing skills. However, in a recent study, Chinese-speaking children with dyslexia were shown to have a disorder that is distinctly different, and likely more severe and complicated, than that of English-speaking children. These differences can be found in both the brain and in the performance of Chinese children on visual and oral language tasks (Siok, Spinks, Jin, & Tan, 2009).

A young girl practices calligraphy.

(Sunabesyou/Fotolia)

Speakers of phonetic languages can hardly imagine what is involved in learning to read and write Japanese, a language with basically three language systems: Kanji, Katakana, and Hiragana. Kanji consists of more than 2,000 logographic characters, often with multiple sounds. Katakana and Hiragana are different forms of a phonetic system in which each character represents a syllable. Katakana is a "simplified" form, whereas Hiragana is the elegant cursive form of this symbol system. Almost all preschoolers pick up the basics of Hiragana at home or in kindergarten, and Katakana is taught in the first three grades. Instruction in Kanji is slowly introduced in the first three grades and continues through sixth grade. This example of Japanese learning to read and write shows very nicely the interaction of different levels of the ecological system in this aspect of language acquisition. Specifically, family and peers in the microsystem aid the learning of Hiragana, as do extended family and families of peers in the exosystem. In combination, these systems assert a combined influence in the mesosystem. When learning Katakana, school and peers are the driving influence in the microsystem, while government-designed curricula (in the exosystem) and the cultural value placed on literacy (in the macrosystem) exert additional influences as one moves to the outer levels of the ecological system. [As an aside, the author's oldest son, Alan, studied at a Japanese university and, as a result of studying and working in the country for more than a decade, became fluent in reading, writing, and speaking the Japanese language. He now uses the language almost daily in his work at an American company.] An ecological system vastly different from the Japanese is described by Pretorius and Naude (2002). In their study of children (5.5–7 years old) in South African townships, they showed that the children's literacy and numerical skills were very poorly developed. The authors speculate that this may be because of the relative lack of emphasis on literacy both in the larger culture (child-rearing practices that do not facilitate parental involvement in literacy development) and in the family (little exposure to reading and writing in the home).

## Points to Ponder

### Learning Language

Infants come into the world with no language at all. In the beginning, they communicate only by crying. In this way, they let those in their family (microsystem) know how they are feeling, if they want attention, if they are hungry, or if their diaper is wet. After months of cooing, babbling begins at about three months, followed soon after by the first words ("mama," "dada"); by twelve months, telegraphic speech or two-word sentences appear ("Daddy read," "mommy eat"), and then full sentences, although not yet grammatically correct ("I felled down and hurted myself"). By the age of six years, the average child knows and can use about 8,000 words! This is one, if not the, most important accomplishments an individual will make—ever. You are unlikely to learn this many new words the rest of your life. Spend some time listening to infants, young children, adolescents, adults, and older adults, and notice differences and similarities in their speech. Listen for regional or foreign accents. Can you identify where they may be from? How does speech vary at different ages? Have you ever visited another culture where you know nothing about the language? Did you feel lost and/or frustrated not being able to make yourself understood or understand others? What did you do? Did you try to use a form of primitive sign language to get your ideas across? Did you do what many travelers do—speak louder (the other person is not deaf; they just don't know what you are saying)—or did you try to make it sound similar to the local language (e.g., "I vant to go to zee hotela")? Neither of these will help! Was another language spoken in your home when you were young? Did you learn some of it? Have you studied another language in school? How successful were you? Do still have opportunities to use it? Are you, your parents, or any friends bilingual? At what age was the second language learned?

# 5.4: Adolescence

## 5.4.1: Formal Operational Thinking

Piaget's stage of formal operations has also been studied cross-culturally, and it is the view of some researchers that individuals in many societies never achieve this type of thinking. For example, a study conducted among Nigerian adolescents by Hollos and Richards (1993), using Piagetian tasks, revealed little use of formal operational thinking.

One of several tasks frequently used to measure cognitive development in the stage of formal operations is the pendulum problem. In the pendulum problem, individuals are shown several pendulums of different weights attached to different lengths of string. When the pendulums are swung, individuals are asked to figure out what determines the speed at which the pendulums swing back and forth. For example, is it the weight, the height from which it is dropped, the force with which it is pushed, the string's length, or perhaps a combination of all of these? According to Inhelder and Piaget (1959), children in the stage of formal operations should be able to solve the pendulum problem through the process of elimination. Several cross-cultural studies have used this problem to observe cognitive changes in formal operations. For example, in studies carried out among adolescents in New Guinea, none of the subjects performed at the formal operational level (Kelly, 1977). Similarly, few adolescents showed formal operational thought when tested in Rwanda (Laurendeau-Bendavid, 1977). However, among Chinese children exposed to the British education system in Hong Kong, formal operational performance was found to be equal to or better than the performance of American or European children (Goodnow & Bethon, 1966). Based on these and similar findings, Piaget (1972) proposed that development of formal operational thinking is influenced by both experience and culture (Rogoff & Chavajay, 1995). As we have seen, events taking place within one's ecological niche frequently determine how one will perceive and behave in a particular ecological setting.

These examples provide added impetus for considering the ecological setting in understanding why behavior, including cognitive activity, is expressed as it is. For example, Cole and Cole (1996) point out that "a lawyer might think in a formal manner about law cases but not when sorting the laundry . . . a baseball manager might employ formal operational thinking to choose his batting lineup but [not when doing] . . . the combination-of-chemicals task" (p. 674). As evidence, they cite a study by Retschitzki (1989) showing that when African men and older boys play a popular board game, Baoule, involving the capture of seeds from opponents, they make use of complex rules, complicated offensive and defensive moves, and skilled calculations. Interviews with skilled Baoule players from Cote d'Ivoire revealed that their strategies in playing this game used the types of logical thinking we usually attribute to formal operations.

The inability to show evidence for the universality of formal operational thinking among adolescents and adults is not confined to non-Western areas. In fact, earlier studies demonstrated that not all adolescents or adults living in Western technological cultures achieve this type of thinking, and that they frequently show low levels of success on formal operational tasks. Even earlier studies conducted by Kohlberg and Gilligan (1971) with subjects in late adolescence reported that only between 30% and 50% of such individuals perform successfully on formal operational tasks. Werner (1979) sums this up by stating, "Formal-operational thinking might not appear at all or might appear in less-generalized form among cultures and individuals whose experience is limited to one or a few specialized or technical occupations. In other words, survival in a particular culture may not call for, nor be influenced by, formal logical thinking. Thus formal thought processes are probably cultural alternatives that can be learned. Humans have the capacity for it, but may not have realized it in order to 'get by' in their particular society" (p. 224). For a review of fifty years of formal operational research, see Bond (1998).

Finally, in a discussion of the socialization of cognition, Goodnow (1990) concludes that Piagetian theory can be applied to the conservation of weight, amount, and volume. However, she goes on to say that "if one's goal is to go beyond these domains—to construct an account of cognitive development that cuts across many domains or that takes place in everyday life—then classical Piagetian theory will certainly need some additions" (pp. 277–278). This, of course, is a position with which we certainly agree and that we encourage other researchers to take into account when conducting future cross-cultural studies of cognition.

As discussed in Chapter 2, formal and informal learning constitutes a large part of child and adolescent socialization. Formal learning environments are also designed to foster cognitive development. However, as we saw in some examples, young people who do not attend schools acquire mathematic and analytical skills through other means. So, how important is formal schooling for cognitive development? A study compared schooled and unschooled children and adolescents in the African nation of Malawi on in their performance on basic cognitive tasks and Raven's Coloured Progressive Matrices (van de Vijver & Brouwers, 2009). The results showed that children who had never attended school had no significant deficits in intelligence and basic information processing skills. Should these results serve as an excuse for adolescence to drop out of school because it does not make a difference anyway? I would discourage such an argument. Even though formal schooling may not enhance intelligence and basic information processing, it still develops verbal abilities and other metacognitive skills such as critical thinking and skill transfer to other domains. *Did any of your peers drop out of school? Do you know what they are doing now? Did some return to get their diplomas?*

# 5.5: Adulthood

## 5.5.1: Reasoning and Decision Making

Most of the research in cross-cultural human development has emphasized cognitive growth in childhood and adolescence. By comparison, few cross-cultural studies have examined cognitive development in adulthood. Piaget believed that formal operational thinking represented the highest level of cognitive development and proposed no additional stages in adulthood. That is, he believed that an adolescent and an adult would think in the same way. However, some developmental psychologists have challenged this belief, arguing for a postformal stage of cognitive development in adulthood. For example, Labouvie-Vief (1986) has suggested that in early adulthood, a change in thinking occurs in which individuals begin to recognize cognitive limitations and may adapt their thinking to the demands of their environment. This process is called **adaptive logic** and involves *balancing critical analyses of objective observations with one's subjective reactions to these observations.* For example, when performing a memory task, older subjects may make a conscious decision to exclude much of the detailed information they remember, believing it may be uninteresting to the researcher or to other listeners. If this is the case, Salthouse (1987) suggests that when measuring cognitive abilities of middle-age adults, we need to employ strategies different than those used with young adults (e.g., experience and expertise). This represents one more challenge for researchers interested in the study of cognitive development.

Another cognitive process that emerges in adulthood is what is called dialectical thinking. **Dialectical thinking** *suggests that for every viewpoint there is an opposing viewpoint and these two can be considered simultaneously.* The ability to synthesize and view opposing ideas holistically to resolve contradiction represents a new level of cognitive flexibility and a deepening of thought, which, in turn, facilitates developmental growth. Researchers have come to consider dialectical and analytical processes (acquired during the formal operational stage) as two coexisting systems that guide human reasoning and decision making (Frankish & Evans, 2009). Within individuals, one system might dominate their reasoning in general, but in a particular situation the dual processing of information may lead to conflicting conclusions (you may have heard people say, "I do not know whether to follow my mind or my heart"). *Can you think of situations in which you have faced similar dilemmas? How did you resolve them? Would you say it was difficult or easy?*

Although it is safe to assume that such basic cognitive processes are universal and develop in all healthy adults, there is also evidence that culture shapes the way these processes are used. In other words, depending on cultural influences, one person might reason analytically and another dialectically when solving a similar problem. For example, East Asians seem to process information more holistically than Europeans. That is, they attend to the object or event itself, along with the surrounding cues or situation. Westerners, in contrast, analyze the object or event, and pay little attention to the context. As a consequence, we also see cultural differences in how people explain, judge, and predict behavior. For example, East Asians tend to attribute the cause of another person's behavior more readily to the situation, whereas Europeans and North Americans think the person's disposition or personality causes behavior. In the first instance, a person might fail a final exam because he or she sat in the back of the classroom and could not understand the teacher's instructions. The person-centered explanation would more likely attribute the person's failure to his or her lack of intelligence.

Some theorists argue that the emphasis on holistic thinking in Eastern cultures has led to a more sophisticated way of dialectical thinking that is more adaptive to a changing environment than the dialectic process that is present in Western thinking (Buchtel & Norenzayan, 2009). Whether there is really a "higher form of dialectical thinking" that develops in response to cultural influences is debatable (Ho, 2000), but considering the discussion in this chapter of ecological influences on cognition, this question is worth further exploration.

# 5.6:  Late Adulthood

As one gets older, one supposedly gets wiser. At middle age and late adulthood, one has greater experience; becomes more sensitive to inconsistencies; and responds differently to social, political, and economic changes. These are generally the years of greatest productivity and self-satisfaction in career, avocation, or family.

Studying and understanding cognition during the late adult years presents unique challenges, in part due to a confounding or intermingling of age and experience. Because the majority of research efforts have been conducted in Western cultures, which are youth oriented, the focus has tended to be on cognitive development among children and adolescents, not on the later years of adulthood. As a result, we still know relatively little about changes in cognitive abilities among adults and even less from a cross-cultural perspective.

## 5.6.1: Intelligence and Cognitive Aging

In their early efforts to investigate changes in cognitive development during middle and late adulthood, Horn and Cattell (1967) proposed a distinction between fluid and crystallized intelligence. **Fluid intelligence** involves *the ability to form concepts, reason abstractly, and apply material to new situations.* It is thought to be biological or intuitive and to be uninfluenced by culture. It is reflected in an individual's ability to make inferences, draw analogies, solve problems, and understand relationships among concepts. **Crystallized intelligence** refers to *an individual's accumulated knowledge and experience in a particular culture* (e.g., ability to react to social situations or respond to classroom tests).

Previous research in developmental psychology indicates that these two types of intelligence unfold in different directions. While fluid intelligence stays the same or declines somewhat throughout adulthood, crystallized intelligence may actually improve.

As researchers have begun to view cognitive aging in cultural contexts, they have challenged the traditional view that the changes in supposedly "hard-wired" cognitive processes are truly a consequence of biological aging and, therefore, unaffected by culture (Park & Hedden, 1999). If it is indeed true that Asians process information more contextually than Westerners, as described in the previous section, Asians should be more responsive to contextual cues when performing memory tasks. This would enhance memory when surrounding cues assist with memory, but detract from performance when contextual cues are distracting or irrelevant. So, depending on the type of memory task that presents itself, Asian elderly may perform better or worse than their Western counterparts. This is an intriguing area worthy of further exploration.

Larger cultural influences are not the only mediating ecological factors in cognitive changes later in life. Social relationships, particularly spousal or partner relationships, play an important role as well. Gerstorf, Hoppmann, Anstey, and Luszcz (2009) followed married couples over a span of eleven years and found interesting correlations between the cognitive functioning of partners. Specifically, husbands' decline in processing speed and memory consistently predicted wives' decline in those functions a year later. The reverse, however, was not the case. Why are wives more susceptible than husbands in being influenced by their partners' decline? The authors offer two possible explanations: (1) cognitively well-functioning husbands may have access to resources (financial or otherwise) that allow the couple to remain active and engaged in older age; and (2) if the husband shows cognitive decline, the opportunities for his wife to engage in activities may be limited as she takes care of him.

The common-sense belief of "use it or lose it" also plays a role in the decline of cognitive performance in older age. First, people who develop a habit of actively seeking cognitively stimulating activities reinforce their existing cognitive skills and even develop new ones. Second, how intensely a person engages in a cognitive task determines how well he or she will perform. This is one reason why older people are encouraged to do crosswords or Sudoku to maintain or improve their memories. In addition, older readers who pause during reading to reflect on what they read will recall more of the contents. [This can serve as a successful strategy for younger people, and I encourage readers to do so while reading this book.] In short, making a habit of engaging frequently and consciously in daily cognitive tasks will contribute to intellectual vitality in later adulthood. As is the case in other areas of development, macro- and microlevel ecological conditions interact with biological factors of cognitive aging.

An overall decline in fluid intelligence may be counteracted by applying accumulated experience (or crystallized intelligence). For example, Yang Tsu, an eighty-four-year-old master of martial arts in China, exhibits great discipline and patience (which took many years to cultivate) when teaching his young, impulsive apprentice, Low Chi Tho, who wants to learn everything very quickly. After some time, Low Chi has come to admire Yang Tsu

and to realize the need to develop a more reflective approach to learning. In short, what might be negatively viewed by some cultures as a slowdown or decline in cognitive response is positively viewed in this case as a necessary quality for achieving success. Our familiarity with cross-cultural research suggests that there are many instances in which a behavior in one culture is viewed quite differently in another. This richness of differences (as well as similarities) provides many opportunities for those interested in pursuing the study of behavior from a cross-cultural, ecological, or sociocultural perspective.

A martial arts instructor teaches his young apprentice.

(Novastock/Stock Connection Blue/Alamy Stock Photo)

The issue of accumulated experience over time has been associated with wisdom. However, does age alone make an individual wiser? Not necessarily. Smith and Baltes (1990) investigated sixty German professionals and divided them into three age groups of twenty-five to thirty-five, forty to fifty, and sixty to eighty-one. Each group was presented with four made-up examples of demanding situations and asked to prepare solutions. Their approaches and solutions were rated by a panel of human services professionals. Of the 240 respondents, eleven scored in the "wise" category but were not necessarily older. In fact, they were found in almost equal numbers in each of the three groups. Wisdom, then, would not appear to be characteristic of any particular age group. In short, individuals do not become wiser simply because they get older. Wisdom takes many forms and varies according to each culture's orientation. In this study. The criterion for determining what constituted wisdom was set by the researchers, who represent a specific cultural orientation that may or may not apply to all cultures. Replication of this study in other cultures might produce some interesting findings.

More recent research on this topic has led Baltes and his colleagues (Baltes & Staudinger, 2000; Kunzmann & Baltes, 2003) to propose several general characteristics associated with wisdom, including the ability to focus on important issues and exercise good judgment, development of a broad base of experiences, and recognition of one's wisdom by others. In addition, Ardelt (2004) suggests that "wisdom-related knowledge has to be *realized* by an individual through a reflection on personal experiences to be called wisdom, and that the wisdom-related knowledge that is written down in texts remains theoretical or intellectual knowledge until a person retransforms it into wisdom. From this perspective, wisdom is a characteristic of people and not of texts" (p. 305).

In the final analysis, it is important to realize that although some aspects of cognitive functioning decline with age, how this change is viewed and evaluated depends largely on one's culture, ecological surroundings, and developmental niche. *Do you have older relatives or friends? Have you noticed any specific declines in their cognitive functioning? What difficulties are they experiencing?*

## 5.6.2: Language and Communication in Later Life

Similar conclusions can be drawn with regard to language use and comprehension in later life. Undoubtedly, some actual changes occur in language with advancing age, particularly when there is a decline of cognitive functions such as memory. For example, older speakers are a little slower and use different strategies in comprehending sentences, and they use less complex sentence structure. However, grammar, vocabulary, and speech production are relatively consistent across the lifespan. Despite these findings, there is the pervasive stereotype that older people are impaired in their communication. In a society in which aging is associated with negative expectations, older adults are confronted

with physical changes of aging (e.g., hearing loss, voice quality, and slowness of movement) that are often interpreted by others as loss of competence. As a consequence, caregivers and others communicate with the older person in "elderspeak": simple words, short sentences, repetition, speaking slowly and in a higher pitch tone of voice (De Bot & Makoni, 2005). Some aspects of elderspeak (e.g., less complex sentence structure) make communication easier for older people. Other aspects (e.g., high pitch voice and slow speech) are often perceived as patronizing and may lead to diminished self-esteem, social withdrawal, and, ultimately, to a decline in communicative competence. Here, negative cultural expectations actually lead to a self-fulfilling prophecy. Consider, once again, the ecological systems approach. Although scientific evidence is lacking, it is conceivable that older adults in cultures that hold their elders in higher esteem will not experience the situation just described. Overall, researchers agree that good quality of interactions is important for the maintenance of language and cognitive skills (e.g., verbal fluency and word recall).

Just as cultural expectations differ in important ways, so do languages. Perhaps aging affects speakers of different languages in different ways. Research on cross-language differences and aging is very sparse and is certainly an area open to further investigation. Kemper (1992) shares a few interesting observations. Some languages are very strict in their structure. For example, English has a fixed word order of subject-verb-object. Other languages, such as Russian and informally spoken Japanese, rely heavily on contextual cues and word order may vary. Kemper points out that the more "contextual" languages may make it easier for older people to comprehend and speak because they do not have to follow complex, strict language rules. This means that older adults who may have problems processing complex sentence structure can still understand and convey the meaning of a spoken sentence by interpreting the larger context.

# Summary: Culture, Language, and Cognition

**Cognition** is a general term referring to thinking, reasoning, decision making, remembering, categorizing, and problem solving. Cultural factors and beliefs found in the interaction among Bronfenbrenner's ecological systems, the developmental niche, and the sociocultural orientation contribute in a variety of ways to cognitive development across the lifespan.

The theories of Piaget, Vygotsky, and others provide a useful framework for conceptualizing cognitive growth and development and its relationship to language and culture. Vygotsky's sociocultural theory emphasizes the strong influence of social and cultural factors on both

cognitive and language development. He introduced the zone of proximal development, which refers to what a child is presently capable of doing and what he or she could potentially do if guided by adults or capable peers. Vygotsky argued that cognitive development is enhanced when instruction is focused on an individual's potential rather than on the level of actual development. According to Vygotsky, the development of egocentric speech, inner speech, and external speech are grounded in one's social and cultural orientation. Vygotsky also emphasized the need for guided instruction (scaffolding) in which adults provide assistance (scaffolds) for children as they attempt to solve difficult problems. Vygotsky's view of language acquisition and sociocultural influences is mirrored in the learning of a second language. Along with a strong developmental influence, we have identified multiple ecological, social, and psychological factors that account for the successful learning of a second, non-native language.

According to Piaget, children's thinking differs significantly from that of adults, which is acquired only after passing through a series of discrete stages. These stages have been studied from a cross-cultural perspective, and research evidence suggests that some aspects (the sequence of stages) may be universal, whereas others (the stage of formal operations) may not.

Cross-cultural investigations of human development have tended to focus primarily on children and adolescents, devoting less attention to middle and late adulthood. At the same time, research in adult cognition has revealed that a fifth stage of cognitive development (postformal thought) may emerge after formal operations. This new thinking allows an individual to move beyond abstract conceptualization and integrate diverse reasoning abilities with pragmatic problem-solving strategies. The work of several researchers suggests that adult cognition is characterized by adaptive logic and dialectical thinking. The ability to synthesize new ideas and realize that there

are at least two sides to every point of view provides adults with more flexibility, problem-solving skills, and a broadening of thought.

Cognitive development in middle and late adulthood follows a different pattern than in childhood and adolescence. Horn and Cattell (1967) have suggested that a distinction be made between fluid and crystallized intelligence. Fluid intelligence is a person's ability to solve problems, think abstractly, and apply new material in creative ways. Crystallized intelligence is learning that is based on experience. Early cross-cultural research indicates that as we get older, fluid intelligence declines and crystallized intelligence increases. More recent research by Baltes and Schaie (1976) disputes this claim and suggests the need to consider cultural and contextual factors when attempting to explain individual differences in cognitive decline during late adulthood.

Although some cognitive decline may influence communication in older age, other factors also influence language competence. Negative views of the elderly embedded in culture and leading to perceived incompetence may be much more influential than actual loss of language competence. Moreover, changes in language competence in older age may be more or less relevant, depending on the characteristics of the language spoken.

## Study Questions

Which developmental and ecological factors play a role in language acquisition and early second-language acquisition?

Cross-cultural research testing Piaget's stages of cognitive development has shown that some aspects of his theory describe universal patterns of development. What aspects of the developmental stages are seemingly universal?

What are "fluid" and "crystallized" intelligence, and how do they develop and change with age?

How does use of language and communication change in later life, and how might different ecological settings help people adapt to those changes?

Have you ever used "elderspeak" to communicate with older relatives or friends? Does it seem to help?

## Developmental Analysis
## Culture, Language, and Cognition

I have often reflected on the differences between my own upbringing and that of my children. Although there are similarities, there are also some striking contrasts—particularly related to language acquisition. I grew up in a predominantly Irish, Catholic community. We all shopped at the same grocery store, attended the same church, and spoke the same language—English. I learned to speak while at home with my mother and honed my

language skills when I entered kindergarten. My peers and I exhibited an ability to sound words out according to the arrangement of letters. Once I had acquired this skill, I felt as if I had gained magical powers! I remember trying to teach my younger sister to speak shortly after she was born. It was extremely frustrating to me that this new little person (who had invaded *my* home) could not even talk.

It was not until I struggled through Latin in the eighth grade that I was exposed to another language. Staring at the letters on the page, I was trying to make sense out of these new patterns—and it did not come easily to me. Sure, I could sound out some of these words (often incorrectly), but what did it all mean? After barely passing the first term's exam, I vowed to stay away from foreign languages. I kept my vow until I ventured off to study in Italy during my junior year in college. I met many people who spoke three, four, and five languages. Quite impressive compared to my one. Fortunately for me, English was often one of the languages spoken!

I began taking Italian language classes shortly after I returned from my study abroad program. It was not easy for me, but I continued learning throughout the courtship with my Italian-born husband, Giorgio. It certainly came in handy when I met my future in-laws for the first time! Between savory mouthfuls of wonderful Italian food, I could effortlessly tell my mother-in-law how delicious her manicotti was. Benissimo!

Giorgio and I made the decision to raise our children in a bilingual environment by exposing them to both English and Italian. Regardless of whether a true "critical period" for language acquisition existed, we both agreed that as children, it would be best for them to learn Italian along with English. Therefore, Giorgio and I spoke both Italian and English in the home. When my mother-in-law came to visit us from Italy, she spoke only Italian. Both of our children now speak Italian fluently and have gone on to learn other languages as well. They thank Giorgio and me for our efforts to raise them in a bilingual environment. They often marvel at how Giorgio and I knew what to do as parents. I tell them that although we had some basic idea of what we were doing, much of our parenting was based on the experiences we had as we went along. Each experience helped us shape our knowledge and parenting approach. Although I think we did a fine job, I often wonder if we could have done better knowing what we know now. I guess that is consistent with the idea that "older is wiser." I definitely feel as if I am *wiser* today—fortunately, I do not feel much older!

# Chapter 6
# Culture, Self, and Personality

*Sergej was happy, agreeable, and easy to care for as a child. He grew up on a* kolkhozy *(collective farm) in the Ukraine, one of the fifteen republics in the former Soviet Union. He was quiet, and even his adolescent years were not characterized by the confusion and psychological turmoil experienced by so many young people. Sergej did well in school, completed an apprenticeship, and, following the breakup of the Soviet Union, now works on his family's small farm. He has been married for several years, and his wife, Tamara, describes him as a "good husband" who works hard, stays at home, and cares for his family.*

*Yuen, born in Guizhou province in southwestern China, was what her mother considered a difficult child. Her moods were unpredictable, and when upset she took a long time to calm down. Yuen never developed a regular sleeping and feeding schedule, making it difficult for her mother to coordinate her work and child care. Her adolescent years were equally challenging. Yuen had few friends and struggled with discipline problems at school. Now in her mid-thirties, she has assumed a leadership position in her work. Occasionally, she has to be reprimanded for her creative and sometimes radical ideas.*

Sergej and Yuen are clearly very different people and showed very distinct character traits as children and as adults. *Were they born with different personalities? Are these differences due to innate cultural patterns of personality? How much do cultural expectations about the course of one's life influence adult personality?* These and other questions are addressed in this chapter by examining issues of personality, self, and individual differences and their embeddedness in a cultural context.

## 6.1: Ecological Context: Temperament, Personality, and self

### 6.1.1: Temperament and Heritability of Traits

Many of the childhood behaviors exhibited by Sergej and Yuen can be explained according to differences in

**temperament**, or *a person's innate characteristic behavioral style or typical pattern of responding to events in the environment.* These patterns are said by many to include such characteristics as introversion (reserved and solitary behaviors) and/or extraversion (energetic, outgoing, and/or talkative behaviors). Even though several attempts at classifying specific elements of temperament have been proposed, researchers have yet to form a general consensus on a model or system. However, individual differences in temperament can be observed in the earliest hours following birth, leading many to believe it is biologically based, while also recognizing that environmental factors (e.g., socialization and parenting approaches) can influence the expression of temperament. For example, although some newborns and infants are irritable and cry frequently, others appear to be good natured and calm. During the first few months of life, some infants are extremely expressive and react to people and events by making sounds and waving their arms; others are less active, may hardly respond to their environment, and appear withdrawn and uninvolved. Frequently, the differences we see in temperament among infants tend to be characteristically consistent throughout individual lives. In fact, some researchers maintain that infant temperament reliably predicts adult personality.

**Personality** can be described as a *unique system of identifiable, characteristic behavioral patterns that distinguish a person from others.* The infant who is shy and anxious around strangers is more likely to be a shy adult than is an infant who curiously approaches strangers. The potentially powerful relationship between infant temperament and adult personality has led many researchers to the conclusion that traits of temperament are, to a significant extent, inherited. They argue that environment and socialization can influence temperament only within the limits initially defined by heredity.

The concept of heritability of temperament has received support from careful studies of twins (identical and fraternal) reared together and apart (DiLalla & Jones, 2000; Segal, 2000, 2012). These studies are based on the hypothesis that identical twins share 100% of their genes and, therefore, should be identical in their temperamental dispositions at birth. In contrast, fraternal twins, similar to other siblings, share only 50% of their genetic makeup and, therefore, should be less similar in their temperament. Yet, similar to identical twins, they share a very similar environment. Studies such as these should be able to provide answers to such questions as the following: (1) *Are identical twins more similar in their temperament than fraternal twins?* (2) *Are identical twins raised in different environments more similar in temperament than are fraternal twins reared together?* (3) *Are fraternal twins (who share half of their genes) more similar to each other than are adopted siblings (who do not share any genes)?*

If the answer to these questions is "yes," then we can conclude that genetic disposition, rather than environment, is responsible for the differences in temperament observed among people. However, to accurately assess the results of twin studies, it is important to understand the way heritability is measured. In general, the degree of heritability is expressed by the **heritability quotient**, which is *an estimate of the percentage of the variability in a given trait that can be attributed to genetic differences.* For example, a heritability quotient of 50% for trait X means that approximately half of the variation, or individual difference, found in a sample is due to genetic differences among these subjects. The remaining half of the variation is assumed to be the result of complex environmental factors or, possibly, unexplained errors in measurement. With this in mind, let us consider some twin research and what it tells us about the inheritability of temperament.

In general, twin studies have produced moderately high heritability quotients. For example, a study of 250 Canadian twins showed broad genetic influence on the five dimensions of neuroticism, extraversion, openness, agreeableness, and conscientiousness. The genetic contribution to trait variation was estimated at 41%, 53%, 61%, 41%, and 44%, respectively (Jang, Livelsy, & Vernon, 1996). Similarly, a study of 350 twins in Minnesota revealed that approximately 40% of the variability among subjects in such traits as stress reaction (related to neuroticism and general anxiousness) and aggression could be attributed to genetics (Bouchard, Lykken, McGue, Segal, & Tellegen, 1990).

Although results such as these suggest that certain temperamental traits are genetically transmitted, they also suggest that, in specific instances, other traits are heavily influenced by socialization within the family environment. After all, a heritability quotient of 40% to 50% also means that 50% to 60% of variation is due to environmental rather than genetic factors. The debate around environmental and genetic influences on temperament continues, and researchers are not yet able to provide a definitive answer as to which plays the more significant role in determining differences in temperament and personality.

One final approach for measuring and understanding temperament is that of Mary K. Rothbart (1981), a well-known temperament researcher who has worked in the field for more than twenty-five years. Using her definition of temperament as "constitutionally based individual differences in reactivity and regulation" (p. XX). Rothbart and Hwang (2005) have developed measures of temperament (in the form of parent- and self-report questionnaires) for each period of the lifespan from infancy to adulthood. In one study, they applied the statistical procedure of factor analysis to data obtained from children ranging in age from three to twelve months. Rothbart and Hwang also describe three broad factors of temperament: (1) *effortful control* characterized by a number of behaviors, including a low threshold for pleasure and perceptual sensitivity, reflecting the extent to which a child can focus attention and not be easily distracted; (2) *surgency/extraversion* characterized by impulsivity and increased levels of activity, reflecting the extent to which a child is considered happy and enjoys "vocalizing"; and (3) *negative affect* characterized by such emotional behaviors as anger, fear, sadness, and frustration. Detailed information about the questionnaires can be found at www.bowdoin.edu/~sputnam/rothbart-temperament-questionnaires/instrument-descriptions. A list of her publications is also listed at www.bowdoin.edu/~sputnam/rothbart-temperament-questionnaires/cv/. [For additional research on temperament, see Rothbart (2011).]

## 6.1.2: The Self: Some Cultural Perspectives

Our unique system of behavioral patterns, or personality, develops over time and is shaped by the interaction between temperament (heritable traits) and the ecological system. As personality develops, it helps lay the foundation for development of the **self-concept**—*the perception of oneself as a person with identifiable behavioral patterns and characteristics, directed by desires, preferences, attributes, and abilities.* The unique structure and content of the self-concept, as well as some of the psychological dynamics related to it, are largely influenced by one's developmental niche and ecological systems (microsystem, mesosystem, exosystem, or macrosystem) in which one finds oneself at a particular time in the lifespan.

Those who write most frequently about the topic of self-concept tend to discuss cultural variations in relation to the dimension of individualism-collectivism. **Individualism** emphasizes the individual with a value of independence and self-reliance; **collectivism** emphasizes the interdependence value of group goals. [See Chapter 1 for a review of these dimensions.] Triandis (1989, 1995), who has written extensively about individualism-collectivism, suggests that culture-specific views of the self result from early exposure to differing values and beliefs. For example, child-rearing patterns in collectivist cultures tend to introduce and reinforce the welfare of the collective over the welfare of the individual. In contrast, parents in individualistic cultures teach their children that the individual's primary goals are achieving independence and establishing a unique self. Based on these fundamentally different approaches, it seems logical that individuals in collectivist and individualistic cultures should vary in how they view themselves. Some authors make a distinction between interdependent and independent selves (Gardiner & Mutter, 1994; Markus & Kitayama, 1991).

Although the concepts of individualism and collectivism may be useful in describing general differences among cultures, critics point out that they disregard within-culture differences and neglect the fact that any culture includes both individualistic and collectivistic beliefs, values, and motives (Turiel, 2004). Applied to the concept of self, this means that a person's self can contain individualistic and collectivistic elements at the same time. In fact, one of the students who read an earlier edition of this book was concerned that she should be relegated to an "individualistic" concept of self just because she grew up in an individualistic culture. For example, she argued convincingly that some aspects of her self-concept and the belief that she is a "good" person are tied to her charity work and helping others. Research confirms this more complex understanding of self. Raeff (2004) reports that late adolescents recognize themselves in relation to others. When asked to describe themselves, most adolescents in Raeff's European American sample used autonomous terms (e.g., I am insightful, I am athletic, and I like to read). However, when they were prompted to explain why these self-characteristics are important, the answers revealed a clear connection between self-characteristics and social relationships. For example, one woman pointed out that being insightful ". . . is very important because communication's obviously a very important thing. . . . You know, and sometimes it's nice to have insight into what somebody else is thinking and feeling" (p. 73). Equally poignant are Li and Yue's (2004) findings that Chinese adolescents can show strong individual goals and ambitions in the realm of learning, despite the generally more collectivistic values present in Chinese culture.

Raeff's (2006a, 2006b, 2006c, 2010) more recent work focuses on the complexities of culture and independence and interdependence in children's developmental experiences with an emphasis on cross-cultural and within-culture variability. For example, among the many important points made in a study of a kindergarten classroom, Raeff (2006a) states that "by defining independence and interdependence as multifaceted and interrelated activity dimensions that reflect cultural conceptions and values, the way is opened for discerning how specific aspects of independent and interdependent behavior may be structured within and across cultures" (p. 554). In a more recent study of independence and interdependence (individualism and collectivism), Raeff (2010) suggests that further research is needed to determine how characteristics of these two behaviors are ". . . understood, valued, and structured in relation to situational factors and societal processes in cultural contexts. . . . Such research would benefit not only from cross-cultural comparisons but also from within-cultural comparisons . . . " (p. 35). This point is given even greater emphasis when she states that she "would be very happy to see a textbook on culture that does not treat individualism and collectivism dichotomously" (C. Raeff, personal communication, March 6, 2014).

*How do you view yourself—as an individualist, a collectivist, or a mixture of the two? What about other members of your family and your friends? Do you change your behavior depending on the situation or group in which you find yourself?*

The ecological model is a useful tool in interpreting these findings. Viewed from this perspective, individual and collective orientations of self can coexist at different levels of the ecological model. Box 6.1 highlights several cultures that have a body of research focused on the concept of the self in relation to cultural values and beliefs—Japan, China, and India.

## Box 6.1 The Self and Personality: Some Cultural Perspectives

### Japan

Japan is generally considered to be a collective culture, where the Japanese place the group above the individual and tend to be other directed. The Japanese are extremely sensitive to, and concerned about, relationships and maintaining harmony (an influence from Confucianism); they stress such values as filial piety, shame (as a method of reinforcing expectations and proper behavior), self-control, emphasis on consensus, and fatalism.

The Japanese view the self as consisting of two parts—the inner self and the outer self, also known as the social self (what is typically shown to others). At the core of the inner self is the *kokoro*, a reservoir of truthfulness and purity that remains private and is not shared with outsiders. Interestingly, the Japanese describe the self in concrete terms that are more contextual and relational than individuals in the United States. For example, although an American may say, "I am shy" (an abstract definition), a Japanese is more likely to say, "I am shy at work" (a contextual definition) or "I am shy with strangers" (a relational definition).

In addition, Japanese behavior often avoids direct communication and careful control over emotions and actions, allowing for the masking of feelings and the appearance of extreme modesty or shyness. The downplaying of one's performance may result in a nonthreatening atmosphere; however, the modesty displayed does not mean that the person lacks confidence or that he or she is shy. The individual may be extremely confident but, according to cultural expectations, he or she does not behave in an outwardly confident manner. Finally, the Japanese tend to be less unrealistically optimistic than Americans. Unrealistic optimism is the tendency for people to believe that, compared to others, they are more likely to experience positive events and less likely to experience negative events. The Japanese do not have this tendency because the attention to the individual that self-enhancement engenders is not valued in Japanese culture.

## China

An interest in understanding personality and the self is not new for the Chinese. An ancient theory held that personality is a result of the interaction of two forces—*yin* (passive, weak, and destructive) and *yang* (active, strong, and constructive)—and the Five Agents or *Wu-using* (metal, wood, water, fire, and earth), each of which has corresponding physical and temperamental characteristics. This is mediated by the Confucian Doctrine of the Mean, which states that there should be a balance of these forces and an avoidance of one-sidedness or extremity to maintain the Mean (moderation). This balance results in all things being in their proper order and thriving. If there is a balance, then the person is active or passive *according to the situation.* If the Doctrine of the Mean is violated, then the person is either extremely passive or extremely active.

A more modern Chinese theory of personality centers on Chinese social orientation or a person's tendency and desire to maintain harmonious relationships with others. An example is dedication to the family that results in Chinese merging their sense of self with the family and not focusing on personal interests, desires, or goals.

Beliefs about personality and the self are also influenced by Confucianism. Confucian personality is viewed as "the becoming process" and not an attained state of being. There is no fixed personality; rather, it is constantly evolving. A person becomes a personality by embodying a life worth living. At the same time, there is a belief in a "boundless" self, and the Chinese see the self as part of a larger vision of the universe.

Finally, although the Chinese focus greater attention on the inner self than individuals in Western cultures, their self-presentation is similar to the Japanese. In other words, the Chinese downplay their successes, engage in self-effacement, are less likely to demonstrate self-serving bias, and mask their feelings in social interactions.

## India

India is predominantly Hindu, with large minorities of Sikhs and Muslims. To understand India's views on the self, an awareness and understanding of Hinduism is extremely helpful. Hinduism is multifaceted and encompasses a body of beliefs, philosophies, worship practices, and code of conduct.

According to Hinduism, all individuals have four basic aims in life that form the basis of Indian values: (1) *kama,* pleasure or enjoyment; (2) *artha,* wealth or success; (3) *dharma,* righteousness, faithful duty or code of conduct; and (4) *moksha,* liberation or salvation. Of these, dharma is the most relevant for the concept of self because it deals with righteousness, faithful duty, or code of conduct. In India rights and duties are defined separately for various segments of the society divided by age and social category (i.e., caste). In fact, the primary term for personhood has been *purusa,* meaning *man,* and the term conveys the privileged status of men.

The Indian view of the self is also related to the "Law of Karma," the guiding principle that assumes lawfulness and order in the physical, biological, mental, and moral realms. According to the law, each person must face the appropriate consequences for his or her actions regardless of whether the actions are good, bad, or indifferent. Because India, similar to many other Asian cultures, is generally a collective society, individuals are not identified by individual traits; they are instead described in terms of social relationships. Responsiveness to the needs of others is viewed as a high moral obligation.

# 6.2:  Infancy

As of today, researchers have not found a definite answer to the question "what influences a person's personality more—temperament or sociocultural factors?" Consequently, most recognize the existence of an intricate relationship between individual temperament and the sociocultural environment. This section discusses some theoretical perspectives that attempt to explain that relationship and how it shapes personality development early in life.

## 6.2.1: Temperament, Ecological Systems, and the Developmental Niche

As pointed out in Chapter 2, a child's developmental environment consists of four basic subsystems: (1) the microsystem, consisting of interactions between the child and his or her immediate environment (e.g., home or day care center); (2) the mesosystem, made up of individual microsystems (e.g., family and preschool); (3) the exosystem, consisting of influential social settings (e.g., parents' place of work); and (4) the macrosystem, comprising customs, values, and laws important to the child's culture. Together, these subsystems provide the individual child with his or her developmental niche, or unique combination of socialization experiences. Each subsystem is influenced by, and in turn influences, a child's individual temperament.

A child's behavior will initiate a specific response from a caregiver in a particular setting (home or preschool). However, these responses differ from one environmental setting to another. For example, a mother's reaction to a child who exhibits irregular sleep and eating patterns differs from North America to East Africa. A North American mother typically pays more attention to an infant who is unpredictable in eating and sleeping patterns, and she arranges her schedule to take care of the child's needs. In contrast, Super and Harkness (1994a) report that mothers in Kokwet, a small farming town in Kenya, interact more with children who operate on a regular daily schedule. Knowing when her baby will be awake and alert, the mother can more easily arrange her many other duties and activities. Kokwet infants who are less predictable in their daily patterns are more often left to the care of an older sister or another caregiver.

This example illustrates how a child's temperament influences the environment. At the same time, however, specific patterns of response exhibited by others in the child's environment may facilitate or inhibit particular behavioral styles on the part of the child, thus making the child–environment relationship a two-way interaction. A fussy child receives more attention from the primary caregiver in most Western cultures, thus potentially rewarding and facilitating the child's dependency on the caregiver. In non-Western cultures, dependency and emotional attachment to the mother are often less pronounced because mothers may not be available to respond with immediate emotional attention to fussy children.

Another theoretical explanation that contributes to the understanding of how temperament, development, and culture relate to one another is that of **goodness of fit**—*the quality of the adaptation, or "match," between a child's temperament and the demands of his or her immediate environment.* This concept was introduced by Thomas and Chess (1977) in an elaborate longitudinal study in which they were able to identify clusters of traits that characterized three different temperament types among infants: (1) the "easy" child (40%), (2) the "difficult" child 10%), and (3) the "slow-to-warm-up" child (15%).

An **easy child** was *characterized by a good mood, regular sleeping and eating cycles, and general calmness.* Mothers considered these babies unproblematic and easy to raise. In addition, they appear to be "...highly adaptive, with positive moods and normal eating and sleeping patterns" (Singer & Navsaria, 2013, p. 1274). In contrast, temperament traits of a **difficult child** included a *negative mood, slow adaptation to and withdrawal from new experiences and people, irregular sleep and feeding patterns, and high emotional intensity.* Moreover, these "difficult" infants were found in later childhood to be less well-adjusted and prone to more behavioral problems. A **slow-to-warm-up child** generally *showed few intense reactions, positive or negative, and tended to be mild and low in activity level.* Thomas and Chess (1977) assert that it is not the individual child's temperament itself that is related to future maladjustment, but rather the match or mismatch of the child's temperament with the environment that predicts problematic behavior. If "difficult" temperament disrupts family routine and leads to negative parental reactions, then negative developmental outcome is likely.

Although this original model of temperament is still used, it has frequently been replaced by others that use a dimensional approach (e.g., Infant Behavior Questionnaire—Revised (IBQ-R) (Garstein & Rothbart, 2003)).

DeVries and Sameroff (1984) further illustrate this concept by describing two individual cases of infants from different parts of Kenya. The case of Hamadi, a Digo boy, demonstrates how an "easy" temperament can lead to poor adjustment due to a mismatch between the boy's temperament and his environment. For example, as an infant, Hamadi was energetic and active and exhibited healthy approach tendencies. He was described as one of the most advanced infants in the entire study. However, after starting school, Hamadi began to withdraw, became shy, and showed clear signs of distress through acting-out behavior.

What caused this transition? Hamadi's parents and teachers reported that Hamadi's temperament did not fit with the cultural expectations of how a Digo boy his age should behave. The efforts of teachers and parents to control his energetic temperament and discourage his curiosity, instead of rewarding his enthusiasm and challenging his intellect, led Hamadi to withdraw and become angry and fearful.

Differences in infant temperament can often be observed side-by-side within the same cultural context.

(Amble Design/Shutterstock)

The second case involves Enkeri, a Masai boy born in the same year as Hamadi. According to traditional temperament measures, Enkeri scored as "difficult." He was the classic "fussy" child—very intense, persistent, overactive, irregular in his daily behavior patterns, and not easily distracted or consolable. In a Western culture, these temperament traits would place Enkeri at risk for future adjustment problems. However, the behaviors that Western mothers dislike and describe as undesirable and difficult are valued highly in Masai society.

The Masai are an agricultural society and often have to struggle for survival in an extremely hostile environment. In times of drought, when herds of cattle and goats are destroyed, infant mortality is high because families cannot rely on the usual supply of milk. Under these kinds of conditions, infants who show "difficult" behavior tend to survive at a higher rate than infants who are quiet and undemanding. Why? Infants who cry are fed and attended to, whereas those who don't are assumed to be content. Consequently, infants who cry a lot are fed more and are in better physical condition, which contributes to their survival. Clearly, the interaction of culture and individuality are different in these two ecological settings, and the resulting behavior and interpretation of it are strongly influenced by the presence of different developmental niches. Before leaving the topic of temperament, a word of caution is in order. Although researchers frequently explain cross-cultural differences in temperament as a result of a particular cultural group's practices and values, Singer and Navsaria (2013) state that ". . . it is important to recognize that these differences may simply be environmental influences in the expression of temperament" (p. 1275). They also point out that research sometimes shows similarities in temperament across cultures, suggesting some traits may, in fact, be universal. As examples, Oakland and Hatzichristou (2010) have found in their studies that children prefer an extroverted social approach to an introverted one; a practical reasoning style to an imaginative one; and an organized approach to decision making when young, but a flexible approach when older. Singer and Navsaria (2013) propose that such similarities across cultures lend further support to the idea that temperament is biologically based but that culture and socialization can, and in many cases do, change temperamental expression.

# 6.3: Childhood

## 6.3.1: The Emerging Self-Concept

*If you were asked to draw a picture of yourself, what would your picture look like? Would it show a single figure in the middle of the page? Would you attempt to portray your most typical features (e.g., hairstyle, clothes, and facial features)? Or, would you show yourself at work, at home, with friends, or with family? The way we think about ourselves, as individual entities or in a social context, is influenced by the cultural*

understanding of who a person is and what characterizes him or her.

In a cross-cultural study of self-concept in Japan and the United States, Cousins (1989) reported that subjects differed in the way they described themselves as individuals. Cousins used the Twenty Statements Test (Kuhn & McPartland, 1954), which asks individuals to write twenty responses to the question, "Who am I?" Results indicated that Americans used psychological attributes such as traits or dispositions ("I am a son" or "I am kind") to describe themselves, whereas Japanese subjects frequently included the larger context when describing who they were. For example, Japanese subjects used more preferences and wishes, social categories, and activities in their self-descriptions ("I will always honor my parents" or "I want to work for my father's company").

Interestingly, the results from this study support several of the major themes we discussed in Chapter 1. For example, in terms of Bronfenbrenner's ecological model, Americans can be said to view the self as part of the microsystem. The individual selects characteristics derived from early interactions between him- or herself as a child and the immediate environment, most notably, the family. This conception reflects the individualistic nature of American culture. The Japanese, in contrast, select characteristics that emerge from interactions in social settings or institutions—that is, in the exosystem or even the macrosystem—where they have come into contact with the customs, values, and laws of their culture. Such behavior reflects a collectivist society. This contrast can be seen in the examples of Sergej and Yuen in the opening vignettes of this chapter.

In another study using the same methodology (the Twenty Statements Test), Bochner (1994) reported similar results when comparing adults from Malaysia (a collectivist culture) with adults from Australia and Britain (individualist cultures). Interestingly, unlike Cousins' study, Malaysians gave more responses referring to personal traits and dispositions than responses associated with social groups, and members of the two other cultures (Australia and Britain) gave more socially oriented responses. However, overall, Bochner's cross-cultural comparison showed significantly fewer personal responses and significantly more group-related responses among Malaysians than in either the Australian or British samples.

Miller (1984) suggested that these differences are developmental in nature (another theme weaving through our topical discussions). He compared adults in North America with Hindus in India. The results seem to replicate other findings: Indians attributed their actions more to contextual factors, whereas Americans explained actions in terms of personal dispositions. In contrast, self-descriptions among young American and Hindu children (eight to eleven years of age) did not differ in any significant way; both groups referred more to context than to personal characteristics. This suggests that Americans, with age, may learn to focus more on the person than on the context when perceiving and evaluating behavior. This also casts some doubt on the definition of the individualism-collectivism dichotomy and its effect on actual behavior (in this case, self-description). After all, it would be naïve to assume that cultural effects on self-concept and behavior could be reduced to two distinct categories of cultural values. This might be an interesting area for future research.

Additional evidence for the early influence of culture comes from a study conducted in the Netherlands (Van den Heuvel, Tellegen, & Koomen, 1992). Moroccan, Turkish, and Dutch children in grades six through eight were asked to describe five things about themselves, about one classmate who is similar to them, and about one classmate who is different from them. As hypothesized by the researchers, children from the two more collectivist cultures (Morocco and Turkey) used more social statements indicating group memberships, social activities, or clearly interpersonal traits (e.g., friendly toward others) when describing themselves or a similar classmate. Dutch children used significantly more psychological attributes such as traits and personal preferences in their descriptions of themselves or a similar classmate. The authors conclude that the significant psychological differences found between individuals with an individualistic cultural background and those with a collectivistic background emerge at an early age and continue to develop across the lifespan.

Development of self-concept is greatly aided by language development and the words we use to describe ourselves. Pronouns such as *me, mine, you, us,* and *them* distinguish between self and others. Through the use of such words, we learn to understand ourselves as unique and different from others. In an early study, Mead (1934) suggested that personal names were at the center of self-concept development. Personal names help identify the self and distinguish oneself from others who are not referred to by that name. In many cultures in which names are carefully selected for their meaning, the person is thought to adopt characteristics associated with that name. These attributes become part of their self-concept. *How often have we met someone with the same name as someone else we know (and perhaps like or dislike) and compared the characteristics of the two individuals? Did your parents choose your name for a special meaning or reason?*

## 6.3.2: Self-Esteem and Self-Efficacy

A recurring question in the study of self-concept is whether we can and should separate how we *think* about ourselves from how we *feel* about ourselves. Some contend that the content of the self-concept and its evaluation, which results in self-esteem, are virtually inseparable. However, other self-concept research increasingly demonstrates that self-esteem may indeed be a distinct aspect of self-concept. From a developmental perspective, it appears that a global sense of self-esteem (perceived self-worth), distinguishable from the descriptive aspects of self, emerges around the age of eight.

Watkins and Dhawan (1989) argue that the distinction or lack of distinction between self-esteem and self-concept may be a cultural phenomenon. In several studies, these investigators examined aspects of the self-concept and self-esteem of children and adults from diverse cultural groups. Similar to previous studies, they found distinct differences between members of Western and Asian cultures. For example, Dhawan and Roseman (1988) reported that 62% of responses of American young adults were classified as self-evaluations compared with 35% of responses among Indians of the same age group. In addition, most of the self-evaluations made by Western subjects were positive rather than negative.

These results, along with others, suggest that the distinction between self-concept and self-evaluation is more pronounced in Asian cultures, whereas both aspects of self are intertwined in Western cultures. Once again, the explanation seems to lie in the individualistic or collectivistic orientation of the cultures involved. If an individual is independent and responsible for his or her success or failure, then a focus on specific positive aspects of the self is an efficient protection against low self-esteem (Gardiner & Mutter, 1994). In contrast, in cultures in which individual success and enhancement are less important, personal attributes and accomplishments are not an immediate source of self-esteem and their value need not be emphasized.

As noted previously, particularly in the discussion of the developmental niche and the ecological systems approach, child-rearing practices and family environment are major contributors to cultural differences. These factors are also believed to be very influential in the development of personality and self-esteem, especially during the first years of life. Therefore, the fact that cultural differences in self-esteem are related to cultural differences in child-rearing should not be surprising. Child-rearing that emphasizes warmth and acceptance, together with consistent rules and achievement expectations, is clearly related to high self-esteem. For example, Olowu (1990) argues that many African children have higher self-esteem than children in Western countries because they enjoy the warmth and acceptance of an extended family. Such parental warmth can be provided by aunts and uncles, as well as by grandparents. Western children, in contrast, frequently rely on one or two caregivers for their self-esteem needs.

In Burkino Faso, a senior Lobi man shows warmth and affection toward a young friend.

(Blue Jean Images/Alamy Stock Photo)

Akande (1999) comes to a similar conclusion after studying the self-esteem in post-apartheid black South African children. He points out that at the core of South African self-esteem is the social group (most notably, the family) that promotes personal achievement, good character ("iwa pele"), influence, prestige, and hegemony.

Social psychologists have argued that we cannot understand a person's self by only considering the general sense of ourselves as a person distinct from another person (self-concept) and our general sense of self-worth (self-esteem). Bandura (1997) explores the construct of "self-efficacy" as an important factor in the development of self. **Self-efficacy** refers to *the general sense of one's ability to master tasks and to direct one's behavior toward a goal.* Although highly correlated with self-esteem (Judge, Erez, Bono, & Thoresen, 2002), self-efficacy adds important insights to our understanding of the developing self.

According to Bandura (1997), self-efficacy, unlike self-esteem, influences personal goals and behavior. When children learn they can influence their environment through their behavior, and they succeed in doing so, they develop a sense of efficacy. This sense of capabilities allows and motivates them to set goals and achieve them. As their world and their ecological systems expand, from family to peers to school, they develop self-efficacy in different domains. For example, the Children's Perceived Self-Efficacy scales (Bandura, 1990) measure self-efficacy in three domains: academic self-efficacy (capable of managing one's learning and mastering academic subjects), social self-efficacy (capable of forming and maintaining social relationships and managing conflicts), and self-regulatory efficacy (capable of resisting social pressure).

In a study involving ten- to fifteen-year-old Italian, Hungarian, and Polish children, Pastorelli and her colleagues (2001) showed that some national differences in academic and social efficacy exist. For example, Hungarian children were more confident in their ability to master

academic subjects but had a lower sense of being able to take charge of their learning than Italians and Poles. The authors point to the differences in educational practices in the different countries, suggesting students may develop high efficacy in subject mastery in an educational system that is highly structured and tightly controlled by teachers and parents. However, these students may perceive a lack of control in choosing and directing their own learning activities. Likewise, the explanation for the tendency of Italian children in this study to perceive themselves as more capable in the social domain than both Hungarian and Polish children may lie in the ecological system. The family exerts the earliest influence in a child's life and provides early opportunities to develop social efficacy. Italian culture is known for its emphasis on strong family relationships throughout life, so it might not be surprising to find that Italian children consider themselves socially competent. They may just have had more opportunities to develop social efficacy within their microsystem.

# 6.4: Adolescence

Adolescence is a particularly interesting period of transition in the lifespan. It begins with biological maturation and ends with society's acceptance of the young person as an adult. Most Western societies have clear social markers that define when a young person is considered mature enough to assume adult responsibilities (e.g., voting in elections) and adult privileges (e.g., driving a car or consuming alcohol). In contrast to many nonindustrialized cultures, adolescence generally lasts several years in most modern Western cultures. Adolescents in non-Western societies assume adult responsibilities much earlier because these societies cannot afford to let their young people be "nonproductive" and engage in idle "self-discovery" for an extended time.

## 6.4.1: Identity Formation

During the adolescent years, young people encounter one of the most important developmental tasks of their lives—the establishment of an individual identity. **Identity** is *a person's self-definition as a separate and distinct individual, including behaviors, beliefs, and attitudes.* Simply stated, the individual is trying to answer the question, "Who am I?" Finding the answer isn't always easy and involves many of those within one's various ecological systems, including family and friends, members of peer groups, and teachers. Some adolescents find the journey particularly difficult and have to deal with serious issues, including antisocial or delinquent behavior. These topics receive attention in the section that follows.

Psychologist Erik Erikson is generally credited with the first complete analysis of identity development (Erikson's stage theory is discussed in detail in Chapter 2;

see Table 2.3). Furthermore, he proposed the integration of identity, social roles, and the broader cultural context (Erikson, 1963). In his cross-cultural research, he collected evidence for the universal existence of identity development, yet the exact process by which individuals achieve an adult identity is influenced by specific contextual factors. The basic premise of identity development across cultures is that it is rooted in the physical and psychological developmental changes an individual experiences during the adolescent period.

It has long been assumed, particularly in Western societies, and most notably in the United States, that the transition to adulthood is a rather painful and psychologically challenging event (Hall, 1904). However, other research shows that the experience of stress during adolescence varies cross-culturally (Offer, Ostrov, Howard, & Atkinson, 1988). Some writers suggest that adolescence is more stressful when individuals are confronted with a large number of choices, as they frequently are in Western cultures. In non-Western societies, in which roles are frequently more clearly defined and choices are more limited, the transition to adulthood appears to be much smoother. For example, if the firstborn child is expected to take over the family business and assume care of the aging parents, it is not necessary to explore multiple social roles to find a suitable adult identity. The important decisions have already been made. In contrast, those societies that value independence offer adolescents numerous opportunities to explore a variety of different social roles, thereby making the search for identity more difficult and of longer duration.

One study serves as an example of the influences of specific contextual factors on identity development. Tzuriel (1992) was interested in knowing whether adolescents exposed to multiple (and sometimes conflicting) sets of norms and expectations experience more identity conflict than adolescents with a less ambiguous environment. Israeli Arabs, who represent a relatively small minority in Israel, grow up experiencing elements of both their traditional culture and the Jewish majority culture. In contrast, Israeli Jews know a more homogeneous culture in which their values and beliefs are reflected and reinforced. Would Israeli Arabs have a more negative view of themselves or express more confusion regarding their identity as a result of their different cultural experiences? Among the six factors of identity examined in this study, Arab youths expressed more self-confidence, a stronger sense of ideological and vocational commitment, and more genuineness. In contrast, Jewish adolescents reported more feelings of alienation and discontent with their appearance and behavior. However, they also recognized that others valued them and their abilities.

These findings suggest that Jewish adolescents experienced a somewhat different struggle in their identity formation than did Arabs. Tzuriel (1992) speculates that the

Personal identity is expressed in interesting ways throughout the world.

(Creatista/Shutterstock)

ambiguous environment, especially among Israeli Arabs, may actually facilitate identity exploration and self-awareness in relation to identity issues. Thus, a seemingly ambiguous environment may have a more positive influence on identity formation than common sense would suggest. With the resolution of the identity conflict, most adolescents achieve an identity with which they are comfortable and adjust their behavior accordingly. For a discussion of the positive effects of cultural identity—high self-esteem; high academic achievement; and low risk for violence, drug abuse, and teen pregnancy—on the lives of immigrant African and Latino Americans, see Ng and Hall (2011).

According to Judith Gibbons (2013), a contemporary question regarding adolescent identity development is the extent to which adolescents ". . . develop dual identities as a result of globalization, and the possible consequences of dual identities . . . from growing up with not only one's own cultural and ethnic heritage, but also global adolescent interests and culture, through music, television, movies, and the Internet" (p. 24). In this regard, Jensen (2011) ". . . has outlined possible risks and benefits of globalization for adolescents, including identity confusion as a possible risk . . . but greater civic involvement as a possible benefit" (p. 24).

## 6.4.2: Social Identity Formation

We tend to view identity as something that is very unique and represents the individual's personal history, experiences, and personality. However, our lives are inextricably connected with those around us—our family, our peers, our coworkers. Viewed from an ecological systems view, groups of people in a given context show a great degree of overlap. It is not surprising, therefore, that part of what we like to think of as our self results from what we share with others. Psychologists call these shared aspects of self "social identities." French psychologist H. Tajfel (1981) defines **social identity** as *"that part of an individual's self-concept which derives from his knowledge of his membership of a social group (or groups) together with the value and emotional significance attached to that membership"* (p. 255).

We tend to belong to multiple groups. Some are assigned to us (e.g., gender and nationality), whereas we choose others (e.g., political affiliation). Among these, ethnic or cultural identity has been singled out as particularly important to self-concept and the psychological functioning of ethnic group members. Phinney, Lochner, and Murphy (1990) suggest that the formation of ethnic or cultural identity is similar to the formation of ego identity as outlined by Erikson. For a discussion of the measurement of ethnic identity, status, and suggestions for future research, see Phinney and Ong (2007).

Ethnic or cultural identity formation appears to take place in three stages. The first stage, generally occurring in adolescence, is characterized by the lack of exploration of ethnic identity. The second stage involves becoming aware of one's ethnicity and actively exploring that ethnicity. At this stage, the person may engage in ethnic group activities, including reading and talking to people about the culture and participating in cultural events. The completion of this stage results in the final stage: ethnic identity achievement. This stage is characterized by a deeper understanding of one's ethnicity and the internalization of ethnic identity into the self. Because this understanding of ethnic identity varies from person to person, according to personal history and ecological systems, the implications for the self-concept and, ultimately, social behavior may also vary. For example, one person may become deeply involved in the activities of his or her ethnic group by maintaining the language, wearing traditional dress, and practicing ethnic rituals and customs. For another person, ethnic identity achievement may result in an intrinsic confidence in his or her ethnicity and not necessarily require strong ethnic involvement.

**CULTURAL INFLUENCES ON SOCIAL IDENTITY** Just as the larger cultural context influences the specific content of adolescents' self-concepts and personal identity, culture also plays an important role in the progression of social identity formation. With regard to ethnic identity as an example of social identity, the position an ethnic group holds in the larger society (minority or majority status) and relationships among ethnic groups are the most influential of these cultural factors (Phinney et al. 1990). In addition, Markstrom (2011), in a study of Native American adolescents, identified three levels of identity—local, national, and global.

Research in the West Indies shows how general cultural conditions and beliefs (i.e., macrosystem) shape the basis from which young people begin their ethnic identity formation. Gopal-McNicol (1995) presented black and white preschool children with black and white dolls. The investigator asked the children questions such as "Which doll would you like to play with?" "Which doll do you want to be?" "Which doll is rich, ugly, pretty?" Similar to research in the United States, nearly five decades earlier (Clark & Clark, 1947), most of the children chose the white doll in response to the positive questions. The author concludes that colonialism, along with the representation of blacks and whites in the media, has made a marked impact on attitudes toward and perceptions of ethnic groups in the West Indies. It is not unreasonable to assume that these attitudes and perceptions play an important role in the eventual ethnic identity formation of those black and white children who participated in the study.

Contemporary adolescents are growing up in a world much more culturally diverse than that of their parents and grandparents. This increased globalization has implications for adolescents in many societies as they attempt to develop and establish their cultural identities. Jensen (2003) suggests that adolescents increasingly form multicultural identities as a result of their exposure to diverse cultural beliefs and behaviors either from firsthand contact with people from other cultures or through the media. She further argues that the process of developing a cultural identity during adolescence in a global society has become more complex and presents more challenges than it did just a generation or two ago.

As an example, Jensen (2003) discusses the changing view of marriage in India. The cultural tradition of arranged marriage in India is deeply rooted in values such as obligation to one's family and conforming to social roles rather than pursuing individual preferences. In today's more global Indian society, young Indian women and men are also exposed to values that emphasize freedom of choice and individual rights. Multiple traditional and nontraditional cultural values and practices influence adolescents' conceptions of who they are and how they fit into the world.

In addition to a general globalization that happens at the macrolevel of the ecological system, cultural influences that occur at the microlevel contribute to personal and social identity. As part of a five-year study, Huntsinger and Jose (2006) discovered some systematic changes in self-reported personality characteristics among second-generation Chinese American and European American adolescents. First, all young people seemed to increase in extraversion and independence during the study period. This seems to be the result of normative developmental influences such as becoming more independent from parents, building social relationship with peers, and defining one's own identity.

Second, the two ethnic groups of adolescents became more similar in their self-reported personality characteristics over the five-year span. At the beginning of the study, the two groups differed significantly in eight of thirteen personality dimensions measured (i.e., emotional stability, excitability, dominance, cheerfulness, shrewdness, apprehension, sensitivity, and withdrawal). Five years later, the same two groups only differed in cheerfulness and boldness. The researchers attribute these changes in part to acculturative influences that may have affected the Chinese American group, in particular, by steering its development toward adopting qualities that are adaptive in the American cultural environment.

As researchers have begun to recognize increasing globalization of the adolescent world, they have come to adopt more complex models to interpret their research findings and understand adolescent identity development. In recent years, developmental researchers have pointed explicitly to ecological systems theory as a useful model to guide research and practice (Spencer, Harpalani, Fegley , Dell'Angelo, & Seaton, 2003; Swanson et al., 2003). In fact, globalization is a good example of a sociohistorical force that is captured by the "chronosystem" in the ecological model (see Chapter 2). As we saw in the preceding discussion of identity formation, the globalization of values, beliefs, and practices permeates all levels of the ecological system and greatly influences individuals' developmental paths. For a recent insightful discussion of the effects of globalization on identity development, see Hindi (2014).

## Points to Ponder

### Finding an Identity

Establishing an identity (*a person's self-definition as a separate and distinct individual, including behaviors, beliefs, and attitudes*) is a lifelong task beginning in infancy and childhood and continuing through one's later adulthood. It can change or be modified multiple times, although Erikson believes the period of adolescence is most crucial in defining it. Ask yourself the question, **"Who am I?"**, and *quickly write down ten answers before reading any further.* **NOW STOP.** Did you write down name, age, relationship (son, daughter, wife, husband, mom, dad, etc.), student, career, nationality, etc? Which did you put first? Now add ten more answers. Ask one or two close friends to give ten answers to the question, "Who are you?" Do they match? Do they see you the way you do? What are the differences? Why? How would you describe your identity now as compared to ten years ago? What has changed? How do you think you might answer this question ten years from now? If you are bicultural, do you have conflicts between the two identities? Is one dominate over another? How would you define your religious, racial, ethnic, and sexual or gender identity?

# 6.5: Adulthood
## 6.5.1: A Time of Stability and Change

Given a secure identity by the early to mid-twenties, along with a set of relatively stable personality dispositions (traits), one might assume that personality would not change much after adolescence. However, distinct patterns of personality development, related to temperament traits, continue to occur. In particular, adults become more agreeable, more conscientious, more emotionally stable, but less extraverted and less open to experience. Numerous studies examining these "Big Five" personality traits have shown this pattern to be surprisingly consistent across many age groups and cultures, including the United States, Germany, South Korea, Italy, Croatia, and Portugal (McCrae & Allik, 2002; McCrae & Costa, 2003; McCrae et al., 1999). See Table 6.1 for a description of these traits. (As a useful memory aid, you may want to note that the first letters of the five traits spell the word "OCEAN".)

The Big Five personality traits were "discovered" when researchers performed statistical analysis on adjectives that describe personality characteristics, as well as on existing personality tests (also based on language). They assumed that natural language, used to communicate differences and similarities between oneself and others, reflects the socially relevant dimensions of personality. Therefore, the analysis of natural language should reveal the characteristics that are important in describing oneself and others. Their analysis showed that all descriptors used in natural language, as well as test items designed to measure personality, can be represented by five common dimensions—the Big Five personality traits. Further

**Table 6.1** The Big Five Personality Traits

| Trait | Description |
| --- | --- |
| Agreeableness | Tendency to be compassionate, cooperative, generous, trusting, sympathetic, and altruistic vs. suspicious, critical, and antagonistic toward others |
| Conscientiousness | Tendency to be well-organized, reliable, hardworking, persistent, ambitious, reliable, and responsible vs. disorganized, negligent, and irresponsible |
| Extroversion | Tendency to be energetic, active, outgoing, and sociable vs. quiet, deliberate, reserved, and less involved in the social world |
| Openness to experience | Tendency to be curious, imaginative, creative, and artistic vs. conventional, unimaginative, and uncreative |
| Neuroticism | Tendency to be emotional, anxious, unstable, temperamental, and worried vs. unemotional, calm, stable, even-tempered, and not easily upset |

SOURCE: Based on Ahadi & Rothbart, 1994; McCrae & Costa, 1990; McCrae & Costa, 2003; McCrae & John, 1992, © Harry Gardiner.

research indicated that these five traits are also found in different languages and different cultures. For more recent research on these traits, see Stankov and Lee (2009) and Novikova (2013).

Robert R. McCrae (2004), one of the main proponents of the Five Factor theory (another name for the Big Five model), even goes so far as to suggest that humans, as a species, have a genetic predisposition to develop in basically the same way, regardless of life experiences or cultural influences. McCrae (2011, July) cites the universal occurrence of the five traits and the seemingly universal pattern of personality change as evidence of a biological basis for personality and personality change.

*Are we destined by biology to become more agreeable, conscientious, and emotionally stable, as well as less sociable and open to experience, relative to when we were younger? Are we bound to change in much the same way as our parents and grandparents did?*

Although there seems to be a universal pattern of adult personality development and change, genetic influences offer one possible explanation. Roberts, Wood, and Smith (2005) adopt such a view. They suggest it is not genetic "hardwiring" that predicts universal patterns of personality development. Rather, it is universally occurring tasks of social living that lead to a shared pattern of personality trait development.

Roberts and his colleagues (2005) argue that "the majority of people in a majority of different cultures go through similar life transitions at roughly the same age" (p. 173). All cultures have defined times at which certain life events are supposed to take place. For example, at some point in their lives, individuals in most cultures are expected to find a partner, start a family, produce offspring, work for a living, and contribute to one's community. These are normative tasks that, similar to Erikson's classic life stages, involve the conflict between acquiring new competencies and maintaining the status quo (see the previous discussion in Chapter 2).

It has been suggested that these normative life tasks affect the adult personality in several ways. First, people adjust more easily to transitions that occur according to normative tasks than to transitions that are "not on time." The unexpected death of a child represents an "off time" event because parents are supposed to be survived by their children. However, the same event, although unexpected, is not considered "off time" in societies with high infant mortality rates. Second, a new stage of life requires changes in behavior that frequently result in personality changes. Young adults who experience their first serious romantic relationship increase their emotional stability and conscientiousness (Neyer & Asendorpf, 2001). In turn, individuals who are more emotionally stable and conscientious tend to have relationships that last longer and are more satisfying (Roberts & Bogg, 2004).

# 6.6: Late Adulthood

## 6.6.1: Personality Changes in Senescence or Illness

Personality traits established throughout life continue to guide behavior into late adulthood. In fact, personality appears to "stabilize" in older age. Johnson, McGue, and Krueger (2005) studied pairs of monozygotic and same-gender dizygotic twins between the ages of fifty and seventy. These adults completed the same personality questionnaires five years apart. Results revealed that personality traits were highly stable over time, and strongly influenced by both genetics and nonshared environment. In their discussion, the authors point out that their study confirms the genetic influences on personality stability. However, they also observed that environmental influences appear to be more important in later life, perhaps because the environment in which people live tends to be more stable later in life. For example, people will have lived within the same community for many years, surrounded by longtime friends and family. Overall, there is much consensus that personality is very stable in older age and any changes that do occur are relatively minimal (Lautenschlager & Foerstl, 2007).

If that is the case, then how does one explain the sometimes highly observable behavior changes in the elderly that are often reported by families or health care professionals? Such changes include increased anxiety, apathy, depression, and hostility. With increasing age, people tend to experience more chronic and severe illnesses. Both the organic changes associated with these illnesses (e.g., Alzheimer's disease) and the stressors related to coping with illnesses can lead to personality changes in older age. Lautenschlaeger and Foerstle (2007) conclude, "Conceptually, personality traits are considered to be stable.[ . . . ]More significant personality changes in old age need to be considered as warning signs for the potential presence of an underlying organic illness, most suspiciously due to different forms of dementia" (p. 66).

As you will see in Chapter 9, the diagnosis of illness, as well as the way individuals respond to illness and cope with it, is largely influenced by the cultural and ecological system. For example, in two comparable samples of elderly individuals suffering from dementia, personality and behavioral disorders were more frequently observed in African Americans in Indianapolis than their African counterparts in Nigeria (Hendrie, Gao, & Baiyewu, 2000). In this case, increased stubbornness, irritability, and anger were more prevalent in American dementia patients than in Nigerian patients. Does this mean dementia affects the personality of individuals in one cultural group more than those in another? Most likely, this difference is a result of cultural expectations about aging, personality, and concepts of deviant behavior.

Just as personality change can be a result of illness, personality is also a predictor of health, illness, and mortality. For example, a longitudinal study of Japanese elderly revealed that conscientiousness, extraversion, and openness were associated with lower mortality rate (Iwasa et al., 2008). The authors speculate that more conscientious people take greater care of their health, more extraverted people are more socially active and have better support systems, and more open people adapt more easily to the changes and challenges of older age.

## 6.6.2: The "Aging" Self

As repeatedly pointed out throughout this book, adults face a number of unique developmental conditions in their later years of life. Aside from the challenges of physical aging, they frequently experience negative stereotypes and ageism. Yet, consistently, the majority of adults maintain a positive self-concept, a sense of well-being, and continue to be productive members of society. This phenomenon seems to be rooted in the developing self, allowing it to remain stable and continuous, and, at the same time, flexible enough to assimilate to changing ecological conditions. Sneed and Whitbourne (2005) synthesize various motivation and self-theories and propose that "age-related changes in adulthood are negotiated through processes of identity assimilation, identity accommodation, and identity balance" (p. 382). In their theory, the successfully aging self is a combination of these three processes.

When faced with information that challenges the existing positive self-concept, a person will initially assimilate the environment in a way that is consistent with the self. For example, an adult suffering from hearing loss may explain his or her failure to have conversations on the telephone with "a bad connection" and, as a consequence, avoid the telephone. This strategy, identity assimilation, maintains a positive sense of self, but limits a person's ability to seek out experiences and may restrict his or her behavior. After some time, assimilation may no longer be functional. Then, a person's well-being comes to depend on the self's ability to adapt to a changing environment. Identity accommodation involves changing the self-concept in response to challenging experiences. However, the accommodating self is less stable, and an inconsistent self is associated with low self-esteem. Thus, neither identity assimilation nor identity accommodation alone is conducive to prolonged well-being. Instead, Whitbourne, Sneed, and Skultety (2002) conclude that identity balance is the most adaptive response to aging. Identity balance allows people to make favorable changes to their self-concept when challenged, while also maintaining a consistent sense of solid identity. This model is echoed in work by Denise Tanner (2007), a professor of social work in Britain, who interviewed several older British adults (ages 70–94) over a period of three years. Qualitative analysis of these interviews revealed that these aging adults indeed employed both assimilation and accommodation strategies to cope with threats to the self.

## Summary: Culture, Self, and Personality

This chapter discusses the development of individual, self, and personality across cultures and in specific cultural contexts. Some aspects of personality and behavior are clearly influenced by innate temperamental dispositions. The ways in which individual temperament is expressed and what is considered acceptable are shown to largely depend on cultural values and practices. The discussion also focuses on cultural variations in the concept of person and self, and their relationship to the early development of self-concept. Although adolescents in most cultures experience the need to establish an identity, the manner in which they accomplish this, as well as the specific issues and behaviors related to it, show great cultural variation. Finally, the question is raised as to whether seemingly universal patterns of personality development in adulthood are the result of "hardwired" developmental processes or universal socially prescribed "normative life tasks." It is also established that both personality and self continue to develop and change throughout life and, in old age, help the individual adapt to the unique challenges in later life.

## Study Questions

Use the examples of Hamadi and Enkeri to describe how children and their environment shape each other and create a "goodness of fit."

Using the ecological model, explain why the concept "individualism-collectivism" is limited in explaining cultural differences in self-concept.

Proponents of the Big Five personality theory claim that our personality changes in a distinctly universal pattern as we get older. What is this pattern?

Describe temperament, how it is measured, and its major characteristics.

# Developmental Analysis
## Culture, Self, and Personality

As you read in this chapter, temperament, ecological systems, and the developmental niche all seem to be intertwined. This was certainly the case with me. At times, my mother said I was an "easy child" because I was usually happy, outgoing, and slept fairly well. I certainly enjoyed my meals, especially desserts, even as an infant in a high chair. However, I could occasionally be a "difficult child," such as when I would insist on climbing trees and jumping to the ground! My younger sister was more difficult than I was—maybe because she was the middle child—and my brother, the youngest, was more "slow-to-warm-up." It is not unusual for a family to have all these types of children. Just when my husband and I (similar to most parents) thought we had learned all we needed to know about successfully raising children, along came the next one who was so different, in many ways, from the previous child. Maybe this is true in your family, too.

Apparently, as a child, I was determined to establish my own personality. I didn't always conform to the norms in terms of clothes, play activities, and school interests. I felt confident in most of my emerging abilities (e.g., doing math and playing sports) and had a good self-concept—often to the point of being stubborn, especially during my adolescent years. I guess you might say I had high self-efficacy. Although our town didn't have the cultural diversity that many places have today, I found a large part of my cultural and ethnic identity in my Irish background (reflected in my red hair, freckles, and sense of humor).

In terms of personality, I have always tended to be extroverted and outgoing, agreeable and trusting, well-organized, hardworking, and ambitious (as reflected in my career accomplishments), curious, creative, and open to new experiences (demonstrated in my travels and efforts at cooking new foods). I see some of these same personality characteristics in our children and grandchildren.

As I approach the seventh decade of my life, I'm generally happy with the person I have become, and as I look back on my early life, I see the many influences that my family, culture, developmental niche, and unique ecological system had on the development of my self-concept and personality. Maybe I would have changed some things—but not many. It's been a good life so far.

# Chapter 7
# Culture and Social Behavior

*Shula grew up in a kibbutz not far from Haifa, Israel, where she lived with her parents and two siblings. Shortly after she was born, her mother returned to her job on the farm, leaving Shula in the care of the kibbutz day care. At day care, Shula built close relationships with the three or four women who were assigned to take care of her. When she was older, Shula spent her mornings in school and her afternoons at the communal area, where she and the other children played and worked under the supervision of adult kibbutz members. Even though her family expected her to stay in the kibbutz, she could not wait to leave to be on her own. She now attends Ben-Gurion University in Beer-Sheva, where she dedicates most of her time to her studies and her political activities.*

*Manami and her parents live in a small apartment on the outskirts of Sapporo, Japan. Even though her father is an engineer, his salary alone barely supports the family. Manami's mother, Midori, gave up her job as an architect when her daughter was born. As a woman who was raised in a traditional Japanese family, Midori decided it was best to stay at home and raise her daughter herself rather than leaving Manami in the care of someone else. Manami has no siblings, and the first year in school was very difficult for her. She missed the undivided attention of her mother and did not get along well with the other children. After a while she built a circle of friends with whom she stayed close all through college. Now in her early thirties, Manami is an independent woman with a career in the competitive business of real estate.*

Shula's and Manami's social and cultural environments were very different from the day they were born. How did these aspects influence their development as social beings? Did the emphasis on collectivism in the kibbutz instill values such as sharing and cooperation in Shula? How do single children such as Manami fare in a collectivist culture? In this chapter, we examine psychological and cultural factors that influence how people relate to their social environment and develop as social beings.

## 7.1: Ecological Context

The ability to form and maintain social relationships is the glue that binds the ecological system. As such, interactions within those relationships shape the individual

throughout life and set the context for development of pro-social and antisocial behavior patterns.

During the first year of life, children actively begin to explore their environment; their curiosity seems almost limitless. To ensure continued learning and growth, the caregiver must encourage this exploration. At the same time, the child must trust that the caregiver is nearby and provides a safe haven when needed. *The emotional bond between child and caregivers that allows children to feel secure and to know to whom they can turn in threatening situations is known as* **attachment**. Early classic ground-breaking studies with baby monkeys (Harlow & Harlow, 1962; Harlow & Zimmermann, 1959) showed that infant–caregiver attachment goes beyond the fulfillment of physical and security needs. In fact, Harlow and others argue that the social interaction that takes place within a secure infant–caregiver relationship is necessary for the development of healthy social behavior. Early social relationships form the foundation for later positive relationships and feelings of security throughout life. In fact, well into old age, the relationship between well-being and social support appears to be largely universal. Comparisons of diverse cultures show a remarkable similarity in patterns of social support from spouses, relatives, adult children, and friends and their influence on well-being.

As to the importance of cross-cultural research, Judith B. Pena-Shaff (2013) emphasizes that the basic premises of attachment theory are strongly supported by such research, and it verifies ". . . context-specific determinants that are imposed by different environments, developmental niches, and parental ethnotheories" (p. 99).

## 7.2: Infancy

### 7.2.1: Child–Caregiver Relationships and Attachment Patterns

The process of attachment over the first two years appears to be similar across different cultures. It is assumed that children have developed an attachment with their caregiver if they show distress when separated from that person.

Ainsworth and Wittig (1969) are credited with developing a standardized event (the **strange situation**) that makes it possible to observe the type of bond a child has with his or her primary caregiver—most frequently, the mother. In the strange situation, a mother and child are placed together in a room equipped with toys. A stranger enters the room and sits quietly in a chair. The stranger begins a conversation with the mother and after a while slowly approaches the child. The mother leaves the room while the stranger keeps interacting with the child. After a few minutes, the mother returns and reunites with the child, and the stranger leaves the room. Another few minutes pass, and the mother leaves the room again. Shortly thereafter, the stranger reenters and tries to distract the child. Finally, the mother returns and reunites with the child.

The child's responses are recorded at specific times during the situation. How close does the child stay to the mother during the initial period? How does he or she react when approached by a stranger in the presence of the mother? How distressed is the child when the mother leaves the room? How does he or she react when alone with the stranger? Is the child happy when reunited with the mother? Specific responses indicate the type of attachment the child has with the primary caregiver.

Ainsworth, Blehar, Waters, and Wall (1978) and Ainsworth (1982) observed that children could be classified according to three categories of behavior patterns when faced with the strange situation. Children classified as *anxious/avoidant* (20%) will not pay much attention to whether the primary caregiver is absent. If they experience distress, then they may turn to a stranger for comfort. On the mother's return, these children do not actively strive to reunite and be close. Children classified as *anxious/resistant* (10%) tend to stay close to their caregiver and become very distressed when the caregiver leaves the room. Even when comforted after the caregiver's return, these children will take a long time to settle down and remain anxious about the caregiver's whereabouts. Finally, *securely attached* (65%–70%) children will be calm and not threatened by strangers in the presence of the caregiver. When the caregiver departs, the distressed child is unlikely to be comforted by a stranger. When the caregiver returns, the child is eager to reunite and will settle down and relax very quickly. According to Pena-Shaff (2013), secure attachment is not only the most common pattern in U.S. children but also across cultures. However, she also notes that "[a] meta-analysis of 32 studies . . . revealed more intracultural differences than intercultural differences in attachment styles, even among samples in the United States" (p. 97). Therefore, it is important, once again, not to assume that ". . . individual samples in one culture are representative of a particular culture or subculture" (p. 97).

*As you think about these types of attachment, can you recall which might describe your early behavior? What about your younger siblings or cousins? If you have young nieces or nephews or friends with young children, you might observe their behavior and see whether you can classify it according to these categories.*

Research in various cultural settings suggests that secure attachment requires a *"secure base"* represented by a primary caregiver with whom the child feels safe when threatened or stressed (Posada et al., 1995). Second, secure attachment further requires that the primary caregiver is *sensitive to subtleties in the child's behavior and responds accordingly* (Van Ijzendoorn & Sagi, 1999). New mothers, for example, learn quickly to distinguish between their child's angry cry and his or her anxious cry. Third, attachment theorists predict that *securely attached children grow up to become socially competent, securely attached, and emotionally stable adults.* The next section discusses each cross-culturally examined theme in attachment.

## 7.2.2: The Secure-Base Hypothesis

The conditions under which a child experiences his or her first social attachment are often determined by the specific cultural setting. These conditions may influence the relationship between caregiver and child considerably. Two of these conditions involve (1) availability of the primary caregiver and (2) the number of other individuals involved in child care. For example, parents' economic circumstances or the structure of the community may require them to work outside the home, leaving the care of the children to family members or others in the community.

Sagi (1990) speculates that the high rate of insecurely attached children in an Israeli kibbutz may be a result of the specific child-rearing arrangements. For example, caregivers in the kibbutz (metaplot) are often assigned to work with three or more infants during the day, while all of the infants are watched by a single caregiver at night (in kibbutzim with communal sleeping arrangements). Sagi argues that this "multiple mothering" leads to inconsistencies in maternal behavior and may result in different (possibly less secure) attachment patterns.

Tronick, Morelli, and Ivey (1992) describe the child-rearing arrangement among the Efe in Zaire. Here, children also enjoy multiple social relationships with other children and adults. However, particularly during the first year, the mother is involved in more than half of the child's social activities. This also means that children spend half of their time with individuals other than their mothers. For example, during the time the mother works away from the camp, her child is left in the exclusive care of other adults or older children. Even when the mother is present, other family members, the children's peers, or other adults are continually engaged in social interactions with the child. In fact, the authors point out that at a given time about ten people are within sight or close hearing range of the child. Unfortunately, there are no data available from this culture describing specific attachment patterns resulting either from these continuous multiple relationships with others or from the close relationship with the mother, although Bailey (1985) indicates that strong father–child attachments were uncommon. However, the authors suggest that the children benefit from this setting in that they develop a multitude of social skills early in life; this leads to better adjustment in social situations later on.

Similarly, Indonesian children enjoy much attention not only from their mother but also from their older siblings. For example, Farver and Wimbarti (1995) found that mothers and older siblings engage in different types of play behavior with young children. In particular, older siblings were more active play partners and facilitated pretend play more often than mothers, thus adding an important dimension of social interaction to the young child's microsystem.

In other settings, mothers keep their infants with them during work. Women in Indonesia, for example, systematically adjust their work patterns to accommodate their children. As we noted previously, several North American Indian societies use the cradleboard (see photo of a Hopi Indian child strapped to a cradleboard in Chapter 3). Niethammer (1977) has written that "all [cradle boards] provide a firm, protective frame on which babies felt snug and secure. A baby in a cradle board could be propped up or even hung in a tree so it could see what was going on and feel part of family activities. After spending much time in their cradle board, Indian children became very attached to them. One Apache mother related that whenever her toddler son was tired or upset he would go and get his cradle board and walk around with it on his back" (p. 15).

Similarly, the Quechua use a **manta pouch** to carry their infants. This is a *backpacklike device that protects the infant from the harsh elements in the Peruvian mountains and provides a secure environment close to the mother.* These and similar devices allow parents to keep their infants near them and to provide the necessary restraint so children's physical activity does not interfere with the mother's work. Today, the use of such baby pouches is a common sight throughout the world, and they are used by mothers and fathers alike. *Did your mother or father use a baby pouch or "sling" with you and/or your siblings when young? If you are a parent, do you use one?*

In conclusion, a "secure base" for healthy attachment may express itself in different ways, depending on the general child care arrangements that are part of the macro- or mesosystems in a child's ecological environment. In setting the stage for the microlevel aspects of parent–child

A Peruvian mother uses a manta pouch to keep her infant near her.

(Kovgabor/Shutterstock)

interactions, the "secure base" is crucial in the development of social relationships and behavior in early childhood.

## 7.2.3: The Sensitivity Hypothesis

Both the infant and the caregiver bring certain characteristics to the caregiver–infant relationship that become a crucial part of the ecological system in which the child grows up. This happens when some of the behaviors and characteristics of the mother (or father) interact with the characteristics of the child to create a unique developmental niche. For example, Richman, Miller, and LeVine (1992) studied the behaviors Mexican mothers showed in response to their infant's distress signals—crying and worried facial expressions. One factor that influenced mothers' responsiveness was their level of education. Mothers with more schooling tended to respond with more talking and facial expressions than mothers with less schooling, who tended to hold their infants more. In explaining these findings, the researchers pointed to earlier research suggesting that mothers with more education generally tend to initiate more verbal interaction with children.

Caregivers also bring their unique cultural beliefs about parenting to the relationship. These beliefs may be culturally influenced and also based on the caregiver's unique experiences. For example, Grossman, Wirt, and Davids (1985) noticed that mothers in their German sample appeared quite unresponsive to their children's crying. Closer observations revealed that this behavior resulted from a shared cultural belief that infants should become independent at an early age and learn that they cannot rely on the mother's comfort at all times. In contrast, traditional Japanese mothers instill a strong sense of dependence or interdependence in their young children by being available at all times. These cultural variations in sensitivity to children's behavior illustrate that although sensitivity may be a universal requirement for secure attachment, the specific ecological systems define the appropriate "sensitive response."

## 7.2.4: Moderators of Attachment and Social Development

What about the assertion (made previously in this chapter) that secure attachment in infancy is necessary for the development of secure attachment patterns over time and competent social behavior?

Much of attachment research over the years supports this claim. Attachment patterns can be stable over long periods of time. This means that a child who is securely attached in infancy is likely to show secure attachment patterns through adolescence and early adulthood (Thompson, 2016). Also, children with secure attachment patterns have higher self-esteem and are more competent in social interactions (Morelli & Rothbaum, 2007). But, again, the relationship is not linear. The following examples illustrate how ecological factors influence the development of attachment over time and across cultures.

Children who experience prolonged social deprivation may reach a point where it becomes difficult to establish secure or even meaningful relationships with others. O'Connor and colleagues (2003) studied Romanian children who spent much of their infancy and childhood in Romanian orphanages. Many of the children who had spent more than six months in an orphanage showed very inconsistent attachment behavior with their new adoptive families. These behaviors ranged from indiscriminant attachment to frequent switching between friendliness and suspicion. In this case, the changes in the children's ecological system result in adverse changes in attachment and social development.

Sharma and Sharma (1999) reviewed studies of children (ages five to eighteen) in India. These studies included street and working children; school dropouts; children of parents with disabilities; children in single-parent families; and children with disabilities, low birth weights, or chronic disease. All of these children in "difficult circumstances" were deemed at risk for psychological and social maladjustment. The researchers also conclude that "at risk" children who were "nestled or vicariously encircled in their family network, seemed to be coping and getting ahead" (p. 412). Although "at risk" from the outside, these children seemed to experience a resilience within their developmental niche that allowed them to develop and maintain a secure attachment, fostering healthy social and psychological development over time.

There is also evidence that broad cultural patterns of individualism/collectivism foster different social

competencies. For example, secure attachment in Japanese culture leads to interdependent social relationships, adherence to social norms, and self-esteem based on other's approval. In Western cultures, secure attachment patterns are more likely associated with autonomy, self-reliance, and self-esteem based on personal competency, reflecting individualistic values (Cheng & Kwan, 2008; Morelli & Rothbaum, 2007). Children expressing these social behaviors are considered healthy and competent in their own respective cultures, but not necessarily in another.

# 7.3: Childhood

When children pass the stage of infancy, they begin to develop social relationships that extend beyond caregivers and the family context, even though the family remains very important. These relationships include children in the immediate neighborhood or at school and frequently become quite complex and multifaceted. We refer to these expanding relationships as children's peer culture. A **peer** is a person of one's own age or status, that is, an equal.

## 7.3.1: Peer Culture and Social Relationships

In their review of relevant research, Corsaro and Eder (1990) identify three central themes that characterize peer culture from early childhood to adolescence. These include (1) dealing with confusion, concerns, fears, and conflicts; (2) resisting and challenging adult rules and authority; and (3) sharing and social participation.

**DEALING WITH CONFUSION, CONCERNS, FEARS, AND CONFLICTS** In the company of their peers, children learn to cope with everyday conflicts and fears through fantasy play (e.g., role playing the defeat of a monster). Children also engage in fantasy play to deal with anxiety and violence. For example, children in several South African communities, where daily life was often interrupted by riots or police raids, played out the violence and aggression they saw around them. Kostelny and Garbarino (1994) explored the drawings of Palestinian children living in Israeli-occupied territories. The drawings of the five- to eight-year-olds frequently showed themes of victimization (e.g., large soldiers with guns threatening small children).

**RESISTING AND CHALLENGING ADULT RULES AND AUTHORITY** Corsaro and Eder (1990) maintain that challenging adult rules serves to establish a sense of independence from parents. At the same time, children strengthen their peer group identity by developing rituals and routines that make fun of adult authority or challenge adult rules. Corsaro (1988) observed frequent violations of Italian and American nursery school rules prohibiting children from bringing toys from home to school. Children attempted to break this rule by bringing in concealed toys or candy, which were then shared with other children who gladly became coconspirators in the violation. Similarly, Marshall (1976) describes a game called "frogs" played by !Kung children. In this game, one participant poses as the "mother," and the others are the "children." While the "mother" pretends to prepare "frogs" as food, the "children" openly refuse to perform tasks, disobey the orders of the "mother," steal the frogs and hide them, and so on. The game ends by the mother chasing the children, who run away in all directions in an effort to avoid being caught.

Aside from challenging rules and authority, it is through games and play that children come to understand concepts of both creating and enforcing rules and cheating and breaking rules. Schwartzman (1983) provides a thoughtful analysis of the socializing function of children's play and includes examples of children in the kibbutz, Australian Aborigine children, Kpelle children in Liberia, and several more.

**SHARING AND SOCIAL PARTICIPATION**  As they get older, children begin to seek the company of other children and enjoy social activities. In interaction with other children and without the presence of adults, they acquire a sense of **cooperation** and sharing. One of the most important settings in which social interaction takes place is that of play and games, which represent a crucial element of the ecological system during childhood. Games such as tag, hopscotch, and jacks, as well as soccer and baseball, are played in similar forms in many cultures. These games facilitate taking turns, cooperation, and negotiation, yet the rules or content may vary with different contexts. Unfortunately, these social interactive games, which also provide exercise, are being rapidly replaced by children—of all ages—spending increasing amounts of time playing solitary games on smart phones, computers, iPads, and other electronic devices. Children in the United States may play soccer (what most of the world refers to as football) in an organized league governed by adults and consisting of set teams, coaches, scheduled match play, and so on. Soccer may also be played without adult participation and with makeshift goals and changing teams in a back alley of São Paulo, Brazil, or in a farmer's field in Nigeria. The social interactions taking place in each of these settings may be quite different. For example, organized sports and games tend to focus on competition, achievement, rules, and success, whereas free play activities tend to focus on participation, equality of players, and adapting or creating

rules to ensure everyone's enjoyment of the game. *What games and sports did you play when you were young? What did you particularly like about each of these? Did your younger or older siblings like the same or different games and sports? Do you believe children play fewer sports today than when you were young?*

Games and play also introduce children to concepts of competition and differential status. Observers of children's peer culture have noted the cultural variation in competitiveness and cooperation in children's play. For example, children in North America generally appear to be more competitive than children in many other societies. However, Domino (1992) found Chinese children to be more concerned than American children about group accomplishment. In this study, children were asked to complete a task in which tokens could be exchanged for various prizes. Depending on the task, tokens could be obtained by working alone or collaboratively. Most of the American children preferred to work individually, trying to accumulate as many tokens as possible for themselves. Chinese children tended to adopt strategies that emphasized collaboration with others rather than individual success.

In another example, Sparkes (1991) used a dyadic (two-person) marble game in which children had the choice to play cooperatively or to compete with each other. Findings showed that Chinese children were more competitive in this situation than American children in the comparison group. Sparkes points out that these differences may be due to the different teaching styles practiced in these cultures. She suggests that the Chinese emphasis on teacher-directed, large-group activities leaves little room for dyadic interactions. As a result, Chinese youngsters may have less experience in negotiating roles and taking turns with a partner. These selected examples demonstrate that cultural differences or similarities in competitive and cooperative behavior may depend on the definition of these concepts and the specific context in which the behavior takes place.

Studies in Africa provide additional cues for environmental factors that may influence cooperative and competitive behavior. Friedman, Todd, and Kariuki (1995) studied 120 Kenyan children from different backgrounds (a middle-class Westernized suburb of Nairobi, poor semiurban Kikuyu, and a poor rural mission village). Results showed that middle-class children behaved competitively, even when cooperation was the most adaptive strategy. Surprisingly, rural children also engaged in competitive behavior. Poor semiurban children from Kikuyu were the most cooperative of all groups. One could speculate that the degree of Westernization corresponds to the degree of individualism found in these settings (i.e., the more individualistic the environment, the greater the emphasis on competition).

The use of the individualism-collectivism dimension as an explanation for cultural differences in competitiveness has sometimes been criticized. As an alternative, Searle-White (1996) proposes a Vygotskian approach. As you may recall from the previous discussion, this framework emphasizes socialization and language as "psychological tools" for mental growth and development. Depending on how these tools are used, children and adults view themselves as being at a point along a continuum of interdependence, where cooperation reflects, in part, the inclination to stay socially connected to others.

This view fits in nicely with our themes of the developmental niche and the ecological systems approach. When children cooperate with others, they work within their developmental niche and recognize that they are interconnected with others. Likewise, in terms of Bronfenbrenner's model, the child interacts with other people within his or her microsystem. At first, this system may be small, involving just a few caregivers. However, as children get older, they do more things with others, expanding their social world. As they become socialized within the mesosystem of the school and the neighborhood, they recognize the benefits of working together to accomplish their academic and personal goals. They learn the rules of cooperative play and practice social behaviors. Later, as children express the cultural values of cooperation and interdependence through language and social behavior, they begin operating within the cultural context of the macrosystem.

Although the topic of play has been studied by some of the most notable researchers in psychology (Piaget, Vygotsky, Bruner, Suomi, and Sutton-Smith), it has not become a centrally important topic in child development. In an effort to change that, Anthony Pellegrini (2015), an expert on play, who has studied the topic for more than thirty years, has prepared a handbook that presents an interdisciplinary guide from a variety of viewpoints (psychology, anthropology, education, history, and evolutionary biology) addressing its definition and theory, methodology, and educational implications for learning and policy. He notes that in terms of theory, Piaget and Vygotsky have had the most influence on the topic for developmental psychologists although their generalizations about play were not rigorously studied and were based only on the children around them (e.g., Piaget's observations of his own two children). Another book (Roopnarine, Patte, Johnson, & Kuschner, 2015) provides an analysis and international perspective on children's play in cultures as diverse as Brazil, Mexico, Australia, Turkey, Sweden, and Estonia, and among Native Americans.

## 7.3.2: Moral Development and Prosocial Orientation

With increased social participation in early childhood, children begin to understand how to relate to others in socially desirable ways. As they acquire the foundations of moral

reasoning and behavior, they begin to understand concepts such as "right" and "wrong." Developmental psychologists have proposed that moral development progresses in stages, with each stage representing more mature reasoning about moral thought and conduct. [For a comprehensive review of moral development, see Vozzola (2014) in the Further Readings section at the end of this book.]

Kohlberg's theory of moral development was introduced in Chapter 2. Morality is generally understood as being two dimensional—one dimension describing "prosocial" judgments, actions, and behaviors that benefit others, including helping, sharing, or comforting, and the second dimension describing judgments, actions, and behaviors that may result in negative consequences for another person or persons. Aggression is considered an expression of this "antisocial" dimension of morality. The next two sections consider ecological systems and how they relate to prosocial and antisocial morality, particularly with regard to culture.

## 7.3.3: Cultural Influences on Caring and Justice Orientation

Kohlberg's definition and assessment of moral reasoning is not accepted by everyone and has been challenged by several researchers (Eckensberger, 1994; Shweder, Mahapatra, & Miller, 1987; Snarey, 1985). In fact, a number of studies suggest that individuals in many non-European cultures, as well as women, exhibit moral reasoning equivalent to that of an adolescent in Kohlbergian terms. Critics argue that an Anglo male bias is built into the model because the highest level of moral development is based on interviews with a 1960s sample of Harvard male undergraduates. In addition, the hypothetical moral dilemmas Kohlberg created to elicit moral reasoning responses and the scoring of the responses may also be culturally biased. Carol Gilligan (1982) specifically pointed to the gender bias in Kohlberg's theory. In her own research, she learned that women's moral thought is *guided by caring and maintaining the welfare of others,* whereas men emphasize *more abstract principles of justice.* Gilligan concludes that women develop a different kind of morality altogether, due to their different socialization. Stack (1974) found a similar **caring orientation** (as opposed to a **justice orientation**) described as "what goes around comes around" in a Midwestern African American community.

Different socialization, parental beliefs, and customs of child care—that is, different aspects of the developmental niche—may explain many research findings in the cultural domain. For example, studies of Buddhist monks showed that young adolescent monks reasoned at stage 2 and even mature adults barely reached stage 4 in Kohlberg's schema (Huebner & Garrod, 1993). Can we conclude that the monks' moral reasoning is less highly developed compared with Western adolescent males? Huebner and Garrod argue that Kohlberg's model is only partially applicable in this context because the Buddhist conception of morality is different than the Western, Christian, liberal democratic view inherent in Kohlberg's theory.

According to the authors, the ideal moral person from a Western perspective is an autonomous individual with strong convictions who stands up for his or her own, as well as others', rights. He or she is an influential individual who uses his or her power to influence others in a "good" way. In contrast, among Buddhists, ideal moral individuals are those who are ultimately connected (to others, the environment, the cosmos) through their compassion and detachment from their own individuality. Buddhist morality is characterized by an understanding of interconnectedness and interdependence and is more reminiscent of Gilligan's caring orientation than Kohlberg's justice orientation.

In a comparative study of adolescents from China, Hong Kong, and England, both Chinese samples showed a stronger orientation toward abiding by the law, as well as being altruistic or affective toward others (Ma, 1989). Ma concludes that this cultural difference may result from the Chinese practice of rearing their children in a more authoritative manner than the English, encouraging them to obey authority and follow norms. At the same time, Chinese cultural values are inherently collectivist, emphasizing human relationships and interdependence.

This discussion of various cultural influences on aspects of moral reasoning demonstrates that moral development may not strictly follow a universal psychological script, as suggested by Kohlberg. Instead, the ecological system in which early social participation takes place shapes individual development of moral thought and behavior.

## 7.3.4: Cultural Influences on Distributive Justice

On the basis of Kohlberg's broad model of moral reasoning, Damon (1973) focused specifically on children's understanding of one aspect of moral reasoning that has important implications for the development of social judgment and social behaviors, namely, **distributive justice—** *the judgment of what constitutes criteria for the fair distribution of goods and resources in society.* Damon presented children ranging in age from four to ten with hypothetical dilemmas that involved the distribution of goods. For example, a school class of children sold their paintings at a fair. How should the earnings be distributed among the children? The answers (e.g., the child who made the most paintings should get the most money) along with the reasoning for the answer (e.g., he or she worked hard and deserves the money) led Damon to propose six levels of distributive justice reasoning development, which occur from early to middle childhood. These are presented in Table 7.1.

**Table 7.1** Damon's Six Levels of Distributive Justice Reasoning Development

| Developmental Level | Reasoning for Distribution of Resources |
|---|---|
| 0-A | The mere expression of a wish: Whoever wants it most gets it. |
| 0-B | External characteristics such as size or age: Whoever is older or bigger gets the most. |
| 1-A | Strict equality regardless of other attributes or actions: Everyone gets the same. |
| 1-B | Reciprocity of behavior or actions: Whoever works hardest gets the most. |
| 2-A | Psychological or material need: Whoever needs it most gets the most. |
| 2-B | Compromise between need and equality: Everyone should get what he or she deserves, which may differ by person or situation. |

The two central concepts in Damon's model, reciprocity and equality, are also conceptualized differently depending on cultural context. In Damon's model, mature reasoning about the just distribution of goods and resources in society is guided by two principles: equality and reciprocity. Equality refers to the judgment that people are equally deserving of receiving resources and goods. Reciprocity refers to the reception of resources either in exchange for a behavior (e.g., work) or to meet a need. At the most mature level of reasoning, children are able to take both equality and reciprocity into account when making judgments about the fair distribution of resources. For example, in India, exchanging helping behavior for money is considered a personal choice, but exchanging helping behavior for previous helping behavior is a social obligation. In contrast, either type of reciprocity is considered a personal choice in the United States.

On the basis of these differences in ecological systems, it would be easy to assume that developmental patterns of distributive justice reasoning may also vary for children in different cultures. Surprisingly, studies in Japan, Sweden, Germany, and the United States indicate that children show similar patterns of distributive justice reasoning, corresponding to Damon's developmental model (Eisenberg, Boehnke, Schuhler, & Silbereisen, 1985; Watanabe, 1986). Other researchers found distinct patterns of distributive justice reasoning in India and Japan, both considered more collectivistic cultures. They found that distributive justice reasoning was guided by equality and need (Krishnan, 1997; Naito, 1994). Even though the results are mixed, differences in ecological systems deserve consideration as a possible explanation for differences in moral reasoning development. For example, Krishnan (1999) proposes an adapted model for distributive justice development, a model that explicitly includes the influence of cultural factors through socialization. (See Figure 7.1.)

**Figure 7.1** Proposed Model for the Influences of Culture, Socialization, and Development on Distributive Justice Reasoning

**SOURCE:** Based on material from "Socialization and Cognitive moral Influences on Justice Rule Preferences: The Case of Indian Culture" by L. Krishman in Culture, Socialization and Human Development: Theory, Research, and Applications in India, T. S. Saraswathi (Ed.), 1999. Thousand Oaks, CA: Sage Publications, © Harry Gardiner.

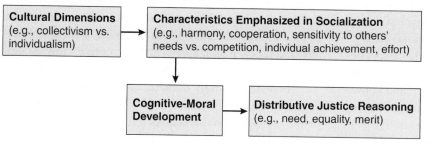

As Takashi Naito (2013) has pointed out that ". . . moral experiences in all cultures are changing with globalization. In the past, people typically experienced moral problems and resolved them based on their cultural values. However, currently people in all cultures have moral development tasks in their lives, demanding resolution of conflicts based on shared concepts, eventually with other cultures" (p. 896).

## 7.3.5: Aggression

Most children in most cultures fight, argue, or aggress against one another (peers or siblings) and against adults (especially parents) at some time during the years of childhood. Learning the differences between appropriate and inappropriate behavior and how to handle hostility and aggression fall within the social realm.

Let us begin by distinguishing between two often misunderstood terms that are frequently used incorrectly to mean the same thing. **Hostility** is *a motive or desire to cause damage or injury*. If someone calls me a name or insults me, then I may want to strike back by returning the insult or by taking something away from that person. I am experiencing hostility. **Aggression**, however, is *an overt action or behavior intended to cause harm, damage, or injury*. If I follow through on my hostile motive and actually use an insult, hit the person, or take something away, then I am acting aggressively.

The form and extent to which such intentions and actions are exhibited depends on many factors, including culture and gender. Research generally shows boys, in most cultures, exhibiting more aggression than girls. Although there is not a great deal of agreement as to why this may be the case, socialization plays a major role, and differences appear to become particularly noticeable between the ages of two and three. An observed increase in aggressive behavior among boys and a corresponding decrease among girls may be related to a greater awareness of one's gender role and a culture's rules regarding the expression of this behavior. (See Chapter 8 for a detailed discussion of the relationship between gender and the development of aggression.)

What causes a particular child to be aggressive? We wish there were a simple answer to this question, but none seems readily available. Some say the cause lies in the evolution of the human species; others, in a child's models (siblings, peers, parents, and the media); still others, in the methods by which one's culture rewards or punishes the expression of aggression. We would certainly agree with Cole and Cole (2001), who suggest that social stressors and ecological factors contribute to some of the individual differences observed in aggressive behavior. Rather than attempting to do what others have been unable to do (adequately explain the causes of childhood aggression), we would prefer to view the topic within a cross-cultural context and discuss similarities and differences across cultures with some detailed illustrations.

Bourguignon (1979) gives an example of two children, a girl of seven or eight and a boy of about six, walking along a path in the mountains of Haiti. The girl is hitting the boy and calling him names. He complains loudly but makes no effort to hit back. Why? We learn that the girl's mother has put her in charge of her younger brother and, modeling her mother's behavior, she is punishing him for being disobedient. Bourguignon explains, "We are dealing with an example of child socialization. Children are beaten to enforce obedience toward elders, a central concern in this society. . . . Haitian society is based on a hierarchy of age and . . . places less stress on differences in sex" (p. 3). The girl is older and so her brother must obey her and pay her respect. She is permitted to hit him, if necessary, to discipline him, and he is not allowed to hit back. In another example, Bourguignon describes a quarrel between two boys in a village in southern France, who are seen insulting and threatening each other. One boy hits the other and then runs away, but is not chased. According to Wylie (1974), who studied the village in which this incident occurred, "If two children start to fight they are immediately separated by any adult who may happen to witness the scene. . . . If it is relatives who separate fighting children, both children are punished. No inquiry is made into the question of which child started the fight or which was in the right. They are both fighting and consequently they are both guilty" (pp. 49–50). Wylie further notes that although French parents discourage physical aggression, they do permit verbal aggression (e.g., insults) as a socially accepted way to deal with anger. According to Bourguignon (1979), adults tend to model this behavior and may themselves "on occasion make a great public show of anger in words and threats, but physical fighting is said to be rare" (p. 2). Researchers have found that children from Sweden, Germany, Indonesia, and the United States differ in their use of aggressive contents when telling stories. For example, stories told by North American children include more aggressive words, aggressive content, unfriendly characters, and aggressive situations compared to those told by children from the other countries studied. The authors suggest that the content of the children's narratives mirrors their experience with and knowledge of aggression in their respective cultures (Farver, Welles-Nyström, Frosch, Wimbarti, & Hoppe-Graff, 1997).

As these examples illustrate, there are certainly considerable cross-cultural differences in the amount of aggressiveness various societies tolerate, first among its young people and later among its adult members. With some effort, it would be possible to draw a continuum with the least aggressive cultures on one end and the most aggressive on the other. Among the least aggressive would be the Inuit of the North American Arctic, the Pygmies of Africa, and the characteristically tranquil and polite Amerindian tribes of Zuni and Blackfoot (Moghaddam, Taylor, & Wright, 1993). At the other end would have to be the Yanomamo, living in the Amazon region of Brazil and Venezuela, often described in anthropological literature as the "most fierce and violent people in the world."

According to Chagnon (1997, 2012, 2013), who was the first anthropologist to report on Yanomamo society and who continued to research their behavior for more than thirty years, aggressiveness is the major determinant of status within the group, and learning the aggressive ways of the society begins at an early age. He relates an example involving a four-year-old boy named Ariwari, whose father encourages him to "beat him on the face and head to express his anger and temper, laughing and commenting on his ferocity. . . . He has already learned that the appropriate response to a flash of anger is to strike someone with his hand or with an object, and it is not uncommon for him to give his father a healthy smack in the face whenever something displeases him [and he is] . . . rewarded by gleeful cheers of assent from his mother and from the other adults in the household" (p. 127).

Why are the Yanomamo so aggressive? According to Chagnon (1997), a great deal of conflict, aggression, and fighting centers around sex, infidelity or suspicion of infidelity, failure to deliver to a suitor a promised wife, revenge, accusations of sorcery, or "harmful magic that 'causes' death" (p. 97).

In contrast, Ember and Ember (2003) cite an example from the Semai of central Malaya, a group known for its timidity, who say, "We do not get angry." The Semai raise their children to be nonviolent and, on the rare occasion that one of them may show anger, do not use physical punishment. With this kind of socialization, children are seldom exposed to aggressive models and, as a result, have no aggressive behavior to imitate. Robarchek and Robarchek (1998) have compared the Semai, one of the world's most peaceful cultures, with the Waorani of Amazonian Ecuador, another of the world's most violent societies. The study is worth noting, especially because the two cultures are similar in their ecological contexts, ways of living, level of technology, and social organization; yet, their attitudes toward violence and their patterns of behavior are at opposite extremes.

There are a variety of methods for evaluating aggression cross culturally. It can be done on the individual level or the cross-national level. As Jennifer Zwolinski (2013) notes, whatever approach one takes to study it, researchers ". . . should be familiar with basic norms for aggression and violence, coping strategies and behaviors, gender roles, and the influence of spirituality and religion in the individual's culture" (p. 36).

**BULLYING**   It is estimated that between 5% and 45% of children worldwide are victimized by ongoing aggressive peer behavior, also described as "bullying" (Pepler et al., 2004). Among the first countries to draw attention to the prevalence and negative effects of bullying was Japan. According to a survey by the Ministry of Education, Culture, Sports, Science and Technology (2006), there were 124,898 reported cases of bullying in Japanese schools: 51,310 cases at junior high schools, 12,307 at high schools, and 384 at special education schools. Most of the bullying took place in primary schools, with 60,897 cases.

This particular pattern of childhood aggression can take on many forms: (1) verbal bullying, including derogatory comments and bad names; (2) bullying through social exclusion or isolation; (3) physical bullying such as hitting, kicking, shoving, and spitting; (4) bullying through lies and false rumors; (5) having money or other things taken or damaged by students who bully; (6) being threatened or being forced to do things by students who bully; (7) racial bullying; (8) sexual bullying; and (9) cyberbullying (via cell phone, Internet, or social media). [Note: The U.S. government has established a website devoted to this topic: http://www.stopbullying.gov/.]

Bullying has detrimental effects on both the bully and the victim, and it has become a prominent concern for teachers, parents, and health professionals in cultures around the world. Victims of peer aggression are susceptible to depression, stress-related illnesses, poor academic performance, and suicide. The aggressor is more likely to drop out of school and engage in drug abuse and criminal activities. Compared to other children, bullies are also at a higher risk for suicide (Kim & Leventhal, 2008). Cyberbullying received worldwide attention with the 2006 suicide by hanging of thirteen-year-old Megan Meier, an American adolescent from Missouri. Her suicide was attributed to cyberbullying on the social networking website MySpace through an account supposedly belonging to a sixteen-year-old male named Josh Evans. In reality, a woman named Lori Drew, the mother of a former friend of Megan, confessed that she and her daughter had created the false account to use Megan's exchange of e-mails with Josh to obtain information about her and then used that information to humiliate her for allegedly spreading gossip about her daughter. Two years later, a federal grand jury indicted Drew on three counts of accessing protected computers without authorization to obtain information to inflict emotional distress and one count of criminal conspiracy. Although Drew was indicted and convicted in 2008 of violations of the Computer Fraud and Abuse Act, an act passed by Congress in 1986, her conviction was reversed on appeal in 2009. However, as a result of the case, several states began consideration of legislation to prohibit harassment over the Internet.

Unfortunately, none of this helped Phoebe Prince, a fifteen-year-old high school student in Massachusetts, who committed suicide in January 2010 after several fellow students inflicted on her *all eight forms of childhood aggression* mentioned here over several months. Six of these students were charged with bullying, involving taunting and harassment via the Internet and textual messaging, statutory rape, and violation of civil rights with bodily injury. They could have faced as much as ten years in prison if convicted. Sadly, their punishment was nearly meaningless. Three of the eighteen-year-olds received probation until their nineteenth birthdays and were required to perform 100 hours of community service, whereas two others only faced probation for one year.

We hope, after reading these examples, you are able to see how one's unique developmental niche and place within a culture's ecological system helps determine the definition and expression of aggressive behavior. It is only by looking at a topic like this from a cross-cultural and developmental perspective that the richness and diversity of human behavior can be fully observed. For an especially useful discussion and approach to studying aggression within a cross-cultural framework, see Chapter 9 in the book by Segall, Dasen, Berry, and Poortinga (1999).

In the lead article of a most important recent special issue of the *American Psychologist*, Hymel and Swearer (2015) review four decades of research on bullying. Their review provides a current understanding of the complexity of the problem, as well as future directions for research and approaches for intervention. Other articles in this special issue address long-term adult outcomes of peer victimization and pathways to adjustment and maladjustment, the development of prevention programs that improve bullying-related outcomes for young people, and a proposal of a social-ecological model for understanding the bullying dynamic and its impact.

# 7.4: Adolescence

## 7.4.1: Family and Peer Influences on Adolescent Social Behavior

As Brown, Greve, and deGuzman (2013) point out, ". . . two theoretical perspectives have driven research in peer relationships cross-culturally" (p. 987). These perspectives are very familiar to us. The first is Bronfenbrenner's ecological theory, which we have learned focuses on culture as a context for an individual's development. Because peer relationships act as a social setting, it is not surprising that children's behaviors reflect their cultural beliefs. The second theoretical perspective is that of Vygotsky, which ". . . focuses on transmission of culture from the social level to the psychological level . . . through guided development with more experienced peers and adults . . ." (p. 987).

Although parents and family continue to play a central role in the lives of young adults, the importance of the **peer group**, *individuals who share certain characteristics (e.g., background, age, status, class) and interact on generally equal terms,* increases considerably during adolescence. Adolescents look to their parents and other adults as models for adult roles and behavior. They look to their peers for opinions, lifestyles, and experiences that are different from those to which they have been exposed through their families. However, adolescents in different cultures seem to perceive their social networks quite differently. A comparison of adolescents in Zimbabwe and the United States showed that parents and friends have different functions in the two cultures (Harrison, Stewart, Myambo, & Teveraishe, 1995). In Zimbabwe, adolescents consider adults (including extended family and teachers) both as mentors and disciplinarians, whereas American youths perceive their relatives as primarily providers of emotional support. Second, Zimbabwean young people feel closer to their siblings, relatives, teachers, and fathers than do Americans, who feel closer to their friends. Finally, African adolescents experience more conflict with their teachers and best friends, whereas American adolescents struggle more with their mothers, fathers, and relatives.

Findings such as these indicate that both parents and peers have a strong influence on the prosocial and antisocial behavior of adolescents, although this influence may vary from culture to culture. For example, the strong orientation toward family among traditional Puerto Rican male adolescents appears to lower their likelihood of engaging in interpersonal violence and illicit drug use (Sommers, Fagan, & Baskin, 1993). In contrast, young men who have acculturated to the majority culture in the United States are more likely to show violent behavior.

There is also some evidence that parental attitudes are related to adolescents' choice of peers. In their study of

European American adolescents, Durbin, Darling, Steinberg, and Brown (1993) found that adolescents with authoritative parents tended to choose peer groups that conformed to the norms their parents valued. For example, these young people gravitated either to groups known as "brains" (the smart students), "populars" (socially active students), or "jocks" (student athletes), depending on parental values. Adolescents from households in which parents were not demanding and less attentive were more likely to engage with peers who did not endorse adult values (e.g., "druggies" or "partiers"). Smith and Blinn Pike (1994) also observed a relationship between social contact and the self-image and attitudes of Jamaican adolescents. Adolescents had stronger overall family relationships, were better adjusted, and had more positive career goals when they chose adults as their socializing partners, compared with adolescents who socialized primarily with their peers.

Parents' attitudes toward drugs and their own use of drugs and alcohol, as well as parent–child communication, were among the strongest predictors for the use of tobacco, alcohol, and other drugs among Spanish adolescents. Recio Adrados (1995) argues that parents and friends act as role models and that their use of and attitudes toward drugs and their relationships with the adolescents predicted drug use by adolescents.

However, peer group influence does not always facilitate delinquent behavior. Although antagonistic friendships frequently foster antisocial behavior, friendships characterized by closeness and prosocial behavior tend to facilitate social adjustment. In particular, peer groups provide social support in achieving social competence. For example, one study demonstrated that Costa Rican peer groups emphasize the generally cooperative and collectivist social attitudes necessary for functioning in the larger society (DeRosier & Kupersmidt, 1991). In contrast, American adolescents often stress the importance of having one "best" friend among peers, reflecting the cultural importance of individuality. *Do you have a "best friend"? How long has this person been your friend? Do you find it easy to make new friends?*

Clearly, young people's cultural definitions of acceptable and unacceptable relationships may sometimes lead to difficulties. Roberts (1994) describes the dilemma African American men experience. The dominant Euro-American culture defines male styles of relating to each other, disregarding the cultural context of relationships experienced by African American men. The white American relationship between men is typically highly competitive, as well as characterized by power and control and a lack of emotion, trust, and connectedness. In contrast, the African American mode of relating emphasizes interconnectedness, caring, and the importance of community over individual needs. Roberts asserts that African

American men must try to integrate two models of relationships that at times are quite incompatible. As a result, their relationships with male (and female) peers are often difficult and fail to provide much-needed social support. Roberts states, "It would seem that the statement 'like a brother' reflects a common expectation among Black men that their relationships with other men reflect the trust, caring, openness, and honesty associated with one's brother. Unfortunately, the majority of the evidence suggests that Black men are not getting (or giving) what they desire and expect in relating to each other" (pp. 387–388).

### Points to Ponder

**The Influence of Peers**

We can think of a *peer* as a person of one's own (or similar) age (likely not more than five years older or younger) or status. A *peer group* consists of a number of individuals having some quality in common (e.g., attending the same school, being in the same work or social group). It is generally a stable group of individuals who interact and share common goals and values, and whose behavior is governed by mutually agreed-on rules. We frequently become members of peer groups when we are children (neighborhood, playground), find their influences greatest during the adolescent years (consider what you have just read), join college or career peer groups in adulthood, and even continue in different peer groups in our later years. Think about the peer groups in which you have been a member. How are they different or similar? Which are you in now? Ask some older people whether peers are important to them now. Observe individuals of different ages and determine whether you think peers are important to them. Visit a senior center and ask members if they have peers and what role they play in their lives. Talk with international students about the influence of peers and parents in their lives—here and in their native culture.

## 7.4.2: Cultural Influences on Adolescent Social Behavior

Arnett (1992, 2004, 2006, 2012) suggests a theoretical framework that is helpful in understanding why adolescent behavior is judged so differently in different cultures. He suggests that the socialization of adolescents is largely influenced by factors other than family and peers within the microsystem. The larger cultural influences include school, community, legal system, cultural beliefs, and the media (meso-, exo-, and macrosystems). According to Arnett, some cultures are characterized by **broad socialization** in which *independence and free self-expression are more highly valued than conformity.* Cultures such as these have no commonly accepted belief systems that judge right and wrong behavior, and deviations from cultural expectations are not severely punished. In these cultures, the range of behavior that falls within the norm is much greater than in so-called **narrow socialization** cultures. The latter clearly *prescribe an ideology that strictly sets forth the basis for right and wrong behavior.* These cultures value conformity and adherence to the standards of the community rather than autonomy, and severely punish deviations from community norms.

Arnett's framework is useful in explaining why behaviors considered delinquent in one society are merely frowned on or even acceptable in others. For example, drinking is unacceptable for adolescents in many kibbutzim in Israel, with the exception of some Jewish festivities, during which moderate alcohol consumption is allowed. In contrast, the attitude toward alcohol consumption by adolescents in Jamaica is casual, and few legal restrictions apply. In Jamaica, adolescent drinking is not a sign of delinquent behavior. Similarly, compared to the United States, adolescents in Spain are able to consume more alcohol per week before they are categorized as "drinkers." Among European countries, the prevalence of weekly drinking varies considerably. For example, adolescents in Greece and Italy drink about twice as much alcohol per week as their counterparts in Ireland. Possible explanations for these variations can probably be found in the cultural differences in beliefs related to alcohol consumption and adult drinking patterns.

An additional factor that needs to be taken into account when defining adolescent social behavior is the status of a given group within the larger culture and this group's attitude toward the majority culture. Gotowiec and Beiser (1993) found a much higher rate of school failure, substance abuse, and suicidal behavior among aboriginal Canadian adolescents than among majority culture adolescents. Similarly, drug consumption patterns of Australian aboriginal peoples differ significantly from that of urban Australians, who represent the majority culture.

Calabrese and Noboa (1995) closely examined Mexican American gang culture. They report that Mexican American adolescents may decide to join a gang as a way of retaining their culture of origin and resisting the majority values found in American public schools. In this case, violence must be interpreted from the standpoint of the minority culture because majority views are rejected. Another example of differential perception of delinquent behavior is the street-fighting code of a minority youth culture in Mexico (*cholo*). The mass media in Mexico choose to portray *cholo* youth as uncontrolled, violent, and destructive. In contrast, Cummings (1994) describes a complex system of *cholo* street-fighting rules based on fairness and honor. This social structure contains rules about who can fight with whom about which matters and under which circumstances. For example, fights only take place when the groups involved are perceived as equal in strength or number; women may intervene on men's behalf, but men never interfere with women's fights.

For an easily accessible website providing a detailed discussion of culture and adolescence in regard to many of the topics covered in earlier chapters, see Chen and Farruggia (2002). Of special interest is the discussion of emerging issues and attempts to answer some of the most important research questions concerning adolescence and culture. One of the issues concerns recent advances in statistical procedures that permit conduction of multigroup comparisons and a more systematic examination of cross-cultural differences in developmental processes such as academic achievement and delinquency. A second issue focuses on the effects of social change and the development of globalization among adolescents, especially in Asian and Eastern European countries, as a result of modern technology such as the Internet, satellite television, computers, and social media. Future research will help us understand how adolescents' cognitive, psychological, and social development is being affected by these changes.

# 7.5: Adulthood

In adulthood, the life tasks change from negotiating one's identity to the generation and maintenance of one's "own life." Erikson calls this stage generativity versus stagnation. This refers to the *generation of something lasting that represents oneself.* A successful mastery of this life task leads to a sense of accomplishment. The accomplishments may be expressed in the form of material wealth, raising children, artistic or intellectual creations, or achieving status within a community. This developmental phase is clearly affected by the individuals' work and social life.

## 7.5.1: Work and Leisure in Middle Adulthood

Cultural beliefs and values influence how individuals come to judge their efforts and accomplishments. Hofstede's (2001; Hofstede, Hofstede, & Minkov, 2010) examination of more than forty countries revealed significant differences in how people in these countries viewed and interpreted work, as well as approached their social relationships at work. In particular, cultures differed on the following four work-related values: power distance, uncertainty avoidance, individualism/collectivism, and masculinity/femininity.

Cultures low on **power distance** put *less emphasis on organizational hierarchy and status between people.* In some cultures, it may be acceptable for a president of a company and a warehouse worker to socialize outside work. Examples of countries low in power distance are Denmark,

Israel, and Austria. Countries high in power distance are Mexico, Venezuela, and India.

The workplace in cultures low in **uncertainty avoidance** tends to *have few rules, policies, and codes that guide workers' communication and interpersonal relations.* In these cultures, a worker's complaints may be handled by different people in a relatively informal way, rather than by an appointed person according to specific procedures. Cultures low in uncertainty avoidance are Singapore, Denmark, and Sweden. Countries with the highest uncertainty avoidance are Greece, Portugal, Belgium, and Japan.

**Collectivism**, according to Hofstede, refers to the *degree to which a culture facilitates conformity, compliance, and the striving for harmony in the workplace.* Peru, Pakistan, Colombia, and Venezuela score high on collectivism, whereas the United States, Australia, Great Britain, and Canada tend to foster more individualistic work values.

Finally, work environments in "**feminine cultures**" *promote gender equality, interpersonal contact, and group decision making.* This dimension can best be described as "working to live" versus "living to work." Scandinavian countries rate the highest in "femininity," whereas Japan, Austria, Italy, and Switzerland tend to promote "masculine" values.

Furnham, Kirkcaldy, and Lynn (1994) studied forty-one nations with regard to seven work-related beliefs. Their results showed that people in North and South America scored highest on work ethic (commitment to work), mastery (need to master problems), savings (importance of saving money), and conformity (identification with the organization and its success). Asian and Eastern countries scored highest on competitiveness (motive to be better than others) and money beliefs (importance of money). In addition, European countries scored lower than non-European countries on all seven dimensions, including achievement (need for excellence).

These beliefs about the work environment are also related to the non-work environment. Studies of leisure activities show that these are both similar and different across cultures. Beatty, Jeon, Albaum, and Murphy (1994) questioned adults in the United States, France, Denmark, and New Zealand about their participation in recreational activities. Findings revealed three consistent clusters: *aesthetic-intellectual* (e.g., reading for pleasure, attending the opera or ballet, or dancing), *sports-action* (e.g., attending sports events or individual sports participation), and *social-entertainment* (e.g., going to the movies, having drinks, and enjoying entertainment). Two additional dimensions that were also examined did not replicate across cultures: *outdoor-nature* (e.g., walking for pleasure or bicycling) and *passive-in-home* (e.g., watching TV and playing sedentary games). The United States and New Zealand were most similar in their leisure activity preferences, with both scoring higher than their European counterparts on the sports-action and social-entertainment dimensions.

Among Chinese adults (Hu, 1995), the first choice for a hobby is reading, followed by social and intellectual activities. Physical exercise is third, tied with other productive activities such as knitting or crafts. One could speculate that leisure activities, defined as the antithesis or opposite of work, provide an environment or context that fulfills needs not met in the workplace. Therefore, one could possibly draw conclusions from predominant work values about the preferences for leisure activities. For example, individuals in cultures that emphasize collectivist work environments may choose to spend their leisure time in solitary activities, as is the case in China. In contrast, people in individualistic societies such as New Zealand, Canada, and the United States, where people work independently and often autonomously, may prefer leisure activities that are social and cooperative. *What kinds of leisure activities are important to you? Are they similar to or different from your work activities?*

## 7.5.2: Sport as a Social Phenomenon

As discussed previously in this chapter, play serves multiple important functions in the social lives of children. The following section outlines how play and games are a central part in the ecological systems of adults in many societies. Games and sport can consist of spontaneous activity or highly organized sport, and participation may range from passive spectator to participating spectator (e.g., referee and coach) to player. Anthropologists and sport historians have identified multiple functions of sport in society. This section summarizes these findings and illustrates how cultural settings shape sporting activities and, at the same time, are shaped by them (for an overview, see Calhoun (1987)). Two of the main historical functions are the practice of economic skills necessary to make a living and military training. The former is expressed in kayaking contests among Eskimos and rodeos among North American cowboys. Boxing, fencing, martial arts, and tug-of-war are classic examples of sports used for building strength, endurance, and skills in the interest of warfare preparation. However, sport and games also serve important social functions.

In many cultures, games or sport can have a ritual or ceremonial function. As such, the game or contest is dedicated to requesting help from, or expressing gratitude toward, a supernatural being. The Native American game of lacrosse or Japanese sumo wrestling is representative of this function. The origins of sumo were religious in nature. The first sumo matches were rituals dedicated to the gods. Along with dances and prayers, sumo matches expressed gratefulness for a bountiful harvest. This ancient sport dates back about 1500 years, and its ritualized character has survived to this day. The *rikishi* (participating sumo wrestlers) enter the ring in their colorful ceremonial aprons (*kesho-mawashi*) and perform a short sumo ritual. After they depart, the wrestlers scheduled to fight enter the ring. Over their *kesho-mawashi*, they wear a large braided hemp rope tied in the back and decorated with patterned paper strips in the front. This kind of decorated rope is a religious symbol that can be found in many Japanese homes and temples. Each sumo wrestler then performs the prefight ceremony with great dignity. He claps his hands to attract the attention of the gods. Then, he extends his arms to the side, palms up to show that he does not carry any weapons. Finally, he lifts first one leg high in the air and brings it down with a thundering stomp on the ground. This move is repeated with the other leg. This maneuver is meant to symbolically drive the evil spirits from the ring. After this, the match begins. Throughout Japan today, sumo wrestlers are honored not only as successful athletes but also as representatives of a small group of individuals who preserve and celebrate religious and cultural traditions. In a culture that is characterized as a tight culture, high in uncertainty avoidance and high in power distance, the sport of sumo emphasizes these cultural values.

A traditional sumo ceremony.

(J. Henning Buchholz/Shutterstock)

At the microsystem level, games and sport serve as recreational and communal activities. They also are an acceptable way of expressing rivalry and settling disputes. On the more distant level of the ecological system, sport expresses social identity and strengthens the sense of unity among members of a culture. Archetti (1999) provides a thorough account of the cultural meaning of sport in Argentina. He discusses football (soccer) as a cultural institution that permeates history, politics, and social and national identity. Archetti describes the evolution of the distinctive style of Argentinian football as a result of two main social forces: British imperialism and the ecological settings in which young Argentinian boys learn to play football. As opposed to the highly organized system of

sport in Britain, most young Argentinian boys learn to play the game in the streets, in confined spaces with uneven surfaces. This setting lets them develop strong dribbling and ball control skills, but little strategy. This leads to a style of football much the opposite of the British style, which is very linear and strategic. Hence, football may be interpreted as a form of expression of independence from the British, and as such, it has become part of Argentinian national identity and pride (macrosystem). The Argentinian football player has also become an idealized role model for male social identity and behavior. Young boys strive toward this ideal and are reinforced by family and peers (microsystem). Spectators rally behind their national team in international competition expressed by uniform colors, national anthems, flags, and other symbols of national pride (exosystem). Victory of the national sports team equals victory of the nation and fills the members of that nation with pride, reinforcing the loyalty and unity of the country at large. This phenomenon of social identification through sports is nowhere more clearly observable than during the Olympic Games, which bring many nations together in competition.

These cultural examples of sport show that this social activity is an important element in the ecological systems of adults who participate (actively or passively). In that capacity, students of human development have to consider sport and games as central to adult social development. For example, as individuals age and make the transition from active to passive participation, their ecological system changes, which, in turn, influences their social behavior.

# 7.6:  Late Adulthood

## 7.6.1: Attachment, Social Support, and Well-Being in Later Adulthood

This chapter previously discussed the importance of attachment patterns in childhood for social competence and self-esteem. In older age, the need for secure attachment and its benefit for social development persists, particularly when relationships are reciprocal and contribute to quality of life and well-being. A cross-national study, involving elder adults from five countries, showed that such relationships were related to greater life satisfaction overall, particularly when they involved family. Adults, who believed they were mostly the recipients of help, were least satisfied (Lowenstein, Katz, & Gur-Yaish, 2007). These relationships seem to be more prevalent in some countries than others. For example, older adults in Israel and Spain perceived their relationships as more reciprocal than elderly in England, Germany, and Norway. Similarly, the elderly in France seem to perceive their relationships to be more reciprocal than their counterparts in the United States—both Caucasian and African American (Antonucci, 1999). Lowenstein et al. (2007) suggest that this may be due to the "more familistic" culture that exists in these cultures, that is, relatively low divorce rate, traditional gender roles, and families living close together and maintaining daily contact.

This cultural explanation for different attachment styles is supported by a study of volunteer participation among postretirement adults in ten European countries. Erlinghagen and Hank (2006) report that people in less familistic, northern European countries (Norway, Denmark, and the Netherlands, with 17%–21% of volunteers) participated in volunteer work at a higher rate than Mediterranean countries (Spain, Italy, and Greece, with 2%–7% of volunteers).

In this later developmental stage of life, the ecological system undergoes changes that affect the relationships that have afforded secure attachment throughout life. Woodward (2004) points out that children leaving home, loss of parents, loss of partner, decline in health, and retirement are all factors that may lead to changes in attachment patterns. Adults in their later years need to adapt to these changes to maintain healthy social behavior and self-esteem.

Attributes of the ecological systems may aid or hinder this adaptation. For example, normative expectations that children care for their elderly parents in Thailand result in the common arrangement that at least one adult child lives in the same household or very close by, thereby providing a minimum level of social support. Even if the caregiving is perceived as demanding, a deep sense of family obligation and emotional bond maintains this system of social connection in old age.

In contrast, shifts in familial positions in Taiwan over time have produced situations in which the daughter-in-law gains more importance in some families than the formerly powerful mother-in-law. With decreased responsibilities, older women have begun to experience feelings of uselessness and reduced social support. This change in social relationships has been related to an increase in suicide risk among the elderly in Taiwan.

Finally, attachment relationships throughout adult life among people who are childless and never married present yet another picture. For the gay, lesbian, and transgendered population, the stigma associated with gender and sexual orientation, in many areas of the world, often leads to separation from the original family. One consequence is that gay and lesbian elders are more likely to live in institutions or alone than their straight cohorts. This places particular importance on the social network and "chosen family," which has been growing as a way of social life in older gay and lesbian communities (Pugh, 2005). Similarly, heterosexual individuals who are childless or who were never married emphasize the importance of friends and other social relations.

Even if motivated to seek out social activities outside the family, the decline in physical mobility or health issues may present an obstacle for the aging person. In response to these limitations, older adults may compensate by emphasizing and choosing more autonomy and independence in their social relationships. This adaptation may be beneficial in dealing with losses of important attachment relationships and physical limitations.

In conclusion, life in late adulthood is more likely to be healthy and fulfilling when attachment needs are met. As such, older adults may benefit most from an environment that provides opportunities for both social participation and independent living, while accommodating changing physical needs.

## Summary: Culture and Social Behavior

Although virtually all social relationships and behavior patterns change over the lifespan, some aspects are more salient at different ages. The types of relationships and behaviors children develop with their primary caregivers early in life set the stage for many social relationships to come. Even though there appear to be universal patterns of "secure base," "caregiver sensitivity," and a correlation between secure attachment and social competence late in life, early attachment patterns are seemingly influenced by caregiving practices and general conditions under which children grow up.

As children learn to communicate, they begin to form more social relationships; these are initially built and later maintained through play. Social relationships require basic behavioral skills such as conflict resolution and cooperation, which involve a general understanding of moral principles. Kohlberg's theory of moral development addresses some important aspects of morality, namely, the understanding of normative principles of justice. However, Gilligan has demonstrated that individuals may also base their moral decisions on nurturance and caring. Although they represent interdependent elements of moral reasoning, the salience of either of these moral orientations may vary from culture to culture.

Along with developing prosocial reasoning and behavior, children and young adolescents are also facing the challenge of managing their own and others' aggressive social behavior. Once again, examples from various cultures illustrate that one's place within a culture's ecological system helps determine the definition and expression of aggressive behavior.

Adolescent social development is marked by an increased influence of peers (in addition to family) on both prosocial and antisocial behavior. However, cultural differences in values and beliefs about appropriate and inappropriate social behavior have to be taken into account when analyzing adolescent social development.

Middle adulthood is dominated by concerns of productivity, which manifest differently depending on values and expectations. As in childhood, the social functions of games and play continue to shape social development in middle and later adulthood. Active and passive participation in sports is part of the ecological system. Finally, social support and satisfying social relationships facilitate well-being and peace of mind in older adulthood.

## Study Questions

Show an understanding of early attachment and conditions in an infant's environment that serve as a basis for social development.

Compare and contrast theories of social development, and discuss their cultural implications.

Comment on cultural influences on parent–child and parent–adolescent relationships. Explain how and why play and games are a vital part of an adult's ecological system.

Discuss the importance of attachment during later adulthood.

## Developmental Analysis
## Culture and Social Behavior

As a young child, I grew up quite attached to my mother. Although I also felt very close to my father, my mother was my primary caregiver. My first memory of being in a strange situation with the absence of my mother was in the local grocery store. I was just two years old and a boisterous walker. I did not want to sit in the cart, so my mother let me walk alongside her. Quite predictably, I began to wander off and soon realized that the flowered skirt I was staring at was not my mother's. The unfamiliar woman knelt down and asked me if I was lost. I began to cry. Nothing would comfort me until I felt the familiar touch of my own mother's arms. Needless to say, I was pleased to sit obediently in the cart during subsequent trips to the grocery store!

My own children grew up in a very different cultural setting. Both my husband and I had careers and were working full time. Circumstances allowed me to stay at home with my daughter for eight months—during which I was the primary caregiver. I was a new mom, but I did not want to admit that I needed any help. I was home alone with Elizabeth, tending to her every need. By the time my son was born, one year later, I had just started a new position as a professor and could not imagine taking leave for so long. We were faced with the question of whether we would put our son, Alexander, into day care at a much earlier age than our daughter. I looked to our families for help. Fortunately, my husband's mother was able to come from Italy and stay with us for an extended period of time. In fact, she stayed for nearly the entire first year of my son's life. As you may know, it is quite common in other cultures for grandparents, aunts, uncles, and cousins to all live together. Many of my friends and colleagues could not imagine having their mother-in-law stay with them for more than a week! I was grateful for the opportunity to continue progressing in my career, while also keeping Alexander and Elizabeth at home with a loving caregiver. Although I was Alexander's mother, his paternal grandmother was his primary caregiver during his early infancy, and they have always shared a special bond.

Together, Elizabeth and Alexander learned about competition and collaboration. At the ages of four and five, I recall watching them struggle to put a puzzle together. They began by dividing up the pieces and racing to see who could put their pieces together first. Soon, they realized that the other sibling may have pieces each of them needed and it would be better to work as a team. Through experiences like this, they learned the importance of cooperation in pursuit of a common goal. However, put a basketball between them and it's an entirely different story! Their competitive drive is obvious during a heated game of hoops.

Our family had an interesting, life-changing, cultural experience many years ago. During one of our many vacations to Brazil, we met a family from Korea. They had just arrived in the country for a brief visit and were having difficulty getting to their hotel. My husband and I were able to help them and shared a meal later that evening. Each year, they send us a gift at the holidays to show their appreciation. When our daughter studied abroad in Korea, they insisted on having her to their home, feeding her, and taking her around the country. For our daughter, this was a wonderful experience. For them, this was their "social obligation." Because we had helped them years before, they felt the need to reciprocate. I was impressed while watching their daughter and Elizabeth interact and seeing how many things they had in common. They were equally consumed with mastering their classes, selecting the right career, and worrying about finding a life partner! I remember being a young girl and sharing such concerns. I am proud to say that it has all worked out for me. I consider marrying Giorgio, raising our lovely children, and having a successful career among my greatest accomplishments.

# Chapter 8
# Culture and Issues of Gender and Sexuality

*Alisa and Alan are middle-age adult siblings who grew up in a small town in the Midwestern United States. As young children, they lived in a single-parent home with their mother, who worked as a secretary. Growing up, they experienced typical gender socialization for that time. Alisa, wearing her favorite party dress, enjoyed playing with her dolls and stuffed animals in her room, whereas Alan, in his sturdy jeans and T-shirt, played rough and tumble games outside. During their school years, Alan was encouraged to study science and went on to become an engineer. Alisa, who did well in school, hoped to have a career too but was raised to see her future role as a wife and mother. Both Alisa and Alan married and had children. One of Alisa's daughters is an astronaut in the American space program and another is a surgeon. Now divorced, Alisa takes care of her elderly mother because Alan lives and works in Japan.*

*When Badal was a ten-year-old boy, he moved with his family from India to England. According to his parents, he was a sociable child who was well mannered and enjoyed spending time at home. Badal's parents were also aware that he dressed and acted in a very feminine manner and often spoke of wanting to be a girl. The parents are non–English-speaking Buddhists and described a belief system that accepts gender ambivalence and the notion that some children are born as a "third gender." At home, Badal was not discouraged from cross-gendered behavior, but at school he was teased by his peers and experienced academic difficulties. He eventually finished school and joined the British Voluntary Service Oversees to work with HIV/AIDS programs in India. Now twenty-four, Badal has remained in India. He has no plans to marry and have children. He sees himself working as a youth counselor and living in his closely knit community of friends, where he is comfortable among a mix of men, women, and transgendered people.*

These three individuals experienced childhood in very different ways, much of it shaped by the norms and beliefs associated with gender. Did Alisa and Alan deliberately "choose" different interests, or were they "assigned" those interests? Did the upbringing experienced by these children influence the choices and preferences all three made in later life? How did culture contribute to these differences in upbringing?

Decades of psychological and anthropological research have produced evidence showing that differences between women and men appear in all known cultures. How many consistent differences exist and to what degree they can be rendered truly "universal" is the subject of much discussion in the field. This chapter presents some of the developmental challenges involved in growing up female or male in different cultures and societies.

Many introductory or developmental textbooks in psychology carefully differentiate the concepts of "sex" and "gender." **Sex** is generally considered to be the *biological aspects of femaleness and maleness*, whereas **gender** refers to the *acquired behavioral and psychological aspects of being a woman or a man.* This nature–nurture distinction provides the illusion of two nearly independent sources of behavior. However, on further review, it becomes clear that the two are not as independent as these definitions might suggest. Rather, it is essential to understand that the relationship between biological sex characteristics and gendered social behavior is much more complex.

Stephanie J. Wong (2013) emphasizes that gender is a "... socially constructed term ... deeply embedded in cultural expectations, norms, and socialization methods. Although gender stereotypes are evident in a variety of cultures, gender is perhaps better conceptualized as multidimensional or occurring on a continuum" (p. 588). She also stresses that the concept is best understood when there is recognition of the role of culture and the influence of the ecological setting.

The World Health Organization further differentiates these terms by stating that "Male" and "Female" are sex categories, whereas "Masculine" and "Feminine" are gender categories (http://www.who.int/gender/whatis-gender/en/).

This chapter introduces some of the issues and theoretical perspectives relevant in gender research today before reflecting on the role gender plays in every stage of a person's life.

# 8.1: Ecological Context: Theoretical Perspectives on Gender Differences

## 8.1.1: Biological Perspectives

It is generally accepted that females and males of any species exhibit distinct biological and physiological differences that are present at birth. Based on this fact, proponents of the biological perspective view the expression of sex in its cultural context (i.e., gender) as predetermined by the genetic, physiological, and neural foundations of biological sex.

Research with mammals and nonprimate populations has provided evidence that prenatal exposure and manipulation of androgens (male "sex hormones" that stimulate or control the development and maintenance of masculine characteristics) and estrogens (female sex hormones) correlate with measurable changes in brain development. In infants and children, these differences align with gender-typical choices of toys and play behavior (Knickmeyer & Baron-Cohen, 2006; Shepard, Michopolous, Toufexis, & Wilson, 2009).

In humans, similar patterns emerge: Studies of prenatal exposure to testosterone show that high testosterone levels correlate with male-typical behaviors in childhood (Auyeung et al., 2009; Hines, 2004). Such biological factors continue to shape behavior throughout life. For example, there is evidence that testosterone level is related to aggressiveness. Because men are known to have higher average levels of testosterone than women, they should be expected to exhibit more aggressive behavior. And, in fact, a review of research on this topic reveals that this is indeed the case (Archer & Mehdikhani, 2004).

However, it is entirely possible that in cultures that encourage aggressive behavior in both genders, women may be more aggressive than men in cultures that discourage aggressive behaviors in general. In addition, there is clear evidence that females show more aggressive behavior than males in certain situations, for example, when protecting their offspring from predators.

Even though the biological research finds convincing evidence that genetic makeup and hormonal exposure predispose the developing brain to gender-typical behaviors, the next section shows that the biological foundations alone are not sufficient to account for sex- and gender-typical behavior throughout life.

## 8.1.2: Evolutionary Perspectives

According to theories of evolution, many gender differences may be explained by an organism's motivation to pass on genes by producing offspring and ensuring the survival of the species at large (Buss, 1994a). Among humans, the particular way in which this is accomplished appears to differ among men and women. Women, who have the ability to produce a limited number of children over a lifetime, put their energy into creating an environment that promotes the survival of a maximum number of children. To accomplish this, many women's activities are directed toward the family and involve food preparation, home maintenance, and creation of a protective network of others who will assist in completing larger tasks and in protecting against enemies (a part of the microsystem). In other words, women create a developmental niche (or a microsystem) that will be most favorable for the development of their children.

In contrast, men can produce an almost unlimited number of children, given the availability of women. According to the evolutionary perspective, men strive to produce as many children as possible because the more they have, the more will be likely to survive. To do this, they have to compete with other men. Under these circumstances, much of their energy is devoted to competing with other men for available women, and the focus is on physical strength and aggressiveness.

Despite these different reproductive strategies, women and men have a common goal; this ensures their children have the greatest possible chance of survival. According to Darwin's "survival of the fittest" doctrine, children have a greater chance of survival if both parents have healthy genes. Consequently, men and women can increase the chances of their children's survival if they mate with a healthy partner. Both men and women enhance and display those characteristics that are evolutionarily attractive in order to be chosen as mates. According to this perspective, men tend to exhibit behavior that conveys strength and sexual prowess, such as engaging in challenging sports and games or displaying symbols of wealth and status—ranging from a Mercedes Benz in Europe to camels in Egypt. Women, however, tend to reinforce symbols of youthfulness and health, such as smooth skin, healthy teeth and hair, and a strong body, to communicate that they are young and fit enough to bear many children. If one accepts this evolutionary view of reproductive strategies, then it may help explain those social behaviors that are considered specific to women and men in most societies.

## 8.1.3: Socialization and Learning Perspectives

Beginning at birth, individuals are socialized into their particular culture and taught the values, beliefs, and behaviors that will permit them to successfully function within it (see Chapter 3). From an early age, as part of the socialization process, children learn to conform to the roles that culture considers consistent with their biological sex. In general, girls are rewarded and praised for exhibiting behavior considered desirable for a woman in that culture and discouraged from showing undesirable, or gender-inappropriate, behavior. In turn, boys are rewarded for "malelike" behavior and ridiculed if they exhibit behaviors reserved for girls or women.

By no means are "feminine" and "masculine" behaviors consistent across cultures. Occasionally, gender-specific norms may interact with cultural norms and modify gender roles. For example, although modesty and humility are viewed in China as culturally important values for all individuals, in other cultures these traits are more desirable, and more expected, in women than in men. For example, Chinese women have been found to be more self-effacing, modest, and less likely to take personal credit for accomplishments than are men, even though the cultural norm requires modesty from both genders. However, other sources suggest that these values, as well as gender socialization, are undergoing significant change in China and in other Asian countries (Hao & Chen, 2014).

In addition to direct reinforcement and punishment, children in most cultures also observe same-sex adult role models and imitate the gender-appropriate behavior exhibited by these models. These behaviors are further reinforced and become internalized as attributes of gender-appropriate behavior patterns. In short, gender concepts are salient at many, if not all, levels of the ecological system and linked to gender differences as they occur in various cultures.

As Gibbons, Stiles, Perez-Prada, Shkodriani, and Medina (1996) have demonstrated, these cultural "systems" influence the gender socialization of children. In their studies, the researchers obtained drawings of the "ideal" woman and the "ideal" man from children and adolescents in several different countries (see Figure 8.1). Although they found a common tendency for the children to portray women as caring for children and the men as occupied in work roles outside the home, the researchers also found specific cultural differences. For instance, adolescents were more

likely to draw the ideal woman in a nontraditional role as businesswoman in cultures with "masculine" work values, and the ideal man in a nontraditional role as caregiver in "feminine" cultures. The latter was the case in Norway, where adolescents more often expect the "ideal" man to participate in housework (Stiles & Gibbons, 1995). The researchers explain this finding by pointing out that Norwegians hold very egalitarian beliefs about the roles and status of women and men in their society and convey these beliefs to their children. Ideals may not always reflect social reality. For example, in highly "masculine" cultures such as Japan, positions of power have been largely held by men. Women have had only limited opportunity to achieve status and power, instead they have tended to remain in subordinate positions, both in the workplace and in private life. However, there is evidence that the role of Japanese women is changing, affecting the image of women throughout Asia.

**Figure 8.1** Drawings of Ideal Women by Children of Various Cultures: (a) by a fourteen-year-old girl from Mexico; (b) by a fifteen-year-old girl from the Netherlands; (c) by a thirteen-year-old boy from Guatemala; (d) by an eleven-year-old boy from Spain.

SOURCE: The thoughts of youth: An international perspective on adolescents' ideal persons by J. L. Gibbons and G. A. Stiles. Copyright © 2004 by Information Age Publishing. Reprinted by permission of Judith L. Gibbons.

In summary, these different perspectives all propose a slightly different explanation for why some behaviors seem to vary with gender. The biological perspective considers gendered behavior a result of underlying biological and physiological processes. The evolutionary perspective describes gendered behavior as the result of evolutionary processes. Gendered behaviors represent behaviors that have evolved as most adaptive, considering both biological attributes and environmental challenges. Finally, socialization and learning theories see gendered behaviors as the result of a person's individual learning history within a specific sociocultural context. None of these perspectives can fully account for the phenomenon of gender differences and how they originated. Nonetheless, each can explain influences on various levels of the ecological system.

Keep this in mind during the upcoming discussion of how issues of sex and gender relate to development in each stage of the lifespan.

## Points to Ponder

### Gender

Think about your childhood and adolescence. When and how did you first become aware that you were a boy or girl? Who influenced you most in determining your gender? In what specific ways? As you look back, do you think you fit a gender stereotype in terms of dress, play, toys, and/or interests? How many siblings did you have in your family—number of boys (and ages) and girls (ages)? Where were you in relation to them? Did they affect the development of your gender role? If you were a girl, were you a "tomboy" and play "boy games"? If a boy, did you play "girl games" with your sisters? Did your parents discourage these behaviors, or did they not mind? How did your mother and father separately influence you? Did your gender play a role in the schools you attended, the friends you played with, the career or jobs you chose? Do you have any friends who are gay, lesbian, bisexual, or transgendered—who may think, feel, look, or act differently from the gender assigned to them by society as a result of their sex? If so, do you know (or can you speculate about) how they became the people they are and how their gender roles developed?

# 8.2:  Infancy

As described in Section 8.1.1, the foundations for behavior are shaped by an intricate interaction of genetic and physiological factors. Even though these biological characteristics vary significantly from person to person, and sometimes the classification of "male" or "female" is

ambiguous at best, culture creates an artificial dichotomy of two mutually exclusive groups. Once the doctor or midwife announces "It's a boy" or "It's a girl," the first major decision in a child's life has been made for him or her. The labels "male" and "female" come with distinctive sets of normative expectations that build a framework for identity and interactions with others in most situations. Furthermore, the assigned membership in one or the other such exclusive category carries great implications for the individual and his or her ecological system.

## 8.2.1: Gender Preference and Gender Ratio at Birth

Within the human population, the distribution of male and female births is approximately equal, with only a slightly higher birthrate for males: 103 male births for every 100 female births (*CIA World Factbook*, 2015).

Yet, there appear to be some striking differences among cultures, as can be observed in recent demographic data (see Table 8.1). These data show that, compared to countries in other parts of the world, in many Asian countries, male births outnumber female births by a larger margin. For example, in China, 110 boys are born for every 100 girls. India (112 boys per 100 girls) shows a similar pattern. Both countries contrast with Brazil and the United States (105 boys born per 100 girls). Although these ratios do not sound vastly different, the absolute numbers are astounding when taking into account total population. In the two population-richest countries combined (China and India), there are *close to 35 million* more male children than female children (ages 0–14 years). In comparison, boys outnumber girls by only 2.5 million in the next two most populated countries combined (the United States and Brazil). Researchers speculate that the cultural tradition of "son preference" along with family planning policies in

**Table 8.1**  Male-to-Female Population Ratios for Selected Countries and the World

| | At Birth | Younger Than 15 | 15–64 | Older Than 65 | Total |
|---|---|---|---|---|---|
| World | 1.07 | 1.06 | 1.02 | 0.78 | 1.01 |
| Brazil | 1.05 | 1.04 | 0.98 | 0.73 | 0.98 |
| China | 1.10 | 1.13 | 1.06 | 0.90 | 1.06 |
| India | 1.12 | 1.10 | 1.06 | 0.90 | 1.06 |
| New Zealand | 1.05 | 1.05 | 1.00 | 0.84 | 0.99 |
| South Africa | 1.02 | 1.00 | 1.02 | 0.69 | 0.99 |
| South Korea | 1.07 | 1.10 | 1.04 | 0.67 | 1.00 |
| Sweden | 1.06 | 1.06 | 1.03 | 0.79 | 0.98 |
| Taiwan | 1.09 | 1.08 | 1.02 | 0.94 | 1.02 |
| United States | 1.05 | 1.04 | 1.00 | 0.75 | 0.97 |

**SOURCE:** World FactBook 2009. Published by CIA.

the former countries have led to this imbalance in male-to-female birth rates.

In 2015, the figures showed only a few slight but not significant changes—some increases and some decreases. For example, the total male-to-female ratio for the world was 1.01, Brazil 0.97, China 1.06, India 1.08, New Zealand 0.99, South Africa 0.98, Sweden 1.00, Taiwan 0.99, and United States 0.97.

According to cultural traditions in many societies, the family name and family property are passed down patrilineally. Sons inherit the family wealth, name, and status, which they will pass on to their sons. Male children are also often expected to support aging parents. A daughter becomes part of her husband's family and no longer has obligations toward her birth parents. In addition, a dowry system may require parents to pay a dowry price to the future husband. This may become a great financial burden for a family with more than one daughter. Within such an ecological system, parents may prefer sons as insurance for financial support and physical security in older age.

By virtue of the value that is placed on male and female offspring, male and female infants are born into very different ecological systems at birth, and these ecological systems influence development throughout life. For example, a newborn son or daughter will likely have different numbers of older brothers or sisters depending on whether there is a cultural preference for male children within the macrosystem and/or the availability of prenatal gender determination technology within the exosystem. Almond and Edlund (2008) found evidence for son preference among families within their analysis of census data in the United States, focusing on statistics for families of Chinese, Korean, and Indian descent. In these families, if the first two children were female, then the third child would be twice as likely to be a boy rather than a girl. Moreover, when at least one of the first two children is a boy, parents are less likely to have a third child.

In the larger population, these practices ultimately have greater social consequences. Male-biased sex ratios have been thought to relate to increased violence and crime among young men, as well as a reduction in unwanted births and female infant mortality.

# 8.3: Childhood

As pointed out in Chapter 3, parents are the primary source of socialization in the lives of young children, and they introduce the important knowledge, values, beliefs, and expected behaviors of the culture. One aspect of this concerns society's expectations regarding appropriate behavior for women and men or gender role stereotypes.

Lucas-Stannard (2013), discussing gender-neutral parenting, presents an approach focusing on a child's self-identity. This book is recommended in the Further Reading section.

## 8.3.1: Gender Socialization

One of the most exhaustive investigations of gender stereotypes and attitudes was conducted by Williams and Best (1990), who found significant differences between male and female stereotypes in each of the twenty-five countries studied. In general, passivity, submissiveness, affiliation, and nurturance were seen as more typical in descriptions of women, whereas activity, dominance, achievement, and aggressiveness were more typical of men. In this study, Williams and Best also found fascinating evidence related to differences in the socialization of gender stereotypes among children five to eleven years of age. For example, across all age groups, children in most countries were more familiar with the male stereotype than with the female, suggesting that male stereotypes are more dominant in their lives and are learned earlier. Only in Brazil, Portugal, and Germany did five-year-old children clearly identify more items associated with the female stereotype. Overall, Williams and Best suggest that gender stereotypes are well established in children by the time they are eight years old. After that age, they serve as powerful "blueprints" for behaviors that are reinforced throughout life. Gender role stereotypes not only promote overt behavior and prescribe types of clothing and social rituals, but they also influence the way in which men and women in a given society view themselves and others. According to these researchers, by the age of nine, children are already applying gender stereotypes in their descriptions of themselves. In the case of the Midwestern siblings Alisa and Alan, both did well in school, and both wanted a career. Yet, Alisa was raised according to the cultural stereotype of women as caregivers. She cared for her husband and two children, and even after her divorce, she continued her role as the caregiver of her elderly mother.

Feminist scholars frequently argue that these gender blueprints socialize women into lower-status roles and dependency due to the differential positions of power either group holds in society. Because, in most known societies, men tend to hold positions of power and to distribute available resources, they frequently have the opportunity to define social roles for both women and men. They also have the potential to use resources and status as rewards. To preserve male social dominance, younger men are rewarded for conforming to the behavior that later enables them to achieve positions of power in society. Among these desirable behaviors are competitiveness, aggressiveness, and dominance. If men conform successfully and "play by the rules," then they will gain power, status, and access to resources.

Women, in contrast, are usually discouraged from exhibiting behaviors that are reserved for men. Instead, an entirely different set of normative behaviors is defined for them. In many cultures, they are expected to be submissive, nurturing, and weak. This feminine ideal is defined by men to preserve male privilege. The idea is that weak and submissive individuals are not likely to compete for resources and power. By conforming to this feminine ideal, women become attractive and gain the recognition of powerful men. In turn, they may be rewarded by receiving indirect access to power and resources. Women who refuse to conform to the female gender role will be denied these resources and status. In this case, the differing social status and power of women and men represent an important part of the ecological system in which children grow up. Power differences between women and men are related to their differential treatment by society, as well as gender differences in behavior.

Being a "homemaker" takes on a new meaning in today's society.

(Poznyakov/Shutterstock)

In polygynous societies, in which it is customary for men to have multiple reproductive partners, the competition among men for women is very strong. In sub-Saharan Africa, young boys are taught to be aggressive and competitive. In societies in which monogamy or even polyandry prevails, the number of reproductive partners is restricted, and men are not engaged in competition to the same extent. For example, the role and socialization of boys in Nyinba, Tibet, are quite different. They are taught cooperation and sharing rather than competition and aggressiveness because they will one day share a common wife and children with one or more men. In addition, polyandrous societies grant women more control over resources and more independence from one particular man. Consequently, socialization of girls focuses more on independence and assertiveness and less on obedience and submissiveness.

More fathers are staying at home to care for their children as mothers enter the workforce.

(Westend61 GmbH/Alamy Stock Photo)

## 8.3.2: Cultural Influences on Female and Male Socialization

Despite widespread similarities in gender role expectations across cultures, there are distinct differences in how gender-related behaviors are transmitted to young girls and boys. Depending on availability of role models, displays of expected role behavior, or influence of socialization agents, children in different cultures experience their socialization differently. Examples of gender role socialization from a variety of cultural perspectives, including Korean, Japanese, Islamic, Indian, Nigerian, and Native American, will serve as illustrations of this point. (See Box 8.1.)

One cannot view the socialization of certain behaviors independently from the cultural context. Cultures define the basic values and ideals (macrosystems), as well as the agents who teach the values and the settings in which they are taught (microsystems). In turn, individuals growing up in this ecological system will shape their environment by adding individual characteristics to that setting, establishing a unique developmental niche. As a consequence, the socialization experiences of individuals in the various cultures described in this chapter have taken very different paths.

# Box 8.1 Cultural Perspectives on Gender Role Socialization

## Korea

In Korean society, women observe the Confucian virtues of the *Rule of Three Obediences*, in which they are required to be obedient to their fathers, husbands, and sons. Parents stress the emotional development of girls, who are expected to be kind and nurturing, and the strength and intellectual development of boys, who are expected to be strong and courageous. The division of responsibilities in the Korean household is segregated by gender, with men providing the financial support and women tending to the house.

Schools are also gender segregated, but both sexes have the opportunity for education. Elementary school attendance is compulsory for both boys and girls, with more boys attending high school and college. Korean schools stress different curricula for males and females, and teachers hold differential expectations based on gender. For example, the curriculum for females is designed to foster feminine traits, and students must take mandatory courses in home economics and subjects geared toward women as consumers and childbearers. The male curriculum promotes masculine traits, and male students are required to take technology-type courses.

Marriage is viewed as a stage that everyone should experience. Adult identification depends on getting married, starting a family, and gaining status in one's profession. Although modern marriages are no longer solely prearranged to continue the family lineage, this does occasionally still occur. Contemporary Korean society views marriage as a way of fulfilling individuals' happiness.

In Korea, the law states that fathers have rights and obligations over their children in case of divorce, and, although some legal action has been taken to reduce paternal rights, they almost always receive custody. As a result, many women who fear losing their children remain in unhappy marriages.

## Japan

Modernization has begun to alter Japan and has affected many areas, including gender. For example, more Japanese women remain single or work outside the home than ever before. However, some customs remain strong. For example, traditionally the eldest male child was responsible for carrying on the family lineage and entitled to an automatic inheritance of the family property. Today, although the oldest son is no longer automatically entitled to the inheritance, he is considered responsible for supporting and caring for aging parents, although, in reality, the daughter-in-law generally provides such care.

Education is extremely important, and, similar to Korea, there is a gender difference. For example, females are under less academic pressure than males. Later, most Japanese men gravitate toward the occupational role while women become committed to the domestic role. The "homebody" or

"professional housewife" is idealized even though 60% of women are in the labor force. Child-rearing remains the most important aspect in Japanese women's lives, and, although more women are working outside the home, this commitment continues, although decreasingly, to exist today.

Finally, women and men both exert a considerable amount of influence but in separate spheres. For example, Japanese women tend to control almost all household duties, including home finances and children's education and, similar to American women, do a disproportionate share of household labor, whereas men more often spend long hours working and commuting.

## Islamic Culture

Although Islam emphasizes the complementary nature of the sexes, what Islam says about men and women may vary in interpretation and practice. Contrary to what some may believe, Islam does not say that women are naturally inferior. In fact, a Muslim woman is entitled to the following rights: (1) independent ownership, (2) to marry whom she likes and to end an unsuccessful marriage, (3) to education, (4) to keep her own identity, (5) to sexual pleasure, (6) to inheritance, (7) to election and nomination to political offices and participation in public affairs, and (8) to respect. However, because sons carry on the family name and daughters do not economically contribute to the family, there is a definite preference for male children. As children, girls help their mothers with the house (an activity discouraged in boys) and have more restrictions placed on them than boys with regard to their behavior.

Marriage in Islam is viewed as a contract between two equal and consenting partners. The wife has a right to stipulate her own conditions and the dowry belongs to her. Islam considers marriage a lifelong commitment, and although divorce is allowed, it is discouraged. When women marry, they enter a new stage of life in which they are sending signals that they are good wives and mothers, and this is a very important way of gathering respect.

Even though the *Qur'an* advocates equal partnership between husband and wife, the husband often assumes the role of authoritarian, and the wife becomes submissive to his wishes and orders—a distinction between what Islam says and its actual practice. Females do have inheritance rights, but they often inherit one-half the part that men do.

Although education is a basic right in Islam for both sexes, educating females has not always been a priority. Recently, efforts have been made to improve female education in some Muslim countries; however, educational opportunities for women, especially in the Middle East, lag behind men. For example, the Islamic world, especially the Arab world, is one of the areas that has the highest rates of illiteracy among women, the lowest level of schooling for females, and the smallest number of women in paid employment.

## India

In India, both age and gender play an important role. Elders, especially elder males, have more status than younger people, and male children are valued more than female children, especially in North India. Marriage is optional for males, but it is considered essential for all girls regardless of their caste, class, religion, or ethnicity; and females are often viewed as visitors because they leave home and reside with the husband's family.

A Hindu woman's role is a series of role relationships as daughter, daughter-in-law, wife, and mother, and she achieves her highest status as mother of a son. A daughter-in-law's status is increased when she gives birth to a boy. Divorce is rare and is considered an admission of a woman's failure as a wife and a daughter-in-law. Brides have impressed on them that walking out of a marriage for any reason will disgrace her parental family. The supervision of daughters-in-law is delegated to their mothers-in-law, who wield considerable power. Thus, older women come under the authority of men, but younger women come under the authority of both men and older women.

Socioeconomic status plays a role in gender and beliefs about men and women. For example, upper-middle-class and upper-class women are likely to have an education and, thus, be exposed to modern (often Western) thought. School is considered essential for boys but not necessarily so for girls, although they are taught to read and write. Instead, girls are often kept at home to care for younger children, especially among lower socioeconomic-level families.

## Nigeria

In infancy, there is little difference in the child-rearing of male and female babies, but gender segregation begins in early childhood. The male child, after the age of six, is involved in secret societies that serve as models of adult society. Girls, however, are not allowed to join.

Children are sent to school when money is available, and boys are enrolled more frequently than girls. However, there has been, in certain parts of the society, a rapid growth in the number of educated females. Although there are many institutions of higher education in Nigeria, a significant proportion of the population still views advanced education as unnecessary for females. The Igbo tribe has been more accepting of female education and changes in female roles than the Hausa tribe.

Women often marry early, usually in their teens, and have large families. Thus, childbearing occupies their fertile years. Nigerian marriage laws acknowledge that the husband is the head of the household and that he has complete authority over his wife and children. Nigerians often practice polygyny, and under Islamic law, a Muslim male can have up to four wives if he can support them. Inheritance is often difficult for women unless they can prove that they helped acquire the material wealth. In some cases, widows are considered property and may be inherited by the husband's oldest male relative.

Finally, there is a difference in the division of labor, with men often involved in cultivating cash crops and blacksmithing, and women, in some areas, selling their weavings and pottery. The Igbo relies on market trade conducted primarily by women as a large part of their economic system. Thus, women's control over local trade helps establish their independence in a culture primarily dominated by men.

## Native American Culture

There are more than 300 distinct tribes of American Indians who primarily live in California, Oklahoma, New Mexico, Arizona, Alaska, North Carolina, and Washington. The tribes vary in customs, language, and type of family structure, as well as in their degree of acculturation and whether they live on reservations or in urban areas. However, despite their great diversity, they are generally viewed as having a number of common values, including (1) sharing, (2) cooperation, (3) non-interference, (4) present time orientation, (5) extended family orientation, and (6) harmony with nature.

Traditionally, great value was assigned to the role of women in Native American society, and they were frequently the primary educators and historians. Life was rooted in spirituality and the extended family, and traditional ideologies stressed the importance of balance and harmony between the genders and the equal contributions of both to maintain the household and the community. For example, men and women share in the work of grazing, agriculture, and crafts and have equal rights of inheritance.

The status of both women and men increases with age, and age and wisdom are revered in both sexes. The Navajo is a matrilineal society (i.e., the mother's clan is of primary importance, and the father's clan is secondary). A Navajo belief is that the people were created from the Changing Woman, who represents the season and the earth, and children of both genders are equally welcomed.

The job of the Navajo father is to provide for his children and to serve as a role model in teaching skills, values, and good behaviors. Mothers teach small children and growing girls. If the father is absent, then the mother's brother assumes some obligations toward her children. Fathers and sons have a more direct relationship than father and daughter.

**SOURCE:** "Culture and Gender" from unpublished manuscript, St. Louis Community College by Vicki Ritts. Copyright © 2001 by Vicki Ritts. Reprinted by permission of Vicki Ritts.

# 8.3.3: Gender Relationships in Childhood

Apart from parents and caregivers, the role of peers in childhood socialization cannot be underestimated. In fact, in most cultures, peer relationships play a role nearly as important as the family. Consequently, same-sex and mixed-sex peer groups provide an effective context for the observation and practice of gender role behaviors. For example, it could be argued that early gender segregation indicates very large differences in normative expectations for women and men in that society; these differences need to be reinforced early. However, mixed-sex peer groups throughout childhood and the relative lack of differential treatment of the two genders may indicate greater equality between the genders in adulthood. A look at different cultures shows that the relationship between gender relations in childhood and adult gender role behavior is not always linear.

There is a large range of cultural variation in the extent to which children's playmates are of both genders or predominantly of the same gender. Gender relations in playgroups range from completely segregated to segregated for part of the time to intergender relations. The makeup of playgroups can be more or less dictated by cultural conventions that include the gender constellation of the groups.

Overall, however, Eleanor Maccoby's (1990, 2002) research suggests that the preference for same-sex playmates is universal, regardless of cultural norms prescribing gender-segregated environments in childhood. Although cultural research on playmate preference is still scarce, a few studies conducted in non-Western cultures seem to confirm Maccoby's claim. Munroe and Romney (2006) analyzed observational data from Belize, Kenya, Nepal, and American Samoa. These four cultures vary in their emphasis on gender differentiation. The Logoli of Kenya and the Newars of Nepal emphasize strict gender-specific roles, rituals, and activities, thus exposing girls and boys to very different socialization experiences. In contrast, among the Garifuna of Belize and in American Samoan society, gender-differentiated socialization is much less pronounced. For example, girls and boys are expected to contribute about equally to work around the house, and there are no gender-specific initiation rites.

The seemingly consistent phenomenon of same-sex preference in playmates lends itself to a biological explanation of gender differences. Due to their predisposition, boys might bond together through activities that facilitate physicality and competition. Girls' pattern of play, in comparison, emphasizes interaction and collaboration. However, biological predisposition toward gender-specific behavior and preferences may only serve as a partial explanation. Harkness and Super (1985) explain these differences in terms of the developmental niche, in which children actively explore and define gender relations within the parameters set by cultural expectations. In addition, unique group processes, inherent in the microsystem of the playgroup, may highlight the expression of gender-specific behaviors. Gauvain and Cole (2008) note that "gender-related behaviors are more evident when children are observed in groups than when they are tested individually" (p. 187).

# 8.4: Adolescence

## 8.4.1: Markers of Sexual Maturation

Much of the change associated with adolescent development centers on **puberty**, *a period of biological transition between childhood and adulthood lasting approximately one to two years.* The physical and physiological changes during puberty are dramatic, having both psychological and social consequences.

In boys, the transition from child to adult may be marked by several physical events, including change in voice, emergence of pubic and facial hair, nocturnal ejaculation, and/or a sudden growth spurt and muscle development. The age at which a boy is granted "adult status" varies greatly by culture, mostly depending on which physical "marker" is used as indicator of physical adulthood. Nonetheless, it is thought that human sexual development, regardless of cultural context, may now begin as early as age ten.

The "landmark event" for girls marking the end of childhood is **menarche**, or *first menstruation.* The importance of viewing menarche within the cultural context and the ecocultural system is illustrated in a study of young girls living at low and high altitudes in Peru. Gonzales and Villena (1996) compared ten- to nineteen-year-old Peruvian girls living in the mountainous regions of Lima with girls of similar age in Cerro de Pasco. Results indicated that those living at higher elevations, where food sources are more limited, experienced the onset of menarche later than those living at sea level in Cerro de Pasco. The authors concluded that although nutrition is an important factor in determining the age at which menarche occurs, one's physical surroundings and developmental niche also need to be considered. Another example of this close interaction between environment and physical development is a study by Proos, Hofvander, and Tuvemo (1991). They observed that the drastic change in environment experienced by Indian girls adopted in Sweden led to an earlier onset of menarche. This earlier onset may affect the women's overall height by cutting short the period of physical growth.

Some cross-cultural researchers have focused on the extent to which exposure to modernization alters the menstrual experience of young girls. In one such study, Fitzgerald (1990) examined three Samoan communities as part of an ongoing stress and health project at the University of Hawaii. One community consisted of residents living in remote traditional villages on the island of Savaii in Western Samoa. A second community, experiencing rapid modernization, was made up of seven villages on the southern coast of the island of Tutuila in American Samoa. The third community was composed of individuals living in affluent neighborhoods in Honolulu, Hawaii. Ninety-three young girls reported on their family medical history, menstrual symptoms, menstrual beliefs and practices, and menstrual experiences. According to Fitzgerald, although the literal translation of the Samoan word for "menstruation" (*ma'imasina*) means "monthly illness," most Samoans view menstruation as a natural part of life—something given to them by God to prepare them for motherhood—over which they have no control. Findings revealed that the more exposed Samoans were to the influences of modernization, the more likely they were to report severe menstrual symptoms. This suggests that as cultures come into greater contact with each other, the values and beliefs of one tend to influence the behaviors of the other.

In this case, the values and beliefs characteristic of the more modern society (Honolulu) tended to affect the menstrual experience of the Samoan islanders. Once again, this tends to support the validity of studying behavior from the perspective of the recurring themes of the ecological model and the developmental niche.

In addition to clear biological markers of sexual maturity, there are distinct cultural markers that indicate a readiness among women and men to find a sexual partner. Biological and cultural markers may or may not coincide, depending on cultural norms. For example, Hindus consider a girl sexually mature with the onset of menstruation. However, a sexually mature unmarried woman living in her father's house is considered unfortunate for all involved, and it is the duty of the father to marry off his daughter as soon as she reaches puberty or even before.

The transition from adolescence to adulthood is often considered a highly spiritual event that is celebrated with elaborate initiation ceremonies. These ceremonies often involve a ritual change of hairstyle, clothing, tattoos, or even circumcision to make the newly gained status as adult visible to all. However, transition to adulthood is not always marked by one single event. Mayan culture, for example, considers young women and men to be sexually mature and allows them to find a mate when they begin to feel sexual desire. Parents or other members of the community do not get involved in the young person's decisions about who or when to marry. This generally does not happen until the ages of sixteen to eighteen for women and twenty for men.

## 8.4.2: Gender, Sexuality, and Cultural Taboos

Once young women and young men are considered sexually mature, they are prepared to experience their first initial sexual encounter. Across cultures, these experiences vary greatly in terms of how strictly they are guided by cultural norms and which forms they take. The expectation of chastity until marriage (particularly for women) is a norm among many cultures. Patriarchal societies and those based on traditional Catholic or Islamic values generally have very strict chastity norms. Consequently, young women have little or no sexual experience or instruction until they marry. In societies in which girls are allowed to explore their sexuality more or less freely, such as the Masai of Kenya or the Hopi Indians of North America, there are some legal or normative rules about the age at which a girl may become sexually active. Usually, the minimum age is no younger than thirteen or fourteen. Chastity norms rarely apply in the same way to young men. Instead, boys are frequently encouraged to engage in various types of activity to practice sexual behavior, satisfy their sexual desires, or express their virility and dominance. Young

men's sexual experience is seen as preparation for a long-term relationship or marriage. It is a well-known practice in some cultures for older women, frequently prostitutes or unmarried women in the community, to instruct adolescent boys in sexual matters.

In some cultures, such as the indigenous societies of North and South America, communication about sexual matters is largely taboo and surrounded by myths, so that adolescents are left to explore their sexuality on their own. In their study of Mayan culture in Guatemala, Bertrand, Ward, and Pauc (1992) report that adolescents receive little education or information about sex. Young girls do not learn about menstruation until they experience menarche and have few sources from which to learn about sexual matters. In contrast, boys learn about physical development in school, from friends, or even from television or movies. Although these are informal sources of information, culturally sanctioned information about marriage is conveyed during a traditional religious ceremony. However, according to their findings, this ceremony is considered primarily a ritual and does not provide practical advice and instruction regarding sexual relations.

In addition to prohibiting sexual intercourse before marriage, some societies have strict taboos about sexual activities. In China, the only sexual behavior considered legal and morally permissible is heterosexual intercourse within a monogamous marriage. Any other behavior is considered illegal. Traditional Hinduism prescribes a very specific definition of sexuality, and following that definition is absolutely essential. Any unnatural sexual activity, including extramarital relations or homosexuality, results in losing one's caste, mutilation, or even death. It should be noted that these norms refer to the strictest followers of traditional Hindu teachings. In modern India, as in many other cultures, the norms themselves, as well as the consequences for breaking them, vary greatly.

Young adolescents in many other cultures are permitted to explore and express their sexuality in a variety of ways. For example, among the Maya in Guatemala, it is common to freely choose one's sexual partner. Parents do not have much to say regarding the selection of a mate or the age of marriage. Nonetheless, Mayan adolescents respect cultural traditions and generally abstain from sexual contact before marriage. Their interactions are typically limited to talking, holding hands, kissing, and embracing.

In cultures in which premarital relations between women and men are not prohibited by cultural norms, they are considered an expression of love and affection. Yet, how love and affection are perceived and expressed is, again, subject to wide cultural variations. In a comparison of college students of four different ethnic backgrounds, Dion and Dion (1993) found that Asian subjects of both genders view love relationships more in terms of friendship and caring than do women and men of European or Anglo-Celtic backgrounds. The authors argue that this view of love is consistent with the notion of self and others in cultures that emphasize collectivism.

In most cultures, the concepts of gender and sexuality are closely related. The cultural norms about what men and women should look like and how they should behave extends to the realm of sexuality. For example, gender-appropriate behavior for women usually includes being attracted to men and engaging in sexual relations with men. Thus, a lesbian woman violates this female gender norm by being attracted to and sexually active with other women. By deviating from the female gender norm, she sheds doubt on her "womanhood." If she does not behave like a "real" woman, then is she a "real" woman? Conversely, a heterosexual man, who happens to be feminine in his appearance or makes a career choice that is more typical for women in his culture, will likely be perceived as gay. If he is gender atypical in his behavior, then it is thought he must also be gender atypical in his sexuality.

Other sexual minorities, such as transgendered individuals and bisexual youth, face similar challenges. In adolescence, when issues of gender and sexuality become particularly salient, young people may struggle with the expression of their gender identity and sexuality. Deviating from gender norms and/or deviating from sexual norms may have serious social and psychological consequences. Interestingly, the extent of the consequences depends on how strictly gender deviation is viewed in a given cultural context. For example, in traditional Latino cultures that value and expect "machismo" from young men and passivity, subservience, and nurturance from young women, those who deviate from these ideals are stigmatized, ostracized, and sometimes the victims of violence. When strict gender norms are less pervasive in a person's ecological system, mild or temporary deviations from gender norms may be tolerated. This might be the case in some contemporary Northern European countries, in which people hold very egalitarian beliefs about the roles and norms for women and men in society; see Stiles and Gibbons (1995), as cited previously in the chapter. Not coincidentally, Scandinavian countries have the most liberal laws concerning sexual minorities.

In recent years, we have heard more about **transgender**—*of or relating to people who have a sexual identity that is not clearly male or clearly female*— individuals as they openly declare their sexuality. Awareness of transgender issues in the media has increased dramatically since 1952 when George (Christine) Jorgensen, an American veteran, announced she had undergone gender reassessment surgery. Within just the past few years, the topic has received increased attention due, in part, to the publicity given a few high-profile individuals (Bruce (Caitlyn) Jenner, Chastity (Chaz) Bono), the presence of transgender characters on television programs and in motion pictures, and the publication of books on the topic. Cross-culturally, we have found transgender individuals in Thailand, India, Iran, Nepal, Vietnam, Indonesia, and other countries. However, it is an area that has not received a great deal of professional research interest. Perhaps with greater attention devoted to it, the situation will change in the future. Of interest to readers may be the website and blog by a mother whose six-year-old son told her at age three that something went wrong when he was born because he is really a girl. See https://gendermom.wordpress.com/.

In this regard, the 3rd annual LGBT (Lesbian, Gay, Bisexual, and Transgender) Research Symposium was held in 2015 at the University of Illinois with a focus on research—challenges and opportunities—for working with these populations and for formulating practices and policies.

Finally, there is an informative article on evidence from the Boston University Medical Center of the biological basis for gender identity that may go a long way in changing physicians' perspectives on transgender medicine and improve health care for these individuals. See Boston University Medical Center (2015, February 13) to be taken directly to their website.

# 8.5: Adulthood

The life tasks that individuals encounter in early and middle adulthood can be considered universal. In any culture, most adults are faced with responsibilities related to child-rearing and providing for themselves and their families. In short, they have to "make a living." How these responsibilities are distributed and what the settings in which people "make a living" look like depends, in large part, on the individual's ecological system. Cultural values, socioeconomic status, and family size are just some examples of ecological influences, as well as characteristics of the developmental niche. This section looks at the specific ways in which gender influences the lives of adults in different cultural environments.

## 8.5.1: Status and the Division of Labor within the Family

Based on universal gender role stereotypes and gender role socialization, the adult roles of women and men are very different. Throughout history, and in almost all known societies, women have taken primary responsibility for child-rearing and housework, whereas men have been responsible for work outside the home. Industrialization and increasing economic pressures have brought about drastic changes that have affected the exclusive nature of this arrangement. Today, agricultural communities can no longer sustain all their families, and many men have to leave their villages and towns to find work in larger cities. As a result, traditional family structure is disrupted and, along with it, traditional gender roles. Women then find it necessary to seek work outside the home to fulfill some of the tasks the departed men leave behind. Also, in highly industrialized countries, technology has made housework much easier and less time consuming, but sometimes more expensive. In many cases, these additional financial needs can only be met by an additional income provided by the woman.

Surprisingly (or maybe not so surprising to some), increased participation of women in the workforce has not led to a significant change in gender roles at home. Numerous studies show that men tend to participate more in housework when their spouse works outside the home. However, even if both spouses are employed full time, child-rearing and housework are still the main responsibilities of the woman. Similar patterns are found in families in the United States, Switzerland, Indonesia, the Philippines, Taiwan, South Korea, and elsewhere.

## 8.5.2: Division of Labor in the Workforce

In addition to the gendered division of labor in the family, women and men are frequently segregated into different occupations in the labor force. Many occupational fields are either female or male dominated. One possible explanation is that those occupations requiring female stereotyped attributes (e.g., nurturance) are female dominated because women have better skills for that work or simply prefer it. For many women and men, these gender-stereotyped occupations represent an important aspect of their developmental niche. Not surprisingly, in many cultures, women tend to be teachers, nurses, or caregivers. Similarly, occupations requiring physical endurance, strength, or assertiveness (e.g., laborer jobs or executive positions) tend to be dominated by males. However, stereotypical gender roles are only one possible explanation for occupational gender segregation.

Occupational fields are also frequently segregated by status. Female-dominated occupations generally have a lower status than male-dominated occupations, regardless of the work involved. For example, activities that involve interpersonal communication and interaction are often associated with women because they tend to have stronger verbal and interpersonal skills. This helps explain why more women than men become teachers, therapists, and social workers. Yet, few women are involved at the highest levels in international politics, science, business, or academia, all of which require a great deal of interpersonal and verbal skills. Badal, mentioned in the opening vignette, who prepared to be a youth counselor in India,

probably has many more female colleagues than male colleagues, unless this occupation is highly regarded in his culture.

High-status occupations typically are better paid and are associated with access to greater resources, resulting in frequent wage and status gaps between some women and men. [In the United States, current discussions of wage inequality are a "hot topic."] As a consequence, women are often economically disadvantaged and dependent on their husbands or other men as financial providers. In fact, it appears that there is a consistent gender difference in how men and women view the relationship between status, money, and pay. Tang (1996) revealed that men in the United States with high money ethic endorsement (MEE)—the psychological importance of money—allocated significantly more money to the highest position and less money to the lowest positions (creating a large pay differential and clearly linking status with money) than did those to whom money was less important. Women's allocation of money was not affected by their MEE. In a subsequent study, Tang, Furnham, and Davis (2000) conducted a cross-cultural comparison of pay differentials (in the United States, Taiwan, and the United Kingdom) as a function of the rater's sex and MEE. Findings showed that Taiwanese allocated more money to different positions than did their British and American counterparts. Men tended to have a significantly higher top/bottom pay differential than women. In another study focusing on the devaluation of women's work, England, Hermsen, and Cotter (2000) found that there is a "wage penalty" for working in occupations that have a higher percentage of women.

In Paslocale, Ecuador, a father and daughter work together making brooms.

(Ian Trower/Alamy Stock Photo)

Many governments have now established public policies and laws that have led to greater gender equality with regard to material and economic differences (i.e., antidiscrimination employment laws). However, differences in the representation of men and women in occupational fields continue to exist. Maria Charles' and Karen Bradley's (2009) study of forty-four societies revealed a surprising trend: In societies that have "regulated" gender equality, occupations are more segregated by gender than in societies with less institutional gender equity. In particular, in such industrially "advanced" countries, men enter the mathematics/engineering occupations in significantly greater numbers than women. The authors argue that economic independence from gender inequality (macrosystem) allows individuals the choice to express their "innate" gendered selves as part of a fundamental identity. The next section explores how the cultural expression of gender reinforces or changes the ecological context in which individual growth and development takes place in adult life.

## 8.5.3: Gender Relations in Social Status and Public Policy

Social and economic stratification is deeply rooted in culture, contributes to gender inequality, and is reflected in relationships within the family. Assuming that economic power equals social power, the family member with the greatest social power will be most dominant within the family and thus be a powerful influence within the microsystem. Asserting this power can mean making financial and social decisions, asserting one's needs, assigning tasks to other family members, and yielding or denying access to resources.

For several centuries, men generally have had more economic and social power than women. Therefore, they are likely to control and shape interpersonal relationships with a spouse and within the family. Although women may manage everyday financial or social affairs, the ultimate power of approval or disapproval for decisions often lies with men, who may or may not choose to exercise this power. Because these status differences are so pervasive, they are often reinforced by the political institutions present within a culture's various ecological settings.

Francoeur and Noonan (2004) perceive some radical changes in this established world order. They argue that there is evidence for a global "sexual revolution," which is bound to change the ways in which people relate and shift gradually toward a new gender equality. The authors provide the following examples of changing "gender culture" around the world: (1) In Finland, the popularity of both marriage and cohabitation are declining. Two national surveys, in 1972 and 1993, show that the fastest-growing lifestyle is couples "living alone together" (LAT) (in a sexual relationship). In these same surveys, LAT couples report being much happier with their personal and intimate lives than married or unmarried cohabiting couples. Similar trends have been reported in Germany and elsewhere.

(2) China has been widely condemned for its one-time one-child-per-family policy, forced abortions, and female infanticide. But because these policies have also created a serious surplus of males, young Chinese women are enjoying an unexpected change in bargaining power and choice in picking the best possible husband. (3) In Latin America, Peruvian women have enthusiastically endorsed a government campaign to make contraception available to all women, especially the poor. In a nation where 90% of the people are Catholic and many rural women have ten or more children, Peru's women are ignoring the pope's ban on contraception and asserting their right to control their own sexual and reproductive lives. (4) In Algeria, Muslim women are turning to personal advertisements to find mates of their own choice, despite strong family disapproval and censorship by fundamentalist Islamic men. (5) There is a growing tradition of financially established single Italian men, "mammoni," who continue living with their parents into their thirties, forties, and beyond, instead of marrying and moving out on their own. Italian husbands and Catholic bishops complain that Italian women are not listening to them anymore. So many Italian women, married and unmarried, are using birth control and having abortions that Italy now has the sixteenth lowest birthrate (9.18 births per 1,000 people) of nations in the world.

These examples lend themselves to the conclusion that gender continues to permeate all levels of the ecological system in adult life. Ultimately, individual development is framed by fundamental beliefs about differences between men and women.

# 8.6:  Later Adulthood

As is the case throughout life, the physical, psychological, and social changes in later adult years affect men and women in similar and different ways. Cultural views of aging, gender, and gender relations shape the ecological system in which older men and women develop.

## 8.6.1: The Experience of Menopause

A major event for women during these years is the experience of menopause. Because menopause, like menarche, is a universal event, it would be easy to assume that all women experience it in the same way. However, based on our previous discussions of Bronfenbrenner's ecological model, we would expect that cultural values, expectations, and context would contribute strongly to shaping the experience—and they do. For example, in previous decades, Europeans and North Americans, among others, frequently described menopause as a "change of life." Many early television programs stereotyped elderly and middle-age women as moody, unpredictable, and depressed. The picture of menopause as presented in contemporary print media does not seem to have significantly improved. Although the frequency of articles on menopause has increased, the information is often insufficient, treated as a negative experience or disease needing medical treatment, frequently containing contradictions and inconsistencies, and ignoring or giving little attention to such factors as race and ethnicity, lifestyle differences, stress, or aging.

Today, most North Americans and, in fact, people in many other countries view menopause very differently. Women's own expectations have changed, and for some, menopause is seen as a liberating experience. Part of this new view can be attributed to changing cultural views of aging. For research that views menopause from a contextual analysis, see Anderson (1999).

Robinson (2002) reviewed cross-cultural studies conducted in Israel, North America, Japan, Peru, the Yucatan, and the Greek island of Evia. Results indicate that there are enormous differences in the experience of menopause among women in the same culture and among women in different cultures. Robinson concludes further that, indeed, menopausal symptoms are the result of not only physical factors but also psychological and cultural influences. From these examples, it becomes clear that both the physical change during menopause itself and the cultural view of menopause shape a woman's experience. Is menopause just another "developmental stage," or is menopause an "illness" that can be treated (e.g., with hormone replacement therapy)? If menopause is an "illness" that warrants treatment, then should we begin to consider hormone treatment for puberty as well, with its many discomforting symptoms (e.g., acne, mood swings, and change in body shape)?

## 8.6.2: Divorce and Widowhood

You may recall from the discussion of cultural views on marriage in Chapter 4 that men and women in later adulthood, in most cultures and religions, consider marriage to be one of the highest sacraments. However, in any society, there will be a number of individuals who do not have a spouse, either because they never married or because they lost their mate through divorce or death.

According to traditional Hindu beliefs, divorce is unacceptable. If men are not content in their marriage, then they are allowed to take a second wife. After their wife's death, men are also permitted to remarry immediately. Widowhood for women, in contrast, carries a strong social stigma. Without her husband, women are considered incomplete and even sinful. They are not allowed to remarry, become social outcasts, and simply await their own death. As a result, some women choose to burn themselves at their husband's funeral to attain spiritual salvation. **Sati**, or *widow immolation,* is a sacred practice (Kumar & Kanth, 2007). Although the current Indian government

strongly discourages this practice, a widow's memory is still held in high regard if she dies within a reasonable time after her husband's death.

Among the Hausa of Northern Nigeria, marriage also plays an important spiritual role. Adults who die while still married are expected to move on to **Lahira**, or *paradise.* Although divorced and widowed adults are stigmatized, they are not met with nearly as much resentment as adults who never marry. Previously married women can still acquire some status by becoming prostitutes and remarrying later, an option denied to women who were never married.

In many Native American societies, a widow secures her livelihood by marrying one of her husband's brothers or another close relative. Divorced women may return to their parents or marry another man. Divorce proceedings are relatively uncomplicated unless wife and husband share a great deal of property or the wife's relatives want to negotiate the return of the bride price paid to the husband. These examples of women in different societies show that even in adulthood, individuals create their own developmental niche in response to cultural norms and expectations associated with, in this case, divorce and widowhood.

When viewing divorce in the larger ecological context, it becomes clear that cultural beliefs about gender roles and gender-typical behavior (macrosystem) shape individual experiences within the family (microsystem). "Divorce is not merely behavior on the microlevel, but is associated with shifting cultures on the macrolevel" (Yodanis, 2005, p. 656). Yodanis argues that the option of divorce, when accepted in society, gives women the power to negotiate equal status in the family. Her study of twenty-two countries revealed that women and men experience more equality in their marriage when divorce is practiced and accepted in their society. In countries that, until recently, outlawed divorce (the Philippines and Ireland) or in which divorce is highly unaccepted (Japan), gender roles within the family tended to be more traditional and unequal in terms of work distribution and decision-making power in the home.

These findings are mirrored in Bulbeck's (2005) description of young people's understanding of gender relations within the larger cultural context. Even though many of the young adults interviewed had not yet established their own families, the cultural beliefs about gender relations within the family were well established. Respondents from Asian cultures (Japan, Korea, and Thailand) tended to emphasize separate roles for men and women within the family. These beliefs were associated with the cultural belief that prescribed gender roles serve the family and society. In contrast, young adults from Australia, the United States, and Canada showed strong support for gender equality in the home based on individual preference.

## 8.6.3: Gender Roles and Status in Old Age

In traditional societies, age is frequently associated with a gain in community status. Older adults are respected and accepted as leaders who bring with them a wealth of life experience. Furthermore, they are frequently thought to have supernatural powers, and they hold important spiritual and religious responsibilities. Finally, both female and male elders are considered important to the socialization process because they pass on the group's cultural heritage to the next generation. In societies in which status is based on age and role as much as gender, older women may actually gain considerable power, both within their families and in society, once they have broken through the "seniority" barrier. This may be the case in Asian societies more so than in Western cultures.

Sangree (1992) examined two societies, with a particular focus on older men and women. The Tiriki of Kenya and the Irigwe of Nigeria are two societies that view their elders with great respect and appreciate the wisdom they bring to the society. On closer examination, Sangree discovered it is not seniority alone that leads to status and influence among these elders. A necessary condition for being recognized as an elder is grandparenthood. To achieve the highest respect as an older person, one has to have at least three living children. Being accepted as an elder represents a gain in status, particularly for Tiriki women. According to cultural norms, Tiriki women cannot be initiated as adults and are denied important positions in the clan or the village. Moreover, their activities are limited to domestic work and farming. As elders, women achieve considerable power and influence by being involved in community affairs, although their contributions are not publicly recognized.

Among the Irigwe, elder status derives from the cultural belief surrounding a mystical relation between death and birth. The Irigwe believe that the soul of a deceased person will eventually be reincarnated as a newborn. The departure of one soul is essential for the creation of a new life. Elders who are approaching death are held in high esteem because their death ensures the continuation of life.

Although Irigwe women are not granted formal leadership in the form of a public office, they nevertheless play a critically important role in community life. In contrast to Tiriki society, women have more opportunities to excel in certain areas and gain public recognition (e.g., as healers or craftswomen). As grandmothers, they achieve even more status and are held in high regard.

With changes brought about by modernization, the gender roles and status of older adults, as well as of younger adults, have changed, particularly in Irigwe society. Sangree (1992) describes how young educated men are taking over community activities formerly conducted by the male and female elders. Such changes are not characteristic of younger women. They are often too busy with their family responsibilities or limited by their lack of education to compete with men for jobs and status.

Among the Tiriki, male elders retain their influence in some local affairs. The culture has preserved the elder males' role as an essential agent in the socialization and initiation of younger males. They are also more involved in their sons' lives because they manage their sons' property while they are away from home for work. The influence and status of female elders are gradually disappearing, and there are fewer opportunities for them to be involved within the community. Overall, the status of Tiriki individuals in late adulthood and how they are viewed increasingly resemble the view held by other modern cultures.

## Summary: Culture and Issues of Gender and Sexuality

This chapter discusses the development of women and men across the lifespan. Whereas some gender differences can be viewed from a biological perspective, the emphasis here is on social and cultural forces that contribute to the psychological development of men and women in different societies. In early childhood, prevailing gender stereotypes already influence the socialization of gendered behavior. Cultural customs and arrangements determine the structure and content of social interaction between boys and girls. These interactions become increasingly important during adolescence, when young people are preparing for their roles as adults. Aside from biological maturity, cultural norms determine when a youth may engage in sexual activity. In addition, cultural rules may dictate mate selection, as well as acceptable or unacceptable sexual activities. The years of adulthood are characterized by clearly stipulated roles and obligations, many of which are defined by gender. Although many of these roles show great similarities across cultures, the status of men and women and their relationships may differ depending on their cultural environment and their unique developmental niche.

# Study Questions

Define the terms "sex" and "gender" and distinguish between them.

Use biological, evolutionary, and social learning perspectives to explain gender differences that are considered universal (e.g., relative strength, body size, aggression, and verbal skills).

Give examples of how factors at the micro-, exo-, and macrolevels of the ecological system explain cultural differences in gender equality during adulthood.

Discuss gender socialization during childhood and some of the influences on it.

Describe the transition from adolescence to adulthood.

Comment on the division of labor within the family and within a culture's labor force.

Consider cultural differences and similarities in divorce and widowhood.

Describe changes in gender roles and status in late adulthood, and give examples.

# Developmental Analysis
## Gender and Sexuality

My life would be very different had I been born a boy or even a girl in another culture with different expectations for women. I have had more freedom and opportunities than women in many other countries. However, as I was growing up, especially during adolescence, I often felt a sense of confusion and lack of direction. I think American society sometimes sends women different messages about what should be most important in life. This is especially true today. Should a young woman focus on marriage and child-rearing or on a career? Can she find a balance among these competing interests? I believe she can, but it certainly is not easy.

All cultures have gender stereotypes that are established early. Boys and girls are frequently expected to conform to them. This was certainly true when I was growing up. One example is the type of toys children are expected to play with. I had my dolls and cooking sets (to help prepare me to be a mother and house-wife), and my brother had his doctor kit and chemistry set (to encourage him to experiment with science and think about a career). Today, boys' and girls' toys are less associated with gender, and everyone learns about computers, plays video games, and has their own iPod (and often cell phone, too).

However, when I was young, my father took me fishing and later taught me how to hunt. Sometimes, I think he wished I'd been a boy, although he never said that. When I was twelve, he had me take Hunter's Safety. I didn't want to because my girlfriends weren't doing it. This is an example of where peers influence gender stereotypes. I am also an avid football fan—unlike many of my female friends. In seventh grade, I wore makeup and skirts. The following year, I changed to jeans and sweatshirts. I was trying to find myself in both extremes and learned I could be both a lady and a tomboy.

My life growing up as a female was quite different from that of my mother. I've been able to do so many more things than she could. For example, I went to college, studied business, traveled abroad, married a man from a different culture, am a mom *and* a professor, and take students on foreign study tours to places such as Guatemala, Egypt, China, and Norway.

My mother and father knew each other as children and married right after high school. Being raised with a strict Catholic background, she knew little about sex and her own sexuality. Although it was embarrassing at times, my girlfriends and I would read magazines, discuss what we read, and try to understand what was happening to our bodies and our changing attitudes toward boys. Naturally, I learned more when I went to college, and when I met my future husband and began to develop an intimate relationship, I learned there are cultural differences in the way people view dating, love, romance, and marriage.

The lives of my son and daughter underwent even more change than I experienced. The same will likely be true for our grandchildren. In terms of gender and sexuality, this is an extremely interesting time in which to live—as you know from your own experiences.

# Chapter 9
# Culture, Health, and Illness

*Hiroki Hashimoto is fourteen and lives with his family in the northern city of Akita on the island of Honshu. He attends a private school, where one of his British teachers, Alison Perrin, is concerned about Hiroki's obsessive neatness, extreme shyness, and apparent lack of many close friends. Based on her previous experiences with adolescents in her own country and during a teaching appointment in Canada, she feels he may have an obsessive—compulsive neurosis, as well as very poorly developed interpersonal skills. She mentions to a Japanese colleague that she is about to recommend that his parents take him to see a child psychologist. Her colleague explains that Hiroki is more likely showing signs of a rather common disorder in Japan known as taijin kyofusho (TKS) syndrome, in which an individual is afraid of offending others while engaged in social situations. Loosely translated as "interpersonal anxiety," or simply "fear of people," TKS appears related to two salient behavior patterns in Japanese culture: an almost universal appearance of shyness or modesty and a great concern with cleanliness.*

*The sun has just appeared over the small village near Huascaran, an extinct volcano and the highest peak in the Andes Mountains, in the Peruvian highlands, where Eric Summerville, an Australian physician, works among the runakuna (native Quechua people). He has just been summoned to the thatched-roof home of a family whose young daughter appears to be suffering from susto, a disorder he has observed many times before among Indian tribes in Peru, Colombia, and Bolivia. Susto (Spanish for fright) is frequently the result of a frightening experience, and its symptoms may include excitability, severe anxiety, depression, rapid heartbeat, and often loss of weight. According to cultural beliefs, it can be caused by a variety of circumstances, including contact with strangers, supernatural spirits, or even "bad air" from cemeteries. The village healer has already made the traditional diagnosis by examining a guinea pig's intestines. Dr. Summerville now assists with the usual treatment of rubbing a variety of plants over the girl's skin, while the healer performs an animal sacrifice to pacify the Earth, where it is believed the girl's soul is trapped.*

Each vignette illustrates a unique cultural orientation to the diagnosis and practice of medicine. In both cases,

making an accurate diagnosis and planning effective treatment are of chief importance. However, the explanations for the behavior and the etiology (causes) of the symptoms differ, as well as the response to the illness and its treatment. In the case of Hiroki, cultural beliefs about social behavior and expectations within his ecological setting play a major role in his symptoms. In Peru, native beliefs about a variety of frightening circumstances lead to a culturally unique diagnosis and treatment, using indigenous methods that are an extension of the developmental niche and shaped by the ecological system.

## 9.1: Ecological Context: Cultural Concepts of Health and Healing

Cultural traditions determine, in large part, how individuals look at their physical and mental health. What is considered healthy behavior in one society may be viewed as unhealthy in another. For example, there are many ways in which people deal with stress and tension (e.g., withdrawal, overt expressions of anger, overeating, or not eating at all). *How do you behave when you experience stress? Which approach to dealing with problems would you consider healthy and which approach would you consider unhealthy?* The answer varies depending on the culture, developmental niche, and interaction among unique ecocultural systems: the individual (microsystem), who lives and interacts with others in a particular village or neighborhood (mesosystem), and the specific cultural health beliefs and practices that help shape what goes on within the wider exosystem and macrosystem.

Culture influences attitudes toward health in a variety of ways. A reciprocal process exists in which cultural beliefs, traditions, and progression of knowledge about health shape the views of a particular society; and the views of society, in turn, determine methods and treatments. Frequently, the symptoms and treatment of an illness are manifested in the beliefs themselves. For example, in remote parts of Sabah and Sarawak in East

Malaysia, an individual who exhibits the symptoms of depression would seek the treatment of a village *bomoh* (medicine man) to remove the charms presumably evoked by jealous clans. In contrast, many North Americans view depression as a biological disorder, explainable as a chemical imbalance in the brain and usually treated with antidepressants. You can imagine how the nature and treatment of depression in either culture might be perceived by the other.

This gives rise to an important concept in cross-cultural psychology discussed previously—the distinction between emic and etic factors. As you may recall, **emic** refers to *culture-specific concepts,* whereas **etic** refers to *culture-general concepts*. In this regard, the symptoms characteristic of certain illnesses in one culture cannot be generalized across cultures. For example, although eating disorders are not unusual among young women in Western countries, such disorders may not be as common in developing countries, where the food supply is scarce. Each culture's delicate balance of ecological systems and developmental niches make up the emic values to be considered when diagnosing and treating illnesses.

In recent years, contemporary researchers have begun moving more toward designing studies that incorporate both of these concepts and thereby explain a particular behavior across cultures (i.e., etic perspective) and at the same time understand how this behavior is meaningful to a specific culture (i.e., emic perspective) (Chao & Lambert, 2013). Such an approach will be better at comparing cultural similarities and differences and draw greater contrast between culture-specific and universal behaviors.

## 9.1.1: Culture-Bound Syndromes

Medical anthropologists and ethnopsychiatrists have known about seemingly unique forms of psychological illnesses for a long time. These researchers observed (1) symptoms of known illnesses that express themselves in unique ways in different cultures and (2) certain illnesses that occur only among members of a specific cultural group. Because the unique patterns of symptoms do not fit any conventional classification system of disorders, these have been largely ignored by the medical community. The revised 5th edition of the *Diagnostic and Statistical Manual of the American Psychiatric Society* (American Psychiatric Association, 2013), reflecting a much more inclusive range of global psychopathology and vastly improved treatment of culture, acknowledges the existence of these culture-bound syndromes and lists twenty-five of the most frequently encountered with detailed definitions, geographic locations, and rates of prevalence among affected populations. Culture-bound syndromes

have been replaced by three concepts: (1) *cultural syndromes*: "clusters of symptoms and attributions that tend to co-occur among individuals in specific cultural groups, communities, or contexts . . . that are recognized locally as coherent patterns of experience" (p. 758); (2) *cultural idioms of distress*: "ways of expressing distress that may not involve specific symptoms or syndromes, but that provide collective, shared ways of experiencing and talking about personal or social concerns" (p. 758); and (3) *cultural explanations of distress or perceived causes*: "labels, attributions, or features of an explanatory model that indicate culturally recognized meaning or etiology for symptoms, illness, or distress" (p. 758). The *DSM-5* views culture-bound syndromes as recurrent, locally specific patterns of abnormal and troubling experiences. Many of these patterns are indigenously considered to be illnesses, and most have local names. Lopez and Ho (2013) suggest that with a world population of more than 7 billion people, there are likely to be many more than just twenty-five such syndromes. (Box 9.1 presents examples of some of the better known syndromes.)

Although the inclusion of culture-bound syndromes represents an improvement in the validity of Western diagnostic systems, current researchers suggest that this is just the foundation for the practice of culturally sensitive medicine. For instance, Azhar and Varma (2000) suggest that a new form of psychotherapy could be used to treat culture-bound syndromes (*koro, amok*) in Malaysia. This treatment is based on Western techniques of cognitive therapy, but includes culture-specific religious beliefs and practices to reduce symptoms and achieve overall well-being.

## 9.1.2: Medical Diagnosis Across Cultures

The emic–etic distinction is germane to another important issue in culture and health—namely, the reliability and validity of diagnostic tests and measurement. Before making a diagnosis, physicians and other health professionals need to consider the medical criteria on which they base their treatment decisions. Often, doctors trained in Western societies use their familiar inventories and diagnostic criteria to evaluate medical conditions in patients from non-Western societies, with a resulting misdiagnosis. The emic- or culture-specific values and beliefs that are part of a particular doctor's ecocultural perspective cannot be readily applied in diagnosing and treating people raised in a culturally different developmental niche. Accurate assessment should take into consideration the beliefs, values, and perceptions of the patient, and doctors should employ culture-specific criteria when diagnosing illnesses.

# Box 9.1 Culture-Bound Syndromes and Psychological Disorders

The way in which individuals view their mental and physical health is determined, in part, by cultural traditions. What is considered healthy in one society may be seen as unhealthy in another. Although psychological disorders can be found in all cultures, the ways in which they are formed and expressed appear to be highly influenced by cultural belief systems and shaped by cultural factors.

## China

*Koro*, found primarily in China (as far back as 3000 BC) and some other South and East Asian countries, is associated with acute anxiety involving the fear that one's genitals (the penis in a man and the vulva and nipples in women) are shrinking and retracting into the body and may result in death. Chinese folk culture provides some insight into the syndrome's origins, which can be found in fears about nocturnal emissions and impotence. These fears originated in the traditional Chinese beliefs about the balance of *yin* (female) and *yang* (male) humors, which held that during masturbation or nocturnal emissions, an unhealthy loss of *yang* was thought to occur and to place an individual in an unbalanced condition.

*Koro* has been identified primarily in younger men, twenty-one to forty years of age. It is believed that guilt and anxiety arise out of real or imagined sexual excesses. People with *koro* demonstrate typical anxiety symptoms such as sweating, breathlessness, and heart palpitations. Men with the disorder have been known to use mechanical devices, such as chopsticks, to try to prevent the penis from retracting into the body. Reassurance by medical professionals that the genitals are not retracting often puts an end to *koro* episodes, and the disorder passes with time. Most cases, however, are handled by traditional medical or folk healers outside the established health care system.

## Japan

*Taijin kyofusho* (TKS) *syndrome* is characterized by an excessive fear and anxiety that a person will behave in ways that will embarrass or offend other people (e.g., blushing, emitting odors, staring inappropriately, or presenting improper facial expressions), resulting in social withdrawal and avoidance. Affecting primarily young Japanese men, the syndrome is believed to be related to an emphasis in Japanese culture on not embarrassing others, as well as deep concerns about issues of shame.

On examining the symptoms of TKS and using a Western diagnostic system, patients with TKS would typically be diagnosed as having anxiety reactions, obsessive—compulsive reactions, or social phobias. Traditional therapy for TKS occurs in the context of a ritual setting and includes physiological applications (sweating and massage), behavioral restrictions (diet), and social support.

## Korea

*Shin-byung* (a divine illness) is a possession syndrome often occurring in the course of a prolonged psychosomatic illness. People believe they are possessed by a dead ancestor and, through a dream or a hallucination, are persuaded to become a shaman, after which the patient becomes "cured" of the ailment. The occurrence of *shin-byung* is reported to be decreasing.

## India

*Dhat* is a disorder affecting Indian males and involves intense fear or anxiety over the loss of semen through ejaculations or through nocturnal emissions. Some men also believe, incorrectly, that semen mixes with urine and is excreted by urinating. In Indian culture, semen is considered to be the elixir of life in both the physical and mystical sense. There is a popular belief that loss of semen drains a man of his vital natural energy, whereas its preservation guarantees health and longevity. Loss of semen through masturbation, excessive sexual intercourse, or nocturnal emission is believed to lead to weakness. The most common symptoms of *dhat* are fatigue, weakness, body aches, severe headaches, depression, anxiety, loss of appetite, and suicidal feelings. Indian males believe that this is caused by heated foods, a fiery constitution, sexual excesses, and the use of intoxicants. A "cooling diet," "cooling medications," and baths are recommended. A tonic may also be given to increase sperm production (Chadda & Ahuja, 1990).

## Nigeria

*"Missing genitals"* is a syndrome that has been reported in Nigeria. The victim of this syndrome, typically a man, might exchange greetings by shaking hands with another man and is suddenly overcome by fear that the genitals have disappeared. It is usually claimed that supernatural forces have been invoked to make the genitals disappear. Although objective examination of the genitals reveals that they are intact, pointing this out to the victim does not convince him (Sijuwola, 1995).

## Latino Culture

*Susto* ("magical fright") is found in some Latino cultures, primarily among the Quechua-speaking Indians of the Andes. It is triggered by a frightening experience, in which the soul is thought to separate from the body and become trapped in the Earth, and the person falls to the ground. Symptoms include loss of appetite and weight, physical weakness, restless sleep, depression, introversion, and apathy. By looking at the intestines of a guinea pig, a healing expert makes the diagnosis and then attempts to appease the Earth through sacrifices so the soul will return to the body.

## Native American Culture

*Amok*, a type of dissociative episode or a sudden change in consciousness or self-identity, is found in traditional Puerto Rican and Navajo cultures in the West. It is marked by a violent or aggressive outburst followed by a period of brooding, often precipitated by a perceived slight or insult. The person, who sometimes experiences amnesia, returns to his or her usual state of functioning following the episode. In the West, the expression "running amuck" refers to an episode of losing oneself and running around in a violent frenzy.

*Windigo*, also known as witiko, is a rare, culture-bound disorder reported among some North American Indian tribes, including the Cree and Ojibwa. It is characterized by symptoms of melancholia and a delusion of transformation into a *witiko* or man-eating monster, who either has a heart of ice or vomits ice, and who will turn the victim into a homicidal cannibal. Cannibalism seldom, if ever, occurs. Suicidal ideation to avoid acting on the cannibalistic urges may take place (Trimble, Manson, Dinges, & Medicine, 1984).

**SOURCE:** "Infusing Culture into Parenting Issues: A Supplement for Psychology Instructors" from unpublished manuscript, St. Louis Community College by Vicki Ritts. Copyright © 2001 by Vicki Ritts. Reprinted by permission of Vicki Ritts.

In an interesting study focusing on illness beliefs, Cook (1994) asked 182 adult Chinese, Indian, and Anglo-Celtic Canadians about their beliefs concerning chronic illness and how it should be treated. He found that each ethnic group viewed the causes and treatment differently, depending on geographical orientation, generation, and age. For example, older first- or second-generation Chinese emphasized a more traditional, spiritual dimension to help explain and treat physical illness, whereas younger Chinese tended to look to biomedical intervention.

When individuals are misdiagnosed, their health generally deteriorates even more. There is little or no relief because treatment is completely ineffective. The chances of this occurring are greatest when physicians and health care professionals from one cultural orientation treat individuals from another. For example, in 1985, more than 100 Cuban refugees were initially rejected from applying for U.S. citizenship because a medical review board composed entirely of American psychiatrists diagnosed them as having antisocial personality disorder. However, this diagnosis was overturned after an official appeal was made to a second medical board composed of physicians and psychiatrists from several different countries. Many of the psychiatrists serving on the initial screening board subsequently admitted not being aware of crucial ethnic and cultural differences when they made their original diagnosis. This should be viewed as a serious warning sign for future diagnosis and treatment of refugees, immigrants, sojourners, and others moving from one culture to another.

Lisa Beardsley (1994) has outlined several reasons for misdiagnoses. A first reason is the use of clinical manuals (e.g., the *DSM-5*) in societies significantly different from the ones for which they were originally intended. For example, although Chinese and American psychiatrists largely agree on some clinical evaluations such as schizophrenia, they disagree on others such as depression and anxiety disorders.

A second reason for misidentifying a health problem frequently centers on the difference in definition between disease and illness behavior. According to Beardsley (1994), **disease** is *a biological process*, whereas **illness behavior** is *a psychological experience and the social expression of disease* (p. 281). This is an important distinction not always understood. She goes on to point out that "cultural variables interact with biological processes, and as a result, there is overlap between culture-specific (emic) and culture-general (etic) features of a disease" (p. 281).

Finally, the use of culturally biased instruments and tests may contribute to misdiagnosis. For example, standardized intelligence tests such as the Stanford-Binet Intelligence Scales, Fifth Edition (Roid, 2003) and the Wechsler Intelligence Scale for Children (WISC-IV) (Wechsler, 2003), as well as personality inventories such as the Minnesota Multiphasic Personality Inventory-2 (MMPI-2) (Butcher, Graham, Ben-Porath, Tellegen, Dahlstrom, & Kaemmer, 2009) were developed for use with specific *American populations* and, even when carefully translated, are not always appropriate for use in other cultures. Consequently, use of these instruments may result in a patient or client receiving ineffective treatment. For example, I once had a Chinese student come to my office in tears because she had been given the results of her MMPI, and the computerized analysis indicated she "demonstrates bizarre behavior and should be institutionalized and treated immediately." Knowing the cultural specificity of certain items on this test used to assess "psychopathological tendencies," I was able to calm her down by showing her how the answers she gave, although reasonable and healthy for her particular culture, were considered inappropriate and unhealthy when given by someone born and raised in the American culture. I strongly recommended that the personnel in the college counseling office, none of whom had had cross-cultural training, not use this instrument as a measure of anything with international students. They took my advice and immediately discontinued its use. As Brislin (1990) aptly states, "It is decidedly a creation of the 'Western' view of etiology and psychiatric classification (and is, therefore, culture-bound); its original normative samples came from small, rural parts of Minnesota (in the United States); and there is little or no 'theory' guiding its cross-cultural use" (p. 69). Nevertheless, the MMPI is available in more than 100 languages and, since the incident mentioned here, has undergone revision and is seen by some as worthy of cross-cultural attention (Butcher, 2006). However, I still agree with Brislin (1990), who argues for caution if employing this instrument because, if misused, it can lead to errors and often to unintended consequences.

The goals of the World Health Organization (WHO) are to promote health, prevent misdiagnoses, and provide medical services to countries throughout the world. One of WHO's major efforts is the Mental Health Program, which is aimed at protecting and promoting mental health. This program consists of four parts: (1) program formulation and evaluation, (2) psychosocial and behavioral factors affecting health and development, (3) organization of services for the prevention and treatment of mental and neurological illnesses, and (4) biomedical research on mental functioning in health and disease. Developing guidelines for improving mental health care and training mental health professionals are also integral parts of this program. As a result of these and other efforts, health care professionals are becoming more culturally sensitive (see Box 9.2).

Success in these efforts requires an understanding of human development from a cross-cultural perspective. The focus of this chapter, therefore, is to investigate how health is mediated by cultural factors across the lifespan. [For a thought-provoking and somewhat controversial discussion of how Western cultures often negatively influence the diagnosis and treatment of psychological disorders throughout the world, see Watters (2010).]

## 9.1.3: Illness, Stress, and Coping

Illness, at any age and in any ecological system, creates considerable stress. We know today that stressful life events affect physical health in complex ways. Behavior, cognition, and emotion interact with the central nervous system and the endocrine system in ways that might suppress or boost the immune system, thus setting the stage for optimal health or risk of illness.

The ability to cope with the stress of illness is not only important for survival, but it is also the foundation for growth and change. You may know people who experienced a seemingly devastating illness at some point in their lives. Yet, they were able to adapt to their limitations and develop abilities and strategies that allowed them to achieve goals. One could argue that coping with and adapting to their illness allows them to grow—they grow not despite the illness but because of it. Hampel and Petermann (2006) showed that children and adolescents with chronic health conditions coped with everyday stressors (e.g., tension with family or friends, school-related issues) better than their healthy counterparts. *Have you or anyone in your family had to deal with a serious illness? What was done? What was the outcome?*

Perhaps adjusting to the stresses related to a chronic illness has helped these children develop coping strategies for stressors in other areas of their lives. The Chinese view of stress emphasizes that it presents both a crisis and an opportunity (for growth) at the same time. In other words, stress is part of life, and adaptation is growth. Yet, individuals and cultural groups differ in how susceptible they are to stress and illness and how they cope with these situations. Ecological factors that shape responses to illness include differences in access to health care, social stigma, and parental modeling of illness behavior. This chapter investigates how health, illness, and response to illness are mediated by cultural factors across the lifespan.

## Box 9.2 Training Health Care Professionals to Be Culturally Sensitive

Although the world's 7 billion inhabitants live in 193 countries and speak more than 6,000 languages, relatively little is known about the effects of culture on health care. In the United States, emergency rooms are treating increasing numbers of individuals from ethnically and culturally diverse backgrounds. For example, in 2010, it was estimated that there were more than 35 million legal immigrants living in the United States, along with approximately 12 million to 20 million illegal immigrants, many speaking little or no English. In an article in *Journal of Pediatrics*, Flores (2000) emphasizes the importance of physicians becoming more sensitive to cultural diversity and provides a framework for understanding the clinical consequences of culture. The specific impact of five cultural components (normative cultural values, language, folk illnesses, parent/patient beliefs, and provider practices) is examined, along with practical solutions to make sure culturally sensitive care is provided to patients. Most important, Flores proposes a model for cultural competency in health care, which can be used to guide clinicians in interactions with any cultural group. Today, hospital staff are taking steps to ensure greater awareness and better understanding of cultural differences. Failure to do this will only increase the possibility of misdiagnosis, as in the case of a Mexican peasant woman who invented her symptoms because she was too embarrassed to describe her real problem (rectovaginal fistula or *an abnormal connection between the rectum and the vagina*). Needless to say, such misunderstanding not only jeopardizes patients' health but also opens up the possibility of a lawsuit. Thus, many physicians are taking courses in multiculturalism and enlisting the help of relatives or friends of patients when making daily rounds. In New York, a Chinatown outreach team from St. Vincent's Hospital is learning about the use of herbal remedies to treat ailments of the elderly. Also, folk healers are recruited at University Hospital in Minneapolis to help serve the large community of Laotian Hmong refugees.

# 9.2: Infancy

Professionals in today's health care delivery systems see infant care as one of their major challenges. Technological advances allow premature and extremely low-birth-weight babies that would not have survived a decade ago to live and grow into healthy children and adults. However, the process is not always easy, and success or failure frequently depends on cultural factors.

## 9.2.1: Risks to Infant Health

Physical development during the prenatal period is critical, and any number of environmental factors can adversely affect this development and increase the odds of giving birth to a child with birth defects. Environmental toxins (aluminum, lead, and carbon dioxide) or **teratogens** (*agents such as chemicals or diseases*) can contribute to the development of physical and mental abnormalities. Even a small amount of alcohol consumed during a critical period of pregnancy may increase a mother's chances of giving birth to a child with physical and cognitive abnormalities. Known as **fetal alcohol syndrome (FAS)**, these abnormalities include an unusually small head, low birth weight, facial deformities, neurological impairments, and signs of impaired intellectual functioning. Although it is difficult to know the precise number of FAS cases throughout the world, it is believed that approximately 1 in every 500 infants is born with the disorder. The result is that FAS contributes significantly to the number of children suffering from mental disabilities. Along these same lines, studies have shown that if an expectant mother uses **crack cocaine** (*a concentrated form of cocaine*) or another addictive drug such as heroin or methadone, it will have the same effect on her fetus that it has on her. The developing fetus is most vulnerable to teratogens during the third to sixth weeks after conception (the critical period), when the central nervous system, heart, arms, and legs are developing.

The most observable indicators of health during the early years of life are the relative increases in height and weight. In this regard, the importance of nutrition during infancy cannot be overemphasized. Nutrition affects changes in physical stature, brain development, and motor skill mastery, as well as other developments. Most of us have seen news reports of chronic malnutrition in many parts of the world. According to the United Nations Children's Fund (UNICEF) (2015), 30,000 children die each day in developing countries from infection and malnutrition due to poverty. This is more than 10 million children each year. In fact, the major cause of child mortality is the malnutrition and dehydration caused by diarrhea.

In January 2014, UNICEF (2015) announced the completion of a nationwide survey of malnutrition in Sudan using the Simple Spatial Survey Methodology (S3M), previously used in Sierra Leone, Niger, and Ethiopia. Results of this survey will allow programs to be tailored to the malnutrition needs of each of the country's eighteen regions.

The incidence of malnutrition among young children, and the short- and long-term effects of physical and psychological trauma associated with it, received worldwide attention following the December 2004 tsunami in Asia and the conflict in Sudan, where thousands of children with severe malnourishment were admitted to therapeutic feeding programs in Darfur since May 2004.

In industrialized countries, bottle feeding is frequently preferred to breastfeeding, in part, because it allows women to pursue individualistic goals and to engage in professional activities. As developing nations become more technologically advanced and increasingly industrialized, there is a reduction in breastfeeding. In some situations, this has resulted in many mothers, especially those living at the poverty level, diluting baby formulas and contributing to their infants' already deficient nourishment.

Breastfeeding young infants is commonly practiced throughout the world.

(Corporation/Alamy Stock Photo)

On a more positive note, the early effects of malnutrition can, in some cases, be lessened and even turned back. For example, Barrett, Radke-Yarrow, and Klein (1982) conducted a follow-up study on a group of Guatemalan children who had been participants in a previous investigation carried out by the Institute of Nutrition of Central America and Panama. These children, suffering from the effects of severe malnutrition, were provided with caloric or nutritional supplements during the first several years of their development. As a result, they were significantly more active, both physically and socially, than children who did not receive such supplements. In a related study involving malnourished Colombian infants, those who received regular food supplements along with home visits were taller and heavier than a comparable group who had not been given such treatment. The former group also demonstrated slightly higher ability in cognitive and social areas. The same reversibility of the effects could be observed in children who spent their first years of life in Romanian orphanages, suffering from physical neglect and malnutrition (Rutter, 1998). The children had been adopted by families in Great Britain, where their environmental conditions improved dramatically. Researchers studied the children's physical and cognitive development at age four and found that most Romanian children had caught up physically with their British counterparts. This was especially true for children who had been adopted before the age of six months.

# 9.3: Childhood

## 9.3.1: Childhood Obesity

Since the 1980s, health care professionals in the United States have become alarmed about the growing problem of obesity in middle childhood. This topic has important implications for the consideration of physical growth and development.

Obesity in middle childhood can lead to serious physical and emotional problems later in life. It can cause considerable respiratory and cardiovascular difficulties and can trigger excessive dieting and consequent complications. In addition, children often reject and ridicule their overweight peers, which negatively affects their self-esteem. **Obesity** is generally considered to be *body weight that is 20% or more over the recommended weight for one's age, gender, and body type*. Even with all the attention given to the importance of keeping one's weight under control, research shows that the incidence of obesity among children has increased dramatically within the past several decades. Cole and Cole (2001) point to a 50% increase among six- to eleven-year-old children and almost as large an increase among twelve- to seventeen-year-old adolescents. The greatest increase for children in the United States has been among Mexican American and African American children and in those living in low-income families.

The National Center for Chronic Disease Prevention and Health Promotion (NCCDPHP) (2011), in the United States, continues to report increases in obesity at all age levels, especially at younger ages. For example, more than one-third of American adults (35.7%) and about 17% (or 12.5 million) of children and adolescents ages two to nineteen years are considered obese.

What causes obesity? Many researchers believe it is caused by a combination of genetic and sociocultural factors as demonstrated in the Human Genome Project. However, this genetic explanation cannot entirely explain obesity; various social factors must also be taken into consideration. For one thing, children often get mixed signals in their culture. In North American society, there is a preoccupation with physical appearance. Being tall and slim are seen as acceptable forms of beauty. Furthermore, some children are likely to observe their parents worrying about overeating and gaining weight. This, in turn, can add to children's confusion about how much food they should eat. There is also a tendency in some cultures for parents to overfeed their children in infancy and early childhood. This is often done in an effort to pacify restless children and as a way to cope with parents' busy schedules. Given the amount of food served in many family restaurants—the "all you can eat" specials—it is not surprising that many overweight children exist, particularly in North America.

Another social factor that contributes to obesity is lack of exercise. This may seem paradoxical because we think of children as running around and being involved in lots of physical activities. However, although *many* children are active, a substantial number of children stay at home and spend many hours taking care of younger siblings, playing video games, watching television, or, more recently, "surfing" the Internet and spending long hours with social media on their iPhones, iPads, and other electronic devices. As a result, many school-age children do not get nearly enough exercise. Kimm and her colleagues (2005), in a nine-year longitudinal study of more than 2,000 white and African American girls, from ages nine and ten to ages eighteen and nineteen, reported that they had a pronounced decline in physical activity and their rate of obesity doubled. The authors recommended that even modest amounts of activity during adolescence can help prevent obesity development and the onset of adult chronic diseases such as high blood pressure and diabetes. They also stress that this problem is not confined to North America but, in fact, represents a "global obesity epidemic." WHO (2016) issued *Fact Sheet 311*, which stated that worldwide obesity had doubled since 1980; that is, more than 1.9 billion adults who were 18 years and older were overweight (with 600 million of these considered obese), 42 million children younger than 5 years were overweight or obese, and most of the world's population lives in countries where being overweight and having obesity kill more people than being underweight or malnourished.

## 9.3.2: Childhood Mental Health

Concerns about mental health are not commonly associated with "childhood." Nonetheless, in recent years, it has become clear that several psychological and developmental disorders may first occur during this early life phase, among them multiple personality disorder, depression, autism, and attention deficit hyperactivity disorder (ADHD).

Viewed from an ecological systems perspective, culture plays a role in how childhood disorders are diagnosed and interpreted within the social context. Studies of autism, depression, and ADHD seem to suggest that, overall, mental health professionals in various countries agree on and correctly recognize the symptoms of these disorders. Although reliable diagnostics can help identify these illnesses, ecological factors influence how family, peers, teachers, and health professionals interpret and deal with these disorders. Teachers, for example, are central in the diagnosis of ADHD because one criterion requires that the symptoms present themselves in at least two different contexts. One context is home, and the other is usually school. A study by Jacobson (2002) showed that teachers in the United States and the United Kingdom correctly identified ADHD-typical behaviors, but the two groups differed significantly in what they considered "appropriate" classroom behaviors. The cultural differences in these children's ecological systems bring into question the interpretation of some ADHD behaviors as "disordered." Another example of the interaction between ecological systems and a child's mental health status is Pribilsky's (2001) discussion of the culture-specific disorder "nervios." This illness occurs among children living in the southern Ecuadorian Andes Mountains. Children suffer from a variety of depression-like symptoms, including melancholy and anger. A common trigger of the illness is children's separation (mainly) from their fathers, who usually migrate to the United States for economic reasons. The author argues that this childhood disorder is clearly defined by changes in lifestyles, family structure, and migration, all representing disturbing changes in the child's ecological system.

### 9.3.3: Ecological Influences on Early Coping Behavior

The ecological conditions in which a child grows up set the stage for many potential health risks and stressors. These conditions include physical factors such as climate, hygienic conditions, and access to vaccinations and medication.

In addition to physical settings and resources, parental characteristics and family dynamics are a very salient aspect of the early ecological system, which influences the ways in which children perceive stress and illness and how they adapt to it. Findings from a landmark longitudinal study conducted by Werner (1989) provide important information on this topic that still has relevancy today.

Beginning in the 1950s, more than 650 infants born on the Hawaiian island of Kauai were monitored for cognitive and emotional development throughout childhood and adulthood. Although most were born without complications and were raised in supportive homes, a substantial number experienced a variety of difficulties, including some perinatal stress and prematurity. The researchers reported

that children raised in supportive and nurturing homes showed more competence than those who were not reared in such environments. Not surprisingly, they also found that premature and low-birth-weight infants developed significantly more slowly when their prenatal problems were combined with impoverished living conditions, dysfunctional family situations, and inadequate parenting. The premature infants who made the greatest progress tended to grow up in families with a lot of physical stimulation, interaction with other family members, and supportive caregiving.

More recently, developmental researchers acknowledge that parenting influences children's coping in multiple phases of the coping process: how and when children may be exposed to a stressor, the appraisal of an event as stressful, modeling stress behavior, and modeling coping behavior (Chao & Wang, 2013). This argument seems to gain some support from Chen and Kennedy (2005), who studied children's coping in different cultural environments. They learned that children of different ethnicities (the sample consisted of European American, Chinese American, and Mexican American children within the United States, and Taiwanese children in their native country) reported different types of stressors, and they also preferred and used different coping strategies. The authors relate these differences to parental characteristics, family dynamics, and early socialization.

Latin American street children help each other survive the challenges of everyday life.

(Florian Kopp/imageBROKER/Alamy Stock Photo)

Chao and Wang (2013) suggest three ways in which culture influences the development of coping strategies, beginning at a young age: (1) suggestions from ". . . parents, schools, society, and media" (notice how these are found in different parts of the ecological system); (2) observation and imitation of previously successful coping behaviors; and (3) facilitation or discouragement of ". . . specific coping activities based on cultural values" (p. 254).

# 9.4: Adolescence

Writing about the hurried child, Elkind (1988) characterizes American youth as growing up too fast too soon and states that "like Superman, Superkid has spectacular powers and precocious competence even as an infant. This allows us to think that we can hurry the little powerhouse with impunity" (p. xii).

The pressure to grow up affects most children at some point, but each culture has its own beliefs about when this is supposed to occur. In some societies, the process is gradual, whereas in others it is abrupt. No matter how smooth the transition might be, it brings with it challenges, possibilities, and health concerns.

**Adolescence**, *the time between childhood and adulthood,* was initially called a period of "storm and stress" by the "father" of modern adolescent psychology, G. Stanley Hall (1904), who described the frequent mood swings and conflict thought to characterize the period. Today, most lifespan psychologists view adolescence as a continuous process rather than a fixed stage in the life cycle.

Adolescence is nevertheless a complex concept shaped by sociocultural beliefs and historical events. For example, just before the start of the twentieth century in the United States, the concept of adolescence did not exist. Young persons were simply expected to take on adult responsibilities and contribute to the welfare of the family as soon as they were physically able to do so. Over time, however, this idea changed, and societies (especially those in the West) became more accepting of adolescence as a distinct stage in adult preparation. In recent years, the period of adolescence has shown signs of expanding so children enter it earlier and stay in it longer—in some cases, well into their early to mid-twenties. For many, biological changes during the adolescent years can be enormously stressful. For example, hormonal changes associated with puberty are frequently accompanied by fluctuations in social and emotional development. For many adolescents, these changes produce only minimal health risks, although, for others, they can contribute to serious health problems, including eating disorders or alcohol and drug addiction. Adolescence is also the time when many severe adult mental disorders begin to manifest themselves.

## 9.4.1: Eating Disorders

Over the years, the topic of adolescent health has taken on new dimensions in cross-cultural human development. Because of the impact childhood illnesses can have on adult development (e.g., obesity and diabetes), international health organizations and relief agencies have devoted increasing attention to the identification of physical and mental illnesses among the world's adolescents. Today, a growing health concern among many professionals is the dramatic rise in the incidence of eating disorders, especially in highly industrialized societies (Miller & Broadwell, 2013).

**Anorexia nervosa** is *an eating disorder*, found primarily among young adolescent girls, *characterized by loss of appetite and extreme loss of weight.* In severe cases, hospitalization becomes necessary, menstruation may stop, and an individual may lose 15% to 25% or more total body weight. It is estimated that between 5% and 15% of anorexic girls die of this disorder each year. By contrast, adolescents suffering from **bulimia nervosa**, again typically young women, *eat extremely large amounts of food and then purge it all by means of self-induced vomiting.* The aim of this behavior is not to lose or gain weight but to maintain a specific weight.

Although in some societies stoutness is associated with good health and prosperity, in others it is not. For example, in parts of Southeast Asia, a plump waistline suggests abundance, wealth, and good fortune. It has been reported that young women of the nomadic Moors of Mauritania or the Annang of Nigeria are force fed because large women are considered the most desirable. In contrast, in North America, being slim and fit is important, whereas being overweight can be embarrassing. An obsession with being thin appears to be especially common among young women. In light of the disproportionally higher incidents of eating disorders in young women as opposed to men, gender is considered a "risk factor" for eating disorders. *Have you or anyone you know suffered from an eating disorder? What did you do about it?*

Anorexia nervosa affects many young women throughout the world.

(Oote Boe 3/Alamy Stock Photo)

**CULTURAL VARIATIONS IN ANOREXIA AND BULIMIA**
Both eating disorders can have serious adverse effects on one's personal health. So, just how common are these disorders in countries throughout the world? Among the cross-cultural studies looking at this problem, findings reveal two predominant trends: (1) eating disorders occur universally, and (2) fewer eating disorders and less dissatisfaction with body image occur in Asian, Middle Eastern, South American, and African cultures, compared to European, North American, and Australian cultures (Miller & Pumariega, 2001). These consistent results over the past decades indicate a relationship between eating disorders and Western cultural ideals of thinness that young women (and sometimes men) believe they need to achieve. A particularly interesting example of the desire for thinness in American society was the celebration of the one-hundredth birthday of the Statue of Liberty. A new coin was issued with a likeness designed to resemble the original, with one exception: Lady Liberty's figure on the new coin had been "slimmed down" to more closely represent the culturally popular Western ideal of feminine thinness.

*Are eating disorders culture-bound syndromes?* Keel and Klump (2003) conducted a thorough review of 1,190 published studies on eating disorders in non-Western cultures. They found that occurrences of anorexia nervosa were reported in every non-Western region of the world, whereas bulimia was restricted to cultures that had been exposed to various Western influences. The authors conclude that these two disorders are distinct in their etiologies (origin and development of a disease): anorexia, a universal illness, appears strongly influenced by genetic predisposition, and bulimia originates from the psychological response to cultural expectations. In short, "culture as a risk factor" seems to be more of a consideration when diagnosing and treating bulimia.

Pike and Borovoy (2004) agree with the notion that culture changes are, in part, the cause for eating disorders (both anorexia and bulimia), but they also contend that culture-specific influences play a particular role in the way the illnesses express themselves and the way they need to be treated. In their study of Japanese women, they describe the histories of two young women with eating disorders, Tomoko and Hiroko. The authors conclude that the eating disorders are rooted in specific Japanese cultural expectations regarding gender roles and beauty ideals. For example, in Hiroko's case, she experiences a conflict between being a "perfect" wife to her alcoholic husband and the desire to disassociate from him. Anorexia nervosa serves as a way to make herself be the perfect wife (by seemingly meeting a beauty ideal of thinness) and, at the same time, become ill and detach from her husband so that she would not be required to fulfill her role as a sexual partner (p. 523). In another example, that places anorexia nervosa in a cultural context. Banks' (1992) exhaustive review of the literature notes an interesting link between anorexia nervosa and **asceticism**, or the religious *practice of self-denial, used to achieve greater spiritual awareness.* In a religious context, symptoms of eating disorders may be expressed in rituals of fasting and vomiting. An interesting study of this type was conducted by Ali and Maharajh (2004), in which an eighteen-year-old Islamic student, enrolled in a Roman Catholic convent, was exposed to ambivalent religious values, which appeared to act as an etiological factor in her development of this disorder.

With regard to the treatment anorexia and bulimia, techniques developed and used in Western cultures often work in other cultures as well. However, because of recognizable differences in family dynamics and interpersonal relationships in other cultures, Miller and Broadwell (2013) recommend the development of new techniques that provide "cultural congruency" . . . "with less emphasis on specific symptoms . . . [because they] . . . are more likely to be efficacious across divergent cultures" (p. 453).

## Points to Ponder

**Eating Disorders**

As pointed out in this chapter, eating disorders, especially anorexia nervosa and bulimia, are common disorders among adolescents in many cultures around the world. There are many reasons for their occurrence. *Have you ever experienced either of these? If so, what were your experiences? If recovered, do you know why you had one or the other or both? Do you have any friends who have experienced these? How did you interact with them regarding the disorder? Did you try to get them help? How did they react? Can you recognize someone who is experiencing one of these disorders?* Obesity is a complex weight disorder influenced by genetics, various medical conditions, social factors, and lifestyle choices. It is perhaps most prevalent in Western societies, especially the United States, but has also seen increases in other cultures in recent years. As before, you may want to make observations in several settings. For example, while grocery shopping, look at the foods people put in their grocery carts and observe their weights. *Who selects more fattening (less healthy) foods—men, women, children, Americans, people from other cultures —and what would you estimate their ages to be? Are the carts of the elderly any better? Spend some time observing children and parents at parks or playgrounds and on the streets. Are they getting sufficient exercise? What do you think can be done to alleviate the obesity problem?*

## 9.4.2: Culture and Sexually Transmitted Diseases and Infections

As adolescents become sexually active, they are more likely to acquire sexually transmitted diseases (STDs) or sexually transmitted infections (STIs) than any other age group. WHO (2011) reported that there are approximately

448 million new cases of STIs worldwide each year among fifteen- to forty-nine-year-old men and women. The largest number of these occurred in South and Southeast Asia, sub-Saharan Africa, and Central and South America, in that order. One STD, in particular, acquired immunodeficiency syndrome (AIDS), which is caused by the human immuno-deficiency virus (HIV), has become a critically important international health issue. Since 1981, when AIDS was first diagnosed in Los Angeles, people with HIV have been found in more than 169 countries. **AIDS** is *a disease that attacks the body's immune system,* leaving an individual weak and susceptible to infections that sometimes prove fatal. According to Hanako Suzuki (2013), 39 million people are currently infected with HIV/AIDS, and it is the fourth lead-ing cause of death in the world. With an increasing number of younger adolescents becoming sexually active and large numbers engaging in unsafe sex, there is serious concern that many have become infected with HIV and may die of AIDS when they reach the third decade of their lives.

Discussion of HIV and AIDS should be made within the context of culture and how it influences the interpreta-tion, diagnosis, and treatment of the disease. Culture is not a passive entity, but rather a dynamic process within which members of a society are continuously acting on their needs and interpreting what they see and experience. One of the major sources of cultural influence throughout the world is the media. In Southeast Asia, the media has devoted con-siderable time and energy to informing and educating the public about the causes and transmission of HIV. However, many local newspapers have a policy of not printing infor-mation about HIV and its relationship to sexual behavior because this sometimes conflicts with religious and cultural beliefs. Instead, in an effort to combat the illegal use and trafficking of drugs, emphasis is often placed on the occur-rence of HIV and AIDS among drug users and their use of dirty needles. Under these circumstances, many people, particularly those who are young, uneducated, and living at the poverty level, will not be adequately informed about the potential sources of contracting the virus, and this igno-rance will substantially contribute to the increasingly large number of AIDS cases throughout the world.

# 9.5: Adulthood

The transition from adolescence to adulthood is more gradual than that from childhood to adolescence. Exactly when an individual becomes an adult is not always clear, and there is likely to be just as much variation within cul-tures as there is among cultures (a point you have read many times throughout this book).

## 9.5.1: Mental Health Issues

In addition to the effects of stress, other mental health issues concern adults. Among these are depression and

schizophrenia. Although it is not our intention to provide a comprehensive analysis of psychopathology in adulthood, we examine some of the different approaches to viewing these illnesses from a cross-cultural perspective.

**DEPRESSION** Each culture has its own beliefs regarding the causes and treatment of illness and stress. This is true for depression as well, and once again, there is often more variation in interpretation within cultures than among cul-tures. For example, in the United States, individuals react in many different ways when hearing that someone is ex-periencing depression. Responses may range from "There's nothing to worry about, he's just a little moody these days. He'll soon be fine" to "She's had a long history of serious depression, just like her mother and father. It seems to run in the family." Because the term tends to be used so freely in everyday conversation and in the media, it is sometimes difficult to recognize the symptoms of depression.

**Depression** is *a serious psychological disorder involving periods of sadness and other negative feelings such as hopeless-ness, despair, sleep disturbance, and loss of energy.* Cultural variations in beliefs about depression and other illnesses have important implications for the health status of indi-viduals worldwide. Health authorities have become increasingly alarmed by the growing number of reported cases of depression among adults. Several years ago, it was estimated that at least 100 million people around the world experience the symptoms of depression each year. This fig-ure is expected to rise as people live longer and as more people are exposed to chronic stress. It is also feared that the sudden exodus of families migrating to new countries and abandoning native customs and traditions, as well as the breakup of the extended family, will result in increased incidences of depression in younger people. Some experts worry that this will lead to a greater consumption of alco-hol and the abuse of drugs, which will only intensify the depression. Obviously, the magnitude of this problem presents enormous public health concerns.

Adolescents experiment with smoking and drinking at increasingly younger ages.

(Kuttig - People/Alamy Stock Photo)

Because depression has varying emotional, physical, and behavioral symptoms, it is common for many cases to go undetected. For this and other reasons, diagnosing and treating depression among young adults continue to be major problems for health care professionals in many cultures. In Western countries, depression is described in terms of being sad, disconnected, and withdrawn. Sometimes, these are accompanied by somatic complaints, such as headaches, stomach cramps, or nausea. However, in parts of India and South Africa, depression is described in quasispiritual or metaphysical terms—"suffering of the spirit." Recent findings suggest that depression in some developing countries is gradually beginning to mimic depressive symptoms seen in the West. It appears that although there are certain culture-specific or emic characteristics associated with depression, there also are several universal (or etic) features and methods of treatment (Stewart, Simmons, & Habibpour, 2012).

WHO (1983) conducted a cross-national study of patients in Canada, Japan, Switzerland, and the Islamic Republic of Iran. Findings revealed a cluster of core depressive symptoms, including long periods of sadness, lack of energy and affect, inability to concentrate, feelings of inadequacy, and loss of self-esteem. Although the frequency and extent of reported depressive cases may vary among cultures, depression remains a major universal problem that usually requires treatment.

In China, depressive episodes and stress-related disorders among adults are often accompanied by somatization. This has also been reported in parts of Latin America, Asia, and Africa. **Somatization** refers to *physical ailments resulting from stress or emotional distress.* One explanation may be that in many collectivistic societies, individuals are discouraged from voicing their psychological complaints in the company of friends or extended family members. Furthermore, depression is viewed as a minor, transient illness not requiring immediate family intervention. Consequently, an individual who experiences a depressive episode is often forced to use somatization to signal distress and thereby gain attention. As Draguns (1990a) states, in the case of depression, "somatization serves as a culturally sanctioned cry for help" (p. 311). Thus, the nature and treatment of depression, similar to many other illnesses, reflects the interaction among ecocultural systems, historical and sociocultural factors, and developmental niche.

Today, depression is often referred to as the "common cold" of psychological disorders, and Prozac (used to treat depression) is one of the most widely prescribed drugs in the world. It is customary to think of depression as a result of living and working in a highly industrialized and hurried society. However, as Draguns (1994) points out, "Depression is not the exclusive property of Judeo-Christian cultures" (p. 168). In fact, depression is probably experienced to some degree in most, if not all, of the world's cultures. Even so, health care professionals have yet to agree on a set of depression symptoms that can be universally applied, and it is unlikely that they ever will because of the role played by cultural variables. Draguns affirms that "[t]he cross-cultural study of depression has not yet progressed to the point of being able to pinpoint the world-wide invariant manifestations of depression" (p. 168).

**SCHIZOPHRENIA**  During the past 200 years, schizophrenia has been one of the most frequently studied psychopathic disorders. **Schizophrenia** refers to *a group of severe psychological disorders characterized by disturbances in thought, perception, and affect or emotion.* Increasing attention has been given to the study of cultural variations in schizophrenia. For example, WHO (1973) began conducting a series of studies in China, Taiwan, Colombia, Czechoslovakia, Denmark, India, Nigeria, the former Soviet Union, the United Kingdom, and the United States. The goal of these investigations has been to determine the extent of schizophrenia, as well as the sociocultural and historical factors surrounding it. Findings have pointed to the identification of several core symptoms, including restricted affect, thinking aloud, lack of insight, poor rapport, incoherent speech, and widespread bizarre delusions. In addition, three symptoms were identified that would not be considered symptoms of schizophrenia: waking early, depressed facial features, and expressions of extreme elation (Draguns, 1990b). Other symptoms reported by Deering (2013) include emotional changes, "odd" behaviors, disorganized speech, and inability to function adequately in daily life.

Subsequent research conducted by WHO (1979) and Sartorius and colleagues (1986) reports a greater likelihood of these symptoms occurring in Colombia, India, and Nigeria than in the other industrialized countries mentioned previously. One explanation may lie in the finding that schizophrenia is inversely proportionate to educational and occupational level. In fact, according to Draguns (1994), poorer and less educated patients in developing countries (e.g., India and Nigeria) recovered most quickly from this illness.

During the past two decades, WHO has continued to conduct cross-cultural research on more than 3,000 schizophrenic patients in more than twenty countries. Results indicate that schizophrenia occurs in nearly all cultures and that the prognosis is better in developing countries than it is in highly industrialized developed countries. Apparently, the support and encouragement provided by extended family members help reduce some of the symptoms associated with schizophrenia.

Schizophrenia has also been studied in India and Nigeria, where the symptoms have been found to be similar to those reported by schizophrenics in Western countries and include hallucinations, delusions, and withdrawal. The separation of the schizophrenic from others and the disruption of the cohesive family system are the most mysterious aspects of this illness to the normal population. It is not the disease itself that is puzzling, but rather the inclination toward withdrawal and obsessive self-focus. The nature of the disease threatens collectivist values and clashes with ecological orientation and developmental niche.

## 9.5.2: Acculturation and Adaptation

The challenge of living, working, or studying in another culture is a common experience for an increasing number of today's young adults. It brings with it stresses that have both physical and psychological consequences for health. Perhaps more so than other life transitions, moving to a different culture changes a person's ecological systems at all levels. Changes in food and climate, language, financial issues, work/study problems, and loss of social network are among the concerns when one moves to a different culture. Therefore, it should not be a surprise that most "sojourners" experience their acculturation as stressful. *Have you spent an extended period of time living in another country? What stresses did you experience? How did you adapt to your new surroundings?*

In recent years, research has shown that **acculturation**—*the process and result of adopting the cultural traits or social patterns of another social group*—is a more complex issue than originally thought (Chun, Organista, & Marin, 2003; Sam & Berry, 2016). For example, it has been shown that acculturation, as described previously, is *not* the same process as **assimilation**—*the rejection of one's native culture in favor of a new one*—with which it is frequently confused. As Nguyen (2013) has clearly shown, acculturation is a bilinear process in which an individual can adopt a new, majority, or host culture while maintaining one's native or minority culture, and thus become bicultural. She goes on to state that in addition to acculturation being bilinear, it is also multidimensional; that is, changes take place in three broad dimensions: ". . . behaviors and practices, values and beliefs, and identity and pride" (p. 8), with each of these, along with language preference, cultural traditions, family socialization, and other variables influencing each other in ". . . multiple domains: home, work, or school" (p. 8). Obviously, this places the process clearly within our ongoing discussion of ecological systems.

Although all acculturation is stressful, we differ in how we perceive stress and how we cope with it. The difference in response to acculturative stress is a result of the dynamics of a person's ecological system earlier in life (e.g., parents' characteristics), as well as the dynamics of the ecological system into which the person enters. Kim and Won (1997) learned that Chinese students reported experiencing more daily stress in their adaptation to a new environment than did Korean and Japanese students in comparable situations. Similarly, among African and Western students studying at Chinese universities, African students reported more stress in their daily lives than Western students, particularly in areas such as climate, finances, reading and writing in Chinese, social activities, and academic performance (Hashim & Zhiliang, 2003).

Cross (1995) focused her research not so much on the perception of acculturative stress, but more on adaptation strategies employed by East Asian and American graduate students at the University of Michigan. Students in the study came from South Korea, the People's Republic of China, Japan, and North America. East Asian students placed more emphasis on community and interdependence than did American students. However, American students exercised strong self-reliance and independence. When adapting to new surroundings, Americans considered expressing oneself and being an autonomic thinker as important cognitive skills. Those East Asian students who showed more preference for independence also used more direct coping strategies when addressing problems related to daily stress. More direct strategies were correlated with reduced level of stress; that is, students of both cultures who were willing to take direct action when confronted with problems of adaptation were less distressed and healthier.

Adult Taiwanese, adjusting to life in the United States, experienced similar adaptation patterns. Ying and Liese (1990) recruited individuals at a seminar designed to prepare them for their overseas study and followed them through their "abroad experience." The researchers inquired about such areas as homesickness, physical complaints, level of control, loneliness, social support, relationship problems, and perception of host country. The results indicated that those adults who took greater risks and became more actively involved during their studies were healthier and better adjusted. They experienced fewer physical difficulties than those who practiced traditional Chinese customs and declined involvement in day-to-day activities on campus. Good adjustment was also related to a sense of control; individuals were more secure when they made decisions on their own, apart from family interference. Conversely, a decline in perceived control was associated with feelings of pressure to comply with family directives to strictly adhere to Chinese traditions. These and other findings lend support for the use of training programs as preparation for study or work abroad experiences. If individuals (e.g., immigrants, refugees, expatriates, and even international exchange students) can learn as much as possible about the ecological system they are about to experience ahead of time, then they may be able to adjust their coping strategies accordingly, making the transition from one culture to another a less stressful experience and minimalize any mental, physical, or psychological difficulties that might arise. Sam and Berry (2016) artfully demonstrate the global contexts of acculturation in a wide range of societies and acculturating groups of people, including expatriates, tourists, immigrants, ethnic minorities, and refugees, while presenting current models and theories of the acculturation process. Anyone wanting to understand the topic of acculturation and its current status would do well to look at their book.

# 9.6:  Later Adulthood

When we think of aging, we frequently have mixed reactions. On the one hand, we think of a group of elderly people enjoying their "golden years" by visiting grandchildren, traveling, and perhaps volunteering. On the other hand, we sometimes perceive the elderly as frail, weak, dependent, and in need of extensive medical care. Certainly, among many North Americans and increasing numbers of older people in other cultures, this can be a disturbing and confusing time. The term **senescence** is used to describe *the process of biological change associated with normal aging.* Although the rate of senescence varies individually, socially, and culturally, few people (if they live long enough) can escape the effects of the aging process.

A better understanding of lifespan development, along with advances in medical technology, has helped expand the life expectancy of the world's population, especially in industrialized nations. For example, in the United States, nearly 14% of the population is sixty-five or older. During the next twenty-five years, this number will double to 72 million people. In addition, the first of 77 million "baby boomers" (those born between 1946 and 1960) turned 65 in January 2011; by 2030, one in five Americans will be sixty-five or older; and by 2050, this number will reach 89 million. It is estimated that every day for the next twenty years, 10,000 Americans will celebrate their sixty-fifth birthday. In 2010, there were an estimated 53,364 Americans older than 100 and 316,600 centenarians throughout the world. The fact that these are among the largest, healthiest, and best educated group of Americans ever to move through and beyond their fifties will present many challenges and opportunities to families, businesses, policymakers, and health care providers, as well as have a significant impact on culture and values for many years to come.

What about the rest of the world's population? Although the population of the world is aging, as of 2001, children still outnumbered the elderly in all major countries except Spain, Italy, Greece, Germany, Japan, and Bulgaria; China had the largest population of elderly; Japan had the highest life expectancy at birth (81 years); there were more older widows than widowers in most countries; and the percentage of elderly living alone in developing countries was much lower than in undeveloped countries (Kinsella & Velkoff, 2001).

## 9.6.1: Disease and Premature Aging

Elderly persons experiencing the normal signs of aging often complain of reduced energy, vision and hearing loss, dried and wrinkled skin, brittle bones, slower reaction time, diminished motor skills, and sometimes a loss of memory. These complaints, some subtle and others less so, are common in most cultures and are often legitimate. However, what about those who age before their time?

Following research conducted on a rare and cruel disease known as Werner's syndrome, scientists at the University of Washington put forth some ideas regarding the aging process. People suffering from this disorder experience all the signs of normal aging, but they do so beginning in their mid-twenties and usually die before they reach their fiftieth birthday. They gray prematurely and develop wrinkled skin, first on the face, and then on their hands, legs, and feet. They catch frequent colds, which often lead to pneumonia, and develop cancer, kidney and heart trouble, and osteoporosis. In addition, they show some of the same symptoms seen in Alzheimer's patients (e.g., problems in concentration, remembering, and decision making). In April 1996, scientists released findings that could be a major breakthrough in explaining why we age. They identified the Werner's gene, the first gene known to cause human aging. Although optimistically cautious, scientists at the National Institute on Aging called this discovery remarkable. Werner's syndrome is estimated to affect 1 in 200,000 individuals in the United States, but 1 in 20,000 to 40,000 in Japan. Scientists are not yet sure why this is the case.

With more accurate identification and treatment of illnesses, as well as rapid advancements in technology, many cultures are experiencing lower mortality rates and longer life expectancies. However, the longer people live, the greater the chance of encountering a major physical or psychological problem. Throughout the world, many elderly die each year from heart disease, cancer, or stroke, and arthritis, osteoporosis, and injuries resulting from falls and other accidents require extended hospitalization or nursing home and hospice care for elderly sufferers.

## 9.6.2: Cultural Views on Dementia and Alzheimer's Disease

*What is the relationship between age and psychological decline? How do a culture's ecocultural system and an individual's developmental niche contribute to the aging process?* As the average lifespan has expanded, we have seen dramatic increases in cases of **dementia** and **Alzheimer's disease**. In the United States, persons diagnosed with Alzheimer's represent about 10% of the population older than sixty-five and as much as 50% of those eighty-five and older. According to WHO (2012), there are currently 35 million people worldwide affected by Alzheimer's disease, and the number will rise to 115 million by 2050 (2012).

In the early stages, Alzheimer's disease resembles normal aging, with periodic memory loss, frequent agitation, problems speaking, and difficulty concentrating for long periods of time. However, as the disease worsens, the signs become more apparent. In the later stages, individuals forget how to perform the most basic tasks of daily living such as changing clothes, eating, and going to the bathroom. They become completely dependent, require twenty-four-hour supervision, and are unable to recognize family members and medical personnel.

Although older age and genetic predisposition may be two of the greatest risk factors in developing the illness, cultural influences may play a role that is not yet fully understood. Ferri (2005) report that 24 million people were afflicted by dementia in 2001, and they present some startling estimates of global prevalence rates for dementia in 2020 (42 million) and in 2040 (81 million). Obviously, such increases and projected numbers require greater cross-cultural awareness at the present time and in the near future. Again, as we have stated before, collection of normative data on a variety of cultural groups will greatly help research efforts and treatment.

An interesting study by Yamada and colleagues (2002) suggests that diet and eating habits may be an additional risk factor. These researchers found a notably higher frequency and severity of symptoms in their Japanese-Brazilian Alzheimer's patients than in comparable samples of Japanese patients. An analysis of patients' dietary patterns revealed that the Japanese—Brazilian diet includes little fish and large amounts of meat—the opposite of the typical Japanese diet. Although one study does not establish dietary patterns as a single risk factor, it certainly points to the desirability of considering ecocultural factors along with biological ones.

*How do caregivers in different cultures respond to an elderly person suffering from Alzheimer's or similar diseases of aging? How do cultural beliefs about family values and relationships influence the course of these diseases?*

Regardless of where it strikes, the devastating effects of Alzheimer's disease affect many people. For example, caring for a loved one with Alzheimer's can be very stressful. This is evident in Strong's (1984) study of caregiver support for Alzheimer's disease patients, in which she compared American Indian and Caucasian caregivers and found that both groups were equally frustrated, angry, guilty, anxious, and helpless. The gradual deterioration of the patient left caregivers in both groups searching for answers. American Indian caregivers were much more communal and interdependent, employing more supportive, although passive, strategies in coping with the stress. For instance, common comments were that "[w]e just have to get used to this. There's nothing you can do about it but

try and make them comfortable." Caucasian caregivers, in contrast, initially tried to handle the situation by themselves, rarely turning to others for help and support.

The difference in the way the two groups responded to the stress of caregiving reflects their culture's ecocultural system and their own developmental niche. Strong (1984) reports the perspective of an American Indian caregiver: "The white man . . . is torn between two ideals; on the one hand he believes in freedom, in minding his own business, and in the right of people to make up their own minds; but on the other hand, he believes that he should be his brother's keeper" (p. 29). In Indian society, taking care of family members is the chief responsibility of each person, and nobody is exempt.

In another study, Cox (1993) conducted personal interviews with eighty-six Hispanic caregivers in New York to examine the ways in which cultural values and norms influence behavior. Her findings concur with those of Strong's, suggesting that family cohesiveness plays a significant role in caregivers' behavior. As with American Indian caregivers, Hispanics appeared to accept passively the stresses of caregiving and believe it is part of their heritage to take care of the afflicted member. At no point did caregivers in either study consider admitting their relative to a nursing home or hospice. *Have you encountered this problem within your own family? How have members of your family dealt with it? If not, how do you think you might deal with it, particularly with regard to an aging parent, grandparent, or other loved one?*

Meng (1991) conducted a survey in China and reported that 96% of elderly persons reside with family members and are cared for until they die. Strong family interdependence and cohesiveness were shown to have a positive impact on the physical and mental health of weak and frail elderly parents living at home. At no point in caring for their aging parents did caregivers consider the possibility of sending them to a medical facility or nursing home. To do so would have brought immediate disapproval and shame from the community. These findings are consistent with those obtained by Frazier and Glascock (1994) in their work with the frail elderly living in a kibbutz community in Israel. Kalu and Kalu (1993) found that frail elderly parents in Nigeria responded somewhat differently. Those who were plagued by physical and mental infirmities retrieved their umbilical cords, buried at birth in their native village. This act is believed to help slow down the aging process. The event is a festive, colorful celebration attended by family members and friends, who surround their loved one with love and support.

As we learn more about the genetic and environmental foundations of Alzheimer's and other diseases common among the elderly, along with methods of treatment from different parts of the world, we can anticipate that cures or better treatments may be found in the future (Reiman, 2014).

These were among the goals discussed at the first Alzheimer's Association International Conference on the Prevention of Dementia held in Washington, DC, in June 2005. In the meantime, efforts to discover why a person's brain at some point in the lifespan begins to self-destruct continue.

In this regard, in March 2014, it was announced that a group of researchers had developed a blood test, based on the analysis of lipids or fatty acids in the bloodstream, that can predict with 90% accuracy the onset of Alzheimer's disease up to three years before its onset. However, there are ethical concerns because this means that one person in ten could be wrongfully diagnosed. Although promising and a major step forward, it still needs additional research (Mapstone et al., 2014).

### 9.6.3: Coping with Chronic Illness in Older Age

Faced with the prospect of failing health and developing chronic illness in older age, coping becomes more critical to the survival and maintenance of one's quality of life in later years. Geriatric researchers Becker and Newsom (2005) provide a good example of how the specific historical, cultural, and social context of African Americans in the United States has shaped their responses to, and coping with, chronic illness later in life. In particular, this segment of the population has developed coping strategies that emphasize reliance on self, community, and spirituality rather than reliance on health services. These coping strategies likely develop in response to ecological systems in which older African Americans often experience economic disadvantages and a lack of access to health services. As a result, they seek out the resources available to them such as the support of family, community, and spiritual leaders. Similarly, Polyakova and Pacquaio (2006) describe how older immigrants from the former Soviet Union bring their cultural values and beliefs about illness and coping to their new cultural environment, building a unique developmental niche. Older immigrants cope with chronic illness by using distractions and by keeping active with hobbies. They also describe family support as important, especially the assurance by family members that the person's illness is just part of life and he or she can deal with the problem successfully.

### 9.6.4: The "Good" Death

There are only two events in life that are truly universally shared by all humans: birth and death. In Chapter 4, we discussed the birth process and the ways it is approached in different cultures. Similarly, concepts of death and dying depend on cultural norms and beliefs. Here, we give particular attention to the notion of the "good" death, which refers to an ideal and desirable end-of-life scenario. Van der Geest (2004) suggests that the similarities across cultures in the idea of what constitutes a "good" death and a "bad" death far outnumber the differences. His study of people's experiences with death in a small rural town in Ghana seems to correspond to accounts from many other societies. In particular, a good death is characterized by dying after a long and well-spent life, after having resolved arguments and conflicts, in the company of loved ones, without pain, and while at peace with one's own death. In contrast, Walter (2003) indicates that cultural norms about the "good" death vary greatly, depending on the depth and content of beliefs, individualistic or collectivistic orientations, and the time it takes to die.

Historical and even contemporary examples describe martyrdom as "good" death. Death is accepted or even sought after as a means to serve a "higher" cause in exchange for rewards in the afterlife. However, between 40% and 75% of Europeans now believe that the present life is the only one. *Would your view of death differ depending on whether your religious beliefs emphasize life after death or rebirth as compared to no afterlife?*

In individualistic societies, individuals emphasize the personal choice of how they should live and die, including the choice of euthanasia. In this context, a "bad" death is one in which the person is unable to make decisions and express his or her desires. In collectivistic societies, the good death will take into consideration the effect on the family and the continued influence of the dead on the lives of the living.

In past centuries, people were expected to die within a few days of becoming sick with a terminal illness. In the twenty-first century, many people (predominantly in developed countries) may be diagnosed with a terminal illness and continue to live for many years. *Can you picture how each scenario will lead to a different preparation for and anticipation of death? What would be a "good" or "bad" death for you or a close member of your family?*

## Summary: Culture, Health, and Illness

When we think about health and related issues, we usually don't consider the many ways these may be affected by culture. *How do cultural beliefs influence one's well-being and ill health?* This chapter explores cultural differences in

health care and beliefs that influence development across the lifespan. It begins with an overview of how standardized tests and diagnostic techniques are often incapable of detecting medical problems in cultures other than those for which they are originally designed. The chapter then discusses the expression of illness symptoms and how they may be interpreted differently across cultures. Furthermore, the way individuals respond to illness and cope with it is also largely influenced by the cultural and ecological system.

Health problems, at birth and shortly afterward (e.g., preterm and low-birth-weight infants), can cause considerable concern for parents in many cultures. Variations in parental cultural beliefs, which have been discussed extensively in previous chapters, play a major role in the way cultures care for problem-birth infants.

Health issues during adolescence focus on the adolescent's search for the perfect body and physical appearance. Cultural variations in the occurrence and treatment of eating disorders such as anorexia and bulimia are examined in depth. STDs and STIs, including AIDS, are also discussed.

In early adulthood, pressures to achieve and to form interpersonal relationships with one's peers are frequently accompanied by the stress of adaptation and acculturation; these stressors produce a variety of medical problems. The ability to maintain a healthy lifestyle grows increasingly

difficult for families that migrate to different countries. Similar difficulties exist for students who pursue formal education in other countries. Several cross-cultural studies involving the resettlement of young adults are examined.

Middle adulthood is sometimes referred to as the "sandwich generation," during which parents attempt to balance their own needs with the physical and emotional needs of their aging parents and growing children. This period can present unique challenges and produce medical problems, including depression and schizophrenia. Cross-cultural research indicates that each culture approaches and treats these illnesses differently, depending on the eco-cultural system and developmental niche.

The last stage in the lifespan, later adulthood, is often viewed as the "golden years," with opportunities for retirement and travel. However, this stage is also characterized by health problems. In the closing section, a cross-cultural comparison of the status of the elderly is addressed, along with cultural practices for nurturing those afflicted with dementia and Alzheimer's disease. In the end, older adults often create an ecological system for themselves that supports them in their adjustment to the health challenges of aging.

## Study Questions

Provide examples of how cultural beliefs and traditions affect the delivery of health care in Western and non-Western cultures.

Define culture-bound syndrome and explain the reciprocal process that exists between cultural beliefs and the methods used to diagnose and treat physical and psychological disorders.

Distinguish between emic and etic aspects of health and culture and discuss how each culture's delicate

balance of ecological systems and developmental niche need to be considered when diagnosing and treating illness.

Discuss research devoted to the relationship between culture and sudden infant death syndrome, childhood mental health, eating disorders, STDs and adolescent drug use, depression, schizophrenia, and dementia.

Consider your personal views of a "good" death and a "bad" death.

## Developmental Analysis
## Culture and Health

My parents and older relatives have often told me that I was a very healthy baby. As I looked at pictures of my younger days, I came to wonder whether "healthy" was another way of saying "plump." I weighed nearly nine pounds at birth, which was quite rare for that era. From the time I was just two months old, I slept in a crib alone in my own bedroom. My parents often teased that they thought I would become an opera singer one day so I could put the strong set of lungs I developed (through countless hours of crying) to good use! Some of the more difficult cries to comfort a baby though are those related to teething. While my siblings and I were teething, my mother's favorite remedy was to put a little brandy on her finger and let us suck on it. The brandy tasted

good and helped numb the feeling of pain in our gums. Not exactly modern medicine, but it seemed to work!

As a child, I remained active by playing outdoors and doing chores on the farm. I was a little larger than the other children my age, but I always felt accepted by my peers and family. Through regular exercise and an eventual growth spurt at age fourteen, I grew into a well-proportioned adolescent. During adolescence, I learned about intoxicants. My parents received a letter from my health teacher, explaining that we were learning about the dangers of drugs at school. The teacher suggested that these messages be reinforced at home. Although the legal drinking age was only eighteen at the time, underage drinking was a problem parents and teenagers had to address. When my parents discussed the dangers of alcohol, tobacco, and other drugs, they spoke about both the legal ramifications and the physical consequences. I learned that my ability to think, breathe, exercise, and even have children could be compromised by the effects of intoxicants. Fortunately, my peer group was strong, and we encouraged one another to stay clear of drugs. (My mother assured me that the brandy I consumed at age one was not detrimental to my health!) As a parent, I was impressed with the public movement to educate children on the dangers of drugs. When my son, Alexander, was fifteen years old, he participated in a school program focused on keeping children's bodies free of drugs. The group hosted alcohol-free parties and dances. He and his friends remained very involved in the program through graduation. These types of programs provide adolescents with useful information, education, and a solid sense of peer support.

Both of our children are grown up now and have young children of their own. It has been delightful to watch our children grow as adults and into the roles of parents. Giorgio and I have also watched our own parents age and pass on. Both of Giorgio's parents passed away about ten years ago of heart disease and cancer, and my father passed away peacefully of old age two years later. My mother is still living and has begun to show early signs of Alzheimer's disease. As a result, we decided to move her to an assisted living facility last year so that she could receive more attentive care. The facility is a wonderful way for my mom to maintain her sense of independence, while also receiving excellent care by health professionals. She is active enough to participate in group activities and receives frequent visits from friends and family.

Giorgio and I have retired and fill our time with travel, visits with family, excursions with friends, and caring for those we love. We feel fortunate to be in good health and spirits. We try to keep our minds and bodies sharp by remaining active in the community and continually gaining new experiences. Last year, we began learning Tae Kwon Do and have earned our yellow belts! Our grandson is catching up to us by attempting to get *his* orange belt!

It has been fun documenting my life in this way and to observe the various cultural influences on my development. I also enjoyed exploring the changing cultural influences my husband Giorgio and I have had on the lives of our own children. Perhaps they, like you, will document their lives and cultural journey as well. I wish you all the best—*buona fortuna!*

# Chapter 10
# Future Trends and Applications

*Phyllidia Ramirez is eleven and lives with her mother, Nina, in a village high in the mountains in the middle of Nicaragua's Central Highlands. Similar to many Nicaraguan women, Nina has lived a large part of her life as a single mother. Her husband, Luis, was a migrant laborer who left home each year for several months to harvest cotton in the lowlands of the Pacific region. The long absences caused serious disruptions, and he abandoned the family when Phyllidia was five years old. Nina and Phyllidia both work part time harvesting coffee. Although schools in the area are underfunded and inadequate, family and kinship are important, and through compadrazgo—a system of "coparenthood" that links parents, children, and godparents—Phyllidia is learning Spanish and weaving skills from her godmother, Maria.*

*Montreal, the largest city in the province of Quebec, differs greatly from the rest of Canada due to the prominence of its French culture and language, as well as the fact that most of its inhabitants belong to the Roman Catholic Church. Michel Lamoureux, thirteen years old, lives here with his mother Sylvie, father Jacques, brother Pierre, and sister Lise. Because his parents are well-to-do, they are able to send their children to private Catholic schools and provide private lessons in foreign language, golf, and tennis. They set high standards for their children and, with careers that frequently keep them away from home, his parents give Michel, the oldest child, a great deal of responsibility for the care of his younger brother and sister.*

Our exploration of "lives across cultures" is nearly over. Before our journey comes to an end, let us briefly revisit our major themes, reconsider some of the theories discussed, and offer suggestions for modifying these to meet the needs of a rapidly changing world. A few simple revisions in specific theoretical positions can help make these theories more useful and appropriate for cross-cultural research. Finally, let us to gaze into our crystal ball and speculate as to where the young field of cross-cultural human development might be heading and make some recommendations for future research as we move toward the end of the second decade of the twenty-first century.

## 10.1: Looking Back: A Review of Major Themes and Theories

This chapter begins with a brief review of the major theories introduced in Chapter 2 and addressed throughout subsequent chapters. The purpose of doing this is to take one last look at the ideas scattered throughout the chapters and to pull them together into a final statement stressing the importance of viewing human development from a cross-cultural perspective and within a cultural context.

The chapter closes with a look at the future—the theories, topics, issues, and research that will help determine the directions that the study of cross-cultural human development may take in the future and how this new knowledge will lead to a better understanding of the effects of culture on behavior and behavior on culture.

### 10.1.1: Ecological Model

As you will recall, the ecological model of Bronfenbrenner focuses on the reciprocal relationships between and among children, their parents, and other family members and their connection with larger social and cultural traditions, as well as the interaction among biological, sociocultural, and psychological factors in human development. Throughout the pages of this book, we have seen, through the use of opening vignettes, how the lives of individuals are deeply embedded in distinctly different ecocultural systems reflecting long-held and well-established patterns of thought and behavior governed by the interaction of micro-, meso-, exo-, and macrosystems (see Figure 2.1 in Chapter 2).

In terms of the microsystem (the cultural setting in which adult–child interactions take place at home or at school), we can see that the young lives of Phyllidia in Nicaragua and Michel in Canada, at the opening of this chapter, have been influenced by their cultural surroundings.

At the same time, parts of each of their microsystems have been in contact with a second, larger circle of influence, the mesosystem, consisting of a number of overlapping social settings that have also influenced the individual development of Phyllidia and Michel. For example, Michel's private tutorial sessions are a routine activity among upper-middle-class families in the educational community in Montreal.

Coffee harvesting is regularly performed by Nicaraguan women and girls.

(Tati Nova photo Mexico/953605/Shutterstock)

Beyond this is the exosystem, consisting of community institutions that individuals experience indirectly. In Michel's case, his private school curriculum reflects the content and skill areas believed to be important in attaining competency, even though he was not directly involved in setting the curricula.

Then, there is the macrosystem made up of the prominent cultural values and attitudes that affect a person's maturation. In Michel's case, religious beliefs provide the foundation for worship and daily living. In Phyllidia's single-parent household, her part-time job and close contact with extended family reflect the values of the macrosystem found in most Nicaraguan villages.

As seen in previous chapters, sometimes several macrosystems operate within a single culture. In Malaysia and Singapore, for example, one macrosystem consists of a rapidly emerging group of young middle-class wage earners who are moving out of their parents' homes in an effort to achieve personal success and financial independence. Another represents the more traditional extended family system, in which parents and grandparents serve as principal caregivers for children, even those well into their adult years.

Because one of the major goals of cross-cultural research is to be aware of the varying influences of culture on behavior by looking at how children interact within their culture's unique ecological system and gradually carve out a developmental niche, it is hoped that the

foundation has been laid for a better understanding of how these forces shape and change development across the cultures considered, as well as those the reader may encounter in the future.

## 10.1.2: Developmental Niche

The concept of a developmental niche has contributed greatly to our understanding of the ways in which different components of a culture work together as a system and how parents and children behave within normal everyday settings.

Applying the developmental niche concept to the vignettes at the opening of this chapter, we can see how Nina's experience as a single mother affects her daughter Phyllidia's views of work and family relationships. Similarly, Michel's parents' expectations regarding his responsibilities toward caring for his younger brother and sister help shape Michel's values and attitudes. Each vignette presents the child's unique developmental niche and how it operates within the larger ecological system (see Figure 2.2 in Chapter 2). Throughout their lives, Phyllidia and Michel will each continue to react and respond to thousands of cultural messages that will eventually become internalized and help them understand their world and themselves.

Although relatively few cross-cultural studies have been specifically designed to compare cultures based on the developmental niche framework, one example is worth noting. Schwarz, Schafermeier, and Trommsdorff (2005) report results of two studies on the relationship among cultural values, parental beliefs, and parenting practices, with a focus on similarities and differences between German and South Korean mothers. Among the findings are those that show South Korean mothers to be less individualistic than German mothers, with a preference for group- and achievement-oriented child-rearing goals. They are also more strict and controlling with their children. The authors emphasize that the results ". . . have shown that child-rearing goals are related to parenting behavior . . . [and] . . . this is in line with some of the assumptions of the developmental niche" (p. 224). We have seen these connections many times throughout this book.

## 10.1.3: Vygotsky's Sociocultural Theory

As we discussed in Chapter 2, Vygotsky offers a contextualist's approach to the study of cognitive development. Although most mainstream Western developmental theories have traditionally viewed individuals as separate from their physical and social environments, Vygotsky believed that human development occurs over time *within* the context of culture. His influential mentor and friend, Alexandria R. Luria (1981), captured the essence of Vygotsky's theory best when he stated, "In order to explain the highly complex forms of human consciousness one must go beyond the human organism. One must seek the origins of conscious activity . . . in the external processes of social life, in the social and historical forms of human existence" (p. 25). Notice the contrast between the strong individualistic assumptions found in much of the psychological research conducted in Western societies and the historical and sociocultural contextualist approach employed by Vygotsky.

If we apply Vygotsky's *zone of proximal development* (the amount of assistance an individual needs from others in contrast to how much he or she can do without help) to this chapter's opening vignettes, then we see that the guided instructions provided by Phyllidia's godmother in the teaching and learning of weaving reflect both the family's ecological surroundings and the godmother's developmental niche. As Maria, the godmother, mentors Phyllidia's apprenticeship, she will move through the zone and increase her weaving skills. Her contributions to the family's collection of woven blankets and other objects strengthen her creativity, while promoting family cohesiveness, cultural identification, and interdependency.

In the case of Michel, he is being carefully trained by his golf coach to develop good putting skills. In the early stages, he needed lots of advice and practice drills to master the basics of good form. As Michel has improved and moved through the zone, demonstrating increased competency, his coach gradually removes the amount of assistance offered until Michel can proceed without further help. In both situations, it is likely that elements of the ecological context—such as climate, types of terrain, urban or rural setting, population density, health care, and other factors—will be intertwined within a variety of social contexts. In short, culture is, to a large extent, a group's response to its physical ecology, ancestral heritage, and developmental niche.

Although Vygotsky's theory does have its problems (little attention to gender differences, lack of emphasis on individuals, and informal research methods), it is certain to receive increased attention from cross-cultural developmental researchers in the decades ahead. This has surely been the case with the theorist discussed in the next section—Jean Piaget.

## 10.1.4: Piaget's Cognitive Developmental Theory

Applying Piaget's theory to our opening vignettes, it is clear that eleven-year-old Phyllidia's ability to re-create her godmother's weaving skills requires that she has the ability to distinguish between types and amounts of materials used, to use symbols creatively, and to infer

cause-and-effect relationships—all characteristics of concrete operational thinking described in Chapter 2. Similarly, Michel's ability to hold the golf club properly and to speculate what will happen if the ball is driven 300 yards or more requires that he be able to make use of hypotheses and form abstractions regarding golf skills. When he is able to do this, he displays some of the characteristics associated with formal operational thinking.

Although each vignette describes life in different cultures, the unique ecological settings, specific developmental niche, and distinctive social interactions experienced by Michel and Phyllidia strongly influence the nature and timing of the development of their cognitive abilities.

## 10.1.5: Kohlberg's Theory of Moral Development

According to Kohlberg, morality is based on a belief in general principles of justice and consists of six levels, ranging from an immature obedience and punishment orientation to an advanced application of universal ethical principles (see Chapter 2 for a detailed description).

Carol Gilligan (1982) severely criticized Kohlberg's approach and suggested that moral reasoning among women is more likely defined by a caring attitude and the maintenance of a network of relationships rather than by rules and abstract principles of justice. However, Gilligan did not take the next logical step and formulate an alternative developmental model that would integrate both orientations (caring and justice) into an understanding of moral development.

From a cross-cultural perspective, Kohlberg's model is clearly limited in its research application. Based on Gilligan's (1982) critique that the justice orientation is not the only way of viewing morality, we wonder how many other moral orientations may be present in other cultures. For example, in Japan, an individual frequently makes moral decisions based on a strict code of honor in which behavior is seen as right because it is the honorable thing to do. A common example involves the resignation of a company's president when someone in the organization behaves badly or commits an immoral act (e.g., overbilling), even though the president had no direct knowledge of, or connection to, the misbehavior. Moral reasoning such as this fits neither the justice nor the caring orientation, and suggests there are significant opportunities for more research in the area of moral development.

In this regard, a rarely cited model of moral development has been put forth by Haan, Aerts, and Cooper (1985). She and her colleagues propose that development of moral reasoning is not determined by general orientations, such as caring or justice, but is the result of understanding the interdependence of self and others that occurs in social interactions. In her model, morality is viewed as a form of social agreement that equalizes individuals' relations with each other, taking into account that when disagreements or disputes arise, all parties make their issues clearly known (Haan, 1991). Thus, moral solutions generally focus on a specific situation, involving a specific group of people, at a given time, and devote careful consideration to what each person needs and deserves, recognizing that these may vary at different times. In other words, the most mature moral reasoner attempts to make a moral decision that balances her needs, desires, strengths, and weaknesses with those of others affected by a particular moral issue. Situations involving conflicting needs frequently become severely emotional because the fundamental form of moral action is dialogue or talk, which often provokes high levels of stress that, in turn, also play a major role in moral decision making. In her research focusing on stressful moral situations, Haan found that individuals who were able to control their emotions, objectively consider a variety of possible solutions, be empathetic, and demonstrate the ability to "cope rather than defend" showed higher levels of moral action. In this view, moral reasoning would take on different forms in different cultures, simply because of wide variations in what is considered a need, desire, strength, or weakness and, unlike many other models of moral development, emphasizes the interactional nature of morality.

The potential usefulness of Haan's (1991) model for the study of moral development across cultures, as well as its relevance to the major themes expressed throughout this book, permit us to study moral reasoning within the context of culture-specific interactions and culture-specific moral issues, resulting in an emic approach to moral development. For example, in a highly individualistic culture such as the United States, most individuals accept as fair the notion that those of greater ability receive higher pay. However, in a collective setting such as the one found in a kibbutz, it may be equally fair that individuals get paid according to their needs, not what they actually earn by their own work. Although both concepts of what is fair or right are valid in each culture, they can only be reasonably evaluated within the appropriate context.

Applying these concepts of moral development to our opening vignettes suggests that Michel's view of what is right or wrong is strongly influenced by the religious values taught as part of his Roman Catholic faith, a centerpiece of the Quebec culture in which he lives. Although the majority of Nicaraguans during the early 1990s were nominally Roman Catholic, the church influenced most Nicaraguans only sporadically at best. Similar to most people living in rural villages far from an organized church, Phyllidia has likely been taught the basics of moral behavior as defined by her parents and community—for example, being nice to others, saying only good things, not stealing, and "having a strong belief in divine power over human affairs . . . reflected in the use of phrases such as 'God willing' or 'if it is God's desire.'"

## 10.1.6: Erikson's Theory of Psychosocial Development

Erikson's theory can be thought of as analogous to a book with eight chapters, and similar to chapters in a "Book of Life," his eight developmental stages follow one another. Sometimes an issue introduced in one chapter is carried over into the next and may not be fully resolved until much later in the book. To understand the story completely and make sense of the plot, the reader must read the eight chapters in chronological order. As infants and children pass through the first four stages of Erikson's theory, they are confronted by a series of psychosocial crises (turning points with two possible resolutions, one positive and one negative) requiring successful resolution if healthy development is to take place at a later stage. These crises center on trust versus mistrust, autonomy versus shame and doubt, initiative versus guilt, and industry versus inferiority. The adolescent and young adult encounters the issue of identity versus role confusion, or identity diffusion. The mature adult first faces the challenge of intimacy versus isolation, followed by generativity versus stagnation or self-absorption. Finally, the older adult needs to resolve issues related to integrity versus despair. Erikson views these crises as a natural development common to everyone, regardless of their culture, through which we come to understand ourselves and our relationships with others. However, as with other stage theories, Erikson's approach is subject to the criticism that stages may vary from one culture to another in the time of occurrence, duration, and content.

Considering what we know about the subjects in our opening vignettes, we might hypothesize that Phyllidia and Michel have both been raised in warm and caring family environments in which they developed the trust that allowed them to explore their surroundings and establish positive social relationships with family members. With supportive parents, they gradually developed control over their behavior, realizing that their intentions could be acted out through imitation of those around them. Michel, guided by his teachers in school, influenced by his golfing instructor in private lessons, and encouraged by his parents to take responsibility for his younger siblings, has developed a strong sense of industry and is on the verge of establishing a strong personal identity. Phyllidia, working part time alongside her mother harvesting coffee and learning her culture's weaving skills from her godmother, feels an equally strong sense of industry and, in the life of her village, is on the verge of womanhood and preparing to assume an adult identity.

Although Erikson's theory works well as a general framework within which some specific lifespan changes can be described and interpreted, it is less useful as a model for cross-cultural experimentation. This is not to say that with some modification and attention to cultural considerations, his ideas could not be usefully applied to human development within the cultural context. In fact, efforts directed at such endeavors might prove quite interesting as we have shown at various places throughout this book. However, an approach that may be even more useful in accounting for the cultural context of lifespan development has been offered by Cantor and her associates (Cantor, Norem, Niedenthal, Langston, & Brower, 1987; Cantor et al., 1991).

Using the concept of "life tasks" (the underlying goals that guide an individual's life or everyday behavior at a given time), Cantor and others (1987) studied a group of undergraduate students in the United States by having them keep records detailing their daily activities. While recording their activities, they also answered questions about the people they were with and their feelings about the activities. Findings revealed that students shared several "life tasks," the two most important being "making friends" and "getting good grades." One advantage of using an approach such as Cantor's in cross-cultural research is that it relies on self-generated "themes" based on people's culture-specific experience. This makes for a more emic approach than imposing a set of preformulated "themes" on individuals, as is the case with Universalist theories such as Erikson's.

We are encouraged by the development of such approaches and urge others to consider using them in formulating their own future cross-cultural human development research efforts.

## 10.2: Where do We go From Here?

No one can know for certain what the field of cross-cultural human development will look in the years ahead. As frequently noted, the literature in mainstream developmental psychology has traditionally emphasized a Western European and North American orientation. For too long, there has been a "psychological research ethnocentrism," that is, the assumption that research findings reported from studies conducted in one culture apply equally well to other cultures. The reader now knows that this is not always true. Yet, Harkness and Keefer (2000) caution that "in our search for cross-cultural validity in comparative research, we must make sure to avoid a new kind of ethnocentrism based on non-Western constructs or measures. Such an approach would be as unrealistic as the former mistake of imposing Western measures on other contexts . . . [and we must avoid the] . . . problem of oversimplification of cultural variability—complete relativism, in which cross-cultural comparisons become impossible" (p. 105).

Although Harkness and Keefer's (2000) point is well taken, it is important to continue to conduct additional indigenous developmental studies. Recent research has demonstrated that concepts first identified indigenously (in one culture, often non-Western) frequently have a significant degree of validity when operationally defined and incorporated into multicultural studies and often broaden our understanding of important issues. For example, Yamuguchi's (2004) study of *amae* has shown that this concept is related to constructs (e.g., attachment) in the United States (and other cultures). Japanese researchers, as well as others, admit that the term **amae**, a Japanese word, is difficult to define. It is generally used to describe *behavior aimed at inducing another person such as a parent, spouse, teacher, boss, or other individual to take care of oneself*. Takeo Doi (1973), the first to discuss the concept, defined it as *indulgent dependency*. In other words, the person who is carrying out *amae* may selfishly beg, plead, or act childishly, knowing that the caregiver will forgive and indulge the person. Although once thought to be unique to Japan, similar behavior has been observed throughout Asia and may have its equivalent in some Western or African countries as well (Smith & Nomi, 2000). Here is an emic or culture-specific concept that, with further research, may be shown to be an etic, universal, or culture-general concept. For these reasons, we welcome additional research conducted on this interesting cultural concept such as the recent work of Niiya, Ellsworth, and Yamaguchi (2006) and Jordan (2005).

Other research worthy of recognition and further investigation includes the work of Cheung and Leung (1998) on indigenous measures of Chinese personality dimensions, and Kwan, Bond, and Singelis (1997) on measurement of relationship harmony. In addition, measures of **budi values** (*generosity, respect, sincerity, and righteousness*) in Malaysia have been shown to account for variances explained by Schwartz's (2011) value survey items (an approach receiving increasing attention among cross-cultural developmentalists). Finally, Boski (2005) has identified **humanism** (defined as *a concern for personal relationships combined with endorsement of personal responsibility and a rejection of materialism*) and **sarmatism** (*a mix of impulsive self-assertion and social hedonism*, deriving from values once espoused by the Polish nobility) as key Polish values.

Although there has been a steady increase in developmental studies in recent years, much of this research still focuses on childhood and adolescence within a Western context. By comparison, relatively few studies have addressed cultural variations in adulthood and old age, and even fewer have examined the end of the lifespan in non-Western societies. With individuals living to increasingly older ages and with the percentage of elderly growing in most cultures, we would certainly benefit from more research on these life stages and behavior within them.

See, for example, the recent examination of elderly widowhood within the family context (Moss & Moss, 2014).

A welcome addition to the applied developmental literature is a volume that focuses on the contemporary culture of Japan, but demonstrates the universality of the research problems discussed (Shwalb, Nakazawa, & Shwalb, 2005). Included among the topics are the effects of video games, *manga*, comics, and television on children's development, literacy acquisition (Japan's rate is nearly 100%), innovative techniques for dealing with children's disabilities, and concern with bullying (a topic on which Japanese researchers have been at the forefront and which was discussed in Chapter 7). One of the strengths of this book is the easy access for international researchers and readers to important findings by contemporary Japanese developmentalists. Another strength is the authors' choice of key issues and an emphasis on how culture guides research and theory and ways in which findings have been shown to have universal applications beyond the culture in which they were found. If only we had more books like this one! It is hoped that the authors' strong emphasis on originality of topics and research approaches, along with attempts at universal applications, will serve as a model for activities in other cultural contexts.

In the next several years, I predict, based on much of what has been discussed in the current book, an increasing interest in viewing human development within an ecological and cross-cultural developmental perspective. Several efforts are at the forefront of this movement. One example is an extensive study by Mishra, Sinha, and Berry (1996) that examines the psychological adaptation of tribal groups in India. Three groups (the Asur, Oraon, and Birhar), differing in settlement and occupation patterns, were compared in terms of cultural lifestyles, patterns of child socialization, cognitive behavior, and acculturation attitudes and experiences. These authors also focus on the application of their findings, this time to problems of acculturative stress. In the decades ahead, I anticipate there will be more studies that focus on the practical application of findings to real-world problems such as immigration and psychological, social, and emotional adjustments to new cultures. I only wish there were more such examples at the present time.

In a review of cultural influences on child development, Super and Harkness (1997) have presented theoretical principles and research evidence in support of three specific approaches that, although varying in focus, emphasize how the environment is dynamic, structured, and integrative. These approaches include their developmental niche concept, which we have referred to extensively throughout this book, Worthman's (1994, 1995) proposed theory of developmental microniche, and Weisner's (2002) work on the ecocultural niche, all of which show promising potential. In another sign of progress, in 2011, a workshop on cultural

niche construction was held at the Konrad Lorenz Institute in Austria to develop new approaches to studying the role of culture in shaping the ecology of humans (and animals) (Laland & O'Brien, 2011). Other workshops have focused on scaffolding in evolution, culture, and cognition (2010), limits of quantification in the sciences (2014), and analyses of human evolution (2015). Other activities of the Konrad Lorenz Institute included brown bag discussions to present research projects in progress, focal seminars with renown experts open to the public, and workshops on key issues presented to international audiences. It is hoped that additional workshops will be held and reports issued in the near future.

In a review of cross-cultural human development research, Gardiner (2004) raised several critical and challenging questions that need to be answered in the near future: *What types of cross-cultural developmental studies will be conducted in the future? How similar or different should these be to current research? In what ways will these studies contribute to our understanding of human development and the ever-changing and increasingly complex world in which people live? What implications will future research findings have for the construction of new developmental theories, and how will these new theories affect the design of even newer studies?* We are, in fact, beginning to see some possible answers to a few of these questions (Smith, 2004).

Finally, there are significant problems in interpreting findings across studies that lack consistency in definitions, approaches, and methodology. We are in need of studies that use culturally sensitive theoretical approaches that look at issues of education, immigration, and acculturation. Such studies will assist in understanding the relationships between ethnicity and culture as they affect mate selection, relationships among siblings, and the roles of grandparents.

In Chapter 3, we focused on what we believe to be one of the most important concepts in human development, namely, socialization. In a review of parental socialization and children's values, Grusec (2002) points out that researchers have significantly altered their theoretical approaches to the study of socialization and introduced more refined and sophisticated methods for measuring its dimensions and outcomes. She states that "[a]t the moment, developmentalists are only beginning to understand how biology, context, and environment interact, and the amount of variance explained in studies is generally not large" (p. 162). However, she asserts that future studies that employ longitudinal designs, larger sample sizes, and variables in interaction "will help to untangle the specific contributions of parent and child to the socialization process . . . [and will] . . . allow the use of causal modeling techniques . . . to suggest the relative contributions of parent and child at given points in time to various outcomes having to do with socialization" (p. 162). Many of these ideas and suggestions for future research are discussed in *Handbook of Socialization* by Grusec and Hastings (2008). Also contributing to a better understanding of parenting and socialization will be additional findings emerging from the field of molecular genetics and the associations beginning to be made between genes and behavioral traits and characteristics (Plomin & Rutter, 1998). Multicultural perspectives on these topics and others will assist in broadening our cross-cultural understanding of the goals and processes of socialization.

In Chapter 4, we looked at families in cultural context and learned that it is a complex topic, including mate selection, marriage and other long-term relationships, birth, transition to parenthood, parental belief systems, grandparenthood, and the need to care for elderly parents. Although a great deal of progress has been made in describing diverse family systems and the variety of cultural contexts in which they develop and thrive, much more remains to be done. For example, we need to broaden our examination of different forms of families (e.g., extended or multigenerational, single-parent, stepfamilies, and families headed by gay and lesbian parents). Cross culturally, we need to encourage indigenous researchers to take an emic (culture-specific) approach to the study of families, parenting, and development to refine and extend our understanding of family dynamics and processes in diverse ecological settings, setting the stage for more etic (universal or cultural general) studies and comparisons.

In their book, *Handbook of Parenting*, Hoghughi and Long (2004) assess the current status of parenting around the world and discuss possible trends affecting parents and children in the twenty-first century. These include the onset of earlier sexual activity in children and parents' role in sex education, increased influence of entertainment media and new technologies on children, increased exposure of children to dysfunctional parenting models in the media, trend for children in their early twenties to continue living (or returning to live) with parents and the effects on all involved, advances in genetic engineering and the ability to create "designer babies," increased family mobility and erosion of neighborhood ties, and increased frequency and severity of children's emotional and behavioral problems throughout the world. Each topic is worthy of further cross-cultural investigation, and we look forward to seeing more such studies in the future.

Advances in reproductive technology (e.g., *in vitro* fertilization (IVF) or "test tube" babies, donor insemination or egg donation, surrogate parenting) have dramatically changed the way in which some families are formed and the manner in which some individuals become parents. Much of this technology is still new enough that we are uncertain how it affects parents and the psychological, social, and emotional development of their children. Golombok (2002) sums it up this way: "Although existing knowledge about the impact of the contemporary reproductive technologies does not give undue cause for concern, there remain many unanswered questions about the consequences for parenting of creating families in this way" (p. 355).

As pointed out previously, the transition to parenthood represents a major change in most people's lives. To understand how this transition takes place, the manner in which parent–child relationships are formed, and the effects on children's development, Cowan, Powell, and Cowan (1998) have proposed that future research employs a family systems model of parenting that collects information on six critical aspects of family functioning, including the quality of relationships: (1) among parents, grandparents, and grandchildren; (2) between siblings; (3) between each parent and child; (4) between nuclear family members and individuals or institutions outside the family (e.g., friends, peers, school, child care, and government); (5) between parents and their roles and communication patterns within the family; and (6) the biological and psychological characteristics of each family member.

What parents know and believe about parenting is, in large part, a result of the way their parents raised them. Although the scientific study of parental beliefs is about fifty years old and has been characterized by a variety of perspectives, Sigel and McGillicuddy-De Lisi (2002) suggest a new approach to the topic that views cognition as the core component, especially the effects on children's cognitive and social development and academic achievement. At the same time, they admit that their approach is controversial with the strongest arguments against it being made by Wachs (2000a). However, they believe their dynamic belief systems model deserves further attention and provides evidence from cross-cultural studies of parental beliefs within specific cultures, across cultures, and between groups from different cultural backgrounds within a society to bolster their view of cultural perspectives. There is much that can be done in this very important area.

There are many questions related to families and parents that might lead to interesting and beneficial research projects. For example, *what do we know about the ecological contexts of new family structures such as gay and lesbian couples with (or without) children or of transnational families living in one culture that communicate through e-mail, travel, and other means with members of their families living abroad? How do families like these deal with issues of identity—how do they define "family," and which values and customs do they decide to maintain, adapt, or reject? How will the expanding global society of cultures influence future family research? Why are some people considered "good" parents and others "poor" parents? What does this mean? What role does age and gender play in parenting? What cultural factors determine the amount and quality of father involvement with their children in different cultures? How can we design more cross-cultural human development research that is experimental rather than correlational? Can we design more longitudinal studies of parenting that incorporate contextual factors that help to sort out the bidirectional and interactive variables involved in parent-child interactions? How does immigration influence parenting styles and practices?*

In their book, *Fathers in Cultural Context*, Shwalb, Shwalb, and Lamb (2013) offer a number of suggestions regarding future cross-cultural research on fathers. For example, they note that there are many countries in which *no* research has been conducted on fathers and suggest pioneering researchers might be the first to do so. Specifically, comparative studies might be made ". . . within Scandinavian welfare states . . . between Brazil and neighbors with common colonial and patriarchal heritage . . . [and] . . . within East Asian states sharing a Confucian/Buddhist heritage . . . " (p. 396). Although preferring an objective and standardized approach to the measurement of fathering, they also recognize the value of multidisciplinary and multimethod approaches. In addition, they encourage a lifespan approach that looks at ". . . how fathers themselves develop over time and how fathers' roles change in relation to their life stages as well as the ages of their children (or the phase in the family lifecycle) . . . " (pp. 396–397). They conclude that such an approach would ". . . enhance fathering research in general, as well as research on fathering in cultural perspective" (p. 297).

In an article on fatherhood in five cultures (Brazil, Bangladesh, Russia, Japan, and Australia), Shwalb and Shwalb (2014) demonstrate and illustrate that fatherhood, fathering, and fathers differ according to eight types of contextual influence, including geographical location, family characteristics, ethnic grouping, long-term historical legacies, family characteristics, economic factors, work-related conditions, societal norms and values, ethnic groupings, and patterns of immigration and emigration. Although stating that overgeneralizations are dangerous, they conclude that there are boundless opportunities for future research on fathering.

For example, Shwalb and Shwalb (2014) suggest a number of specific directions, including the effects of alcoholism and other behaviors on Russian fathering, the changing role of Brazilian fathers, the influence of Islam on fathering, and comparisons of religious influences on fathering (e.g., Hindu vs. Muslim and Catholic vs. Protestant). They conclude their important article with the following comment: "Future worldwide research on fathers must therefore pay attention to changing ecologies and cultures, and to men's role as agents of social change, as we focus on how cultures influence fathers and vice versa. It is undeniable that the international body of work on fathering has already begun to grow and mature significantly in recent years. We predict that the future of such scholarship will be challenging and promising, and that it will enrich cross-cultural understanding of socialization and childrearing in family contexts" (p. 17).

In the latter part of Chapter 4, we devoted attention to grandparenthood and the roles played by grandparents in several cultures, including those of Japan, China, and the United States. Although information on this topic has grown rapidly over the past twenty years, there are limitations, including limited methodology (interviews or structured questionnaires), narrow range of cultures (primarily in the United States), and a lack of theoretical structuring. To improve and extend our knowledge of grandparenting, we need to use a wider range of methods (e.g., naturalistic home observations of grandparent–grandchild interactions, children's drawings of grandparents, and essays written about them), employing more cultures (e.g., those in Asia, Africa, and Latin America), and greater use of theoretical frameworks, like those mentioned previously, to interpret new and previously collected data. As cross-cultural researchers reach later adulthood and become grandparents themselves, we may begin to see more research on these topics.

In addition to these, even less is known about stepgrandparenthood, the role of grandparents in lesbian and gay families, and the extended intergenerational role of great-grandparenthood. There are numerous opportunities to explore these topics in a wide variety of cultural and cross-cultural contexts.

In Chapter 5, we learned that individuals throughout the world tend to use the same or similar cognitive processes, but that cultural differences distinguish the way they are employed in specific cultural contexts. Our understanding of the relationship between culture and cognition requires a careful synthesis of what is currently known about these topics. Norbert Ross (2003), who knows both cognitive anthropology and cognitive psychology well, has provided such a synthesis in his book—*Culture and Cognition: Implications for Theory and Method*—and suggests a number of useful directions for future investigation that are not only interesting but could also be quite productive.

Williams and Sternberg (2001), building on the ideas of Vygotsky and Rogoff, have set forth ten lessons parents can use to maximize children's cognitive abilities (e.g., recognizing what can and cannot be changed, aiming to *meaningfully challenge* them, and teaching them to take responsibility both for their successes and their failures).

Regarding the topic of children's temperament discussed in Chapter 6, individual differences can be observed in the earliest hours following birth, become more apparent during infancy, and remain an important although often modifiable influence (depending on age, gender, social and cultural factors, and parental characteristics) on later developments in behavioral, social, and cognitive areas.

As to future research, Rothbart and Bates (1998) point out that even the best contemporary measures of temperament are inadequate, and future research should be directed at the development of measures with better construct validity—the extent to which a test measures the construct it is designed to measure (e.g., temperamental characteristics of Indonesian infants). See also the work of Rothbart and Hwang (2005). Efforts should also be made to examine parental expectations before the birth of a child to determine how these may influence socialization strategies employed with a child's actual behavior after birth. For example, imagine you are expecting a child. You or your mate may be "hoping for" a boy or a girl. When the baby arrives, whether it is or isn't the gender you expected, you may already have preconceived ideas about how the child will behave and how you will react to those behaviors, which may or may not be appropriate. Knowing more about temperament, the characteristic styles of children and typical parental patterns of responding, will help you to be a more effective parent as you provide socialization experiences appropriate to the culture and world in which your newborn child will live. Recall the interesting ideas of Kara Smith (2005) on prenatal socialization and prebirth gender talk discussed in Chapter 3.

Carefully designed longitudinal studies, beginning at infancy, may help to explain observed gender and cultural differences in temperament. In addition, a number of researchers have drawn attention to the importance of replicating previous parent-temperament interaction findings to be certain they are accurate—an argument we have made several times with regard to other types of research findings as well.

Putnam, Sanson, and Rothbart (2002) recommend that future research on temperament can be greatly improved by moving away from global measures (e.g., "difficult," "easy," and "slow-to-warm-up"), which can vary significantly from one study to another, to more specific measures (e.g., irritability, fear, self-regulation, and shyness). This suggests another promising area—the testing of hypotheses that focus on specific combinations of parenting characteristics and temperament traits (e.g., how fear might lead to a lessening of aggressive responses). These authors also note that almost all temperament research has focused on mothers and, with changes in parental roles, more attention should be given to the caregiving role of fathers and others (e.g., grandparents and extended family members).

Finally, and perhaps of greatest importance to those interested in human development within cultural contexts, is the issue of the generalizability of findings. Almost all of the research on temperament, with the exception of a few anthropological studies (e.g., Margaret Mead's work in New Guinea), has been conducted in individualistic Western cultures. As Kitayama and Markus (1994) have

suggested, individuals raised in more collectivist cultures (e.g., those in Asia, Africa, and among Indian tribes in the United States and Canada) are more frequently identified by their relationship to various groups, and, as a result, variations in temperament may, therefore, be less noticeable and relevant. We suggest that indigenous researchers should carefully examine the relationship between temperament and parenting within their cultures to expand our understanding of this crucial topic and provide parents with relevant information as they attempt to deal with their children's developing personalities. Putnam et al. (2002) have expressed it well: "The task then for the parent and the practitioner is to foster 'respect for the individuality and integrity of each child, and flexibility in creating environments that may lead to positive outcomes for them and for us'" (p. 272).

In Chapter 7, we discussed some aspects of culture and social behavior. What kinds of developments might we expect in the future, particularly from a cross-cultural perspective? Smith, Bond, and Kagitcibasi (2006) have suggested several possible areas of interest, including (1) expansion of our cultural theory base (e.g., consideration of cultural factors contributing to aggression and conflict resolution, as well as movement from Western, individualized theories of development to non-Western, collectivized theories of relatedness and interdependence), (2) universalization of social science measures (e.g., movement away from predominantly American instruments written in English to development of "cultural scripts" consisting of simple sentences that capture cultural norms from the point of view of "natives" and expresses these norms in terms of universal human concepts), and (3) diversification of input (e.g., greater interdisciplinary and cultural cooperation among social scientists in both the development of research projects and authorship of published writings). The authors speculate that attention to a number of dimensions of cultural variation is beginning to emerge. These include increasing contributions by Asian researchers from collectivist cultures interested in comparative studies, examination of relationships between cultural masculinity/femininity and measures of sexual norms and behaviors, as well as gender-related beliefs represented by the work of Hofstede (1996, 2001; Hofstede & Hofstede, 2004), and studies of values at the individual and cultural level (Knafo & Schwartz, 2003; Schwartz, 1995). In an expansion of his pioneering research on cultural values, Hofstede and Hofstede (2004; Hofstede, 2010) maintain that individuals carry around "mental programs," developed within the family during the years of early childhood, containing elements of national culture, reinforced in organizations and schools. The clearest expression of these "programs" can be found in the cluster of values that characterize and distinguish one cultural group from another. According to Smith and Bond (1999), these changes had to "await the diffusion of 'Western' psychology to different cultural milieux and the nurturing of local psychologists who are capable of challenging the biases of the discipline in its own terminology, using its established procedures" (p. 322). Now that cross-cultural social psychology has reached this stage, the authors believe there will be "an intellectual synergy that will enable us to transcend the limitations imposed by our different cultural origins. We may then be able to claim that we have a more truly universal understanding of humanity's social behaviour" (p. 323).

Another topic receiving considerable attention in Chapter 7 was attachment. In the view of Waters and Cummings (2000), "Cross-cultural research on key issues in attachment theory is one of the most exciting prospects for the next generation of attachment research" (p. 169). Rothbaum and Morelli (2005) express a similar view by pointing out the necessity of understanding how "biological dispositions to develop attachments and real environments in which these attachments occur are co-mingled" (p. 119). They suggest a multimethod approach to look at cultural variations that will lead to better understanding of child security and caregiver behavior. For more information on recent attachment measures and a discussion of issues and difficulties in assessing the topic of attachment, refer to http://www.psychology.sunysb.edu/attachment/measures/measures_index.html. For a comprehensive review of theory, research, and clinical applications, see the Second Edition of the *Handbook of Attachment* by Cassidy and Shaver (2008) and *Different Faces of Attachment: Cultural Variations on a Universal Human Need* by Otto and Keller (2014).

In the latter book, Otto and Keller (2014) state that future research should focus on ". . . systematic research programs to study intra- and intercultural variations . . . [in attachment] . . . in order to predict children's future developmental achievements" (p. 311).

The authors put forth a proposal to study attachment as a biocultural construct involving several phases: (1) conceptions of attachment and caregiver–child relationships from indigenous perspectives, using focus group discussions and qualitative and semistructured interviews, should be constructed; (2) families and their children should be observed longitudinally over the first year by a variety of methods in their natural social environments; (3) an assessment of the indigenous conceptions of attachment and their characteristics, in terms of behavioral and neurophysiological measures, should be conducted when the children are one year old. Such a research program would greatly enhance our understanding of attachment.

As we saw in Chapter 8, issues of gender and sexuality have been of increasing interest in cross-cultural psychology and anthropology. Best and Williams (2001) have provided one of the most comprehensive reviews of research on culture and gender. Based on their knowledge

of these issues, they pose a number of questions and challenges for the future of cross-cultural gender research. First, Best and Williams express surprise that more of the cross-cultural research on gender is not "theory driven," that is, based on hypotheses derived from current theories (e.g., social learning, cognitive developmental, and gender schema). They suggest conducting longitudinal studies in societies experiencing rapid changes in socioeconomic development to determine if gender concepts change in theoretically predicted directions. Second, Best and Williams note that the relationship between cultural practices (e.g., initiation rites or rites of passage), frequently studied by anthropologists, and individual development (more often the focus of psychologists), needs greater research attention. The authors argue, as I have before, that psychologists and anthropologists, with shared interests in understanding how culture affects human behavior, should work more closely together and, thereby, learn from each other. Best and Williams express this well when they suggest that "[p]erhaps the growing field of cultural psychology, together with cross-cultural psychology, will provide a bridge between disciplines, recognizing that culture serves as both an independent and an organizing variable" (p. 212).

In Chapter 9, we noted that when it comes to health and related issues, we often do not consider the many ways these might be affected by culture. In their *Handbook of Cultural Health Psychology*, two Canadian researchers, Kazarian and Evans (2001), have set forth a conceptual framework that considers the interface between health behavior and cultural psychology, a necessary step for the advancement of a more culturally competent and ethnically sound approach to health. Some of the topics discussed by contributors to this handbook are (1) approaches to multiculturalism, the relationship between culture and health, and the need to understand variations in health concepts and practices in multicultural societies, including the physical, popular, and folk sectors; (2) provider–patient relationships and the success or failure of treatments that are frequently embedded in cultural differences in individualism and collectivism and the illness models and cultural expectations for health care that result from these differences; (3) the need to more fully integrate the role of culture into the critical topics of health promotion and disease prevention, areas from which it has been conspicuously absent; (4) health concerns of Latinos (e.g., heart disease, HIV/AIDS, cancer, and diabetes); (5) clinical issues encountered by professionals working with native peoples, specific health-related issues they face, and a proposal for a "culturally congruent model" that integrates the values and beliefs of the target groups (e.g., present-time orientation, harmony with nature, sharing, respect for elders, and nonmaterialism); and (6) discussion of the principles of Confucianism and

Taoism as they apply to beliefs about health and illness and some of the ways in which the cultural context shapes both collective and individual health behaviors in traditional and contemporary Chinese societies.

This collection still provides a state-of-the-art understanding of what is known and not known about the rapidly emerging field of cultural health psychology, along with valuable detailed suggestions for designing much-needed multicultural studies to expand the field and lead to important findings related to each of the health issues discussed.

Gurung (2011) expresses a desire for more research on how health and behavior are influenced by cultural differences. He notes that ". . . [m]ainstream psychology has tended to be blind to culture . . . because of the belief that there are commonalities to human behavior that transcend culture" (p. 271). He urges more ". . . theoretical and practical implications of a focus on the collective context—the family, peers, community, and culture, of the individual" (p. 271). This is a point we have stressed throughout this book and that we would like to see expanded on in the future.

In another timely effort, Tinsley, Markey, Ericksen, Oritz, and Kwasman, (2002) reviewed and attempted to integrate research findings concerned with specific ways parents try to promote children's health in a variety of cultural settings. They examine traditional approaches to child health care and more contemporary developmental models. Tinsley et al. also discuss parents' socialization of children's sick role and wellness behaviors. The authors conclude that health research is limited (e.g., focusing on mother's role in health promotion). They would like to see more attention given to the role of fathers, and the influence of entire families as they function in a cultural and ecological context. The recent book on *Fathers in Cultural Context* by Shwalb, Shwalb, and Lamb (2013) begins to add to this literature as it looks at the changing roles of fathers in such cultures as Japan, China, Malaysia, Africa, Brazil, and elsewhere.

In another effort to understand and explain the relationship between culture and health, Maclachlan (2006) introduces new techniques for assessment and treatment of disorders found in a variety of cultures. Making use of psychological, anthropological, sociological, and medical research, the author provides case studies and guidelines for good practice that show promise for future research.

An area of the world that has not received as much cross-cultural attention as it deserves, particularly in light of recent global events, is the Middle East/North Africa, sometimes referred to as MENA. In fact, until recently we have known relatively little about the people living in this important region of the world. A major contribution to our understanding of the societies and cultures that exist here, along with insights into their struggles with traditions and modernity, self and identity, stereotypes and

misunderstandings, and the universality and unique behaviors that characterize their citizens, are discussed in a book by Gary Gregg (2005) titled *The Middle East: A Cultural Psychology*. Most important, he provides a "social ecology" of psychological development and explores development across the same life stages as we have from infancy to adulthood. His contributions are theoretical, empirical, and pragmatic, and they add significantly to our cross-cultural understanding of societies we do not know very well but certainly should. In addition, the majority of the reported research has been conducted by Arab-Muslim scholars and has previously been unavailable to Westerners and others.

Gregg (2005) closes with thoughtful suggestions for further research based on the writings of indigenous scholars with a focus on emic-etic influences on development. Among the priorities that researchers might consider are care practices among the growing urban poor, mastering of the "honor-modesty" system, the nature and consequences of patriarchal or authoritarian parenting styles, and adolescent dealings with the contradictory worldviews associated with tradition and modern institutions, as well as their effect on identity formation. The book contains a wealth of ideas that can be applied not only to the study of MENA cultures but also to other cultures as well. Readers may also enjoy and gain insight from Gregg's (2007) book on *Culture and Identity in a Muslim Society*, in this case, Morocco. Consisting of six eighteen-hour interviews with eleven eighteen- to twenty-eight-year-olds, it proposes a three-level theory of personality that seeks to extend Erikson's theory of identity development in late adolescence and early adulthood.

Abdel-Satta Ibrahim (2013), president of the Egyptian Union for Psychological Professions, comments on some of the challenges, indigenous and cross-cultural, confronting psychologists in many contemporary Arab nations. These include limited opportunities for growth, lack of recognition for their work, and professional conflicts with other disciplines. Nevertheless, some local and global recognition is being received for their contributions in education, mental health services, and cultural decision making. He is hopeful that, in the not too distant future, their work will begin to reach the level it has in other more developed countries.

In bringing the fifth edition of *Lives Across Cultures* (Gardiner, 2008) to a close, we said that "[c]ross-cultural study of development frequently resembles a confused mosaic of often contradictory findings. Yet therein lies the promise and excitement of future endeavors. . . . Much more needs to be done, and as the cross-cultural perspective reveals, discovery of similarities and dissimilarities in human behavior will make our understanding both easier and more difficult" (p. 310). This was true then, and it is even truer today.

Ahead of us lie tremendous challenges and opportunities. Speculating about where our cross-cultural journey will take us next is difficult. Wherever we go, it is certain to be an interesting and exciting adventure. Perhaps some of you will be the pioneer theorists and researchers who take us to the next point on this journey. We look forward eagerly to that day.

## Summary: Future Trends and Applications

In this final chapter, we look back at the major theories introduced at the beginning of our journey into human development and comment on their usefulness for explaining cultural similarities and differences in behavior across the lifespan. These include the ecological systems approach and developmental niche, as well as the work of Piaget, Vygotsky, Erikson, and Kohlberg. I conclude with my view of some of the current challenges in the field of cross-cultural human development and promising directions the field will (or should) take as it attempts to expand our knowledge and understanding of a most fascinating topic—ourselves.

## Study Questions

Comment critically on the theories of Kohlberg and Erikson, and explain how these theories might be made more useful to cross-cultural researchers.

Explain why there is a need to conduct more comparative cross-cultural studies of human development.

Describe some of the examples of the type of cultural research the author recommends be conducted in the future.

If you were to conduct cross-cultural human development studies, what topics of interest would you select?

# Glossary

**Accommodation**    Process of adjusting or modifying existing schemes to account for new ideas and information. (See **assimilation**.)

**Aggression**    Overt action or behavior intended to cause harm, damage, or injury. (See **hostility**.)

**Alzheimer's disease**    Progressive neurological disease resulting in memory loss, judgment, and cognitive functioning.

**Anorexia nervosa**    Eating disorder primarily among young adolescent girls characterized by loss of appetite and extreme loss of weight. (See **bulimia nervosa**.)

**Assimilation**    Process by which new information and ideas are incorporated or fitted into existing knowledge or schemes.

**Attachment**    Emotional bond between child and caregivers that allows children to feel secure and to know to whom they can turn in threatening situations.

**Back translation**    Research procedure for achieving linguistic equivalence when conducting cross-cultural studies.

**Bulimia nervosa**    Primarily found in young women who eat extremely large amounts of food and then purge it all by self-induced vomiting.

**Childhood**    End of infancy, about 1.5 years, to the beginning of adolescence, about 11 to 12 years, depending on the particular culture.

**Chronosystem**    Last and least defined level of the ecological model focusing on time and sociohistorical conditions affecting a child's behavior.

**Cognition**    Process of obtaining knowledge, including perceiving, recognizing, reasoning, thinking, and judging.

**Collectivist culture**    Consists of people who consider the group to be most important, with an emphasis on cooperation, traditions, and common goals and values (e.g., South America, Africa, and much of Asia). (See **individualistic culture**.)

**Cosleeping**    A child sleeping with a parent.

**Cross-cultural comparison**    When individuals from at least two different cultural groups are measured and compared on some aspect of behavior.

**Cross-cultural goals**    (1) Testing or extending the generalizability of existing theories and findings, (2) exploring other cultures for variations not part of one's own cultural experience, (3) integrating and applying findings to cultural settings and societies, and (4) applying research findings across professional disciplines.

**Cross-cultural perspective**    Understanding human behavior based on cross-cultural research within cultural contexts.

**Cross-cultural psychology**    Systematic study of human development and behaviors that become established in individuals growing up in particular cultures.

**Crystallized intelligence**    Individual's accumulated knowledge and experience in a particular culture. (See **fluid intelligence**.)

**Cultural human development**    Cultural similarities and differences in developmental processes and their outcomes expressed by behavior of individuals and groups.

**Culture**    Cluster of learned and shared beliefs, values, practices, behaviors, symbols, and attitudes that characterize people and are communicated from one generation to another.

**Culture-bound syndrome**    Culture-specific illness found only in specific societies or cultures.

**Dependent variable (DV)**    Subject's response or the behavior being measured in an experiment. (See **independent variable**.)

**Depression**    Serious psychological disorder with sadness and other negative feelings (e.g., despair, sleep disturbance, hopelessness, and loss of energy).

**Developmental niche**    Framework, developed by Harkness and Super, for understanding how various aspects of a culture guide the developmental process by focusing on the child as the unit of analysis within his or her sociocultural setting or context.

**Dialectical thinking**    Idea that for every viewpoint there is an opposing viewpoint, and these can be considered simultaneously.

**Difficult child**    Characterized by a negative mood, slow adaptation, withdrawal from new experiences and people, and irregular feeding and sleeping patterns.

**Easy child**    Characterized by a good mood, regular eating and sleeping cycles, and general calmness.

**Ecological model**    Approach developed by Urie Bronfenbrenner that views behavior and development as a shared function of the individual and the larger contemporary and historical contexts of society and time in which one is born and lives his or her life. (See **chronosystem, exosystem, macrosystem, mesosystem,** and **microsystem**.)

**Emics**    Culture-specific concepts that generally focus on a single culture. (See **etics**.)

**Ethnocentrism**    Tendency to judge other people and cultures by one's own standards and to believe the behavior, norms, values, customs, and other characteristics of one's own group are natural, correct, and valid, whereas those of others are unnatural, incorrect, and invalid.

**Ethnotheories**    Parents' cultural belief systems about the nature of children, the processes of development, and the meaning of behavior.

**Etics**    Universal or culture-general concepts that compare and contrast cultures. (See **emics**.)

**Exosystem**   Third level of the ecological model consisting of formal settings that influence one's behavior (e.g., parents' place of work).

**Fluid intelligence**   Biological ability to form concepts, reason abstractly, and apply material to new situations. (See **crystallized intelligence**.)

**Formal learning**   Knowledge generally acquired in a structured setting (e.g., school). (See **informal learning**.)

**Gender**   Acquired behavioral and psychological aspects of being a woman or a man.

**Goodness of fit**   Match between a child's temperament and the demands of his or her immediate environment.

**Group marriage**   All women and men in a group are married simultaneously to each other.

**Heritability quotient**   Estimate of the percentage of the variability in a given trait that can be attributed to genetic differences.

**Hostility**   Motive or desire to cause damage or injury. (See **aggression**.)

**Human development**   Changes in physical, psychological, and social behavior experienced by individuals across the lifespan from conception to death.

**Human Genome Project (1990–2003)**   Identification of the 20,000 to 25,000 genes in human DNA and analysis of the roles they play in a variety of physical illnesses and psychological conditions.

**Identity**   Individual's self-definition as a separate and distinct person, including behaviors, beliefs, and attitudes.

**Independent variable (IV)**   Condition introduced into or systematically manipulated in an experiment by the researcher. (See **dependent variable**.)

**Individualism-collectivism (IND-COL)**   Approach to describing, explaining, and understanding similarities and differences in a variety of cultural contexts.

**Individualistic culture**   Consists of people responsible to themselves and their family and whose individual achievement are most important (e.g., the United States and most European cultures). (See **collectivist culture**.)

**Informal learning**   Knowledge generally acquired by means of observation and imitation. (See **formal learning**.)

**Language**   System of symbols used to communicate information and knowledge.

**Macrosystem**   Fourth level of the ecological model consisting of the customs, values, and laws considered important in the child's culture, determining acceptable and unacceptable behaviors.

**Manta pouch**   Backpacklike device that protects an infant from the harsh elements in the Peruvian mountains and provides a secure environment close to the mother.

**Mesosystem**   Second level of the ecological model consisting of two or more microsystems linking information, knowledge, and attitudes from one setting to another (e.g., home and day care, day care and school, or family and peer group).

**Microsystem**   First level of the ecological model closest to the child where the child has direct (face-to-face) contact with family, home, day care center, or preschool, resulting in dependence, independence, cooperation, competition, etc.

**Monogamy**   One man married to one woman.

**Moral dilemmas**   Hypothetical incidents involving conflicts between an individual's needs or desires and rules of society.

**Newborn**   Term applied to babies from birth through the first two weeks.

**Obesity**   Generally considered body weight 20% or more above the recommended weight for one's age, gender, and body type.

**Peer**   Individual of similar age and sometimes the same gender.

**Peer group**   Individuals who share certain characteristics (e.g., background, age, status, class) and interact on generally equal terms.

**Personality**   Unique system of identifiable and characteristic behavioral patterns that distinguish one person from another.

**Polyandry**   One woman married to several men.

**Polygyny**   One man married to several women.

**Puberty**   Period of biological transition between childhood and adulthood lasting approximately one to two years.

**Rites of passage**   Ceremonies or rituals ("coming-of-age" experiences) that recognize or symbolize an individual's movement from one status to another.

**Scaffolding**   Temporary support or guidance given a child by parents, older siblings, peers, or other adults in solving a problem.

**Scheme**   An organized pattern of thought or action applied to persons, objects, or events in an effort to make sense of them.

**Schizophrenia**   Group of severe psychological disorders characterized by disturbances in thinking, perception, and emotion.

**Self-concept**   Perception of oneself as an individual with identifiable behavioral patterns and characteristics.

**Self-efficacy**   General sense of one's ability to complete tasks and to direct behavior toward a goal.

**Senescence**   Process of biological change associated with normal aging.

**Sex**   Biological aspects of femaleness and maleness.

**Slow-to-warm-up child**   Characterized by few positive or negative reactions and mild and low in activity level.

**Social identity**   Part of an individual's self-concept that derives from knowledge of membership in a social group or groups.

**Socialization**   Process by which an individual becomes a member of a particular culture and takes on its beliefs, values, and other behaviors to function within it.

**Sociocultural theory of development**   Theory of cognitive development proposed by Lev Vygotsky in which thinking and reasoning emerge through activity in social environments.

**Somatization**   Physical ailments resulting from stress or emotional distress.

**Strange situation**   Standardized event allowing observation of child's bond with caregiver. Temperament an individual's innate characteristic behavioral style or typical pattern of responding to events in the environment.

**Theory**   Set of hypotheses (guesses) or assumptions about behavior.

**Theory of cognitive development**   Jean Piaget's comprehensive theory of the nature and development of intelligence.

**Theory of moral development**   Six-stage theory developed by Lawrence Kohlberg to explain a child's moral reasoning and ethical behavior. (See **moral dilemmas**.)

**Theory of psychosocial development**   Eight-stage theory of personality development and social behavior covering the lifespan proposed by Erik Erikson.

**Transgender**   Individual with a gender identity differing from one's assigned sex.

**Zone of proximal development (ZPD)**   Difference between what children can achieve independently and/or with guidance and instruction.

# References

Abdel-Khalek, A. M., & Soliman, H. H. (1999). A cross-cultural evaluation of depression in children in Egypt, Kuwait, and the United States. *Psychological Reports, 85*, 973–980.

Abdulcadira, J., Margairarazb, Boulvaina, M., & Irion, O. (2011). Care of women with female genital mutilation/cutting—A review. *Swiss Medical Weekly, 140*, 13137.

Abela, A., & Walker, J. (2014). Global changes in marriage, parenting and family life: An overview. In A. Abela & J. Walker (Eds.), *Contemporary issues in family studies: Global perspectives on partnerships, parenting, and support in a changing world* (pp. 5–15). Oxford, UK: Wiley & Sons.

Adelson, J. (1985). Observations on research in adolescence. *Genetic, Social, and General Psychology Monographs, 111*, 249–254.

Ahadi, S. A., & Rothbart, M. K. (1994). Temperament, development, and the big five. In C. F. Halverson, Jr., G. A. Kohnstamm, & R. P. Martin (Eds.), *The developing structure of temperament and personality from infancy to adulthood* (pp. 189–207). Hillsdale, NJ: Erlbaum.

Ainsworth, M., Blehar, M., Waters, E., & Wall, S. (1978). *Patterns of attachment*. Hillsdale, NJ: Basic Books.

Ainsworth, M. D. S. (1982). Attachment: Retrospect and prospect. In C. M. Parks & J. Stevenson-Hinde (Eds.), *The place of attachment in human behavior* (pp. 3–30). New York: Basic Books.

Ainsworth, M. D. S., & Wittig, B. A. (1969). Attachment and exploratory behavior of one-year-olds in a strange situation. In B. M. Foss (Ed.), *Determinants of infant behavior IV* (pp. 111–136). London: Methuen.

Akande, A. (1999). Intercultural and cross-cultural assessment of self-esteem among youth in twenty-first century South Africa. *International Journal for the Advancement of Counselling, 21*, 171–187.

Aldous, J., Mulligan, G. M., & Bjarnason, T. (1998). Fathering over time: What makes the difference? *Journal of Marriage and Family, 60*(4), 809–820.

Ali, A., & Maharajh, H. D. (2004). Anorexia nervosa and religious ambivalence in a developing country. *The Internet Journal of Mental Health, 2*(1). Retrieved from http://ispub.com/IJMH/2/1/12092#

Almond, D., & Edlund, L. (2008). Son-biased sex ratio in the 2000 United States Census. *Proceedings of the National Academy of Sciences USA, 105*(15), 5681–5682.

American Psychiatric Association. (2013). *Diagnostic and statistical manual of mental disorders* (Rev. 5th ed.). Washington, DC: Author.

Anderson, J. A. (1999). Hot flashes or power surges? A contextual analysis of menopause and its meaning. *Dissertation Abstracts International: Section B: The Sciences and Engineering, 60*(6-B), 2979.

Andersson, G., & Noack, T. (2011). Legal advances and demographic developments of same-sex unions in Scandinavia. *Zeitschrift fur Familienforshung* [Journal of Family Research].

Antonucci, T. C. (1990). Social supports and social relationships. In R. H. Binstock & K. George (Eds.), *Handbook of aging and the social sciences* (3rd ed., pp. 205–226). New York: Academic Press.

Antonucci, T. C. (1994). Attachment in adulthood and aging. In M. B. Sperling & W. H. Berman (Eds.), *Attachment in adults: Clinical and developmental perspectives* (pp. 256–272). New York: Guilford Press.

Archer, J., & Mehdikhani, M. (2004). Sex differences in aggression in real-world settings: A meta-analytical review. *Review of General Psychology, 8*, 291–322.

Archetti, E. P. (1999). *Masculinities: Football, polo, and the tango in Argentina*. Oxford, UK: Berg.

Ardelt, M. (2004). Wisdom as expert knowledge system. *Human Development, 47*(5), 257–285.

Arnett, J. (1992). Reckless behavior in adolescence: A developmental perspective. *Developmental Review, 12*, 339–373.

Arnett, J. J. (2004). Adolescence in the 21st century: A worldwide survey. In U. P. Gielen & J. L. Roopnarine (Eds.), *Childhood and adolescence in cross-cultural perspective* (pp. 277–294). New York: Guilford Press.

Arnett, J. J. (2006). *Adolescence and emerging adulthood: A cultural approach* (3rd ed.). Upper Saddle River, NJ: Prentice Hall.

Arnett, J. J. (Ed.). (2006). *International encyclopedia of adolescence*. London: Routledge.

Arnett, J. J. (2009). *Adolescence and emerging adulthood: A cultural approach* (4th ed., Books a la Carte). Upper Saddle River, NJ: Prentice Hall.

Arnett, J. J. (2012). *Human development: A cultural approach*. Boston: Pearson.

Atkinson, P., & Delamont, S. (Eds.). (2006). *Narrative methods*. London: Sage.

Auyeung, B., Baron-Cohen, S., Ashwin, E., Knickmeyer, R., Taylor, K., Hackett, G., et al. (2009). Fetal testosterone predicts sexually differentiated childhood behavior in girls and boys. *Psychological Science, 20*(2), 144–148.

Ayachi, S. (2014). Mate selection and marriage stability in the Maghreb. In A. Abela & J. Walker (Eds.), *Contemporary issues in family studies: Global perspectives on partnerships, parenting, and support in a changing world* (pp. 317–327). Oxford, UK: Wiley & Sons.

Azhar, M. Z., & Varma, S. L. (2000). Mental illness and its treatment in Malaysia. In I. Al-Issa (Ed.), *Al-Junūn: Mental illness in the Islamic world* (pp. 163–186). Madison, CT: International Universities Press.

Azuma, H. (2005). Foreword. In D. W. Shwalb, J. Nakazawa, & B. J. Shwalb (Eds.), *Applied developmental psychology: Theory, practice, and research from Japan* (pp. xi–xvii). Greenwich, CT: Information Age.

Bailey, R. C. (1985). *The socioecology of Efe pygmy men in the Ituri forest, Zaire* (Doctoral dissertation, Harvard University).

Baltes, P. B. (1987). Theoretical propositions of life-span developmental psychology: On the dynamics between growth and decline. *Developmental Psychology, 23*, 611–626.

Baltes, P. B., & Schaie, K. W. (1976). On the plasticity of intelligence in adulthood and old age: Where Horn and Donaldson fail. *American Psychologist, 31*(10), 720–725.

Baltes, P. B., & Staudinger, U. M. (2000). Wisdom. *American Psychologist, 55*, 122–136.

Bandura, A. (1990). *Multidimensional scales of perceived academic efficacy*. Stanford, CA: Stanford University.

Bandura, A. (1997). *Self-efficacy: The exercise of control*. New York: Freeman.

Banks, C. G. (1992). 'Culture' in culture-bound syndromes: The case of anorexia nervosa. *Social Science and Medicine, 34*(8), 867–884.

Barlow, K., & Chapin, B. L. (2010). The practice of mothering: An introduction. *Ethos, 38*(4), 324–338.

Barnard, K., & Solchany, J. (2002). Mothering. In M. H. Bornstein (Ed.), *Handbook of parenting, Volume 3: Being and becoming a parent* (pp. 3–26). Mahwah, NJ: Erlbaum.

Barnard, K. E., & Martell, L. K. (1995). Mothering. In M. H. Bornstein (Ed.), *Handbook of parenting* (Vol. 3, pp. 3–26). Mahwah, NJ: Erlbaum.

Barnlund, D. C., & Araki, S. (1985). Intercultural encounters: The management of compliments by Japanese and Americans. *Journal of Cross-Cultural Psychology, 16*, 9–26.

Barrett, D. E., Radke-Yarrow M., & Klein, R. E. (1982). Chronic malnutrition and child behavior: Effects of early caloric supplementation on social and emotional functioning at school age. *Developmental Psychology, 18*(4), 541–556.

Basseti, B., & Cook, V. (2011). Language and cognition: The second language user. In V. J. Cook & B. Basseti (Eds.), Language and bilingual cognition (pp. 143–190). Oxford, UK: Psychology Press.

Beach, L. R. (2010). *The psychology of narrative thought*. Bloomington, IN: Xlibris Corporation.

Beardsley, L. M. (1994). Medical diagnosis and treatment across cultures. In W. J. Lonner & R. Malpass (Eds.), *Psychology and culture* (pp. 279–284). Boston: Allyn & Bacon.

Beatty, S. E., Jeon, J., Albaum, G., & Murphy, B. (1994). A cross-national study of leisure activities. *Journal of Cross-Cultural Psychology, 25*, 409–422.

Becker, G., & Newsom, E. (2005). Resilience in the face of serious illness among chronically ill African Americans in later life. *Journal of Gerontology: Series B: Psychological Sciences and Social Sciences, 60*, 214–223.

Belsky, J. (1985). Exploring individual differences in marital change across the transition to parenthood: The role of violated expectations. *Journal of Marriage and the Family, 47*, 1037–1044.

Bergen, D. (2007). *Human development: Traditional and contemporary theories*. NJ: Prentice Hall.

Berry, J. W. (1983). The sociogenesis of social sciences: An analysis of the cultural relativity of social psychology. In B. Bain (Ed.), *The sociogenesis of language and human conduct* (pp. 449–458). New York: Plenum.

Berry, J. W., & Dasen, P. (Eds.). (1974). *Culture and cognition*. London: Methuen.

Berry, J. W., Poortinga, Y. H., Breugelmans, S. M., Chasiotis, A., & Sam, D. (2011). *Cross-cultural psychology: Research and applications* (3rd ed.). Cambridge, UK: Cambridge University Press.

Berry, J. W., Poortinga, Y. H., & Pandey, J. (Eds.). (1997). *Handbook of cross-cultural psychology, Volume 1: Theory and method* (2nd ed.). Boston: Allyn & Bacon.

Berry, J. W., Poortinga, Y. H., Segall, M. H., & Dasen, P. R. (2002). *Cross-cultural psychology* (2nd ed.). Cambridge, UK: Cambridge University Press.

Bertrand, J. T., Ward, V., & Pauc, F. (1992). Sexual practices among the Quiche-speaking Mayan population of Guatemala. *International Quarterly of Community Health Education, 12*, 265–282.

Best, D. L., & Williams, J. E. (2001). Gender and culture. In D. Matsumoto (Ed.), *The handbook of culture and psychology* (pp. 195–219). New York: Oxford University Press.

Bharti, B., Malhi, P., & Kashyap, S. (2006). Patterns and problems of sleep in school going children. *Indian Pediatrics, 43*(1), 35–38.

Birdsong, D., & Molis, M. (2001). On the evidence for maturational constraints in second-language acquisition. *Journal of Memory and Language, 44*, 235–249.

Birren, J. E., & Schaie, K. W. (Eds.). (1995). *Handbook of psychology and aging*. San Diego: Academic.

Bishop, B. (2004). *Globalisation and women in the Japanese workforce*. London: Routledge Curson.

Bochner, S. (1994). Cross-cultural differences in the self-concept. A test of Hofstede's individualism/collectivism distinction. *Journal of Cross-Cultural Psychology, 25*, 273–283.

Bolton, R. (1994). Sex, science, and social responsibility: Cross-cultural research on same-sex eroticism and sexual intolerance. *Cross-Cultural Research, 28*, 134–190.

Bond, T. G. (1998). Fifty years of formal operational research: The empirical evidence. *Archives de Psychologie, 66*, 221–238.

Borgatti, S. P. (1992). ANTHROPAC 4.0: *Methods guide*. Columbia, SC: Analytic Technologies.

Bornstein, M. H. (1995). Parenting infants. In M. H. Bornstein (Ed.), *Handbook of parenting* (Vol. 1, pp. 3–39). Mahwah, NJ: Erlbaum.

Bornstein, M. H. (2000). Infant to conversant: Language and non-language processes in developing early communication. In N. Budwig, I. C. Uzgiris, & J. V. Wertsch (Eds.), *Communication: An arena of development (pp. 109–129)*. Stamford, CT: Ablex.

Bornstein, M. H. (2002). Parenting infants. In M. H. Bornstein (Ed.), *Handbook of parenting* (Vol. 1, 2nd ed., pp. 3–43). Mahwah, NJ: Erlbaum.

Bornstein, M. H., Tal, J., Rahn, C., Galperin, C. Z., Pecheux, M. G., Lamour, M., et al. (1992). Functional analysis of the contents of maternal speech to infants of five and thirteen months in four cultures: Argentina, France, Japan, and the United States. *Developmental Psychology, 28*, 593–603.

Bornstein, M. H., Tal, J., & Tamis-LeMonda, C. S. (1991). Parenting in cross-cultural perspective: The United States, France, and Japan. In M. H. Bornstein (Ed.), *Cultural approaches to parenting* (pp. 69–90). Hillsdale, NJ: Erlbaum.

Boski, P. (2005). Humanism–materialism: Century-long Polish cultural origins and twenty years of research in cultural psychology. In U. Kim, K.-S. Yang, & K.-K. Hwang (Eds.), *Indigenous and cultural psychology* (pp. 373–402). New York: Springer.

Boston University Medical Center. (2015). Transgender: Evidence on the biological nature of gender identity. *ScienceDaily*. Retrieved from www.sciencedaily.com/releases/2015/02/150213112317.html

Bouchard, T. J., Lykken, D. T., McGue, M., Segal, N. L., & Tellegen, A. (1990). Sources of human psychological differences: The Minnesota study of twins reared apart. *Science, 250*, 223–228.

Bourguignon, E. (1979). *Psychological anthropology: An introduction to human nature and cultural differences.* New York: Holt, Rinehart & Winston.

Brannigan, M. C. (Ed.). (2004). *Cross-cultural biotechnology.* Lanham, MD: Rowman & Littlefield.

Brislin, R. (Ed.). (1990). *Applied cross-cultural psychology.* Newbury Park, CA: Sage.

Brislin, R. (1993). *Understanding culture's influence on behavior.* New York: Harcourt Brace Jovanovich.

Bronfenbrenner, U. (1967). Response to pressure from peers versus adults among Soviet and American school children. *International Journal of Psychology, 2*, 199–207.

Bronfenbrenner, U. (1970). *Two worlds of childhood: U.S. and U.S.S.R.* New York: Russell Sage Foundation.

Bronfenbrenner, U. (1975). Reality and research in the ecology of human development. *Proceedings of the American Philosophical Society, 119*, 439–469.

Bronfenbrenner, U. (1977). Toward an experimental ecology of human development. *American Psychologist, 32*, 513–531.

Bronfenbrenner, U. (1979). *The ecology of human development: Experiments by nature and design.* Cambridge, MA: Harvard University Press.

Bronfenbrenner, U. (1986). Ecological systems theory. In R. Vasta (Ed.), *Annals of child development* (Vol. 6, pp. 187–251). Greenwich, CT: JAI Press.

Bronfenbrenner, U. (1989). Ecological systems theory. In R. Vasta (Ed.), *Six theories of child development* (Vol. 6, pp. 187–250). Greenwich, CT: JAI Press.

Bronfenbrenner, U. (1993). The ecology of cognitive development: Research models and fugitive findings. In R. H. Wozniak & K. W. Fischer (Eds.), *Development in context: Acting and thinking in specific environments* (pp. 3–44). Hillsdale, NJ: Erlbaum.

Bronfenbrenner, U. (1994). Ecological models of human development. In T. Husen & T. N. Postlethwaite (Eds.), *International encyclopedia of education* (2nd ed., Vol. 3, pp. 1643–1647). Oxford, UK: Pergamon/Elsevier Science.

Bronfenbrenner, U. (1999). Environments in developmental perspective: Theoretical and operational models. In S. L. Friedman & T. D. Wachs (Eds.), *Measuring environment across the life span.* Washington, DC: American Psychological Association.

Bronfenbrenner, U. (2000). Ecological systems theory. In A. Kazdin (Ed.), Encyclopedia of psychology (Vol. 3, pp. 129–133). New York: Oxford University Press.

Bronfenbrenner, U. (Ed.). (2005). *Making human beings human.* Thousand Oaks, CA: Sage.

Bronfenbrenner, U., & Morris, P. (1998). The ecology of developmental processes. In R. M. Lerner (Ed.), *Handbook of child psychology, Volume 1: Theoretical models of human development* (5th ed., pp. 993–1028). New York: Wiley.

Brooks, P. J., Jia, X., Braine, M. D. S., & Da Graca Dias, M. (1998). A cross-linguistic study of children's comprehension of universal quantifiers: A comparison of Mandarin Chinese, Portuguese, and English. *First Language, 18*, 33–79.

Bross, F., & Pfaller, P. (2012). The decreasing Whorf-effect: A study in the classifier systems of Mandarin and Thai. *Journal of Unsolved Questions, 2*(2), 19–24.

Brown, B. B., Lohr, M. J., & Trujillo, C. (1990). Multiple crowds and multiple life-styles: Adolescents' perceptions of peer-group stereotypes. In R. E. Muuss (Ed.), *Adolescent behavior and society* (4th ed., pp. 30–36). New York: McGraw-Hill.

Brown, J. R., Greve, K., & deGuzman, M. R. T. (2013). Peer relationships. In K. D. Keith (Ed.), *The encyclopedia of cross-cultural psychology* (pp. 986–988). Hoboken, NJ: Wiley-Blackwell.

Bryce, C., Boschi-Pinto, C., Shibuja, K., & Black, R. E. (2005). WHO estimates of the causes of death in children. *Lancet, 365*, 1147–1152.

Buchtel, E. E., & Norenzayan, A. (2009). Thinking across cultures: Implications for dual processes. In J. Evans & K. Frankish (Eds.), *In two minds: Dual processes and beyond* (pp. 217–238). New York: Oxford University Press.

Budwig, N., Wertsch, J. V., & Uzgiris, I. C. (2000). Introduction: Communication, meaning, and development: Interdisciplinary perspectives. In N. Budwig, I. C. Uzgiris, & J. V. Wertsch (Eds.), *Communication: An arena of development* (pp. 1–16). Stamford, CT: Ablex.

Bulbeck, C. (2005). "The mighty pillar of the family": Young people's vocabularies on household gender arrangements in the Asia-Pacific region. *Gender Work and Organization, 12*, 14–31.

Bushong, L. J. (2013). *Belonging everywhere and nowhere: Insights into counseling the globally mobile.* Fishers, IN: Mango Tree International Services.

Buss, D. M. (1994a). *The evolution of desire: Strategies of human mating.* New York: Basic Books.

Buss, D. M. (1994b). Mate preferences in 37 cultures. In W. J. Lonner & R. Malpass (Eds.), *Psychology and culture* (pp. 197–201). Boston: Allyn & Bacon.

Buss, D. M. (2003). *The evolution of desire: Strategies of human mating* (Rev. ed.). New York: Basic Books.

Buss, D. M. (2007). The evolution of human mating. *Acta Psycholica Sinica, 39*(3), 502–512.

Buss, D. M. (2015). *Evolutionary psychology: The new science of the mind* (5th ed.). New York: Psychology Press.

Buss, D. M., & Schmitt, D. P. (1993). Sexual strategies theory: An evolutionary perspective on human mating. *Psychological Review, 100*, 204–232.

Butcher, J. N. (2006). *MMPI-2: A practitioner's handbook.* Washington, DC: American Psychological Association.

Butcher, J. N., Graham, J. R., Ben-Porath, Y. S., Tellegen, Y., Dahlstrom, Y., & Kaemmer, B. (2009). *Minnesota Multiphasic Personality Inventory-2 (MMPI-2).* Minneapolis: University of Minnesota Press.

Calabrese, R. L., & Noboa, J. (1995). The choice for gang membership by Mexican-American adolescents. *High School Journal, 78*, 226–235.

Calhoun, D. W. (1987). *Sport, culture, and personality* (2nd ed.). Champaign, IL: Human Kinetics.

Cantor, N., Norem, J. K., Langston, C. A., Zirkel, S., Fleeson, W., & Cook-Flannagan, C. (1991). Life tasks and daily life experience. *Journal of Personality, 59*, 425–451.

Cantor, N., Norem, J. K., Niedenthal, P. M., Langston, C. A., & Brower, A. M. (1987). Life tasks, self-concept ideals, and cognitive strategies in a life transition. *Journal of Personality and Social Psychology, 53*, 1178–1191.

Caravolas, M. (2008). The nature and causes of dyslexia in different languages. In M. J. Snowling & C. Hulme (Eds.), *The science of reading: A handbook* (pp. 336–355). Malden, MA: Blackwell.

Carey, G. (2003). *Human genetics for the social sciences.* Thousand Oaks, CA: Sage.

Caselli, C., Casadio, P., & Bates, E. (1999). A comparison from first words to grammar in English and Italian. *Journal of Child Language, 26*, 69–111.

Cassidy, J., & Shaver, P. R. (Eds.). (2008). *Handbook of attachment* (2nd ed.). New York: Guilford Press.

Centers for Disease Control and Prevention (CDC). (2010, March 25). Breast-feeding varies by race, place. *USA Today.* Retrieved from http://usatoday30.usatoday.com/news/health/2010-03-25-breastfeeding_N.html

Central Intelligence Agency (CIA). (2009). *The world factbook.* Washington, DC: Author.

Central Intelligence Agency (CIA). (2013). *The world factbook.* Washington, DC: Author.

Chadda, R. K., & Ahuja, N. (1990). Dhat syndrome. *British Journal of Psychiatry, 156*, 577–579.

Chagnon, N. A. (1997). *Yanomamo* (5th ed.) (Case Studies in Anthropology). Fort Worth, TX: Holt, Rinehart & Winston.

Chagnon, N. A. (2012). *Yanomamo* (6th ed.) (Case Studies in Anthropology). Independence, KY: Cengage Learning.

Chagnon, N. A. (2013). *Noble savages: My life among two dangerous tribes—the Yanomamo and the anthropologists.* New York: Simon & Schuster.

Chao, R., & Lambert, K. (2013). Emic-etic approach. In K. D. Keith (Ed.), *The encyclopedia of cross-cultural psychology* (pp. 469–471). Hoboken, NJ: Wiley-Blackwell.

Chao, R., & Wang, C. (2013). Coping and coping styles. In K. D. Keith (Ed.), *The encyclopedia of cross-cultural psychology* (pp. 253–255). Hoboken, NJ: Wiley-Blackwell.

Chao, R., & Tseng, V. (2002). Parenting of Asians. In M. H. Bornstein (Ed.), *Handbook of parenting* (Vol. 4, pp. 59–93). Mahwah, NJ: Erlbaum.

Charles, M., & Bradley, K. (2009). Indulging our gendered selves? Sex segregation by field of studying 44 countries. *American Journal of Sociology, 114*(4), 924–976.

Chen, C., & Farruggia, S. (2002). Culture and adolescent development. In W. J. Lonner, D. L. Dinnel, S. A. Hayes, & D. N. Sattler (Eds.), *Online readings in psychology and culture* (Unit 11, Chapter 2). Bellingham: Center for Cross-Cultural Research, Western Washington University. Retrieved from www.wwu.edu/culture/Chen_Farruggia.html

Chen, J.-L., & Kennedy, C. (2005). Cultural variations in children's coping behavior, TV viewing time, and family functioning. *International Nursing Review, 52*, 186–195.

Cheng, S., & Kwan, K. W. K. (2008). Attachment dimensions and contingencies of self-worth: The moderating role of culture. *Personality and Individual Differences, 45*(6), 509–514.

Cheung, K., & Leung, K. (1998). Indigenous personality measures: Chinese examples. *Journal of Cross-Cultural Psychology, 29*, 233–248.

Chisholm, J. S. (1983). *Navajo infancy.* New York: Aldine.

Chiu, M. L., Feldman, S. S., & Rosenthal, D. A. (1992). The influence of immigration on parental behavior and adolescent distress in Chinese families residing in two western nations. *Journal of Research on Adolescence, 2*(3), 205–239.

Christensen, K., Doblhammer, G., Rau, R., & Vaupel, J. W. (2009). Aging populations: The challenges ahead. *Lancet, 374*(9696), 1196–1208.

Chua, A. (2011). *Battle hymn of the tiger mother.* New York: Penguin Books.

Chun, K. M., Organista, P. B., & Marin. G. (2003). *Acculturation: Advances in theory, measurement, and applied research.* Washington, DC: American Psychological Association.

Cieciuch, J., & Schwartz, S. H. (2012). The number of distinct basic values and their structure assessed by PVQ-40. *Journal of Personality Assessment, 94*(3), 321–328.

*Clark, K. B., & Clark, M. P. (1947). Racial identification and preference in Negro children.* New York: Holt.

Cole, M. (1998). *Cultural psychology: A once and future discipline.* Cambridge, MA: Belknap Press of Havard University.

Cole, M. (2005). Using cross-cultural psychology to design after-school educational activities in different cultural settings. In W. Friedlmeier, P. Chakkarath, & B. Schwarz (Eds.), *Culture and human development* (pp. 53–71). New York: Psychology Press.

Cole, M., & Cole, S. R. (1993). *The development of children* (2nd ed.). New York: Freeman.

Cole, M., & Cole, S. R. (1996). *The development of children* (3rd ed.). New York: Freeman.

Cole, M., & Cole, S. R. (2001). *The development of children* (4th ed.). New York: Worth.

Coleman, J. (2014). Parenting teenagers. In A. Abela & J. Walker (Eds.), *Contemporary issues in family studies: Global perspectives on partnerships, parenting, and support in a changing world* (pp. 203–214). Oxford, UK: Wiley & Sons.

Colin, V. L. (1996). *Human attachment.* New York: McGraw-Hill.

Collier, R., & Sheldon, S. (2008). *Fragmenting fatherhood: A socio-legal study.* Oxford, UK: Hart.

Comer, J. (2006). *When roles reverse: A guide to parenting your parents.* San Francisco: Hampton Roads.

Computer Fraud and Abuse Act (CFAA). (1986). 18 U.S.C. § 1030.

Condon, J. C. (1984). *With respect to the Japanese.* Yarmouth, ME: Intercultural Press.

Connolly, M. (1990). Adrift in the city: A comparative study of street children in Bogota, Colombia and Guatemala City. In N. Boxhill (Ed.), *Homeless children: The watchers and the waiters* (pp. 129–149). New York: Haworth Press.

Cook, P. (1994). Chronic illness beliefs and the role of social networks among Chinese, Indian, and Anglo-Celtic Canadians. *Journal of Cross-Cultural Psychology, 25*, 452–465.

Cooley, C. H. (1902). *Human nature and the social order.* New York: Scribner's.

Corman, H. H., & Escalona, S. K. (1969). Stages in sensori-motor development: A replication study. *Merrill-Palmer Quarterly, 15*(4), 351–361.

Correa-Chavez, M., Mejia-Arauz, R., & Rogoff, B. (2015). *Children learn by observing and contributing to family and community endeavors: A cultural paradigm* (Vol. 49) (Advances in Child Development and Behavior). New York: Academic Press.

Corsaro, W. A. (1988). Routines in the peer culture of American and Italian nursery school children. *Social Education, 61,* 1–14.

Corsaro, W. A., & Eder, D. (1990). Children's peer cultures. *Annual Review in Sociology, 16,* 197–220.

Cosgrove, J. (1990). Towards a working definition of street children. *International Social Work, 33,* 185–192.

Cousins, S. D. (1989). Culture and self-perception in Japan and the United States. *Journal of Personality and Social Psychology, 56,* 124–131.

Cowan, P. A., Powell, D., & Cowen, C. P. (1998). Parenting interventions: A family systems perspective. In W. Damon, I. E. Sigel, & K. A. Renninger (Eds.), *Handbook of child psychology* (5th ed., pp. 3–72). New York: Wiley.

Cox, C. (1993). Hispanic culture and family care of Alzheimer's patients. *Health and Social Work, 18*(2), 92–101.

Crosnoe, R., Crosnoe, R., & Johnson, M. K. (2011). Research on adolescence in the twenty-first century. *Annual Review of Sociology, 37,* 439–460.

Cross, S. E. (1995). Self-construals, coping, and stress in cross-cultural adaptation. *Journal of Cross-Cultural Psychology, 26,* 673–697.

Crystal, D. S., Watanabe, H., & Chen, R. (2000). Reactions to morphological deviance: A comparison of Japanese and American children and adolescents. *Social Development, 9,* 40–61.

Cummings, L. L. (1994). Fighting by the rules: Women street-fighting in Chihuahua, Mexico. *Sex Roles, 30,* 189–198.

Cushner, K. (1990). Cross-cultural psychology and the formal classroom. In R. W. Brislin (Ed.), *Applied cross-cultural psychology* (pp. 98–120). Newbury Park, CA: Sage.

D'Abreu, R. C., Mullis, A. K., & Cook, L. A. (1999). The resiliency of street children in Brazil. *Adolescence, 34*(136), 745–751.

Damon, W. (1973). Early conceptions of positive justice as related to the development of logical operations. *Child Development, 46,* 301–312.

Dasen, P. R. (1972). Cross-cultural Piagetian research: A summary. *Journal of Cross-Cultural Psychology, 7,* 75–85.

Dasen, P. R. (1984). The cross-cultural study of intelligence: Piaget and the Baoule. *International Journal of Psychology, 19,* 407–434.

Dasen, P. R. (2003). Theoretical frameworks in cross-cultural developmental psychology: An attempt at integration. In T. S. Saraswathi (Ed.), *Cross-cultural perspectives in human development: Theory, research, and applications* (pp. 128–165). New Delhi: Sage India.

Dasen, P. R., & Heron, A. (1981). Cross-cultural tests of Piaget's theory. In H. C. Triandis & A. Heron (Eds.), *Handbook of cross-cultural psychology* (Vol. 4, pp. 295–342). Boston: Allyn & Bacon.

Dasen, P. R., Inhelder, B., Lavellee, M., & Retschitzki, J. (1978). *Naissance de l'intelligence chez l'enfant Baoule de Côte d'Ivoire.* Berne: Hans Huber.

Day, N. (2013). *No big deal but this researcher's theory explains everything about how Americans parent.* Retrieved from http://www.slate.com/blogs/how_babies_work/2013/04/10/parental_ethnotheories_and_how_parents_in_america_differ_from_parents_everywhere.html

Day, R. D., & Lamb, M. B. (Eds.). (2004). *Conceptualizing and measuring father involvement.* Mahwah, NJ: Erlbaum.

De Bot, K., & Makoni, S. (2005). *Language and aging in multilingual contexts.* Clevedon, UK: Multilingual Matters, Ltd.

Deering, C. G. (2013). Schizophrenia. In K. D. Keith (Ed.), *The encyclopedia of cross-cultural psychology* (pp. 1129–1131). Hoboken, NJ: Wiley-Blackwell.

Delaney, C. H. (1995). Rites of passage in adolescence. *Adolescence, 30,* 891–897.

Dennis, W. (1973). *Children of the crèche.* New York: Appleton-Century-Crofts.

Dentan, R. K. (1968). *The Semai: A nonviolent people of Malaya.* New York: Holt, Rinehart & Winston.

DeRosier, M. E., & Kupersmidt, J. B. (1991). Costa Rican children's perceptions of their social networks. *Developmental Psychology, 27,* 656–662.

de St. Aubin, E., McAdams, D. P., & Kim, T.-C. (Eds.). (2003). *The generative society: Caring for future generations.* Washington, DC: American Psychological Association.

DeVries, M. W., & Sameroff, A. J. (1984). Culture and temperament: Influences on temperament in three East African societies. *American Journal of Orthopsychiatry, 54,* 83–96.

Dex, S., & Sabates, R. (2015). Multiple risk factors in young children's development. *Children and Society, 29*(2), 95–108.

Dhawan, N., & Roseman, I. J. (1988). *Self-concept across two cultures: India and the United States.* Paper presented at the ninth conference of the International Association for Cross-Cultural Psychology, Newcastle, Australia.

DiLalla, L. F., & Jones, S. (2000). Genetic and environmental influences on temperament in preschoolers. In V. J. Molfese & D. Molfese (Eds.), *Temperament and personality development across the life span* (pp. 33–55). Mahwah, NJ: Erlbaum.

Dion, K. L., & Dion, K. K. (1993). Gender and ethnocultural comparisons in styles of love. *Psychology of Women Quarterly, 17,* 463–473.

Diop, A. M. (1989). The place of the elderly in African society. *Impact of Science on Society, 153,* 93–98.

Doi, T. (1973). *The anatomy of dependence.* Tokyo: Kodansha International.

Doka, K. J., & Mertz, M. E. (1988). The meaning and significance of great-grandparenthood. *Gerontologist, 28*(2), 192–197.

Domino, G. (1992). Cooperation and competition in Chinese and American children. *Journal of Cross-Cultural Psychology, 23*(4), 456–467.

Doucet, A. (2006). *Do men mother? Fatherhood, care, and domestic responsibility.* Toronto: University of Toronto Press.

Draguns, J. G. (1990a). Applications of cross-cultural psychology in the field of mental health. In R. Brislin (Ed.), *Applied cross-cultural psychology* (pp. 302–324). Newbury Park, CA: Sage.

Draguns, J. G. (1990b). Normal and abnormal behavior in cross-cultural perspective: Toward specifying the nature of their relationship. In J. J. Berman (Ed.), *Nebraska symposium on motivation 1989* (pp. 236–277). Lincoln: University of Nebraska Press.

Draguns, J. G. (2001). Pathological and clinical aspects. In L. L. Adler & U. P. Gielen (Eds.), *Cross-cultural topics in psychology* (2nd ed., pp. 247–262). Westport, CT: Praeger.

Draguns, J. G., & Tanaka-Matsumi, J. (2003). Assessment of psychopathology across and within cultures: Issues and findings. *Behaviour Research and Therapy, 41,* 755–776.

Durbin, D. L., Darling, N., Steinberg, L., & Brown, B. B. (1993). Parenting style and peer group membership among European-American adolescents. *Journal of Research on Adolescence, 3,* 87–100.

Dybdahl, R. (1996, August). *The child in context: Exploring childhood in Somalia.* Paper presented at the Twenty-Sixth International Congress of Psychology, Montreal.

Dybdahl, R. (2001). Children and mothers in war: An outcome study of a psychological intervention program. *Child Development, 72,* 1213–1230.

Dybdahl, R. (2002). *Bosnian women and children in war: Experiences, psychological consequences and psychosocial intervention* (Doctoral thesis, University of Tromsø, Norway).

Dybdahl, R. (2005). Psychosocial assistance to civilians in war— the Bosnian experience. In L. Barbanel & R. Sternberg (Eds.), *Psychosocial intervention in times of crisis.* New York: Springer.

Dybdahl, R., & Hundeide, K. (1998). Childhood in the Somali context: Mothers' and children's ideas about childhood and parenthood. *Psychology and Developing Societies, 10,* 131–145.

Eckensberger, L. H. (1994). Moral development and its measurement across cultures. In W. J. Lonner & R. S. Malpass (Eds.), *Psychology and culture* (pp. 71–78). Boston: Allyn & Bacon.

Edwards, C. P. (1989). The transition from infancy to early childhood: A difficult transition, and a difficult theory. In V. R. Bricker & G. H. Gossen (Eds.), *Ethnographic encounters in Southern Mesoamerica: Essays in honor of Evon Z. Vogt, Jr.* (pp. 167–175). Austin: University of Texas.

Edwards, C. P. (1996). Parenting toddlers. In M. H. Bornstein (Ed.), *Handbook of parenting* (Vol. 1, pp. 41–63). Hillsdale, NJ: Erlbaum.

Eisenberg, N., Boehnke, K., Schuhler, P., & Silbereisen, R. K. (1985). The development of prosocial behavior and cognitions in German children. *Journal of Cross-Cultural Psychology, 16,* 69–82.

Eisenberg, N., & Valiente, C. (2004). Elaborations on a theme: Beyond main effects in relations of parenting to children's coping and regulation. *Parenting: Science and Practice, 4,* 319–323.

Elder, G. H. (2000). The life course. In E. F. Borgatta & R. J. V. Montgomery (Eds.), *Encyclopedia of sociology* (2nd ed., Vol. 3, pp. 1614–1622). New York: Macmillan.

Elder, G. H., & Giele, J. Z. (Eds.). (2009). *The craft of life course research.* New York: Guilford Press.

Elder, G. H., Modell, J., & Parke, R. D. (Eds.). (1993). *Children in time and place.* New York: Cambridge University Press.

Eldering, L. (1995). Child rearing in bicultural settings: A culture-ecological approach. *Psychology and Developing Societies, 7,* 133–153.

Elkholy, A. (1981). The Arab American family. In C. Mindel & P. Habenstein (Eds.), *Ethnic families in America: Patterns and variations* (pp. 145–162). New York: Elsevier.

Elkind, D. (1988). *The hurried child: Growing up too fast too soon.* Reading, MA: Addison-Wesley.

Ellis, R. (1994). *The study of second-language acquisition.* Oxford, UK: Oxford University Press.

Ellison, P. T. (Ed.). (2001). *Reproductive ecology and human evolution.* New York: Aldine de Gruyter.

Ember, C. R., & Ember, M. (2000). *Cross-cultural research methods.* Walnut Creek, CA: AltaMira Press.

Ember, C. R., & Ember, M. (2003). *Cultural anthropology* (11th ed.). Englewood Cliffs, NJ: Prentice Hall.

Emerick, Y. (2000). *The holy Qur'an in today's English.* Baltimore, MD: Amirah.

Engels, J. (1993). *Pocket guide to pediatric assessment* (2nd ed.). St. Louis, MO: Mosby.

England, P., Hermsen, J. L., & Cotter, D. (2000). The devaluation of women's work: A comment on Tam. *American Journal of Sociology, 105,* 1741–1751.

Engle, P. L., Zeitlin, M., Medrano, Y., & Garcia, L. M. (1996). Growth consequences of low-income Nicaraguan mothers' theories about feeding 1-year-olds. In S. Harkness & C. M. Super (Eds.), *Parents' cultural belief systems* (pp. 428–446). New York: Guilford Press.

Enright, R. D., Franklin, C. C., & Manheim, L. A. (1980). Children's distributive justice reasoning: A standardized and objective scale. *Developmental Psychology, 16,* 193–202.

Epstein, J. L. (1983). Longitudinal effects of family–school–person interactions on student outcomes. *Research in Sociology of Education and Socialization, 4,* 101–107.

Erikson, E. H. (1963). *Childhood and society* (2nd ed.). New York: Norton.

Erikson, E. H. (1982). *The life cycle completed.* New York: Norton.

Erikson, E. H., Erikson, J. M., & Kivnick, H. Q. (1986). *Vital involvement in old age.* New York: Norton.

Erlinghagen, M., & Hank, K. (2006). The participation of older Europeans in volunteer work. *Ageing and Society, 26*(4), 567–584.

Evans, G. W., Li, D., & Whipple, S. P. (2013). Cumulative risk and child development. *Psychological Bulletin, 139*(6), 1342–1396.

Falbo, T. (1991). The impact of grandparents on children's outcomes in China. *Marriage and Family Review, 16*(3–4), 369–376.

Farver, J. A. M., Welles-Nyström, B., Frosch, D. Wimbarti, S., & Hoppe-Graff, S. (1997). Toy stories: Aggression in children's narratives in the United States, Sweden, Germany, and Indonesia. *Journal of Cross-Cultural Psychology, 28*(4), 393–420.

Farver, J. A. M., & Wimbarti, S. (1995). Indonesian children's play with their mothers and older siblings. *Child Development, 66,* 1493–1503.

Fasold, R. (1999). *Ebonic need not be English (ERIC issue paper).* Washington, DC: ERIC Clearinghouse on Languages and Linguistics.

Fay, W. B. (1993). Families in the 1990s. *Marketing Research, 5*(1), 47.

Ferguson, E. D. H., Maurer, J. A., Matthews, S. B., & Peng, K. P. (2013). Asian culture in transition: Is it related to reported parenting styles and transitivity of simple choices? *Journal of Applied Social Psychology, 43*(4), 730–740.

Ferri, C. P. (2005). Global prevalence of dementia: A Delphi consensus study. *Lancet, 366*(9503), 2112–2117.

Fingerman, K. L. (2004). The role of offspring and children-in-law in grandparents' relationships with grandchildren. *Journal of Family Issues, 25*, 1026–1049.

Fischer, R., Ferreira, M. C., Assmar, E., Redford, P., Harb, C., Glazer, S., et al. (2009). Individualism-collectivism as descriptive norms: Development of a subjective norm approach to cultural measurement. *Journal of Cross-Cultural Psychology, 40*, 187–213.

Fishbein, H. D. (1984). *The psychology of infancy and childhood: Evolutionary and cross-cultural perspectives*. Hillsdale, NJ: Erlbaum.

Fitzgerald, M. H. (1990). The interplay of culture and symptoms: Menstrual symptoms among Samoans. *Medical Anthropology, 12*, 145–167.

Flanagan, C. A., & Eccles, J. S. (1993). Changes in parents' work status and adolescents' adjustment to school. *Child Development, 64*, 246–258.

Fleming, J., Watson, C., McDonald, D., & Alexander, K. (1991). Drug use patterns in Northern Territory Aboriginal communities, 1986–1987. *Drug and Alcohol Review, 10*, 367–380.

Flores, G. (2000). Culture and the patient–physician relationship: Achieving cultural competency in health care. *Journal of Pediatrics, 136*, 14–23.

Flouri, E. (2005). *Fathering and child outcomes*. New York: Wiley & Sons.

Francis-Connally, E. (2000). Toward an understanding of mothering: A comparison of two motherhood stages. *American Journal of Occupational Therapy, 54*, 281–289.

Francoeur, R. T., & Noonan, R. J. (2004). Global trends: Some final impressions. In R. T. Francoeur & R. J. Noonan (Eds.), *The continuum complete international encyclopedia of sexuality* (pp. 1373–1376). New York: Continuum. http://www.kinseyinstitute.org/ccies/ Retrieved from http://www.indiana.edu/~kinsey/ccies/globaltrends.php

Frankish, K., & Evans, J. St. B. T. (2009). The duality of mind: An historical perspective. In J. St. B. T. Evans & K. Frankish (Eds.), *In two minds: Dual processes and beyond* (pp. 1–30). Oxford, UK: Oxford University Press.

Frazier, C. L., & Glascock, A. P. (1994). Aging and old age in cross-cultural perspective. In L. L. Adler & U. P. Gielen (Eds.), *Cross–cultural topics in psychology* (pp. 103–111). Westport, CT: Praeger.

Freeman, D. (1983). *Margaret Mead and Samoa*. Cambridge, MA: Harvard University Press.

Friedlmeier, W., Chakkarath, P., & Schwarz, B. (Eds.). (2005). *Culture and human development*. New York: Psychology Press.

Friedman, A., Todd, J., & Kariuki, P. W. (1995). Cooperative and competitive behavior of urban and rural children in Kenya. *Journal of Cross-Cultural Psychology, 26*(4), 374–383.

Friedman, S. L., & Wachs, T. D. (Eds.). (1999). *Conceptualization and assessment of environment across the lifespan*. Washington DC: American Psychological Association.

Furnham, A., Kirkcaldy, B. D., & Lynn, R. (1994). National attitudes to competitiveness, money, and work among young people: First, second, and third world differences. *Human Relations, 47*(1), 119–132.

Gander, M. J., & Gardiner, H. W. (1981). *Child and adolescent development*. Boston: Little, Brown.

Garbarino, J. (1985). *Adolescent development: An ecological perspective*. Columbus, OH: Merrill.

Garbarino, J. (2000). The soul of fatherhood. *Marriage and Family Review, 29*, 11–21.

Gardiner, H. W. (1966). *Newspapers as personalities: A study of the British national daily press*. (Unpublished doctoral dissertation, University of Manchester, UK).

Gardiner, H. W. (1994). Child development. In L. L. Adler & U. P. Gielen (Eds.), *Cross-cultural topics in psychology* (pp. 61–72). New York: Praeger.

Gardiner, H. W. (1995, March/April). The life of a Buddhist monk. *Calliope: World history for young people*. Peterborough, NH: Cobblestone.

Gardiner, H. W. (1996). *Cross-cultural content in contemporary developmental textbooks*. Paper presented at the Thirteenth Congress of the International Association for Cross-Cultural Psychology, Montreal, Canada.

Gardiner, H. W. (2001a). Child and adolescent development. In L. L. Adler & U. P. Gielen (Eds.), *Cross-cultural topics in psychology* (2nd ed., pp. 63–79). Westport, CT: Greenwood.

Gardiner, H. W. (2001b). Culture, context, and development. In D. Matsumoto (Ed.), *The handbook of culture and psychology* (pp. 101–117). New York: Oxford University Press.

Gardiner, H. W. (2016). Cross-cultural human development: Follow the yellow brick road In search of new approaches for the 21st century. In U. P. Gielen & J. L. Roopnarine (Eds.), *Childhood and adolescence* (2nd ed., pp. 464–471). Westport, CT: Greenwood Press.

Gardiner, H. W. (2008). *Lives across cultures: Cross-cultural human development* (5th ed.). Boston, MA: Allyn & Bacon.

Gardiner, H. W., & Gardiner, O. S. (1991). Women in Thailand. In L. L. Adler (Ed.), *Women in cross-cultural perspective* (pp. 174–187). New York: Praeger.

Gardiner, H. W., & Mutter, J. D. (1994). *Measuring multicultural awareness and identity: A model*. Paper presented at the twenty-third annual meeting of the Society for Cross-Cultural Research, Santa Fe, NM.

Garstein, M. A., & Rothbart, M. K. (2003). Studying infant temperament via the Revised Infant Behavior Questionnaire. *Infant Behavior and Development, 26*, 64–86.

Gauvain, M., & Cole, M. (2008). *Readings on the development of children* (5th ed.). New York: Worth.

Georgas, J., Berry, J. W., van de Vijver, F. J. R., Kagitcibasi, C., & Pooringa, Y. H. (2006). *Families across cultures: A 30-nation psychological study*. Cambridge, UK: Cambridge University Press.

Gerstorf, D., Hoppmann, C. A., Anstey, K. J., Luszcz, M. A. (2009). Dynamic links of cognitive functioning among married couples:

Longitudinal evidence from the Australian longitudinal study of ageing. *Psychology and Ageing, 24*(2), 296–309.

Gibbons, J. (2013). Adolescence. In K. D. Keith (Ed.), *The encyclopedia of cross-cultural psychology* (pp. 23–32). Hoboken, NJ: Wiley-Blackwell.

Gibbons, J. L., Stiles, D. A., Perez-Prada, E., Shkodriani, G. M., & Medina, M. (1996, February). *Adolescents' beliefs about women's and men's roles in Iceland, Mexico, Spain, and the United States.* Paper presented at the 25th annual meeting of the Society for Cross-Cultural Research, Pittsburgh, PA.

Gibson, J. T., Westwood, M. J., Ishiyama, F. I., Borgen, W. A., Showalter, S. M., Al-Sarraf, Q., et al. (1991). Youth and culture: A seventeen nation study of perceived problems and coping strategies. *International Journal for the Advancement of Counselling, 14*, 203–216.

Gielen, U., & Jeshmaridian, S. S. (1999). Lev S. Vygotsky: The man and the era. *International Journal of Group Tensions, 28*(3), 273–301.

Gielen, U., & Roopnarine, J. (2004). Families in global perspective. Boston: Pearson.

Gilligan, C. (1982). *In a different voice: Psychological theory and women's development.* Cambridge, MA: Harvard University Press.

Gire, J. T. (2002). How death imitates life: Cultural influences on conceptions of death and dying. In W. J. Lonner, D. L. Dinnel, S. A. Hayes, & D. N. Sattler (Eds.), *Online Readings in Psychology and Culture* (Unit 14, Chapter 2), Bellingham: Center for Cross-Cultural Research, Western Washington University. Retrieved from http://www.wwu.edu/culture/gire.html

Gladwin, T., & Sarason, S. B. (1953). *Truk: Man in paradise.* (Viking Fund Publications in Anthropology, No. 20). New York: Wenner-Gren Foundation for Anthropological Research. Retrieved from http://onlinelibrary.wiley.com/doi/10.1525/aa.1955.57.5.02a00540/pdf

Goldberg, S. (1972). Infant care and growth in urban Zambia. *Human Development, 15*, 77–89.

Golombok, S. (2002). Parenting and contemporary reproductive technologies. In M. H. Bornstein (Ed.), *Handbook of parenting* (2nd ed., Vol. 3, pp. 339–360). Mahwah, NJ: Erlbaum.

Gonzales, G. F., & Villena, A. (1996). Body mass index and age at menarche in Peruvian children living at high altitudes and at sea level. *Human Biology, 68*(2), 265–276.

Goodnow, J. J. (1990). The socialization of cognition. In J. W. Stigler, R. A. Shweder, & G. Herdt (Eds.), *Cultural psychology: Essays on comparative human development* (pp. 259–286). Cambridge, UK: Cambridge University Press.

Goodnow, J. J., & Bethon, G. (1966). Piaget's tasks: The effects of schooling on intelligence. *Child Development, 37*, 573–582.

Gopal-McNicol, S. (1995). A cross-cultural examination of racial identity and racial preference of preschool children in the West Indies. *Journal of Cross-Cultural Psychology, 26*, 141–152.

Gotowiec, A., & Beiser, M. (1993). Aboriginal children's mental health: Unique challenges. *Canada's Mental Health, 41*(4), 7–11.

Green, E. G. T., Deschamps, J.-C., & Paez, D. (2005). Variation in individualism and collectivism within and between 20 countries: A typological analysis. *Journal of Cross-Cultural Psychology, 36*(3), 321–339.

Green, J. A., Irwin, J. R., & Gustafson, G. E. (2000). Acoustic cry analysis, neonatal status and long-term developmental outcomes. In R. G. Barr, B. Hopkins, & J. A. Green (Eds.), *Crying as a sign, a symptom, and a signal* (pp. 137–156). New York: Cambridge University Press.

Green, M., & Piel, J. A. (2010). *Theories of development: A comparative approach* (2nd ed.). Boston: Allyn & Bacon.

Greenfield, P. M., & Cocking, R. R. (1994). *Cross-cultural roots of minority child development.* Hillsdale, NJ: Erlbaum.

Gregg, G. S. (2005). *The Middle East: A cultural psychology.* New York: Oxford University Press.

Gregg, G. S. (2007). *Culture and identity in a Muslim society.* New York: Oxford University Press.

Grossman, B., Wirt, R., & Davids, A. (1985). Self-esteem, ethnic identity, and behavioral adjustment among Anglo and Chicano adolescents in West Texas. *Journal of Adolescence, 8*, 57–68.

Grossmann, K. E., Grossman, K. G., & Waters, E. (Eds.). (2005). *Attachment from infancy to adulthood: The major longitudinal studies.* New York: Guilford Press.

Grusec, J. E. (2002). Parental socialization and children's acquisition of values. In M. H. Bornstein (Ed.), *Handbook of parenting* (Vol. 5, 2nd ed., pp. 143–167). Mahwah, NJ: Erlbaum.

Grusec, J. E., & Hastings, P. D. (Eds.). (2008). *Handbook of socialization.* New York: Guilford Press.

Gurung, R. A. R. (2011). Cultural influences on health. In K. D. Keith (Ed.), *Cross-cultural psychology: Contemporary themes and perspectives* (pp. 260–273). Chichester, UK: Wiley-Blackwell.

Haan, N. (1991). Moral development and action from a social constructivist perspective. In W. M. Kurtines & J. L. Gewirtz (Eds.), *Handbook of moral behavior and development, Volume 1: Theory* (pp. 251–273). Hillsdale, NJ: Erlbaum.

Haan, N., Aerts, E., & Cooper, B. B. (1985). *On moral grounds: The search for a practical morality.* New York: New York University Press.

Hagestad, G. O. (2000). Adult intergenerational relationships (Chap. 4). In *United Nations Economic Commission for Europe (UNECE)* (Ed.), *Generations and gender programme—Exploring future research and data collection options.* New York/Geneva: Author.

Hakoyama, M., & MaloneBeach, E. E. (2013). Predictors of grandparent–grandchild closeness: An ecological perspective. *Journal of Intergenerational Relationships, 11*(1), 32–49.

Hakuta, K., Bialystok, E., & Wiley, E. (2003). Critical evidence: A test of the critical-period hypothesis for second-language acquisition. *Psychological Science, 14*, 31–38.

Hall, G. S. (1904). *Adolescence.* New York: Appleton-Century-Crofts.

Hall, G. S. (1922). *Senescence: The last half of life.* New York: Appleton-Century-Crofts.

Hamilton, C. E. (2000). Continuity and discontinuity of attachment from infancy through adolescence. *Child Development, 71*, 690–694.

Hamon, R. R., & Ingoldsby, B. B. (Eds.). (2003). *Mate selection across cultures.* Thousand Oaks, CA: Sage.

Hampel, P., & Petermann, F. (2006). Perceived stress, coping, and adjustment in adolescents. *Journal of Adolescent Health, 38,* 409–415.

Hao, Z., & Chen, S. (2014). *Social issues in China: Gender, ethnicity, labor, and the environment.* New York: Springer.

Harkness, S. (2005). Themes and variations: Parental ethnotheories in seven Western cultures. In K. Rubin (Ed.), *Parental beliefs, parenting, and child development in cross-cultural perspectives* (pp. 61–80). New York: Psychology Press.

Harkness, S., Hughes, M., Muller, B., & Super, C. M. (2005). Entering the developmental niche: Mixed methods in an intervention program for inner-city children. In T. S. Weisner (Ed.), *Discovering successful pathways in children's development: Mixed methods in the study of childhood and family life* (pp. 329–358). Chicago: The University of Chicago Press.

Harkness, S., & Keefer, C. H. (2000). Contributions of cross-cultural psychology to research and interventions in education and health. *Journal of Cross-Cultural Psychology, 31,* 92–109.

Harkness, S., Moscardino, U., Bermudez, M. R., Zylicz, P. O., Welles-Nystrom, B., Blom, M., et al. (2006). Mixed methods in international collaborative research: The experiences of the international study of parents, children, and schools. *Cross-Cultural Research, 40,* 1–18.

Harkness, S., & Super, C. M. (1985). The cultural context of gender segregation in children's peer groups. *Child Development, 56,* 219–224.

Harkness, S., & Super, C. M. (1995). Culture and parenting. In M. Bornstein (Ed.), *Handbook of parenting* (Vol. 2, pp. 211–234). Hillsdale, NJ: Erlbaum.

Harkness, S., & Super, C. M. (Eds.). (1996). *Parents' cultural belief systems: Their origins, expressions, and consequences.* New York: Guilford Press.

Harkness, S., & Super, C. M. (2003). Culture and parenting. In M. Bornstein (Ed.), *Handbook of parenting* (2nd ed., Vol. 2, pp. 253–280). Mahwah, NJ: Erlbaum.

Harkness, S., & Super, C. M. (2012). The cultural organization of children's environments. In L. C. Mayes & M. Lewis (Eds.), *The Cambridge handbook of environment in human development* (pp. 498–516). Cambridge, UK: Cambridge University Press.

Harkness, S., & Super, C. M. (2015). Beyond the randomized control trial: Mixed methods that matter for children's healthy development in cultural context. In M. C. Hay (Ed.), *Methods that matter: Integrating mixed methods for more effective social science research* (pp. 130–156). Chicago: The University of Chicago Press.

Harkness, S., & Super, C. M., & Mavridis, C. J. (2011). Parental ethnotheories about children's socioemotional development. In X. Chen & K. H. Rubin (Eds.), *Socioemotional development in cultural context* (pp. 73–98). New York: Guilford Press.

Harkness, S., Super, C. M., Mavridis, C. J., Barry, O., & Zeitlin, M. (2013). Culture and early childhood development: Implications for policy and programs. In P. R. Britto, P. L. Engle, & C. M. Super (Eds.), *Handbook of early childhood development research and its impact on global policy* (pp. 142–160). New York: Oxford University Press.

Harlow, H. F., & Harlow, M. K. (1962). Social deprivation in monkeys. *Scientific American, 207,* 136–146.

Harlow, H. F., & Zimmermann, R. R. (1959). Affectional responses in the infant monkey. *Science, 130,* 421–432.

Harris, J. R. (2006). *No two alike.* New York: Norton.

Harrison, A. O., Stewart, R. B., Myambo, K., & Teveraishe, C. (1995). Perceptions of social networks among adolescents from Zimbabwe and the United States. *Journal of Black Psychology, 21,* 382–407.

Hashim, I. H., & Zhiliang, Y. (2003). Cultural and gender differences in perceiving stressors: A cross-cultural investigation of African and Western college students in Chinese colleges. *Stress and Health, 19,* 217–225.

Hatfield, E., & Rapson, R. L. (2005). *Love and sex: Cross-cultural perspectives.* Lanham, MD: University Press of America.

Heath, S. B., Street, B. V., & Mills, M. (2008). *On ethnography: Approaches to language and literary research.* New York: Teachers College Press.

Heinicke, C. M. (1995). Determinants of the transition to parenting. In M. H. Bornstein (Ed.), *Handbook of parenting* (Vol. 3, pp. 277–303). Mahwah, NJ: Erlbaum.

Hendrie, H. C., Gao, S., & Baiyewu, O. (2000). A comparison of symptoms of behavioral disturbances in Yoruba and African American individuals with dementia. *International Psychogeriatrics, 12*(Suppl. 1), 403–408.

Hendry, J. (1986). *Becoming Japanese.* Honolulu: University of Hawaii Press.

Hendry, J. (1993). Becoming Japanese: The arenas and agents of socialization. In R. H. Wozniak (Ed.), *Worlds of childhood reader.* New York: HarperCollins.

Herman, D. R., Taylor, B. M., Adams, E., Cunningham-Sabo, L., Duran, N., Johnson, D., & Yakes, E. (2014). Life course perspective: Evidence for nutrition. *Maternal and Child Health Journal, 18*(2), 450–461.

Hindi, G. (2014). The effects of globalization on identity [Special issue]. *European Scientific Journal, 1,* 531–538.

Hines, M. (2004). *Brain gender.* New York: Oxford University Press.

Ho, D. Y. F. (2000). Dialectical thinking: Neither Eastern nor Western. *American Psychologist, 55,* 1064–1065.

Hobbs, D., & Wright, R. (Eds.). (2006). *The Sage handbook of fieldwork.* London: Sage.

Hofstede, G. (1996). *Masculinity, religion, gender and sex.* Paper presented at 13th Congress of the International Association for Cross-Cultural Psychology, Montreal, Canada.

Hofstede, G. (2001). *Cultures consequences: Comparing values, behavior, institutions, and organizations across cultures* (2nd ed.). Thousand Oaks, CA: Sage.

Hofstede, G., & Hofstede, G. J. (2004). *Cultures and organizations: Software of the mind* (2nd ed.). New York: McGraw-Hill.

Hofstede, G., Hofstede, G. J., & Minkov, M. (2010). *Cultures and organizations: Software of the mind* (3rd ed.). New York: McGraw-Hill.

Hoghughi, M., & Long, N. (Eds.). (2004). *Handbook of parenting.* Thousand Oaks, CA: Sage.

Hollos, M., & Richards, F. A. (1993). Gender-associated development of formal operations in Nigerian adolescents. *Ethos, 21,* 24–52.

Honigman, B. (2012, November 29). 100 Fascinating social media statistics and figures from 2012. *The Huffington Post.* Retrieved from http://www.huffingtonpost.com/brian-honigman/100-fascinating-social-me_b_2185281.html

Hoope-Bender, P., Campbell, J., Fauveau. V., & Matthews, Z. (2011). The state of the world's midwifery 2011: Delivering health, saving lives. *International Journal of Gynecology and Obstetrics, 114*(3), 211–212.

Horn, J. L., & Cattell, R. B. (1967). Age differences in fluid and crystalized intelligence. *Acta Psychologica, 26*, 107–129.

Hrdy, S. (1999). *Mother nature: Material instincts and how they shape the human species.* New York: Ballantine Group.

Hrdy, S. (2009). *Mothers and others: The evolutionary origins of mutual understanding.* Cambridge, MA: Harvard University Press.

Hsu, F. L. K. (1985). The self in cross-cultural perspective. In A. J. Marsella, G. DeVos, & F. L. K. Hsu (Eds.), *Culture and self: Asian and Western perspectives* (pp. 24–55). New York: Tavistock.

Hsu, F. L. K., Watrous, B. G., & Lord, E. M. (1961). Culture pattern and adolescent behaviour. *International Journal of Social Psychiatry, 7*, 33–53.

Hu, Y.-H. (1995). Elderly suicide risk in family context: A critique of the Asian family care model. *Journal of Cross-Cultural Psychology, 10*, 199–217.

Huebner, A. M., & Garrod, A. C. (1993). Moral reasoning among Tibetan monks: A study of Buddhist adolescents and young adults in Nepal. *Journal of Cross-Cultural Psychology, 24*, 167–185.

Huntsinger, C. S., & Jose, P. E. (2006). A longitudinal investigation of personality and social adjustment among Chinese American and European American Adolescents. *Child Development, 77*, 1309–1324.

Hymel, S., & Swearer, S. M. (2015). Four decades of research on school bullying: An introduction [Special issue]. *American Psychologist, 70*(4), 293–299.

Ibrahim, A.-S. (2013). Arab world psychology. In K. D. Keith (Eds.), *The encyclopedia of cross-cultural psychology* (pp. 88–94). Hoboken, NJ: Wiley-Blackwell.

Inatani, F., Maehara, T., & Tasuda, A. (2005). Japanese grandparenthood and psychological well-being. *Hellenic Journal of Psychology, 2*(3), 199–224.

InCultureParent Staff. (2012, March 5). Breastfeeding around the World. *InCultureParent* [Online magazine]. Retrieved from www.incultureparent.com/2012/03/breastfeeding-around-the-world

Inhelder, B., & Piaget, J. (1959). *The early growth of logic in the child: Classification and seriation.* New York: Harper & Row.

Isralowitz, R. E., & Hong, O. T. (1990). Singapore youth: The impact of social status on perceptions of adolescent problems. *Adolescence, 98*, 357–362.

Iwasa, H., Masui, Y., Gondo, Y., Inagaki, H., Kawaai, C., & Suzuki, T. (2008). Personality and all-cause mortality among older adults dwelling in a Japanese community: A five-year population-based prospective cohort study. *American Journal of Geriatric Psychiatry, 16*, 399–405.

Jablensky, A., Sartorius, N., Ernberg, G., Anker, M., Korten, A., Cooper, J. E., et al. (1992). Schizophrenia: Manifestations, incidence and course in different cultures. A World Health Organization ten-country study. *Psychological Medicine Monograph Supplement, 20*, 1–97.

Jacobson, K. (2002). ADHD in cross-cultural perspective: Some empirical results. *American Anthropologist, 104*, 283–286.

Jahoda, G. (1982). *Psychology and anthropology: A psychological perspective.* London: Academic Press.

Jahoda, G. (1986). A cross-cultural perspective on developmental psychology. *International Journal of Behavioral Development, 9*, 417–437.

Jahoda, G. (2009). The climate for and status of cross-cultural psychology in the 1960s. *Online Readings in Psychology and Culture, 1*(1). Retrieved from http://dx.doi.org/10.9707/2307-0919.1001

Jahoda, G., & Krewer, B. (1997). History of cross-cultural and cultural psychology. In J. W. Berry, Y. H. Poortinga, & J. Pandey (Eds.), *Handbook of cross-cultural psychology: Theory and method* (Vol. 1, pp. 1–42). Boston: Allyn & Bacon.

Jang, K. L., Lively, W. J., & Vernon, P. A. (1996). Heritability of the big five personality dimensions and their facet: A twin study. *Journal of Personality, 64*, 577–591.

Jenni, O. G., & O'Connor, B. B. (2005). Children's sleep: An interplay between culture and biology. *Pediatrics, 115*, 204–216.

Jensen, L. (2003). Coming of age in a multicultural world: Globalization and adolescent cultural identity formation. *Applied Developmental Science, 7*, 188–195.

Jensen, L. A. (2011). Navigating local and global worlds: Opportunities and risks for adolescent cultural identity development. *Psychological Studies, 56*, 62–70.

Jiang, D., Chan, M. C. H., Lu, M., & Fung, H. H. (2015). Grandparenthood and the changing nature of social relationships. In N. Pachana (Ed.), *Encyclopedia of geropsychology* (pp. 1–8). New York: Springer.

Johnson, J. S., & Newport, E. L. (1989). Critical period effects in second-language learning: The influence of maturational state on the acquisition of English as a second language. *Cognitive Psychology, 21*, 60–99.

Johnson, W., McGue, M., & Krueger, R. F. (2005). Personality stability in late adulthood: A behavioral genetic analysis. *Journal of Personality, 73*, 523–551.

Jordan, B. (1978). *Birth in four cultures: A cross-cultural investigation of childbirth in Yucatan, Holland, Sweden and the United States.* St. Albans, VT: Eden Women's Publications.

Jordan, B., & Davis-Floyd, R. (1993). *Birth in four cultures: A cross-cultural investigation of childbirth in Yucatan, Holland, Sweden and the United States* (4th ed.). Prospect Heights, IL: Waveland Press.

Judge, T. A., Erez, A., Bono, J. E., & Thoresen, C. J. (2002). Are measures of self-esteem, neuroticism, locus of control, and generalized self-efficacy indicators of a common core construct? *Journal of Personality and Social Psychology, 83*, 693–710.

Kalu, W., & Kalu, O. (1993). Nigeria. In L. L. Adler (Ed.), *International handbook on gender roles* (pp. 228–243). Westport, CT: Greenwood Press.

Kamara, A. I., & Easley, J. A., Jr. (1977). Is the rate of cognitive development uniform across cultures? A methodological critique with new evidence from Themne children. In P. R. Dasen (Ed.), *Piagetian psychology: Cross-cultural contributions* (pp. 26–63). New York: Gardner/Wiley.

Kasuya, H. (2002). Bilingual context for language development. In S. Blum-Kulka & C. E. Snow (Eds.), *Talking to adults: The contribution of multi-party discourse to language acquisition* (pp. 299–325). Mahwah, NJ: Erlbaum.

Kazarian, S. S., & Evans, D. R. (2001). *Handbook of cultural health psychology*. San Diego: Academic Press.

Kazdin, A. E. (Ed.). (2000). *Encyclopedia of psychology*. Washington, DC: American Psychological Association.

Keel, P. K., & Klump, K. L. (2003). Are eating-disorder culture-bound syndromes? Implications for conceptualizing their etiology. *Psychological Bulletin, 5,* 747–769.

Keith, K. D. (2013). *The encyclopedia of cross-cultural psychology* (3 vols.). Hoboken, NJ: Wiley-Blackwell.

Keller, H., & Greenfield, P. M. (2000). History and future of development in cross-cultural psychology. *Journal of Cross-Cultural Psychology, 31,* 52–62.

Kelly, M. (1977). Papua New Guinea and Piaget—An eight-year study. In P. R. Dasen (Ed.), *Piagetian psychology: Cross-cultural contributions* (pp. 169–202). New York: Gardner Press.

Kemper, S. (1992). Language and aging. In F. I. M. Craik & T. A. Salthouse (Eds.), *The handbook of aging and cognition* (pp. 213–270). Hillsdale, NJ: Erlbaum.

Kenkel, W. F. (1985). *The family in perspective* (5th ed.). Houston: Cap and Gown Press.

Kim, K., & Won, H. (1997). Students' stress in China, Japan and Korea: Transcultural study. *International Journal of Social Psychiatry, 43,* 87–94.

Kim, S., Wang, Y., Orozco-Lapray, D., Shen, Y., & Murtuza, M. (2013). Does 'tiger parenting' exist? Parenting profiles of Chinese Americans and adolescent development outcomes. *Asian American Journal of Psychology, 4*(10), 7–18.

Kim, U., Yang, K. S., & Hwang, K. K. (Eds.). (2006). *Indigenous and cultural psychology: Understanding people in context*. New York: Springer.

Kim, Y. S., & Leventhal, B. (2008). Bullying and suicide: A review. *International Journal of Adolescent Medicine and Health, 20,* 133–154.

Kimm, S. Y., Glynn, N. W., Obarzanek, E., Kriska, A. M., Daniels, S. R., Barton, B. A., et al. (2005). Relation between the changes in physical activity and body-mass index during adolescence: A multicentre longitudinal study. *Lancet,* www.thelancet.com*366*(9482), 301–307.

Kinsella, K., & Velkoff, V. A. (2001). U.S. Census Bureau, Series P95/01-1, *An Aging World: 2001*. Washington, DC: U.S. Government Printing Office. Retrieved from http://www.census.gov/prod/2001pubs/p95-01-1.pdf

Kirmayer, L. J., & Minas, H. (2000). The future of cultural psychiatry: An international perspective. *Canadian Journal of Psychiatry, 45,* 438–446.

Kitayama, S., & Markus, H. (Eds.). (1994). *Culture and emotion*. Washington, DC: American Psychological Association.

Klineberg, O. (1980). Historical perspectives: Cross-cultural psychology before 1960. In H. C. Triandis & W. W. Lambert (Eds.), *Handbook of cross-cultural psychology* (Vol. 1, pp. 1–14). Boston: Allyn & Bacon.

Knafo, A., & Schwartz, S. H. (2003). Parenting and adolescents' accuracy in perceiving parental values. *Child Development, 74*(2), 595–611.

Knerr, W., Gardner, F., & Culver, L. (2011). *Reducing harsh and abusive parenting and increasing positive parenting in low- and middle-income countries: A systematic review*. Pretoria, South Africa: Oak Foundation and South African Medical Research Council.

Knickmeyer, R. C., & Baron-Cohen, S. (2006). Fetal testosterone and sex differences. *Early Human Development, 82,* 755–760.

Koerner, E. F. K. (2000). Towards a 'full pedigree' of the 'Sapir-Whorf hypothesis': From Locke to Lucy. In M. Pütz & M. H. Verspoor (Eds.), *Explorations in linguistic relativity* [Current issues in linguistic theory 199]. Amsterdam: John Benjamins. doi:10.1075/cilt.199.03koe

Kohlberg, L. (1981). *Essays on moral development* (Vol. 1). New York: Harper & Row.

Kohlberg, L., & Gilligan, C. (1971). The adolescent as philosopher: The discovery of self in a post-conventional world. *Daedalus, 100,* 1051–1086.

Kornhaber, A. (1996). *Contemporary grandparenting*. Thousand Oaks, CA: Sage.

Kostelny, K., & Garbarino, J. (1994). Coping with the consequences of living in danger: The case of Palestinian children and youth. *International Journal of Behavioral Development, 17,* 595–611.

Krishnan, L. (1999). Socialization and cognitive–moral influences on justice rule preferences: The case of Indian culture. In T. S. Saraswathi (Ed.), *Culture, socialization and human development: Theory, research, and applications in India*. Thousand Oaks, CA: Sage.

Krishnan, L. (2011). Culture and distributive justice: General comments and some insights from the Indian context. In G. Misra (Ed.), *Handbook of psychology in India* (pp. 205–225). New Delhi: Oxford University Press.

Kroeber, A. L., & Kluckhohn, C. (1952). *Culture, part III:* Papers of the Peabody Museum of Harvard University. Cambridge, MA: Harvard University Press.

Kuhl, P. K., Conboy, B. T., Coffey-Corina, S., Padden, D., Rivera-Gaxiola, M., & Nelson, T. (2008). Phonetic learning as a pathway to language: New data and native language magnet theory expanded (NLM-e). *Philosophical Transactions of the Royal Society B, 363,* 979–1000.

Kuhn, M. H., & McPartland, T. S. (1954). An empirical investigation of self-attitudes. *American Sociological Review, 19*(1), 68–76.

Kumar, V., & Kanth, S. (2007). Bride burning in India. In P. M. Verity (Ed.), *Violence and aggression around the globe* (pp. 147–177). Hauppauge, NY: Nova Science.

Kunzmann, U., & Baltes, P. B. (2005). The psychology of wisdom. *Personality and Social Psychology Bulletin, 29,* 1104–1119.

Kwan, V. S. Y., Bond, M. H., & Singelis, T. M. (1997). Pancultural explanations for life-satisfaction: Adding relationship harmony to self-esteem. *Journal of Personality and Social Psychology, 73,* 1038–1051.

Labouvie-Vief, G. (1986). *Mind and self in lifespan development.* Paper presented at the annual meeting of the Gerontological Association of America, Chicago.

Laland, K., & O'Brien, M. (2011, September). *Cultural niche construction*. 27th Altenberg Workshop in Theoretical Biology, Konrad Lorenz Institute for Evolution and Cognition Research, Altenberg, Austria.

Lalor, K. J. (1999). Street children: A comparative perspective. *Child Abuse and Neglect*, 23, 759–770.

Lamb, M. E. (Ed.). (1987). *The role of the father: Cross-cultural perspectives*. Hillsdale, NJ: Erlbaum.

Lamb, M. E. (Ed.). (2004). *The role of the father in child development* (4th ed.). New York: Wiley & Sons.

Lambert, L. (2014). *Research for indigenous survival: Indigenous research nethodology in the behavioral sciences*. Pablo, MT: Salish Kootenai College.

Lambert, W. W. (1971). Cross-cultural backgrounds to personality development and the socialization of aggression: Findings from the six cultures study. In W. Lambert & R. Weisbrod (Eds.), *Comparative perspectives on social psychology* (pp. 49–61). Boston: Little, Brown.

Lancy, D. (1980). Work and play: The Kpelle children during rapid cultural change. In D. F. Lancy & B. A. Tindall (Eds.), *The anthropological study of play: Problems and prospects*. West Point, NY: Leisure Press.

Lansford, J. E. (2012). Cross-cultural and cross-national parenting perspectives. In V. Maholmes & R. B. King (Eds.), *The Oxford handbook of poverty and child development* (pp. 656–677). New York: Oxford University Press.

Laurendeau-Bendavid, M. (1977). Culture, schooling, and cognitive development: A comparative study of children in French Canada and Rwanda. In P. R. Dasen (Ed.), *Piagetian psychology: Cross-cultural contributions* (pp. 123–168). New York: Gardner Press.

Lautenschlager, N. T., & Foerstl, H. (2007). Personality change in old age. *Current Opinion in Psychiatry*, 20, 62–66.

Leaper, C., & Friedman, C. K. (2007). The socialization of gender. In J. E. Crusec & P. D. Hastings (Eds.), *Handbook of socialization: Theory and practice* (pp. 561–587). New York: Guilford Press.

Lefrancois, G. R. (1996). *The lifespan* (5th ed.). Belmont, CA: Wadsworth.

Lennartsson, C. (1999). Social ties and health among the very old in Sweden. *Research in Aging*, 21, 657–681.

Lerner, R., Brennan, A. L., & Noh, E. R. (1998). *The parenting of adolescents and adolescents as parents: A developmental contextual perspective*. Retrieved from http://parenthood.library.wisc.edu/Lerner/Lerner.html

le Roux, J., & Smith, C. S. (1998). Psychological characteristics of South African street children. *Adolescence*, 33(132), 891–899.

Levy, B. S., Wilkinson, F. S., & Marine, W. M. (1971). Reducing neonatal mortality rate with nurse midwives. *American Journal of Obstetrics and Gynecology*, 109, 50–58.

Levy, R. (1996). Essential contrasts: Differences in parental ideas about learners and teaching in Tahiti and Nepal. In S. Harkness & C. M. Super (Eds.), *Parents' cultural belief systems: Their origins, expressions, and consequences* (pp. 123–142). New York: Guilford Press.

Lewin, K. (1935). *A dynamic theory of personality*. New York: McGraw-Hill.

Lewis, J. R., & Ozaki, R. (2009). Amae and mardy: A comparison of two emotion terms. *Journal of Cross-Cultural Psychology*, 40(6), 917–934.

Lewis, M. P., Simons, G. F., & Fennig, C. D. (Eds.). (2013). *Ethnologue: Languages of the world* (17th ed.). Dallas: SIL International.

Li, J., & Yue, X. (2004). Self in learning among Chinese children. *New Directions in Child and Adolescent Development*, 104, 27–43.

Liu, X. C, Liu L. Q., & Wang, R. Z. (2003). Bedsharing, sleep habits, and sleep problems among Chinese school-aged children. *Sleep*, 26, 89–94.

Lonner, W. J. (2005). The psychological study of culture: Issues and questions of enduring importance. In W. Friedlmeier, P. Chakkarath, & B. Schwarz (Eds.), *Culture and human development* (pp. 9–25). New York: Psychology Press.

Lonner, W. J., & Malpass, R. (Eds.). (1994). *Psychology and culture*. Boston: Allyn & Bacon.

Lopez, I., & Ho, A. (2013). Culture-bound (or culturally salient?): The role of culture in disorder. In K. D. Keith (Ed.), *The encyclopedia of cross-cultural psychology* (pp. 355–362). Hoboken, NJ: Wiley-Blackwell.

Lourenco, O., & Machado, A. (1999). In defense of Piaget's theory: A reply to 10 common criticisms. *Psychological Review*, 103(1), 143–164.

Low, B. S., Hazel, A., Parker, N., & Welch, K. (2008). Influences on women's reproductive lives: Unexpected ecological underpinnings. *Cross-Cultural Research*, 42, 201–219.

Lowenstein, A., Katz, R., & Gur-Yaish, N. (2007). Reciprocity in parent–child exchange and life satisfaction among the elderly: A cross-national perspective. *Journal of Social Issues*, 63, 865–883.

Lucas-Stannard, P. (2013). *Gender neutral parenting*. Dallas: Verity Press.

Luria, A. R. (1981). *Language and cognition* (J. V. Wertsch, Ed.). New York: Wiley Intersciences.

Lusk, M. (1992). Street children of Rio de Janeiro. *International Social Work*, 35, 293–305.

Lykken, D. T. (2000). Reconstructing fathers. *American Psychologist*, 55, 681–682.

Ma, H. K. (1989). Moral orientation and moral judgment in adolescents in Hong Kong, Mainland China, and England. *Journal of Cross-Cultural Psychology*, 20, 152–177.

Maccoby, E. E. (1990). Gender and relationships. A developmental account. *American Psychologist*, 45, 513–520.

Maccoby, E. E. (1998). *The two sexes: Growing up apart, coming together*. Cambridge, MA: Harvard University Press.

Maccoby, E. E. (2002). Gender and group processes: A developmental perspective. *Current Directions in Psychological Science*, 11, 55–58.

MacDorman, M., & Singh, G. (1998). Midwifery care, social and medical risk factors, and birth outcomes in the USA. *Journal of Epidemiology Community Health*, 52, 310–317.

Maclachlan, M. (2006). *Culture and health*. New York: John Wiley & Sons.

MacLeod, R. B. (1947). The phenomenological approach to social psychology. *Psychological Review*, 54, 193–210.

Madrona, L., & Madrona, M. (1993). The future of midwifery in the United States. *NAPSAC News*, Fall-Winter, 30.

Main, M., & Solomon, J. (1990). Procedures for identifying infants as disorganized/disoriented during the Ainsworth strange situation. In M. Greenberg, D. Cicchetti, & E. M. Cummings (Eds.), *Attachment in the preschool years: Theories,* research, and intervention (pp. 121–160). Chicago: The University of Chicago Press.

Mapstone, M., Cheema, A. K., Fiandaca, M. S., Zhong, X., Mhyre T. R., MacArthur, L. H., et al. (2014). Plasma phospholipids identify antecedent memory impairment in older adults. Nature Medicine, 20, 415–418.

Markstrom, C. A. (2011). Identity of American Indian adolescents: Local, national, and global considerations. Journal of Research on Adolescents, 21(2), 519–535.

Markus, H., & Kitayama, S. (1991). Culture and the self: Implications for cognition, emotion, and motivation. Psychological Review, 98, 224–253.

Marshall, L. (1976). The !Kung of Nyae Nyae. Cambridge, MA: Harvard University Press.

Marsiglio, W., & Cohan, M. (2000). Contextualizing father involvement and paternal influence: Sociological and qualitative themes. Marriage and Family Review, 29, 75–95.

Mascolo, M. F., Misra, G., & Rapisardi, C. (2004). Individual and relational conceptions of self in India and the United States. New Directions in Child and Adolescent Development, 104, 9–26.

Matchinda, B. (1999). The impact of home background on the decision of children to run away: The case of Yaounde city street children in Cameroon. Child Abuse and Neglect, 23, 245–255.

Matsumoto, D. (2000). Culture and psychology: People and the world (2nd ed.). Belmont, CA: Wadsworth.

Matsumoto, D. (Ed.). (2001). The handbook of culture and psychology. New York: Oxford University Press.

Matsumoto, D., & Juang, L. (2008). Culture and psychology (4th ed.). Belmont, CA: Wadsworth.

Matsumoto, D., & van de Vijver, F. J. R. (Eds.). (2011). Cross-cultural research methods in psychology. New York: Cambridge University Press.

Matsumoto, D., & Yoo, S. H. (2006). Toward a new generation of cross-cultural research. Perspectives on Psychological Science, 1(3), 234–250.

Mayes, L., & Lewis, M. (2012). The Cambridge handbook of environment in human development. New York: Cambridge University Press.

McCrae, R. R. (2004). Human nature and culture: A trait perspective. Journal of Research in Personality, 38, 3–14.

McCrae, R. R. (2011, July). Robert R. McCrae talks about personality traits across diverse cultures. [Fast Moving Front Commentary]. Science Watch. Retrieved from http://archive.sciencewatch.com/dr/fmf/2011/11julfmf/11julfmfMcCr/

McCrae, R. R., & Allik, J. (Eds.). (2002). The five-factor model of personality across cultures. New York: Kluwer Academic/Plenum.

McCrae, R. R., & Costa, P. T., Jr. (1990). Personality in adulthood. New York: Guilford Press.

McCrae, R. R., & Costa, P. T., Jr. (2003). Personality in adulthood: A five-factor theory perspective (2nd ed.). New York: Guilford Press.

McCrae, R. R., Costa, P. T., Jr., de Lima, M. P., Simoes, A., Ostendorf, F., Angleitner, A., et al. (1999). Age differences in personality across the adult life span: Parallels in five cultures. Developmental Psychology, 35, 466–477.

McCrae, R. R., & John, O. P. (1992). An introduction to the five-factor model and its applications. Journal of Personality, 60, 175–216.

McDade, T. M., & Worthman, C. M. (2004). Socialization ambiguity in Samoan adolescents: A model for human development and stress in the contest of cultural change. Journal of Research on Adolescence, 14(1), 49–72.

McGann, P. J. (1999). Skirting the gender normal divide: A tomboy life story. In M. Romero & A. J. Stewart (Eds.), Women's untold stories: Breaking silence, talking back, voicing complexity (pp. 105–124). New York: Routledge.

McKenna, J. (2002). Breastfeeding and bedsharing: Still useful (and important) after all these years [Special issue]. Mothering, 28–37.

McKenna, J. (2012). Sleeping with your baby: A parent's guide to cosleeping. Washington, DC: Platypus Media.

McKenna, J. J., & Gettler, L. T. (2015). There is no such thing as infant sleep, there is no such thing as breastfeeding, there is only breastsleeping. Acta Paediatrica. doi:10.1111/apa.13161

McLeod, S. A. (2014). Lev Vygotsky. Retrieved from www.simplypsychology.org/vygotsky.html

Mead, G. H. (1934). Mind, self, and society. Chicago: The University of Chicago Press.

Mead, M. (1973). Coming of age in Samoa: A psychological study of primitive youth. New York: American Museum of Natural History. (Original work published 1928.)

Meng, J. M. (1991). The pattern of family and quality of life. Journal of Gerontology, 3, 135–140.

Meyers, S. A. (1993). Adapting parent education programs to meet the needs of fathers: An ecological perspective. Family Relations, 42(4), 447–453.

Miller, J. G. (1984). Culture and the development of everyday social explanation. Journal of Personality and Social Psychology, 46, 961–978.

Miller, M. N., & Pumariega, A. J. (2001). Culture and eating disorders: A historical and cross-cultural review. Psychiatry, 64, 93–110.

Miller, R. L., & Broadwell, R. M. (2013). Eating disorders. In K. D. Keith (Ed.), The encyclopedia of cross-cultural psychology (pp. 451–455). Hoboken, NJ: Wiley-Blackwell.

Ministry of Education, Culture, Sports, Science and Technology. (2006). Bullying trends in public and private schools: Number of schools and number of cases reported. Tokyo, Japan. Retrieved from http://www8.cao.go.jp/youth/whitepaper/h20honpenhtml/html/b1_sho1_2.html (In Japanese)

Minkler, M., & Roe, K. (1991). Preliminary findings from the grandmother caregiver study of Oakland, California. Berkeley: University of California Press.

Mishra, R. C., Sinha, D., & Berry, J. W. (1996). Ecology, acculturation, and psychological adaptation. Thousand Oaks, CA: Sage.

Mitchell, R., Myles, F., & Marsden, E. (2013). Second language learning theories. New York: Routledge.

Moghaddam, F. M., Taylor, D., & Wright, S. C. (1993). Social psychology in cross-cultural perspective. New York: Freeman.

Molitor, A., & Eckerman, C. O. (1992). Behavioral cues of distress/avoidance in preterm infants. Paper presented at the International Conference on Infant Studies, Miami, Florida.

Morelli, G. A., Rogoff, B., Oppenheim, D., & Goldsmith, D. (1992). Cultural variation in infants' sleeping arrangements: Questions of independence. *Developmental Psychology, 28,* 604–613.

Morelli, G. A., & Rothbaum, F. (2007). Situating the child in context: Attachment relationships and self-regulation in different cultures. In S. Kitayama & D. Cohen (Eds.), *Handbook of cultural psychology* (pp. 500–527). New York: Guilford Press.

Morinaga, Y., Frieze, I. H., & Ferligoj, A. (1993). Career plans and gender-role attitudes of college students in the United States, Japan, and Slovenia. *Sex Roles, 29,* 317–334.

Morris, V. (2014). *How to care for aging parents.* New York: Workman.

Moss, M. S., & Moss, S. Z. (2014). Widowhood in old age: Viewed in a family context. *Journal of Aging Studies, 29,* 98–106.

Mundy-Castle, A. C., & Okonji, M. D. (1976). *Mother–infant interaction in Nigeria.* Unpublished manuscript, University of Lagos, Nigeria.

Munroe, R. L., & Romney, A. K. (2006). Gender and age differences in same-sex aggregation and social behavior: A four-culture study. *Journal of Cross-Cultural Psychology, 37,* 3–19.

Muuss, R. E. (1988). *Theories of adolescence* (5th ed.). New York: Random House.

Muuss, R. E. (1996). *Theories of adolescence* (6th ed.). New York: McGraw-Hill.

Muuss, R. E., & Porton, H. D. (1998). *Adolescent behavior and society: A book of readings* (5th ed.). New York: McGraw-Hill.

Mwamwenda, T. S. (1992). Cognitive development in African children. *Genetic, Social, and General Psychology Monographs, 118*(1), 7–72.

Naito, T. (1994). A survey of research on moral development in Japan. *Cross-Cultural Research, 28,* 40–57.

Naito, T. (2013). Moral development. In K. D. Keith (Ed.), *The encyclopedia of cross-cultural psychology* (pp. 891–897). New York: Wiley.

National Center for Chronic Disease Prevention and Health Promotion (NCCDPHP). (2011, July 22). *The obesity epidemic* [Online video]. Available from http://www.cdc.gov/cdctv/diseaseandconditions/lifestyle/obesity-epidemic.html

Nesdale, D., & Naito, M. (2005). Individualism-collectivism and the attitudes to school bullying of Japanese and Australian students. *Journal of Cross-Cultural Psychology, 36,* 537–556.

Newland, L. A., Chen, H.-H., Coyl-Shepherd, D. D., Liang, Y.-C., Carr, E. R., Dykstra, E, & Gapp, S. C. (2013). Parent and child perspectives on mothering and fathering: The influence of eco-cultural niches. *Early Child Development and Care, 183*(3–4), 534–552.

Neyer, F. J., & Asendorpf, J. B. (2001). Personality-relationship transaction in young adulthood. *Journal of Personality and Social Psychology, 81,* 1190–1204.

Ng, J., & Hall, G. C. N. (2011). Cultural influences of adolescence. *Encyclopedia of Adolescence,* 45–51.

Nguyen, A.-M. T. (2013). Acculturation. In K. D. Keith (Eds.), *The encyclopedia of cross-cultural psychology* (pp. 7–12). Hoboken, NJ: Wiley-Blackwell.

Niethammer, C. (1977). *Daughters of the earth: The lives and legends of American Indian women.* New York: Macmillan.

Niiya, Y., Ellsworth, P. C., & Yamaguchi, S. (2006). Amae in Japan and the United States: An exploration of a "culturally unique emotion." *Emotion, 6*(2), 279–295.

Noller, P., & Atkin, A. (2010). *Family life in adolescence.* London: Routledge.

Novikova, I. A. (2013). Big five (The five-factor model and the five-factor theory). In K. D. Keith (Ed.), *The encyclopedia of cross-cultural psychology* (pp. 136–138). Hoboken, NJ: Wiley-Blackwell.

Nunes, T., Schliemann, A. D., & Carraher, D. W. (1993). *Street mathematics and school mathematics.* Cambridge, UK: Cambridge University Press.

Nurmi, J. E. (1991). How do adolescents see their future? A review of development of future orientation and planning. *Developmental Review, 11,* 1–59.

Nyiti, R. M. (1982). The validity of "cultural differences explanations" for cross-cultural variation in the rate of Piagetian cognitive development. In D. A. Wagner & H. W. Stevenson (Eds.), *Cultural perspectives on child development.* San Francisco: Freeman.

Oakland, T., & Hatzichristou, C. (2010). Temperament styles of Greek and US children. *School Psychology International, 31*(4), 422–437.

Obukhova, L. F. (2012). Vygotsky and developmental psychology in his and our time. *Cultural-Historical Psychology, 1,* 51–58.

Ochs, E. (1988). *Culture and language development.* Cambridge, UK: Cambridge University Press.

O'Connor, T. G., Marvin, R. S., Rutter, M., Olrick, J. T., Pritner, P. A., & the English and Romanian Adoptees Study Team. (2003). Child–parent attachment following early institutional deprivation. *Development and Psychopathology, 15,* 19–38.

Offer, D., Ostrov, E., Howard, K. I., & Atkinson, R. (1988). *The teenage world: Adolescents' self-image in ten countries.* New York: Plenum.

Okedu, K., Rembe, S., & Anwo, J. (2009). Female genital mutilation: A human rights perspective. *Journal of Psychology in Africa, 19*(1), 55–62.

Olowu, A. A. (1990). The self-concept in cross-cultural perspective. In A. A. Olowu (Ed.), *Contemporary issues in self-concept studies.* Ibadan, Kenya: Shaneson C. I., Ltd.

Olson, L. K. (1994). *The graying of the world: Who will care for the frail elderly?* New York: Routledge.

Otto, H., & Keller, H. (2014). *Different faces of attachment: Cultural variations on a universal human need.* Cambridge, UK: Cambridge University Press.

Oyserman, D., Coon, H. M., & Kemmelmeier, M. (2002). Rethinking individualism and collectivism: Evaluation of theoretical assumptions and meta-analysis. *Psychological Bulletin, 128*(1), 3–72.

Packer, M. J. (2008). Is Vygotsky relevant? Vygotsky's Marxist psychology. *Mind, Culture, and Activity, 15*(1), 8–31.

Palmer, J. A. (2001). *Fifty modern thinkers on education: From Piaget to the modern day.* London: Taylor & Francis.

Park, D. C., & Hedden, N. R. (1999). Aging, culture, and cognition. *Journal of Gerontology, Series B: Social Sciences, 54*(2), 75–84.

Parke, R. D. (2000). Father involvement: A developmental psychological perspective. *Marriage and Family Review, 29,* 43–58.

Parke, R. D. (2002). Fathers and families. In M. H. Bornstein (Ed.), *Handbook of parenting* (2nd ed., Vol. 3, pp. 27–74). Mahwah, NJ: Erlbaum.

Parmar, P., Harkness, S., & Super, C. M. (2004). Asian and Euro-American parents' ethnotheories of play and learning: Effects on pre-school children's home routines and school behavior. *International Journal of Behavioral Development, 28*(2), 97–104.

Pastorelli, C., Caprara, G. V., Barbaranelli C., Rola, J., Rosza, S., & Bandura, A. (2001). The structure of children's perceived self-efficacy: A cross-national study. *European Journal of Psychological Assessment, 17,* 87–97.

Pellegrini, A. D. (2015). *The Oxford handbook of the development of play.* Cambridge, UK: Oxford University Press.

Pena-Shaff, J. B. (2013). Attachment. In K. D. Keith (Eds.), *The encyclopedia of cross-cultural psychology* (pp. 96–101). Hoboken, NJ: Wiley-Blackwell.

Pepler D., Craig W., Yuile A., & Connolly J. (2004). Girls who bully: A developmental and relational perspective. In M. Putallaz & K. L. Bierman (Eds.), *Aggression, antisocial behavior, and violence among girls: A developmental perspective* (pp. 90–109). New York: Guilford Press.

Pew Research Center. (2013). The *global divide on homosexuality: Greater acceptance in more secular and affluent countries.* Retrieved from http://www.pewglobal.org/files/2013/06/Pew-Global-Attitudes-Homosexuality-Report-FINAL-JUNE-4-2013.pdf

Phinney, J. S., Lochner, B., & Murphy, R. (1990). Ethnic identity development and psychological adjustment in adolescents. In A. Stiffman & L. Davis (Eds.), *Ethnic issues in adolescent mental health* (pp. 53–72). Newbury Park, CA: Sage.

Phinney, J. S., & Ong, A. D. (2007). Conceptualization and measurement of ethnic identity: Current status and future directions. *Journal of Counseling Psychology, 54,* 271–281.

Piaget, J. (1972). Intellectual evolution from adolescence to adulthood. *Human Development, 15,* 1–12.

Pike, K. M., & Borovoy, A. (2004). The rise of eating disorders in Japan: Issues of culture and limitations of the model of "Westernization." *Culture, Medicine, and Psychiatry, 28,* 493–531.

Pillemer, D. B., & White, S. H. (Eds.). (2005). *Developmental psychology and social change.* New York: Cambridge University Press.

Plomin, R., & Rutter, M. (1998). Child development, molecular genetics, and what to do with genes once they are found. *Child Development, 69,* 1223–1242.

Pollitt, E., Gorman, K. S., Engle, P. L., Martorell, R., & Rivera, J. (1993). Early supplemental feeding and cognition: Effects over two decades. *Monographs of the Society for Research in Child Development, 58*(7), 1–99; discussion 111–118.

Pollock, D. C., & Van Reken, R. E. (2009). *Third culture kids: Growing up among worlds* (Rev. ed.). Yarmouth, ME: Intercultural Press.

Polyakova, S. A., & Pacquaio, D. F. (2006). Psychological and mental illness among elder immigrants for the former Soviet Union. *Journal of Transcultural Nursing, 17,* 40–49.

Posada, G., Gao, Y., Wu, F., Posada, R., Tascon, M., Schöelmerich, A., et al. (1995). The secure-base phenomenon across cultures: Children's behavior, mothers' references, and experts' concepts. *Monographs of the Society for Research in Child Development, 60*(2–3, Serial No. 244), 27–48.

Pretorius, E., & Naude, H. (2002). A culture in transition: Poor reading and writing ability among children in South African townships. *Early Childhood Development and Care, 172,* 439–449.

Pribilsky, J. (2001). Nervios and "modern childhood": Migration and shifting contexts of child life in the Ecuadorian Andes. *Childhood: A Global Journal of Child Research, 8,* 251–273.

Price-Williams, D. R., Gordon, W., & Ramirez, M., III. (1969). Skills and conservation: A study of pottery-making children. *Developmental Psychology, 1,* 769.

Proos, L. A., Hofvander, Y., & Tuvemo, T. (1991). Menarchael age and growth pattern of Indian girls adopted in Sweden. I. Menarcheal age. *Acta Pediatrica Scandinavia, 80*(8–9), 852–858.

ProQuest. (2013). *The statistical abstract of the United States.* Bethesda, MD: ProQuest.

Pugh, S. (2005). Assessing the cultural needs of older lesbians and gay men: Implications for practice. *Practice, 17*(3), 207–221.

Putnam, S. P., Sanson, A. V., & Rothbart, M. K. (2002). Child temperament and parenting. In M. H. Bornstein (Ed.), *Handbook of parenting* (2nd ed., Vol. 1, pp. 255–277). Mahwah, NJ: Erlbaum.

Quah, S. R. (2008). *Families in Asia: Home and kin* (2nd ed.). London: Routledge.

Raeff, C. (2004). Within-culture complexities: Multifaceted and interrelated autonomy and connectedness characteristics in late adolescent selves. *New Directions in Child and Adolescent Development, 104,* 61–78.

Raeff, C. (2006a). Individuals in relation to others: Independence and interdependence in a kindergarten classroom. *Ethos, 34,* 521–557.

Raeff, C. (2006b). Multiple and inseparable: Conceptualizing the development of independence and interdependence. *Human Development, 49,* 96–121.

Raeff, C. (2006c). *Always separate, always connected: Independence and interdependence in cultural contexts of development.* Mahwah, NJ: Erlbaum.

Raeff, C. (2010). Independence and interdependence in children's developmental experiences. *Child Development Perspectives, 4*(1), 31–36.

Recio Adrados, J. L. (1995). The influence of family, school, and peers on adolescent drug misuse. *International Journal of the Addictions, 30,* 1407–1423.

Reiman, E. M. (2014). Alzheimer's disease and other dementias: Advances in 2013. *Lancet Neurology, 13*(1), 3–5.

Retschitzki, J. (1989). Evidence of formal thinking in Baule airele players. In D. M. Keats, D. Munro, & L. Mann (Eds.), *Heterogeneity in cross-cultural psychology* (pp. 234–243). Amsterdam: Swets & Zeitlinger.

Rhode, D. L. (Ed.). (2003). *The difference "difference" makes: Women and leadership.* Stanford, CA: Stanford University Press.

Richerson, P. J., & Boyd, R. (2004). *Not by genes alone: How culture transformed human evolution.* Chicago: The University of Chicago Press.

Richman, A. L., LeVine, R. A., New, R. S., Howrigan, G. A., Welles-Nystrom, B., & LeVine, S. (1988). Maternal behavior to infants in five cultures. In R. A. LeVine, P. M. Miller, & M. M. West (Eds.), *Parental behavior in diverse societies: New directions for child development* (pp. 81–97). San Francisco: Jossey-Bass.

Richman, A. L., Miller, P. M., & LeVine, R. A. (1992). Cultural and educational variations in maternal responsiveness. *Developmental Psychology, 28*, 614–621.

Riessman, C. K. (2007). *Narrative methods for the human sciences.* Thousand Oaks, CA: Sage.

Robarchek, C. A., & Robarchek, C. J. (1998). Reciprocities and realities: World views, peacefulness, and violence among Semai and Waorani. *Aggressive Behavior, 24*, 123–133.

Roberts, B. W., & Bogg, T. (2004). A longitudinal study of the relationships between conscientiousness and the social-environmental factors and substance-use behaviors that influence health. *Journal of Personality, 72*, 325–353.

Roberts, B. W., Wood, D., & Smith J. L. (2005). Evaluating five-factor theory and social investment perspective on personality trait development. *Journal of Research in Personality, 39*, 166–184.

Roberts, G. W. (1994). Brother to brother: African American modes of relating among men. *Journal of Black Studies, 24*, 379–390.

Robinson, G. (2002). Cross-cultural perspectives on menopause. In A. E. Hunter & C. Forden (Eds.), *Readings in the psychology of gender: Exploring our differences and commonalities* (pp. 140–149). Needham Heights, MA: Allyn & Bacon.

Rogoff, B. (1990). *Apprenticeship in thinking: Cognitive development in social context.* New York: Oxford University Press.

Rogoff, B. (2003). *The cultural nature of human development.* New York: Oxford University Press.

Rogoff, B. (2011). *Developing destinies: A Mayan midwife and town* [Child development in cultural context]. New York: Oxford University Press.

Rogoff, B., & Chavajay, P. (1995). What's become of research on the cultural basis of cognitive development? *American Psychologist, 50*, 859–873.

Roid, G. H. (2003). *Stanford-Binet Intelligence Scales* (5th ed.). Boston: Houghton Mifflin Harcourt.

Roopnarine, J. L., & Carter, D. B. (1992). *Parent–child socialization in diverse cultures.* Norwood, NJ: Ablex.

Roopnarine, J. L., Patte, M., Johnson, J. E., & Kuschner, D. (Eds.). (2015). *International perspectives on children's play.* London: Open University Press/McGraw Hill.

Ross, N. O. (2003). *Culture and cognition: Implications for theory and method.* Thousand Oaks, CA: Sage.

Rothbart, M. K. (1981). Measurement of temperament in infancy. *Child Development, 52*, 569–578.

Rothbart, M. K. (2011). *Becoming who we are: Temperament and personality in development.* New York: Guilford Press.

Rothbart, M. K., & Bates, J. E. (1998). Temperament. In N. Eisenberg (Ed.), *Handbook of child psychology* (5th ed., Vol. 3, pp. 105–176). New York: Wiley.

Rothbart, M. K., & Hwang, J. (2005). Temperament. In A. J. Elliot & C. S. Dweck (Eds.), *Handbook of competence and motivation* (pp. 167–184). New York: Guilford Press.

Rothbaum, F., & Morelli, G. (2005). Attachment and culture: Bridging relativism and universalism. In W. Friedlmeier, P. Chakkarath, & B. Schwarz (Eds.), *Culture and human development* (pp. 100–123). New York: Psychology Press.

Rothbaum, F., Weisz, J., Pott, M., Miyake, K., & Morelli, G. (2000). Attachment and culture: Security in the United States and Japan. *American Psychologist, 55*, 1093–1104.

Rubin, K. H., Bukowski, W. M., & Laursen, B. (Eds.). (2009). *Handbook of peer interactions, relationships, and groups.* New York: Guilford Press.

Rutter, M. (1998). Developmental catch-up, and deficit, following adoption after severe global early privation. English and Romanian Adoptees (ERA) Study Team. *Journal of Child Psychology and Psychiatry, and Allied Disciplines, 39*(4), 465–476.

Ryan, E. B., Giles, H., Bartolucci, G., & Henwood, K. (1986). Psycholinguisitc and social psychological components of communication by and with the elderly. *Language and Communication, 6*, 1–24.

Sabates, R., & Dex, S. (2013). The impact of multiple risk factors on young children's cognitve and behavioural development. *Children and Society, 29*(2), 95–108.

Sagi, A. (1990). Attachment theory and research in cross-cultural perspective. *Human Development, 33*, 10–22.

Sagi-Schwartz, A., & Aviezer, O. (2005). Correlates of attachment to multiple caregivers in kibbutz children from birth to emerging adulthood: The Haifa longitudinal study. In K. E. Grossmann, K. Grossmann, & E. Waters (Eds.), *Attachment from infancy to adulthood: The major longitudinal studies* (pp. 165–197). New York: Guilford Press.

Sahin, N., & Sahin, N. H. (1995). Dimensions of concerns: The case of Turkish adolescents. *Journal of Adolescence, 18*, 49–69.

Salthouse, T. A. (1987). The role of experience in cognitive aging. In K. W. Schaie & K. Eisdorfer (Eds.), *Annual review of gerontology and geriatrics* (Vol. 7, pp. 135–158). New York: Springer.

Sam, D. L., & Berry, J. W. (2016). *Cambridge handbook of acculturation psychology* (2nd ed.). Cambridge, UK: Cambridge University Press.

Sangree, W. H. (1992). Grandparenthood and modernization: The changing status of male and female elders in Tiriki, Kenya, and Irigwe, Nigeria. *Journal of Cross-Cultural Gerontology, 7*, 331–361.

Saraswathi, T. S. (Ed.). (2003). *Cross-cultural perspectives in human development.* Thousand Oaks, CA: Sage.

Sartorius, N. R., Jablensky, A., Korten, A., Ernberg, G., Anker, M., Cooper, J. E., et al. (1986). Early manifestations and first contact incidence of schizophrenia in different cultures: A preliminary report on the initial evaluation phase of the WHO Collaborative Study on Determinants of Outcome of Severe Mental Disorders. *Psychological Medicine, 16*, 909–928.

Scabini, E., Marta, E., & Lanz, M. (2006). *The transition to adulthood and family relations.* New York: Psychology Press.

Schlegel, A., & Barry, H., III. (1991). *Adolescence: An anthropological inquiry.* New York: Free Press.

Schlegel, A., & Barry, H., III. (2015). Leaving childhood: The nature and meaning of adolescent transition rituals. In L. A. Jensen (Ed.), *The Oxford handbook of human development and culture: An interdisciplinary perspective* (pp. 327–340). New York: Oxford University Press.

Schugurensky, D. (2000). *The forms of informal learning: Towards a conceptualization of the field*. Retrieved from http://www.oise.utoronto.ca/depts/sese/csew/nall/res/19formsofinformal.html

Schwartz, M. A., & Scott, B. M. (2010). *Marriages and families: Diversity and change* (6th ed.). Boston: Prentice Hall.

Schwartz, S. H. (1995). Are there universal aspects in the structure and contents of human values? *Journal of Social Issues, 50*, 19–46.

Schwartz, S. H. (2011). Studying values: Personal adventures, future directions. *Journal of Cross-Cultural Psychology, 42(2)*, 307–319.

Schwartz, T. (1981). The acquisition of culture. *Ethos, 9*, 4–17.

Schwartzman, H. B. (1983). Socializing play: Functional analysis. In J. C. Harris & R. J. Park (Eds.), *Play, games, and sports in cultural contexts*. Champaign, IL: Human Kinetics.

Schwarz, B., Schafermeier, E., & Trommsdorff, G. (2005). Relations between value orientation, childrearing goals, and parenting: A comparison of German and South Korean mothers. In W. Friedlmeier, P. Chakkarath, & B. Schwarz (Eds.), *Culture and human development* (pp. 203–230). New York: Psychology Press.

Schwarz, S., & Hassebrauck, M. (2012). Sex and age differences in mate selection. *Human Nature, 23(4)*, 447–466.

Scully, E. (2002). Social constraints and language learning: Filipina immigrants in Japan. *Race Ethnicity and Education, 5*, 397–418.

Searle-White, J. (1996). Personal boundaries among Russians and Americans: A Vygotskian approach. *Cross-Cultural Research, 30(2)*, 184–208.

Segal, N. L. (2000). *Entwined lives: Twins and what they tell us about human behavior*. New York: Plume.

Segal, N. L. (2012). *Born together—Reared apart: The landmark Minnesota Twin Study*. Boston: Harvard University Press.

Segall, M. H. (1979). *Cross-cultural psychology*. Belmont, CA: Wadsworth.

Segall, M. H., Dasen, P. R., Berry, J. W., & Poortinga, Y. H. (1999). *Human behavior in global perspective* (2nd ed.). Boston: Allyn & Bacon.

Segall, M. H., Lonner, W. J., & Berry, J. W. (1998). Cross-cultural psychology as a scholarly discipline: On the flowering of culture in behavioral research. *American Psychologist, 53*, 1101–1110.

Segalowitz, S. J., & Schmidt, L. A. (2003). Developmental psychology and the neurosciences. In J. Valsiner & K. Connolly (Eds.), *Handbook of developmental psychology* (pp. 48–71). London: Sage.

Serpell, R. (1993). *The significance of schooling: Life-journeys in an African society*. New York: Cambridge University Press.

Sharma, N., & Sharma, B. (1999). Children in difficult circumstances: Familial correlates of advantage while at risk. In T. S. Saraswathi (Ed.), *Culture, socialization, and human development: Theory, research, and applications in India* (pp. 398–418). Thousand Oaks, CA: Sage.

Shepard, K., Michopolous, V., Toufexis, D. J., & Wilson, M. E. (2009). Genetic, epigenetic, and environmental impact on sex differences in social behavior. *Physiology and Behavior, 97*, 157–170.

Shostak, M. (1981). *Nissa: The life and words of a !Kung woman*. Cambridge, MA: Harvard University Press.

Shwalb, D. W., Nakazawa, J., & Shwalb, B. J. (Eds.). (2005). *Applied developmental psychology: Theory, practice, and research from Japan*. Greenwich, CT: Information Age.

Shwalb, D. W., Nakazawa, J., Yamamoto, T., & Hyun, J. H. (2003). Fathering in Japanese, Chinese, and Korean cultures: A review of the research literature. In M. E. Lamb (Ed.), *The role of the father in child development* (4th ed., pp. 146–181). New York: Wiley.

Shwalb, D. W., & Shwalb, B. J. (2014). Fatherhood in Brazil, Bangladesh, Russia, Japan, and Australia. *Online Readings in Psychology and Culture, 6*(3). Retrieved from http://dx.doi.org/10.9707/2307-0919.1125

Shwalb, D. W., Shwalb, B. J., & Lamb, M. E. (Eds.). (2013). *Fathers in cultural context*. New York: Routledge.

Shweder, R., Mahapatra, M., & Miller, J. G. (1987). Culture and moral development. In J. Kagan & S. Lamb (Eds.), *The emergence of morality in young children* (pp. 1–82). Chicago: The University of Chicago Press.

Sigel, I. E. (Ed.). (1985). *Parental belief systems: The psychological consequences for children*. Hillsdale, NJ: Erlbaum.

Sigel, I. E., & McGillicuddy-De Lisi, A. V. (2002). Parental beliefs are cognitions: The dynamic belief system model. In M. H. Bornstein (Ed.), *Handbook of parenting: Being and becoming a parent* (pp. 485–508). Mahwah, NJ: Erlbaum.

Sigel, I. E., McGillicuddy-De Lisi, A. V., & Goodnow, J. J. (Eds.). (1992). *Parental belief systems: The psychological consequences for children* (2nd ed.). Hillsdale, NJ: Erlbaum.

Sijuwola, O. A. (1995). Culture, religion, and mental illness in Nigeria. In I. Al-Issa (Ed.), *Handbook of culture and mental illness* (pp. 65–72). Madison, WI: International Universities Press.

Singer, J. S., & Navsaria, N. (2013). Temperament. In K. D. Keith (Ed.), *The encyclopedia of cross-cultural psychology* (pp. 1272–1275): Hoboken, NJ: Wiley-Blackwell.

Siok, W. T., Spinks, J. A., Jin, Z., & Tan, L. H. (2009). Developmental dyslexia is characterized by the co-existence of visuospatial and phonological disorders in Chinese children. *Current Biology, 19*(19), R890–R892.

Smith, D. E., & Blinn Pike, L. (1994). Relationship between Jamaican adolescents' drinking patterns and self-image: A cross-cultural perspective. *Adolescence, 29*, 429–437.

Smith, H. W., & Nomi, T. (2000). Is Amae the key to understanding Japanese culture? *Electronic Journal of Sociology*. Retrieved from http://www.sociology.org/content/vol005.001/smith-nomi.html

Smith, J., & Baltes, P. B. (1990). Wisdom-related knowledge: Age/cohort differences in response to life-planning problems. *Developmental Psychology, 26*(3), 494–505.

Smith, K. (2005, March 22). Prebirth gender talk: A case study in prenatal socialization. *Women and Language*. Retrieved from http://www.redorbit.com/news/health/158908/prebirth_gender_talk_a_case_study_in_prenatal_socialization/

Smith, P. B. (2004). Nations, cultures, and individuals: New perspectives and old dilemmas. *Journal of Cross-Cultural Psychology, 35*, 6–12.

Smith, P. B., & Bond, M. H. (1999). *Social psychology across cultures* (2nd ed.). Boston: Allyn & Bacon.

Smith, P. B., Bond, M. H., & Kagitcibasi, C. (2006). *Understanding social psychology across cultures: Living and working in a changing world*. Thousand Oaks, CA: Sage.

Smith, P. K. (1991). Introduction: The study of grandparenthood. In P. K. Smith (Ed.), *The psychology of grandparenthood: An international perspective* (pp. 1–16). London: Routledge & Keagan Paul.

Smith, P. K. (1995). Grandparenthood. In M. H. Bornstein (Ed.), *Handbook of parenting* (Vol. 3, pp. 89–112). Mahwah, NJ: Erlbaum.

Smith, P. K. (2005). Grandparents and grandchildren. *The Psychologist, 18*, 684–687.

Smith, P. K., & Drew. L. M. (2002). Grandparenthood. In M. H. Bornstein (Ed.), *Handbook of parenting* (2nd ed., Vol. 3, pp. 141–172). Mahwah, NJ: Erlbaum.

Smith, P. K., & Drew, L. M. (2004). Grandparenting and support networks. In M. S. Hoghughi & N. Long (Eds.), *The handbook of parenting: Theory, research, and practice* (pp. 146–159). London: Sage.

Snarey, J. R. (1985). Cross-cultural universality of socio-moral development: A critical review of Kohlbergian research. *Psychological Bulletin, 97*, 202–232.

Sneed, J. R., & Whitbourne, S. K. (2005). Models of the aging self. *Journal of Social Issues, 61*, 375–388.

Solomon, G. B. (1997). Fair play in the gymnasium: Improving social skills among elementary school children. *Journal of Physical Education, Recreation, and Dance, 68*, 22–25.

Sommers, I., Fagan, J., & Baskin, D. (1993). Sociocultural influences on the explanation of delinquency for Puerto Rican youths. *Hispanic Journal of Behavioral Sciences, 15*, 36–62.

Sorkhabi, N. (2012). Parenting socialization effects in difference cultures: Significance of directive parenting. *Psychological Reports, 110*(3), 854–878.

Sparkes, K. K. (1991). Cooperative and competitive behavior in dyadic game-playing: A comparison of Anglo-American and Chinese children. *Early Child Development and Care, 68*, 37–47.

Spencer, M. B., Harpalani, V., Fegley, S., Dell'Angelo, T., & Seaton, G. (2003). Identity, self, and peers in context: A culturally sensitive developmental framework for analysis. In R. Lerner, F. Jacobs, & D. Wertlieg (Eds.), *Handbook of applied developmental science* (Vol. 1, pp. 123–142). Newbury Park, CA: Sage.

Spock, B., & Rothenberg, M. B. (1992). *Dr. Spock's baby and child care.* New York: Pocket Books.

Stack, C. B. (1974). *All our kin: Strategies for survival in a black community.* New York: Harper & Row.

Stankov, L., & Lee, J. (2009). Large-scale cross-cultural studies of cognitve and noncognitive constructs. *Learning and Individual Differences, 19*(3), 327–329.

Steinberg, L. (1987). Impact of puberty on family relations: Effects of pubertal status and pubertal timing. *Developmental Psychology, 23*, 451–460.

Steinberg, L. (1988). Reciprocal relation between parent–child distance and pubertal maturation. *Developmental Psychology, 24*, 122–128.

Steinberg, L., Darling, N. E., & Fletcher, A. C. (1995). Authoritative parenting and adolescent adjustment: An ecological journey. In P. Moen, G. H. Elder, Jr., & K. Luscher (Eds.), *Examining lives in context: Perspectives on the ecology of human development* (pp. 423–466). Washington, DC: American Psychological Association.

Steinberg, L., & Silk, J. S. (2002). Parenting adolescents. In M. H. Bornstein (Ed.), *Handbook of parenting* (2nd ed., Vol. 1, pp. 103–133). Mahwah, NJ: Erlbaum.

Sternberg, R. J., & Grigorenko, E. (Eds.). (2004). *Culture and competence: Contexts of life success.* Washington, DC: American Psychological Association.

Steube, A. M., Rich-Edwards, J. W., Willett, W. C., Manson, J. E., & Michels, K. B. (2005). Duration of lactation and incidence to type 2 diabetes. *Journal of the American Medical Association, 294*, 2601–2610.

Stevenson, H. W., Chen, C., & Lee, S. (1991). Chinese families. In J. L. Roopnarine & D. B. Carter (Eds.), *Parent–child socialization in diverse cultures* (pp. 17–33). Norwood, NJ: Ablex.

Stevenson, H. W., & Stigler, J. W. (1992). *The learning gap: Why our schools are failing and what we can learn from Japanese and Chinese education.* New York: Simon & Schuster.

Stewart, S. M., Simmons, A., & Habibpour, E. (2012). Treatment of culturally diverse children and adolescents with depression. *Journal of Child and Adolescent Psychopharmacology, 22*(1), 72–79.

Stigler, J., & Fernandez, C. (1995). Learning mathematics from classroom instructions: Cross-cultural and experimental perspectives. In C. Nelson (Ed.), *Contemporary perspectives on learning and development: Twenty-seventh Minnesota symposium on child psychology* (pp. 103–130). Hillsdale, NJ: Erlbaum.

Stiles, D. A., & Gibbons, J. L. (1995). *Gender role expectations of Norwegian adolescents.* Paper presented at the twenty-fourth annual meeting of the Society for Cross-Cultural Research, Savannah, Georgia.

Strom, R., Strom, S., Collinsworth, P., Sato, S., Makino, K., Sasaki, Y., et al. (1995). Grandparents in Japan: A three-generational study. *International Journal of Aging and Human Development, 40*(3), 209–227.

Strom, R. D., & Strom, S. K. (2000). Intergenerational learning and family harmony. *Educational Gerontology, 26*, 261–283.

Strom, R. D., Strom, S. K., Wang, C., Shen, Y., Griswold, D., Chan, H., et al. (1999). Grandparents in the United States and the Republic of China: A comparison of generations and cultures. *International Journal of Aging and Human Development, 49*, 279–317.

Strong, C. (1984). Stress and caring for elderly relatives: Interpretations and coping strategies in an American Indian and White sample. *Gerontologist, 24*(3), 251–256.

Sullivan, R. (2004). (Ed.) *Focus on fathering.* Melbourne, Australia: AECR Press.

Super, C. M. (2005). The globalization of developmental psychology. In D. B. Pillemer & S. H. White (Eds.), *Developmental psychology and social change* (pp. 11–33). New York: Cambridge University Press.

Super, C. M., & Harkness, S. (1982). The infants' niche in rural Kenya and metropolitan America. In L. L. Adler (Ed.), *Cross-cultural research at issue* (pp. 47–55). New York: Academic Press.

Super, C. M., & Harkness, S. (1986). The developmental niche: A conceptualization of the interface of child and culture. *International Journal of Behavioral Development, 9*, 545–570.

Super, C. M., & Harkness, S. (1994). The developmental niche. In W. J. Lonner & R. Malpass (Eds.), *Psychology and culture* (pp. 95–99). Boston: Allyn & Bacon.

Super, C. M., & Harkness, S. (1997). The cultural structuring of child development. In J. W. Berry, P. R. Dasen, & T. S. Saraswathi

(Eds.), *Handbook of cross-cultural psychology* (2nd ed., Vol. 2, pp. 1–39). Boston: Allyn & Bacon.

Super, C. M., & Harkness, S. (1999). The environment as culture in developmental research. In S. L. Friedman & T. D. Wachs (Eds.), *Measuring environment across the life span* (pp. 279–323). Washington, DC: American Psychological Association.

Super, C. M., & Harkness, S. (2002). Culture structures the environment for development. *Human Development, 45*, 270–274.

Super, C. M., & Harkness, S. (2003). The metaphors of development. *Human Development, 46*, 3–23.

Super, C. M., Harkness, S., Barry, O., & Zeitlin, M. (2011). Think locally, act globally: Contributions of African research to child development. *Child Development Perspectives, 5*(2), 119–125.

Suzuki, H. (2013). Sexually transmitted diseases. In K. D. Keith (Ed.), *The encyclopedia of cross-cultural psychology* (pp. 1173–1175). Hoboken, NJ: Wiley-Blackwell.

Suzuki, T. (1998). Children's comprehension of Japanese passives: A different perspective. In E. Clark (Ed.), *The Proceedings of the Twenty-Ninth Annual Child Language Research Forum* (pp. 91–100). Stanford, CA: Center for Study of Language and Information.

Swanson, D. P., Spencer, M. B., Harpalani, V., Dupree, D., Noll, E., Ginzburg, S., et al. (2003). Psychosocial development in racially and ethnically diverse youth: Conceptual and methodological challenges in the 21st century. *Developmental Psychopathology, 15*, 743–771.

Tajfel, H. (1981). *Human groups and social categories.* Cambridge, UK: Cambridge University Press.

Tamis-LeMonda, C. S., Baumwell, L., & Cabrera, N. J. (2014). Fathers' role in children's language development. In N. J. Cabrera & C. S. Tamis-LeMonda (Eds.), *Handbook of father involvement* (2nd ed., pp. 135–150). Mahwah, NJ: Erlbaum.

Tan, A., Stone, O., et al. (Producers), & Wang, W. (Director). (1993). *The joy luck club* [Motion picture]. United States: Buena Vista Studio.

Tang, T. L.-P. (1996). Pay differential as a function of rater's sex, money ethic, and job incumbent's sex: A test of the Matthew Effect. *Journal of Economic Psychology, 17(1)*, 127–144. doi:10.1016/0167-4870(95)00038-0

Tang, T. L.-P., Furnham, A., & Davis, G. M.-T. W. (2000). A cross cultural comparison of pay differentials as a function of rater's sex and money ethic endorsement: The Matthew Effect revisited. *Personality and Individual Differences, 29*(4), 685–697. Retrieved from http://dx.doi.org/10.1016/S0191-8869(99)00225-1

Tanner, D. (2007). Starting with lives: Supporting older people's strategies and ways of coping. *Journal of Social Work, 7*, 7–30.

Thomas, A., & Chess, S. (1977). *Temperament and development.* New York: Brunner/Mazel.

Thomas, R. M. (1999). *Human development theories: Windows on culture.* Thousand Oaks, CA: Sage.

Thomas, R. M. (2001). *Recent theories of human development.* Thousand Oaks, CA: Sage.

Thomas, W. I., & Znaniecki, F. (1927). *The Polish peasant in Europe and America.* New York: Knopf.

Thompson, R. A. (2016). Early attachment and later development: Reframing the questions. In J. Cassidy & P. R. Shaver (Eds.), *Handbook of attachment* (3rd ed). New York: Guilford Press.

Tien, H. Y., & Lee, C. F. (1988). New demographics and old designs: The Chinese family and induced population transition. *Social Science Quarterly, 69*, 605–628.

Tinsley, B. J., Markey, C. N., Ericksen, A. J., Oritz, R. V., & Kwasman, A. (2002). Health promotion for parents. In M. H. Bornstein (Ed.), *Handbook of parenting* (2nd ed., Vol. 5, pp. 311–328). Mahwah, NJ: Erlbaum.

Tomasik, M. J., & Silbereisen, R. K. (2011). Globalization and adolescence. In B. B. Brown & M. J. Prinstein (Eds.), *Encyclopedia of adolescence* (pp. 109–117). Philadelphia: Elsevier.

Triandis, H. C. (1989). The self and social behavior in differing cultural contexts. *Psychological Bulletin, 96*, 506–520.

Triandis, H. C. (1995). *Individualism and collectivism.* Boulder, CO: Westview Press.

Triandis, H. C. (2008). *Fooling ourselves: Self-deception in politics, religion, and terrorism.* Santa Barbara, CA: Greenwood Press.

Trimble, J. E., Manson, S. M., Dinges, N. G., & Medicine, B. (1984). American Indian concepts of mental health: Reflections and directions. In P. B. Pedersen, N. Sartorius, & A. J. Marsella (Eds.), *Mental health services: The cross-cultural context* (pp. 199–220). Beverly Hills: Sage.

Tronick, E. Z., Morelli, G. A., & Ivey, P. K. (1992). The Efe forager infant and toddler's pattern of social relationships: Multiple and simultaneous. *Developmental Psychology, 28*, 568–577.

Trottier, K., Recknow, J., & Ferraro, F. R. (2013). Dementia. In K. D. Keith (Ed.), *The encyclopedia of cross-cultural psychology* (pp. 379–383). Hoboken, NJ: Wiley-Blackwell.

Trudge, J. R. H., Mokrova, I., Hatfield, B. E., & Karnik, R. B. (2009). Uses and misuses of Bronfenbrenner's ecocultural theory of human development. *Journal of Family Theory and Review, 1*, 198–210.

Turiel, E. (2004). Commentary: Beyond individualism and collectivism: A problem or progress? *New Directions in Child and Adolescent Development, 104*, 91–100.

Tylor, E. B. (1871). *Primitive culture* (2 vols.). London: Murray.

Tzuriel, D. (1992). The development of ego identity at adolescence among Israeli Jews and Arabs. *Journal of Youth and Adolescence, 21*, 551–571.

Ungar, M. (2002). A deeper, more social, ecological social work practice. *Social Service Review, 76*(3), 480–497.

United Nations Children's Fund (UNICEF). (2001). *Progress since the world summit for children—A statistical review.* New York: United Nations Publications.

United Nations Children's Fund (UNICEF). (2003). *The state of the world's children, 2003.* New York: United Nations Publications.

United Nations Children's Fund (UNICEF). (2009). *The state of the world's children, 2009.* New York: United Nations Publications.

United Nations Children's Fund (UNICEF). (2012). *The state of the world's children, 2012.* New York: United Nations Publications.

United Nations Children's Fund (UNICEF). (2015). *The state of the world's children, 2015.* New York: United Nations Publications.

United Nations Educational, Scientific and Cultural Organization (UNESCO). (2002). *UNESCO universal declaration on cultural diversity*. Retrieved from http://unesdoc.unesco.org/images/0012/001271/127162e.pdf

United States Census Bureau. (2001). *Household and family statistics: 2000*. Washington, DC: Author. Retrieved from https://www.census.gov/prod/2001pubs/c2kbr01-8.pdf

University of Iowa Health Sciences. (2009, February 14). Education and money attract a mate; chastity sinks in importance. *ScienceDaily*. Retrieved from www.sciencedaily.com/releases/2009/02/090205182737.html

Uzgiris, I. C., & Raeff, C. (1995). Play in parent–child interactions. In M. H. Bornstein (Ed.), *Handbook of parenting, Volume 4: Social conditions and applied parenting* (pp. 221–242). Mahwah, NJ: Erlbaum.

Valdez, A. (2009). *Mexican American girls and gang violence: Beyond risk*. New York: Palgrave Macmillan.

Van Acker, J., Oostrom, B., Rath, B., & de Kemp, R. (1999). Street children in Nairobi: Hakuna Matata? *Journal of Community Psychology, 27*, 393–404.

Van den Heuvel, H., Tellegen, G., & Koomen, W. (1992). Cultural differences in the use of psychological and social characteristics in children's self-understanding. *European Journal of Social Psychology, 22*, 353–362.

Van der Geest, S. (2004). Dying peacefully: Considering good death and bad death in Kwahu-Tafo, Ghana. *Social Science and Medicine, 58*, 899–911.

van de Vijver, F. J. R. (2001). The evolution of cross-cultural research methods. In D. Matsumoto (Ed.), *The handbook of culture and psychology* (pp. 77–97). New York: Oxford University Press.

van de Vijver, F. J. R., & Brouwers, S. A. (2009). Schooling and basic aspects of intelligence: A natural quasi-experiment in Malawi. *Journal of Applied Developmental Psychology, 30*(2), 67–74.

van de Vijver, F. J. R., Chasiotis, A., & Breugelmans, S. M. (2011). *Fundamental questions in cross-cultural psychology*. Cambridge, UK: Cambridge University Press.

van de Vijver, F. J. R., & Leung, K. (2000). Methodological issues in psychological research on culture. *Journal of Cross-Cultural Psychology, 31*, 33–51.

Van Ijzendoorn, M. H., & Sagi, A. (2008). Cross-cultural patterns of attachment: Universal and contextual dimensions. In J. Cassidy & P. R. Shaver (Eds.), *Handbook of attachment: Theory, research, and clinical applications* (2nd ed., pp. 713–734). New York: Guilford Press.

Veale, A. (1992). Toward a conceptualization of street children: The case from Sudan and Ireland. *Troaire Developmental Review* (Dublin), 107–128.

Viberg, O., & Gronlund, A, (2013). Cross-cultural analysis of users' attitudes toward the use of mobile devices in second and foreign language learning in higher education: A case from Sweden and China. *Computers and Education, 69*, 169–180.

Visano, L. (1990). The socialization of street children: The development and transformation of identities. *Sociological Studies of Child Development, 3*, 139–161.

Vondra, J., & Belsky, J. (1993). Developmental origins of parenting: Personality and relationship factors. In T. Luster & L.

Okagaki (Eds.), *Parenting: An ecological perspective* (pp. 1–33). Hillsdale, NJ: Erlbaum.

Vozzolo, E. (2014). *Moral development: Theory and applications*. New York: Routledge.

Vygotsky, L. (1968). *Thought and language* (Rev. ed.). Boston: MIT Press.

Vygotsky, L. S. (1978). *Mind in society: The development of higher psychological processes*. Cambridge, MA: Harvard University Press.

Wachs, T. D. (2000a). *Necessary but not sufficient: The respective roles of single and multiple influences of individual development*. Washington, DC: American Psychological Association.

Wachs, T. D. (2000b). Linking nutrition and temperament. In V. J. Molfese & D. L. Molfese (Eds.), *Temperament and personality development across the life span* (pp. 57–84). Mahwah, NJ: Erlbaum.

Wainryb, C. (2006). Moral development in culture: Diversity, tolerance, and justice. In M. Killen & J. G. Smetana (Eds.), *Handbook of moral development* (pp. 211–240). Mahwah, NJ: Erlbaum.

Walker, J. (2014). The transition to parenthood: Choices and responsibilities. In A. Abela & J. Walker (Eds.), *Contemporary issues in family studies: Global perspectives on partnerships, parenting, and support in a changing world* (pp. 119–135). Oxford, UK: Wiley & Sons.

Walter, T. (2003). Historical and cultural variants on the good death. *British Medical Journal, 327*, 218–220.

Watanabe, Y. (1986). Distributive justice development. *Japanese Journal of Educational Psychology, 34*, 84–90.

Waters, E., & Cummings, E. M. (2000). A secure base from which to explore the environment. *Child Development, 71*, 164–172.

Watkins, D., & Dhawan, N. (1989). Do we need to distinguish the constructs of self-concept and self-esteem? *Journal of Social Behavior and Personality, 4*, 555–562.

Watson, J. L., & Caldwell, M. L. (Eds.). (2005). *The cultural politics of food and eating*. Oxford, UK: Wiley-Blackwell.

Watters, E. (2010). *Crazy like us: The globalization of the American psyche*. New York: Free Press.

Wechsler, D. (2003). *Wechsler Intelligence Scale for Children - Fourth Edition (WISC-IV)*. San Antonio, TX: The Psychological Corporation.

Wei, M., Russell, D. W., Mallinckrod, B., & Zakalik, R. A. (2004). Cultural equivalence of adult attachment across four ethnic groups: Factor structure, structured means, and associations with negative mood. *Journal of Counseling Psychology, 51*, 408–417.

Weiner, I. B., & Craighead, W. W. (2010). *The Corsini encyclopedia of psychology* (4 vols.). New York: Wiley.

Weinfield, N., Sroufe, L. A., & Egeland, B. (2000). Attachment from infancy to early adulthood in a high-risk sample: Continuity, discontinuity, and their correlates. *Child Development, 71*, 695–702.

Weisner, T. S. (2002). Ecocultural understanding of children's developmental pathways. *Human Development, 45*, 272–281.

Weisner, T. S. (2010). John and Beatrice Whiting's contributions to the cross-cultural study of human development: Their values, goals, norms, and practices. *Journal of Cross-Cultural Psychology, 41*(4), 499–509. doi:10.1177/0022022110362720

Werker, J. F., & Hensch, T. K. (2015). Critical periods in speech perception: New directions. *Annual Review of Psychology, 66*, 173–196.

Werner, E. E. (1979). *Cross-cultural child development.* Belmont, CA: Wadsworth.

Werner, E. E. (1989). Children of the garden island. *Scientific American, 260*, 101–111.

Whitbourne, S. K., Sneed, J. R., & Skultety, K. M. (2002). Identity processes in adulthood: Theoretical and methodological challenges. *Identity, 2*, 29–45.

White, M. (1993). *The material child: Coming of age in Japan and America.* New York: Free Press.

Whiting, B. B. (1963). *Six cultures: Studies of child rearing.* Cambridge, MA: Harvard University Press.

Whiting, B. B., & Edwards, C. P. (1988). *Children of different worlds: The formation of social behavior.* Cambridge, MA: Harvard University Press.

Whiting, B. B., & Whiting, J. W. M. (1975). *Children of six cultures: A psycho-cultural analysis.* Cambridge, MA: Harvard University Press.

Whorf, B. L. (1956). *Language, thought and reality.* Cambridge, MA: MIT Press.

Williams, J., & Best, D. (1990). *Sex and psyche: Gender and self viewed cross-culturally.* Newbury Park, CA: Sage.

Williams, J., Satterwhite, R. C., & Best, D. L. (1999). Pan-cultural gender stereotypes re-visited: The five-factor model. *Sex Roles, 40*, 513–525.

Williams, W. M., & Sternberg, R. J. (2001). How parents can maximize children's cognitive abilities. In M. H. Bornstein (Ed.), *Handbook of parenting* (2nd ed., Vol. 5, pp. 169–194). Mahwah, NJ: Erlbaum.

Wink, J., & Putney, L. G. (2001). *A vision of Vygotsky.* Boston: Allyn & Bacon.

Wolf, A. P. (1978). *Studies in Chinese society.* Stanford, CA: Stanford University Press.

Wolf, M. (1972). *Women and the family in rural Taiwan.* Stanford, CA: Stanford University Press.

Wolfe, W. S., Campbell, C. C., Frongillo, E. A., Haas, J. D., & Melnik, T. A. (1994). Overweight schoolchildren in New York state: Prevalence and characteristics. *American Journal of Public Health, 84*, 807–813.

Wong, S. J. (2013). Gender. In K. D. Keith (Ed.), *The encyclopedia of cross-cultural psychology* (pp. 586–589). Hoboken, NJ: Wiley-Blackwell.

Wong, S. J. (2013). Gender. Woodward, J. (2004). Attachment theory and ageing. In M. Green & M. Scholes (Eds.), *Attachment and human survival* (pp. 53–70). London: Karnac Books.

World Health Organization (WHO). (1979). *Schizophrenia: An international follow-up study.* New York: Wiley.

World Health Organization (WHO). (1983). *Depressive disorders in different cultures: Report of the WHO collaborative study of standardized assessment of depressive disorders.* Geneva: Author.

World Health Organization (WHO). (2008). *Female genital mutilation.* Fact Sheet 241. Geneva: Author.

World Health Organization (WHO). (2010). *Female genital mutilation.* Geneva: Author.

World Health Organization (WHO). (2011). *Sexually transmitted infections.* Retrieved from http://www.who.int/mediacentre/factsheets/fs110/en/index.html

World Health Organization (WHO). (2012). *Dementia: A public health priority.* Geneva: Author.

World Health Organization (WHO). (2016, June). *Obesity and overweight.* Fact Sheet 311. Retrieved from http://www.who.int/mediacentre/factsheets/fs311/en/

Worthman, C. M. (1994). Developmental microniche: A concept for modeling relationships of biology, behavior, and culture in development. *American Journal of Physical Anthropology, 18*(Suppl.), 210.

Worthman, C. M. (1995). Biocultural bases of human variation. *ISSBD Newsletter, 27*(1), 10–13.

Wylie, L. (1974). *Village in the Vaucluse* (3rd ed.). Cambridge, MA: Harvard University Press.

Yamada, T., Kadekaru, H., Matsumoto, S., Inada, H., Tanabe, M., Moriguchi, E. H., et al. (2002). Prevalence of dementia in the older Japanese-Brazilian population. *Psychiatry and Clinical Neuroscience, 56*, 71–75.

Yamaguchi, S. (2004). Further clarifications of the concept of *amae* in relation to dependence and attachment. *Human Development, 47*(January–February), 28–33.

Yang, C. K., & Hahn, H. M. (2002). Cosleeping in young Korean children. *Journal of Developmental Behavioral Pediatrics, 23*, 151–157.

Yang, J.-A. (1999). An exploratory study of Korean fathering of adolescent children. *Journal of Genetic Psychology, 160*, 55–68.

Yi, S. H. (1993). Transformation of child socialization in Korean culture. *Early Childhood Development, 85*, 17–24.

Ying, Y., & Liese, L. (1990). Initial adaptation of Taiwan foreign students to the U.S: The impact of prearrival variables. *American Journal of Community Psychology, 18*, 825–845.

Yodanis, C. (2005). Divorce culture and marital gender equality: A cross-national study. *Gender and Society, 19*, 644–659.

Zarit, S. H., & Eggebeen, D. J. (1995). Parent–child relationships in adulthood and old age. In M. H. Bornstein (Ed.), *Handbook of parenting* (Vol. 1, pp. 119–140). Hillsdale, NJ: Erlbaum.

Zarit, S. H., & Eggebeen, D. J. (2002). Parent–child relationships in adulthood and later years. In M. H. Bornstein (Ed.), *Handbook of parenting* (2nd ed., Vol. 1, pp. 135–161). Mahwah, NJ: Erlbaum.

Zavershneva, E. (2002). The Vygotsky family archive: New findings. *Journal of Russian and East European Psychology, 48*(1), 34–60.

Zhang, Y., Proenca, R., Maffel, M., Barone, M., Leopold, L., & Friedman, J. M. (1994). Positional cloning of the mouse obese gene and its human homologue. *Nature, 372*(6505), 425–432.

Zook, J. M., Chapman, B., Wang, J., Mittelman, D., Hofmann, O., Hide, W., et al. (2014). Integrating human sequence data sets provides a resource of benchmark SNP and indel genotype calls. *Nature Biotechnology, 32*, 246–251. doi:10.1038/nbt.2835

Zwolinski, J. (2013). Aggression. In K. D. Keith (Ed.), *The encyclopedia of cross-cultural psychology* (pp. 34–38). Hoboken, NJ: Wiley-Blackwell.

# Further Readings

## Chapter 1

Dave Barry. (1993). *Dave Barry Does Japan* [Reissue]. New York: Random House.

An irreverent view of Japanese culture by one of America's premiere humorists. Witty and sometimes insightful. Contains discussion of such topics as "Failing to Learn Japanese in Only Five Minutes (Very much good morning, Sir)," "Lost in Tokyo (Looking for plastic squid)," and "Humor in Japan (Take my tofu! Please!)."

Michael Brannigan. (Ed.). (2004). *Cross-Cultural Biotechnology*. Plymouth, UK: Rowman & Littlefield.

Fifteen essays from international academics and practitioners address a broad range of legal, ethical, and social issues in biotechnology, underscoring the relevance of cultural values. Topics include the International Human Genome Project and research ethics in East Asia.

Shaun Gallager. (2013). *Experimenting with Babies: 50 Amazing Science Projects You Can Perform On Your Kid*. New York: Perigree.

Innovative hands-on guide to activities for curious parents based on scientific research with hypotheses, instructions, and illustrations to encourage motor, language, behavioral, and cognitive development. Interesting to all readers.

Ariel Heryanto. (2008). *Popular Culture in Indonesia*. Oxford, UK: Routledge.

An examination of popular culture in Indonesia, the most populous Muslim nation and the third largest democracy in the world. It shows how the "multilayered and contradictory" processes of identity formation are linked to popular culture. A significant addition to the literature on Asian popular culture.

Richard Lerner. (2015). *Handbook of Child Psychology and Developmental Science* (7th ed.). New York: Wiley.

The definitive guide to the field of developmental science, with four volumes, and now in its seventh edition. It is available in book, e-book, and electronic reference form. It will be useful reading for those interested in psychology, anthropology, sociology, and neuroscience.

Walter Lonner. (2013). Chronological Benchmarks in Cross-Cultural Psychology. Foreword to the Encyclopedia of Cross-Cultural Psychology. *Online Readings in Psychology and Culture*, 1(2). Available at http://dx.doi.org/10.9707/2307-0919.1124.

Lonner, a leader in cross-cultural psychology, provides a chronological perspective on the significant events and developments that have contributed to the current status of the field.

Terri Morrison & Wayne A. Conaway. (2006*). Kiss, Bow, or Shake Hands* (2nd ed.). Avon, MA: Adams Media.

Updated and expanded guide to international behaviors. Most useful for business travelers, but also of value for tourists and travelers or anyone living or interacting with a culture other than their own. Very informative.

James Shreeve. (2006). *The Greatest Journey. National Geographic*, 209(3), 60–73.

A very readable account of genes, DNA, migration, and the origins of modern human life and culture.

The Human Genome Project. For an overview of the project, see https://www.genome.gov/12011238/an-overview-of-the-human-genome-project/.

Visit this website for information about this project—its history, research, publications, educational resources, and new programs based on data and resources from The Human Genome Project, The Microbial Project, and systems biology.

## Chapter 2

Urie Bronfenbrenner. (2005). *Making Human Beings Human: Bioecological Perspectives on Human Development*. Thousand Oaks, CA: Sage.

The culminating work by the author, consisting of twenty-three articles written over six decades that describe the historical development of his groundbreaking model. Contains recommendations for future research and applications for the design of social programs and policies for promoting positive development of children and families throughout the world.

Douglas Raybeck. (1996). *Mad Dogs, Englishmen, and the Errant Anthropologist: Fieldwork in Malaysia*. Prospect Heights, IL: Waveland Press.

A lively account of the author's adventures and misadventures while doing fieldwork, with vivid descriptions of Kelantanese society and culture, kinship, linguistics, and gender relations. Provides a real sense of how an anthropologist conducts and gathers reliable information in cultural settings where often "things go awry."

Susan Goldstein. (2000). *Cross-Cultural Explorations: Activities in Culture and Psychology*. Boston: Allyn & Bacon.

This book contains nine chapters with ten activities each revolving around case studies, self-administered scales, mini-experiments, and a collection of content-analytic, observational, and interview data allowing "hands-on" experience. Of particular interest is a chapter on "Culture and Psychological Research" that explores major issues and techniques in the conduct of cross-cultural research.

Walter J. Lonner & Roy Malpass. (1994). *Psychology and Culture*. Boston: Allyn & Bacon.

Each of the forty-three short (five- to six-page), easy-to-read chapters on various aspects of cross-cultural psychology provides personal insights into the ways in which the authors carried out their research, often with revealing comments on the mistakes they made.

F. J. R. van de Vijver. (2000). Types of Cross-Cultural Studies in Cross-Cultural Psychology. In W. J. Lonner, D. L. Dinnel, S. A. Hayes, & D. N. Sattler (Eds.), *Online Readings in Psychology and*

*Culture* (Unit 11, Chapter 2). Bellingham: Center for Cross-Cultural Research, Western Washington University. Available at www.wwu.edu/culture/Chen_Farruggia.htm.

This easily accessible online article classifies cross-cultural studies along three dimensions and provides examples and illustrations of cross-cultural methodology.

Gita L. Vygodskaya. His Life [Translated from Russian]. *School Psychology International, 16.* Available at http://webpages.charter.net/schmolze1/vygotsky/gita.html.

In this unique article, Lev Vygotsky's daughter provides a view of her father as a person and psychologist and, in so doing, helps provide a context for understanding his thinking and the development of his theory. Most unusual, but extremely interesting.

## Chapter 3

Naomi Baumslag & Dia L. Michels. (2008). *Milk, Money, and Madness: The Culture and Politics of Breastfeeding.* Santa Barbara, CA: Praeger.

The authors convincingly present the medical, cultural, psychological, and economic benefits of breastfeeding to mothers, infants, and the general population. A fascinating, informative, and highly readable book.

Jude Cassidy & Philip R. Shaver (Eds.). (2008). *Handbook of Attachment* (2nd ed.). New York: Guilford Press.

Cutting-edge theory and research findings on attachment across a wide range of ages and contexts. An indispensable guide for understanding this crucial developmental process.

Joan E. Grusec & Paul D. Hastings (Eds.). (2006). *Handbook of Socialization.* New York: Guilford Press.

Almost all you want to know about socialization, including historical and methodological perspectives; its effects across the lifespan (within and outside the family); and relationship to gender, cognition, emotional competence, and prosocial development.

John Loughery. (1995). *Into the Widening World: International Coming-of-Age Stories.* New York: Persea Books.

An edited anthology of twenty-six short stories from twenty-two countries focusing on the adolescent experience and emergence of adulthood. Visit the sun-baked alleys of Cairo, the terrifying forests of war-time Nigeria, a hidden grove in Jamaica, a turkey farm in Canada, and a young woman facing an arranged marriage in Malaysia. Fascinating, insightful, and informative reading.

James J. McKenna. (2012). *Sleeping with Your Baby: A Parent's Guide to Cosleeping.* Washington, DC: Platypus Media. Also see http://cosleeping.nd.edu/.

Trusted advice from the world's foremost authority on sleeping with your baby, based on scientific studies spanning more than twenty-five years.

Dennis O'Neil. (n.d.). *Cultural Anthropology Tutorials.* Available at http://anthro.palomar.edu/tutorials/cultural.htm.

This website offers tutorials on a variety of topics related to socialization, including culture, language, social control, culture change, social and political organization, and processes of socialization.

Barbara Rogoff. (2011). *Developing Destinies: A Mayan Midwife and Town.* New York: Oxford University Press.

An engaging story of a Mayan sacred midwife, Chona Perezof, who in her eighty-five years has successfully blended traditional cultural practices with new approaches to preserve and extend cultural heritage. Provides extensive photographs and accounts of Mayan family life, medical practices, birth, child development, and learning. Interesting reading.

InCultureParent. Available at www.incultureparent.com/about.

An online magazine for parents raising "little global citizens." Features articles on language, tradition, culture, and parenting around the world, including raising multilingual and multicultural children. Its stated goal is to "foster greater understanding across cultures through the lens of parenting." A wide variety of interesting articles.

## Chapter 4

Patricia Crawford & Sharika Bhattacharya. (2014). Grand Images: Exploring Images of Grandparents in Picture Books. *Journal of Research in Childhood Education, 28*(1), 128–144.

Interesting examination of 220 children's picture books published over a twenty-year period as sources of socialization messages, cultural diversity, and depictions of aging, employment, hobbies, and child custody arrangements.

Robbie E. Davis-Floyd & Carolyn F. Sargent (Eds.). (1997). *Childbirth and Authoritative Knowledge: Cross-Cultural Perspectives.* Berkeley, CA: University of California Press.

This interdisciplinary book extends the work of Brigitte Jordan on the ecology of birth. In a series of essays, authors present first-hand ethnographic research findings on reproduction and childbirth in sixteen different societies and cultures.

Nicholas Day. (2013). *Baby Meets World: Suck, Smile, Touch, Toddle: A Journey Through Infancy.* New York: St. Martin's Press.

Organized around activities that dominate the early days of an infant's life, yet seen from a variety of perspectives—personal, cross-cultural, historical, and scientific—this book provides a fresh (and often humorous) view of parents and infants.

Raeann R. Hamon & Bron B. Ingoldsby (Eds.). (2003). *Mate Selection Across Cultures.* Thousand Oaks, CA: Sage.

An exploration of mate selection in Ecuador, Trinidad, Ghana, Egypt, Turkey, Spain, and more, with chapters authored by experts in each country. Chapters include case studies, vignettes, photographs of courtship and wedding traditions, and original research and methodologies used by contributing authors. Lively and interesting for student readers and others.

Arthur Kornhaber. (2004). *The Grandparent Solution: How Parents Can Build a Family Team for Practical, Emotional, and Financial Success.* San Francisco, CA: Jossey-Bass.

This groundbreaking book, based on more than thirty years of research, gives families the tools needed for grandparents to offer support for their children while finding the appropriate degree of involvement with grandchildren.

Robert Levine, Suguru Sato, Tsukasa Hashimoto, & Jyoti Verma. (1995). Love and Marriage in Eleven Cultures. *Journal of Cross-Cultural Psychology, 26,* 554–571.

What kinds of views do college students have on the topics of love and marriage? This study reports on students from India,

Pakistan, Thailand, Mexico, Brazil, Japan, Hong Kong, the Philippines, Australia, England, and the United States.

Tom Luster & Lynn Okagaki (Eds.). (2005). *Parenting: An Ecological Perspective* (2nd ed.). Mahwah, NJ: Erlbaum.

This book, centering on Bronfenbrenner's model, summarizes the latest research findings on parenting. Includes ecological perspectives on developmental origins of parenting, roles of mothers and fathers, marital relationships, social networks, socioeconomic status and ethnicity, and parental socialization of children's behaviors.

*GrandFamilies: The Contemporary Journal of Research, Practice and Policy.* Available at http://scholarworks.wmich.edu/grandfamilies/.

This online journal is dedicated to topics related to grandparents raising grandchildren. It provides a forum for quality, evidence-based research with sound scholarship, knowledge, skills, and best practices from the field for scholars, clinicians, policymakers, educators, program administrators, and family advocates.

David W. Shwalb & Barbara J. Shwalb. (2014). Fatherhood in Brazil, Bangladesh, Russia, Japan, and Australia. *Online Readings in Psychology and Culture, 6*(3). Available at http://dx.doi.org/10.9707/2307-0919.1125.

The authors demonstrate and illustrate that fatherhood, fathering, and fathers differ according to eight types of contextual influence, including geographical location, family characteristics, ethnic grouping, and so on. However, they conclude that overgeneralizations are dangerous. They conclude that there are boundless opportunities for future research in this area.

David W. Shwalb, Barbara J. Shwalb, & M. E. Lamb (Eds.). (2013). *Fathers in Cultural Context.* New York: Routledge.

International experts discuss the latest research on fathering from every continent and cultures representing more than half the world's population. Contains personal stories, maps, and photos to create an engaging view of each culture. References more than 1,000 studies on fathering.

## Chapter 5

J. Altarriba. (2002). Bilingualism: Language, Memory, and Applied Issues. *Online Readings in Psychology and Culture, 4*(2). Available at http://dx.doi.org/10.9707/2307-0919.1034.

Bilingualism, or the knowledge of more than one language, is prevalent throughout the world; however, much of the cognitive literature on language processing and memory retrieval has included participants who are monolingual speakers. This online chapter introduces the ways in which bilingualism has been investigated in the areas of autobiographical memory, memory recall, and communication in applied settings, and offers suggestions for further research.

Roberta M. Golinikoff, Kathy Hirsh-Pasek, & Diane Eyer. (2004). *Einstein Never Used Flashcards: How Our Children Really Learn—And Why They Really Need to Play More and Memorize Less.* Emmaus, PA: Rodale Books.

Authors and child psychologists address key areas of development, including language, social skills, math, reading, and self-awareness, explaining the learning process from a child's point of view. Provides forty age-appropriate games for

creative play, better than today's high-tech and expensive gadgets and toys.

Sandra G. Kouritzin. (1999). *Face(t)s of First Language Loss.* Mahwah, NJ: Erlbaum.

This book contributes to the understanding of first language loss in both immigrant and indigenous communities by providing insight into the process and the factors contributing to it; defining from an insider perspective what it means to "lose" a language; and analyzing the perceived consequences of first language loss in terms of social, academic, emotional, and economic factors. Five different storytellers relate the histories of their first language while learning English.

John Korte. (1995). *White Gloves: How We Create Ourselves Through Memory.* New York: Free Press.

Drawing on research on cognition and clinical psychology, the author, in an intriguing, readable, and jargonfree manner, illustrates the nature of memory from childhood to old age, including first memories, photographic memories, memories of dreams, and repressed memory.

Barbara Rogoff. (1990). *Apprenticeship in Thinking.* New York: Oxford University Press.

This book overflows with examples of parents leading their children through rough and calm cognitive seas to new levels of thinking. Illustrations of daily activities performed in scores of cultures fill almost every page of this book, which was written by one of the most prominent proponents of the cultural context perspective.

## Chapter 6

A. Timothy Church & Marcia S. Katigbak. (2002). Studying Personality Traits Across Cultures: Philippine Examples. *Online Readings in Psychology and Culture, 4*(4). Available at http://dx.doi.org/10.9707/2307-0919.1039.

This online chapter reviews the questions addressed by researchers who study personality traits across cultures, including whether traits are used in all cultures to understand persons and their behavior, the universality versus culture-specific traits, the validity of imported and indigenous measures of personality traits, and the meaningfulness of trait comparisons across cultures. Evidence relevant to these questions is summarized for one collectivistic culture—the Philippines.

Sigmund Freud. (1961). *Civilization and Its Discontents* (Vol. 21). London: Hogarth.

One of the most important writings on the interaction between personality and culture by one of the most creative and influential contributors to the field of psychology.

Robert R. McCrae. (2002). Cross-Cultural Research on the Five-Factor Model of Personality. *Online Readings in Psychology and Culture, 4*(4). Available at http://dx.doi.org/10.9707/2307-0919.1038.

An online chapter discussing the Five-Factor Model, its use across cultures, and some recent research findings.

The Big Five Personality Test. Available at http://www.outofservice.com/bigfive/.

If you are interested in learning more about the Big Five personality traits mentioned in this chapter, then you can take a free, anonymous, online test that will help you understand the traits as they relate to your personality www.outofservice.com/bigfive/.

Mary K. Rothbart. (2011). *Becoming Who We Are: Temperament and Personality in Development*. New York: Guilford Press.

A comprehensive examination of the role temperament plays in the development of personality and psychopathology across the lifespan. Written in direct and readable style, the book also reviews childhood intervention programs.

Nancy L. Segal. (2012). *Born Together—Reared Apart: The Landmark Minnesota Twin Study*. Boston: Harvard University Press.

The much-anticipated original study of the identical "Jim twins" separated at birth, raised in different families, and united at age thirty-nine only to discover a multitude of shared physical, psychological, and personal characteristics. Extremely interesting and informative read.

## Chapter 7

Cheryl Bentsen. (1989). *Masai Days*. New York: Anchor Books.

The author provides a close-up look at this traditional African culture. This book is not so much a scholarly account as an informative and lively view of Masai everyday life. Among other things, the reader learns about the concerns of two young boys torn between traditional and modern ways, young adult women and their social network, and young men who take great pride in their role as warriors.

Emily Brazelon. (2014). *Sticks and Stones: Beating the Culture of Bullying and Rediscovering the Power of Character and Empathy*. New York: Random House.

A groundbreaking, enlightening, and deeply researched book that takes the reader from cafeterias to courtrooms to Facebook, defining what bullying is and is not. Perceptive, accessible, and much needed.

Sandra L. Calvert & Barbara J. Wilson (Eds.). (2012). *The Handbook of Children, Media, and Development*. Hoboken, NJ: Wiley-Blackwell.

Up-to-the-moment research by an interdisciplinary group of experts analyzing the impact contemporary media are having on social interactions, learning, and healthy development of today's children. Impressive and thought provoking.

Carol Gilligan. (1998). *In a Different Voice: Psychological Theory and Women's Development*. Boston: Harvard University Press.

Gilligan's seminal work demonstrating that women speak in a different voice than men due to societal and cultural expectations and influences.

Carol Gilligan. (2013). *Joining the Resistance*. Boston: Polity.

Gilligan reflects on her evolution in thinking and presents her latest ideas on gender and human development.

Gert Jan Hofstede, Paul B. Pedersen, & Geert Hofstede. (2002). *Exploring Culture: Exercises, Stories, and Synthetic Cultures*. Boston: Intercultural Press.

A guidebook to Hofstede's five dimensions of culture, providing more than seventy-five exercises, stories, dialogues, and simulations that make them easy to remember and understand for educators, trainers, and students.

Robert Kaminski & Judy Sierra. (1995). *Children's Traditional Games: Games from 137 Countries and Cultures*. Phoenix, OH: Oryx Press.

The authors provide practical educational activities based on folk games from more than 130 countries and cultures. Although the book is designed mainly as a practical reference book for teachers, it also discusses the function of games in childhood development and their cultural importance, the types of games found around the world, and the rationale for using folk games in the classroom.

Robert V. Levine. (2003). Measuring Helping Behaviors Across Cultures. *Online Readings in Psychology and Culture*, 5(3). Available at http://dx.doi.org/10.9707/2307-0919.1049.

This online chapter focuses on some of the special challenges and difficulties in conducting cross-cultural research, including a series of studies in which helpfulness toward strangers was assessed in thirty-six cities across the United States and twenty-three large cities around the world. Situations included seeing whether passersby would alert a pedestrian who dropped a pen, offer to help a pedestrian with a hurt leg, and assist a blind person to cross the street.

Robert R. Sands (Ed.). (1999). *Anthropology, Sport, and Culture*. Westport, CT: Bergin & Garvey.

This unique collection of research on culture and sport discusses issues such as ethnicity, identity, ritual, and culture change, as well as the effect of environment and genes. The book illustrates the importance of studying sport as a universal phenomenon that both shapes, and is shaped by, its cultural context.

Elizabeth Vozzola. (2014). *Moral Development: Theory and Applications*. New York: Routledge.

Comprehensive and readable review of classic and contemporary theories of moral development with applications and examples that help apply theory to real-world situations.

## Chapter 8

Nicholas M. Teich. (2012). *Transgender 101: A Simple Guide to a Complex Issue*. New York: Columbia University Press.

A book that brings clarity and understanding to the range of issues faced by of transgendered individuals, their friends, family, and society. Conversational in tone, easy to read, educational, and entertaining at the same time.

Caroline B. Brettell & Carolyn F. Sargent. (2004). *Gender in Cross-Cultural Perspective* (4th ed.). New York: Prentice Hall.

This reader introduces learners to the most significant topics in the field of gender—drawing from classic sources, as well as from the most recent, diverse literature on gender roles and ideology around the world. It features broad geographical coverage and the most current research available. An extensive range of topics.

John Colapinto. (2000). *As Nature Made Him: The Boy Who Was Raised as a Girl*. New York: HarperCollins.

The story of a couple who arranged for one of their twin sons to undergo sex reassignment. The case, initially proclaimed a success, was considered a landmark in explaining the shaping of human sexual identity. However, thirty years later, the subject tells of his participation in an experiment in psychosexual engineering gone wrong. When informed of his medical history, at age fourteen, the subject decided to live as a male and shares his eventual triumph in asserting his sense of self against his medically and surgically imposed identity. Fascinating reading.

Joanne Eicher & Lisa Ling. (2005). *Mother, Daughter, Sister, Bride: Rituals of Womanhood*. Washington, DC: National Geographic Society.

This book celebrates the defining connections among women and honors their differences—from Quinceañera parties commemorating a Hispanic girl turning fifteen, to prewedding henna ceremonies in the Middle East, to American traditions such as the debutante ball, and to the coming-of-age rituals of Mende girls in Sierra Leone. Illustrated with photographs from the National Geographic archives. A fascinating look at the historical, cultural, emotional, and personal impact of women's rituals and ritual practices.

Paige Lucas-Stannard. (2013). *Gender Neutral Parenting*. Dallas, TX: Verity Press.

This book suggests parents should allow children a variety of behavioral choices, let them explore and make decisions, and provide strategies for supporting them in a world of changing stereotypes.

David P. Schmidt. (2002). Are Sexual Promiscuity and Relationship Infidelity Linked to Different Personality Traits Across Cultures? Findings from the International Sexuality Description Project. *Online Readings in Psychology and Culture, 4*(4). Available at http://dx.doi.org/10.9707/2307-0919.1041.

More than 17,000 participants responded to self-reported measures of sexuality and personality. Analyses across fifty-eight cultures from fifty-two nations revealed that romantic relationship infidelity was significantly associated with disagreeableness and low levels of conscientiousness across most cultures. Sexual promiscuity was related to extraversion across many, but not most, cultural regions. Discussion questions focus on patterns of findings and why regional differences in sexuality–personality linkages seem to exist.

Suzzane LaFont. (2002). *Constructing Sexualities: Readings in Sexuality, Gender, and Culture*. New York: Prentice Hall.

This collection introduces readers to a broad range of ideas and theories and encourages critical thinking about the relationships among sexuality, gender, and culture. The readings include descriptions of variations in sexual and gender ideologies, expressions of sexuality, gender diversity, and global issues. Gay rights, transgendered movements, female genital mutilation, male circumcision, AIDS, sex tourism, and other current issues are addressed.

## Chapter 9

Centers for Disease Control and Prevention (CDC). (2013). The State of Aging and Health in America 2013. Atlanta: CDC, U.S. Department of Health and Human Services. Available at http://www.cdc.gov/aging/pdf/state-aging-health-in-america-2013.pdf.

Most recent CDC data on key indicators of health, well-being, and mental health among America's elderly.

Shahé S. Kazarian & David R. Evans. (Eds.). (2001). *Handbook of Cultural Health Psychology*. San Diego, CA: Academic Press.

This collection provides a state-of-the-art understanding of what is known and not known about the rapidly emerging field

of cultural health psychology. The editors take a multicultural approach, providing a diversity of perspectives by acknowledged experts on a wide range of crucial topics. Case studies are well designed and helpful in highlighting the major concepts within the chapters.

David B. Morris. (1998). *Illness and Culture in the Postmodern Age*. Berkeley, CA: University of California Press.

In a narrative account, the author follows the concept of health and illness through modern history into the late twentieth century, providing a context for talk about health and illness, medicine, and suffering. Anyone who wants to understand why people get sick differently in different cultures and what's making us sick here and now will enjoy this book.

Renee Rose Shield & Stanley M. Aronson. (2003). *Aging in Today's World: Conversations Between an Anthropologist and a Physician*. New York: Berghahn Books.

In a unique approach, each author explores a different aspect of aging in alternating chapters, in turn followed by a commentary by the other. The authors interrupt each other within chapters to raise questions, contradict, ask for clarification, and explore related ideas—emphasizing the dynamic nature of their ideas about age. Finally, a third "voice," that of a random old man, periodically "speaks" to remind the authors of their limited understanding of the subject.

Ronald C. Simons & Charles C. Hughes. (Eds.). (1985). *The Culture-Bound Syndrome: Folk Illnesses of Psychiatric and Anthropological Interest*. Dodrecht, Netherlands: D. Reidel.

One of the best available compilations on culture-bound syndromes from many areas around the world.

Eunkook M. Suh & Shigehiro Oishi. (2002). Subjective Well-Being Across Cultures. *Online Readings in Psychology and Culture, 10*(1). Available at http://dx.doi.org/10.9707/2307-0919.1076.

This online chapter suggests that all individuals strive to be happy. How they pursue this ultimate human goal, however, seems to vary in interesting ways across cultures. Three key findings have emerged from recent scientific research: (1) individualist cultures are happier than collectivists, (2) psychological attributes characterizing the self (e.g., self-esteem, self-consistency) are more relevant to the happiness of Western individualists than to the happiness of collectivists, and (3) the self-judgment of happiness is anchored on different types of cues and experiences across cultures.

## Chapter 10

Roy D'Andrade. (2000). The Sad Story of Anthropology 1950–1999. *Cross-Cultural Research, 34*, 219–232.

The author discusses how changing political attitudes over the past fifty years have affected the field of anthropology and its effectiveness as a discipline and what directions it might take in the future.

Wolfgang Friedlmeier, Pardeep Chakkarath, & Beate Schwarz. (2005). *Culture and Human Development*. New York: Psychology Press.

This book provides an interdisciplinary approach to key developmental processes, with particular focus on theoretical and methodological issues in cross-cultural research. An invaluable source of information and very readable.

Gary S. Gregg. (2005). *The Middle East: A Cultural Psychology.* New York: Oxford University Press.

A book that provides a long overdue synthesis of psychological research on Middle Eastern and North African societies. Readers will become familiar with the lives of individuals in this critical region of the world who are attempting to resolve differences between adherence of traditional values and the attraction of Westernized lifestyles.

Heidi Keller & Patricia M. Greenfield. (2000). History and Future of Development in Cross-Cultural Psychology. *Journal of Cross-Cultural Psychology, 31,* 52–62.

It provides a view of the future of cross-cultural human development and how developmental issues and methods can be used to advance theory and research.

David Shwalb, Jun Nakazawa, & Barbara J. Shwalb (Eds.). (2005). *Applied Developmental Psychology: Theory, Practice, and Research from Japan.* Greenwich, CT: Information Age.

This book consists of sixteen chapters in which the editors and authors provide valuable insights into theories, approaches, and applications of findings in a non-Western culture that have important implications for other cultures. Not only are the presentations original, but they are also easy to read and understand.

# Credits

## Text Credits

**Chapter 1** Excerpt on p. 2 From "The Acquisition of Culture" by Theodore Schwartz in Ethos, Volume 9, Issue 1, Pages 4–17. Published by John Wiley & Sons, © 1981; Excerpt on p. 2 From "The Sociogenesis of Social Sciences: An Analysis of the Cultural Relativity of Social Psychology" by John W. Berry in The Sociogenesis of Language and Human Conduct. Published by Springer, © 1983; Excerpt on p. 2 From Handbook of Cross-Cultural Psychology, Volume 1: Theory and Method, 2e by John W. Berry (Editor), Janak Pandey (Editor), Ype H. Poortinga (Editor). Published by Allyn & Bacon, © 1997; Excerpt on p. 2 The Science of the Culture" in Primitive Culture, 2e by Edward Burnett Tylor. Published by John Murray, 1871; Excerpt on p. 2 From UNESCO Universal Declaration on Cultural Diversity. Published by UNESCO, © 2002; Excerpt on p. 3 From "Foreword" by Hiroshi Azuma in Applied Developmental Psychology: Theory, Practice, and Research from Japan by David W. Shwalb,(editor), Jun Nakazawa(editor) , Barbara J. Shwalb(editor). Published by Information Age Publishing, © 2005; Excerpt on p. 4 From "Cross-Cultural Psychology As A Scholarly Discipline: On The Flowering Of Culture" by Marshall H. Segall, Walter J. Lonner and John W. Berry in Behavioral Research, Vol 53, issue- 10, pp. 1101–1110. Published by American Psychological Association, © 1998; Excerpt on p. 4 From "Historical Perspectives: Cross-Cultural Psychology before 1960" by O. Klineberg in Handbook of Cross-cultural Psychology by Harry Charalambos Triandis. Published by Allyn and Bacon, © 1980; Excerpt on p. 4 From "History of Cross-Cultural and Cultural Psychology" by Gustav Jahoda, Brend Krewer in Handbook of Cross-Cultural Psychology: Theory and Method by John W. Berry, Ype H. Poortinga, Janak Pandey. Published by John Berry, © 1997; Excerpt on p. 4 From Psychology and Anthropology: A Psychological Perspective by Gustav Jahoda. Published by Academic Press, © 1983; Excerpt on p. 7 From Cross-Cultural Psychology: Human Behavior in Global Perspective by Marshall H. Segall. Published by Brooks/Cole Publishing Company, © 1979; Excerpt on p. 9 From "Developmental Psychology and the Neurosciences" by Sidney J.Segalowitz, Louis A. Schmidt in Handbook of Developmental Psychology by Jaan Valsiner, Kevin J Connolly. Published by Sage, © 2003; Excerpt on p. 9 From Human Genetics for the Social Sciences by Gregory Carey. Published by SAGE Publications, © 2002.

**Chapter 2** Excerpt on p. 13 From No Two Alike: Human Nature and Human Individuality by Judith Rich Harris. Published by W.W. Norton & Company, © 2006; Excerpt on p. 13 From "Environments in Developmental Perspective: Theoretical and Operational Models" by Urie Bronfenbrenner in Measuring Environment Across the Life Span: Emerging Methods and Concepts by Sarah L. Friedman, Theodore D. Wachs. Published by American Psychological Association, © 1999; Excerpt on p. 14 From American Psychologist, Vol 32, pp. 513–531. Published by American Psychological Association, © 1977; Excerpt on p. 14 From Making Human Beings Human: Bioecological Perspectives on Human Development 1e by Urie Bronfenbrenner. Published by Sage Publications, © 2005; Figure 2.1 on p. 15 Alan Gardiner © 2016. Based on data from The Ecology of Human Development by Urie Bronfenbrenner; Excerpt on p. 16 From Theories of Adolescence, 6e by Rolf Muuss. Published by McGraw-Hill Humanities, © 1996; Excerpt on p. 16 From Measuring Environment Across the Life Span: Emerging Methods and Concepts by Sarah L. Friedman, Theodore D. Wachs. Published by American Psychological Association, © 1999; Excerpt on p. 16 From Theories of Adolescence, 6e by Rolf Muuss. Published by McGraw-Hill Humanities, © 1996; Excerpt on p. 16 From Making Human Beings Human: Bioecological Perspectives on Human Development by Urie Bronfenbrenner. Published by SAGE Publications, © 2005; Excerpt on p. 17 From "Themes And Variations: Parental Ethnotheories In Seven Western Cultures" by Sara Harkness in Parenting Beliefs, Behaviors, and Parent-Child Relations: A Cross-Cultural Perspective by Kenneth H. Rubin, Ock Boon Chung. Edts. Published by Psychology Press, © 2005; Excerpt on p. 17 From "The Developmental Niche" by Charles M. Super, Sara Harkness from Psychology and Culture by W. J. Lonner & R. Malpass. Published by Allyn & Bacon, © 1994; Table 2.1 on p. 17 Harry Gardiner, Lives Across Cultures: Cross-Cultural Human Development, 6e, 9780134629445, © 2018; Excerpt on p. 18 From "Culture and Parenting" by Charles M. Super, Sara Harkness in Handbook of Parenting: Volume 2: Children and Parenting by Charles M. Super, Sara Harkness. Published by Lawrence Erlbaum, © 1995; Figure 2.2 on p. 18 Handbook of Cross-Cultural Psychology Vol 2, 2e by John W. Berry, T. S. Saraswathi, Pierre R. Dasen. Copyright © 1997, by Allyn and Bacon. Reprinted by permission of John Berry; Excerpt on p. 18 From "The Child in Context: Exploring Childhood in Somalia," paper presented by Ragnhild Dybdahl at the Twenty-Sixth International Congress of Psychology, Montreal, August 1996. Reprinted by permission; Excerpt on p. 18 From "The Developmental Niche" by Charles M. Super, Sara Harkness in Psychology and Culture by Walter J. Lonner, Roy S. Malpass. Published by Allyn and Bacon, © 1994; Excerpt on p. 20 From "The Environment as Culture in Developmental Research" by Charles M. Super, Sara Harkness in Measuring Environment Across the Life Span: Emerging Methods and Concepts by Sarah L. Friedman, Theodore D. Wachs. Published by American Psychological Association, ©1999; Excerpt on p. 20 Harry Gardiner, Lives Across Cultures: Cross-Cultural Human Development, 6e, 9780134629445, © 2018; Table 2.2 on p. 20 Harry Gardiner, Lives Across Cultures: Cross-Cultural Human Development, 6e, 9780134629445, © 2018; Excerpt on p. 21 From Human Development Theories: Windows on Culture, 1e by R. Murray Thomas. Published by Sage Publications, © 1999; Excerpt on p. 21 From "In Defense of Piaget's Theory: A Reply to 10 Common Criticisms" by Orlando Lourenso, Armando Machado in Psychological Review, Vol. 103, No.1, pp. 143–164. Published by American Psychological Association, © 1999; Excerpt on p. 22 From Human Development Theories:

Windows on Culture, 1e by R. Murray Thomas. Published by Sage Publications, © 1999; Table 2.3 on p. 23 Harry Gardiner, Lives Across Cultures: Cross-Cultural Human Development 6e,9780134629445, © 2018; Table 2.4 on p. 23 Harry Gardiner, Lives Across Cultures: Cross-Cultural Human Development, 6e, 9780134629445, © 2018; Excerpt on p. 22 From Making Human Beings Human: Bioecological Perspectives on Human Development, 1e by Urie Bronfenbrenner. Published by Sage Publications © 2005; Excerpt on p. 26 From Culture and Psychology: People Around the World, 2e by David Matsumoto. Published by Wadsworth Publishing, © 2000; Excerpt on p. 26 From "History and Future of Development in Cross-Cultural Psychology" by Heidi Keller, Patricia M. Greenfield in Journal of Cross-Cultural Psychology, Vol. 31 no.1, pp. 52–62. Published by Sage Publications, © 2000; Excerpt on p. 27 From "The Environment as Culture in Developmental Research" by Charles M. Super, Sara Harkness in Measuring Environment Across the Life Span: Emerging Methods and Concepts by Sarah L. Friedman, Theodore D. Wachs. Published by American Psychological Association, © 1999; Excerpt on p. 27 From Theories of Adolescence, 6e by Rolf Muuss. Published by McGraw-Hill, © 1996; Excerpt on p. 27 From "The Environment as Culture in Developmental Research" by Charles M. Super, Sara Harkness in Measuring Environment Across the Life Span: Emerging Methods and Concepts by Sarah L. Friedman, Theodore D. Wachs. Published by American Psychological Association, © 1999; Excerpt on p. 28 From "The Ecology of Developmental Processes" by Urie Bronfenbrenner, Pamela A. Morris in Handbook of Child Psychology: Vol 1: Theoretical Models of Human Development, 5e by William Damon, (Ed) Richard M. Lerner, (Ed). Published by John Wiley & Sons Inc, © 1998

**Chapter 3** Excerpt on p. **28** From Parent-child Socialization in Diverse Cultures by Jaipaul L. Roopnarine, D. Bruce Carter (editors). Published by Ablex Publishing Corporation, © 1992; Excerpt on p. **31** From The Cultural Nature of Human Development by Barbara Rogoff. Published by Oxford University Press, © 2003; Excerpt on p. **31** From Understanding Culture's Influence on Behavior by Richard W. Brislin. Published by Harcourt Brace Jovanovich College Publishers, © 1993; Excerpt on p. **33** From Handbook of Parenting: Volume 2 Biology and Ecology of Parenting, 2e by Marc H. Bornstein. Published by Erlbaum, © 1995; Excerpt on p. **33** From Handbook of Parenting: Volume I: Children and Parenting by Marc H. Bornstein. Published by Erlbaum, © 2002; Excerpt on p. **35** From Dr. Spock's Baby and Child Care, 6e by Benjamin Spock, Michael B. Rothenberg. Published by Pocket Books, © 1992; Excerpt on p. **35** From Dr. Spock's Baby and Child Care, 6e by Benjamin Spock, Michael B. Rothenberg. Published by Pocket Books, © 1992; Excerpt on p. **36** From Growth Consequences of Low-income Nicaraguan Mothers' Theories about Feeding 1–year-olds by Patrice L Engle, Marian Zeitlin, Yadira Medrano, Lino Garcia M in Parents' Cultural Belief Systems: Their Origins, Expressions, and Consequences by Sara Harkness, Charles M. Super. Published by Guilford Press, © 1996; Excerpt on p. **38** From "Cross-cultural Psychology and the Formal Classroom" by K. Cushner in Applied Cross-Cultural Psychology by Richard W. Brislin. Published by Sage Publications, © 1990; Excerpt on p. **38** From "Cross-cultural Psychology and the Formal Classroom" by K. Cushner in Applied Cross-Cultural Psychology by Richard W. Brislin. Published by Sage Publications, © 1990; Excerpt on p. **39** From The Development of Children, 3e by Michael Cole, Sheila R. Cole. Published by W.H. Freeman, ©

1996; Excerpt on p. **40** From Female Genital Mutilation. Published by World Health Organisation, © 2010; Excerpt on p. **41** From The Development of Children, 2e by Michael Cole, Sheila R. Cole. Published by Freeman, © 1993; Excerpt on p. **44** From Parent-Child Socialization in Diverse Cultures by Jaipaul L. Roopnarine(author), D. Bruce Carter(editor). Published by Ablex Publishing Corporation, © 1992.

**Chapter 4** Excerpt on p. **46** From "Mate Preferences in 37 Cultures" by David M. Buss in Psychology and Culture by Walter J. Lonner and Roy S. Malpass. Published by Pearson Education, © 1994; Excerpt on p. **46** From The Family in Perspective, 5e, by William F. Kenkel. Published by Cap and Gown Press, © 1985; Figure 4.1 on p. **47** Love and Sex: Cross-cultural Perspectives by Elaine Hatfield and Richard L. Rapson, Copyright © 2005 by University Press of America. Reprinted by permission of Rowman & Littlefield Publishing Group; Excerpt on p. **47** From "Mate Preferences in 37 Cultures" by David M. Buss in Psychology and Culture by Walter J. Lonner and Roy S. Malpass. Published by Pearson Education, © 1994; Excerpt on p. **48** From "Mate Selection and Marriage Stability in the Maghreb" by Sabah Ayachi in Contemporary Issues in Family Studies: Global Perspectives on Partnerships, Parenting and Support in a Changing World by Angela Abela and Janet Walker. Published by Contemporary Issues in Family Studies: Global Perspectives on Partnerships, Parenting and Support in a Changing World , © 2014; Excerpt on p. **49** From Verse (4:3) Qur'an; Excerpt on p. **49** From "Sex, Science, and Social Responsibility: Cross-Cultural Research on Same-Sex Eroticism and Sexual Intolerance" by Ralph Bolton in Cross-Cultural Research, Volume 28, No: 2, pp. 134– 190, Published by SAGE Publications, © 1994; Excerpt on p. **49** From The Global Divide on Homosexuality, Published by Pew Research Center, © 2013; Excerpt on p. **50** From Nisa, the Life and Words of a !Kung Woman by Marjorie Shostak and Nisa, Published by Harvard University Press, © 1981; Excerpt on p. **51** From " Women in Thailand" in Women in Cross-cultural Perspective edited by Leonore Loeb Adler, Published by Greenwood Publishing Group, © 1991; Excerpt on p. **51** From Birth in Four Cultures: A Crosscultural Investigation of Childbirth in Yucatan, Holland, Sweden, and the United States, 4e by Brigitte Jordan, Published by Waveland Press, © 1992; Excerpt on p. **51** From Birth in four cultures: a crosscultural investigation of childbirth in Yucatan, Holland, Sweden, and the United States by Brigitte Jordan, Published by Eden Press, © 1978; Excerpt on p. **52** From Birth in four cultures: a crosscultural investigation of childbirth in Yucatan, Holland, Sweden, and the United States by Brigitte Jordan, Published by Eden Press, © 1978; Excerpt on p. **52** From The Family in Perspective, 5e, by William F. Kenkel, Published by Cap and Gown Press, © 1985; Excerpt on p. **52** From "Determinants of the transition to parenting" by C. M. Heinicke in Handbook of parenting. Volume 3, Status and social conditions of parenting by Marc H. Bornstein, Published by Lawrence Erlbaum & Associates, © 1995; Excerpt on p. **53** From "Exploring individual differences in marital change across the transition to parenthood: The role of violated expectations" by Jay Belsky in Journal of Marriage and Family, Volume 47, Issue 4, pp. 1037–1044, Published by National Council on Family Relations, © 1985; Excerpt on p. **53** From "The Transition to Parenthood: Choices and responsibilities" by J .Walker in Contemporary Issues in Family Studies: Global Perspectives on Partnerships, Parenting and Support in a Changing World, by Angela Abela and Janet Walker, Published by John Wiley & Sons Inc, © 2013;

Excerpt on p. **53** From "Parenting Infants" in Handbook of Parenting: Children and Parenting edited by Marc H. Bornstein, Published by Lawrence Erlbaum & Associates, © 1995; Excerpt on p. **53** From "Improving Positive Parenting Skills and Reducing Harsh and Abusive Parenting in Low- and Middle-Income Countries: A Systematic Review" by Wendy Knerr, Frances Gardner and Lucie Cluver in Prevention Science, Volume 14, Issue 4, pp 352–363, Published by society of prevention research, © 2013; Excerpt on p. **53** From "Developmental Origins of Parenting: Personality and Relationship Factors" by Tom Luster and Lynn Okagaki in Parenting: an Ecological Perspective, Published by Lawrence Erlbaum & Associates, © 1993; Excerpt on p. **54** From Parents' Cultural Belief Systems: Their Origins, Expressions, and Consequences by Sara Harkness, Charles M. Super, Published by Guilford Press, © 1996; Box on p. 54 "Infusing Culture into Parenting Issues: A Supplement for Psychology Instructors" from unpublished manuscript, St. Louis Community College by Vicki Ritts. Copyright © 2001 by Vicki Ritts. Reprinted by permission of Vicki Ritts; Excerpt on p. **55** From "Mothering" by K. E.Barnard and & Martell, L. K in Handbook of Parenting: Children and Parenting by Marc H. Bornstein in Handbook of Parenting: Children and Parenting, Published by Lawrence Erlbaum & Associates, © 1995; Excerpt on p. **55** From Parents' Cultural Belief Systems: Their Origins, Expressions, and Consequences by Sara Harkness, Charles M. Super, Published by Guilford Press, © 1996; Excerpt on p. **55** From "Mothering" by K. E.Barnard and & Martell, L. K in Handbook of Parenting: Children and Parenting by Marc H. Bornstein in Handbook of Parenting: Children and Parenting, Published by Lawrence Erlbaum & Associates, © 1995; Figure 4.2 on p. **55** Copyright © Alan V. Gardiner. Reprinted by permission of Alan V. Gardiner; Excerpt on p. **55** Based on Barnard, K. E., & Martell, L. K. (1995). Mothering. In M. H. Bornstein (Ed.), Handbook of parenting (Vol. 3, pp. 3–26). Mahwah, NJ: Erlbaum, © Harry Gardiner; Excerpt on p. **55** Based on Hrdy, S. (2009). Mothers and others: The evolutionary origins of mutual understanding. Cam-bridge, MA: Harvard University Press; Hrdy, S. (1999). Mother nature: Material instincts and how they shape the human species. New York: Ballantine Group, © Harry Gardiner; Excerpt on p. **56** From "The Practice of Mothering: An Introduction" by Kathleen Barlow and Bambi L. Chapin in Ethos Volume 38, Issue 4, Pp 324–338, Published by American Anthropological Association, © 2010; Excerpt on p. **56** From "From Fathers and Families" by R.D Parke in Handbook of Parenting: Volume 3: Being and Becoming a Parent, 2e, by Marc H Bornstein, Published by Lawrence Erlbaum & Associates, © 2002; Excerpt on p. **57** From "From Fathers and Families" by R.D Parke in Handbook of parenting. Volume 3, Being and becoming a parent, by Marc H Bornstein, Published by Lawrence Erlbaum & Associates, © 2002; Excerpt on p. **57** From "Parenting Teenagers" by J.Coleman in Contemporary Issues in Family Studies: Global Perspectives on Partnerships, Parenting and Support in a Changing World by Angela Abela and Janet Walker, Published by John Wiley & Sons Inc, © 2013; Excerpt on p. **58** From The Material Child: Coming of Age in Japan and America by Merry I. White, Published by Free Press, © 1993; Excerpt on p. **58** From Theories of Adolescence, 5e by Rolf E. Muuss, Published by The McGraw-Hill Companies, © 1988; Excerpt on p. **58** From Theories of Adolescence,6e by Rolf E. Muuss, Published by The McGraw-Hill Companies, © 1996; "Although the macrosystem; Excerpt on p. **58** From Theories of Adolescence,6e by Rolf E. Muuss, Published by

The McGraw-Hill Companies, © 1965; Excerpt on p. **59** From Adolescence: An Anthropological Inquiry, by Alice Schlegel and Herbert Barry, Published by Free Press, © 1991; Excerpt on p. **59** From The Material Child: Coming of Age in Japan and America by Merry I. White, Published by Free Press, © 1993; Excerpt on p. **59** From "Leaving childhood: The nature and meaning of adolescent transitional rituals" by A.Shlegel, & H.Barry in The Oxford Handbook of Human Development and Culture: An Interdisciplinary Perspective by Lene Arnett Jensen, Published by Oxford University Press, © 2015; Excerpt on p. **60** From "Parent–child relationships in adulthood and old age" by Zarit, S. H., & Eggebeen, D. J in Handbook of Parenting: Volume I: Children and Parenting by Marc H. Bornstein, Published by Lawrence Erlbaum & Associates, © 1995; Excerpt on p. **60** From "Introduction: The study of grandparenthood" by P.K Smith in Handbook of parenting Volume 3 Status and social conditions of parenting by Marc H. Bornstein, Published by Taylor & Francis, © 1995; Excerpt on p. **61** From "The Role of Offspring and In-Laws in Grandparents' Ties to Their Grandchildren" by Karen L. Fingerman in Journal of Family Issues volume 25, Issue 8 pp. 1026–1049, Published by SAGE Publications, © 2004; Excerpt on p. **61** From Contemporary Grandparenting by Arthur Kornhaber, Published by SAGE Publications, © 1995; Excerpt on p. **61** From The Material Child: Coming of Age in Japan and America by Merry I. White. Published by Free Press, © 1993; Excerpt on p. **62** From Studies in Chinese Society by Arthur P. Wolf. Published by Stanford University Press, © 1978; Excerpt on p. **62** From "The Impact of Grandparents on Children's Outcomes in China" by Toni Falbo in Marriage & Family Review, Vol.16, Issue 3–4, pp. 369–376. Published by Taylor & Francis Online, © 1991; Excerpt on p. **62** From "Chinese Families" in Parent-Child Socialization in Diverse Cultures by Jaipaul L. Roopnarine. Published by Ablex Publishing Corporation, © 1992; Excerpt on p. **63** From Contemporary Grand parenting by Arthur Kornhaber. Published by Sage Publications, © 1996; Box 4.2 on p. 63 "Culture and Aging" from unpublished manuscript, St. Louis Community College by Vicki Ritts. Copyright © 2001 by Vicki Ritts. Reprinted by permission of Vicki Ritts.

**Chapter 5** Excerpt on p. **69** From "From Cross-cultural tests of Piaget's theory" by P. R Dasen and A.Heron in Handbook of cross-cultural psychology, 4e by Harry Charalambos Triandis, Published by Pearson Education, © 1981; Excerpt on p. **69** From Cross-cultural child development: a view from the planet Earth by Emmy E. Werner, Published by Brooks Cole Publishing Co, © 1979; Excerpt on p. **70** From " Fathers' role in children's language development" by Tamis-LeMonda, C. S., Baumwell, L. Cabrera in Handbook of Father Involvement: Multidisciplinary Perspectives, 2e, by Natasha J. Cabrera and Catherine S.Tamis-LeMonda, Published by Routledge Ltd, © 2014; Excerpt on p. **71** From "Bilingual context for language development"in Talking to Adults: The Contribution of Multiparty Discourse to Language Acquisition, edited by Shoshana Blum-Kulka and Catherine E. Snow , Published by Psychology Press & Routledge, © 2002; Table 5.1 on p. **72** Based on material from The Study of SecondLanguage Acquisition by R. Ellis, 1994. Oxford, U.K.: Oxford University Press, © Harry Gardiner; Excerpt on p. **73** From "The validity of "cultural differences explanations" for cross-cultural variation in the rate of Piagetian cognitive development" by R. M. Nyiti in Cultural Perspectives on Child Development by Daniel A. Wagner and Harold William Stevenson, Published by W.H. Freeman

& Company Publisher, © 1982; Excerpt on p. **76** From The Development of Children, 3e by Michael Cole and Sheila Cole, Published by W.H. Freeman & Company Publishers, © 1996; Excerpt on p. **76** From Cross-cultural child development: a view from the planet Earth by Emmy E. Werner, Published by Brooks Cole Publishing Co, © 1979; Excerpt on p. **76** From "The socialization of cognition" edited by James W. Stigler, Richard A. Schweder and Gilbert Herdt in Cultural Psychology: Essays on Comparative Human Development, Published by Cambridge University Press, © 1990; Excerpt on p. **79** From "Wisdom as expert knowledge system" by Monika Ardelt in Human Development, Volume 47, Issue 5, pp. 257–285, Published by University of Florida, © 2004.

**Chapter 6** Excerpt on p. **84** From "Within-Culture Complexities: Multifaceted and Interrelated Autonomy And Connectedness Characteristics In Late Adolescent Selves" by Catherine Raeff in New Directions for Child and Adolescent Development Volume 2004, Issue 104, pp: 61–78. Published by John Wiley and Sons, © 2004; Excerpt on p. **84** From "Individuals in Relation to Others: Independence and Interdependence in a Kindergarten Classroom" by Catherine Raeff in Ethos, Vol. 34, No. 4, pp. 521–557. Published by American Anthropological Association, © 2006; Excerpt on p. **84** From "Independence and Interdependence in Children's Developmental Experiences" by Catherine Raeff in Child Development Perspectives, Vol 4, Issue 1, pp: 31–36. Published by Society for Research in Child Development, © 2010; Box 6.1 on p. **84** "Personality, the Self, and Culture" from unpublished manuscript, St. Louis Community College by Vicki Ritts. Copyright © 2001 by Vicki Ritts. Reprinted by permission of Vicki Ritts; Excerpt on p. **86** From "Temperament" from The Encyclopedia of Cross-Cultural Psychology by Kenneth D. Keith (Editor). Published by Wiley-Blackwell, © 2013; Excerpt on p. **87** From "Temperament" from The Encyclopedia of Cross-Cultural Psychology by Kenneth D. Keith (Editor). Published by Wiley-Blackwell, © 2013; Excerpt on p. **90** From "Adolescence" by Judith Gibbons from The Encyclopedia of Cross-Cultural Psychology by Kenneth D. Keith (Editor). Published by Wiley-Blackwell, © 2013; Excerpt on p. **90** From "Navigating Local and Global Worlds: Opportunities and Risks for Adolescent Cultural Identity Development" by Lene Arnett Jensen in Psychological Studies, Vol 56, Issue 1, pp 62–70. Published by Springer International Publishing, © 2011; Excerpt on p. **91** From Racial Identification and Preference in Negro Children by Kenneth B. Clark, Mamie P. Clark. Published by Henry Holt and Company, © 1947; Excerpt on p. **92** Based on Ahadi & Rothbart, 1994; McCrae & Costa, 1990; McCrae & Costa, 2003; McCrae & John, 1992, © Harry Gardiner; Excerpt on p. **93** From "Evaluating Five Factor Theory and Social Investment Perspectives on Personality Trait Development" in Journal of Research in Personality, Volume 39, Issue 1, pp: 166–184. Published by Elsevier, © 2005; Excerpt on p. **93** From "Personality Change in Old Age" in Current Opinion in Psychiatry, Volume 20, Issue 1, pp: 62–66. Published by Lippincott Williams & Wilkins, Inc., © 2007; Excerpt on p. **94** From "Models of the Aging Self" by Joel R. Sneed, Susan Krauss Whitbourne in Journal of Social Issues, Volume 61, Issue 2, pp: 375–388. Published by John Wiley & Sons, © 2005.

**Chapter 7** Excerpt on p. **96** From "Attachment" by Pena-Shaff in The Encyclopedia of Cross-Cultural Psychology by Kenneth D. Keith (Editor). Published by Wiley-Blackwel, Copyright © 2013; Excerpt on p. **97** From "Attachment" by Pena-Shaff in The Encyclopedia of Cross-Cultural Psychology by Kenneth D. Keith (Editor). Published by Wiley-Blackwel, © 2013; Excerpt on p. **98** From Daughters of the Earth: The Lives and Legends of American Indian Women by Carolyn J. Niethammer. Published by Macmillan, © 1977; Excerpt on p. **99** From "Children in Difficult Circumstances: Familial Correlates of Advantage While at Risk" by N. Sharma, B. Sharma in Culture, Socialization and Human Development: Theory, Research, and Applications in India by T. S. Saraswati. Published by Sage Publications, © 1999; Excerpt on p. **103** From "Moral Development" by Takashi Naito in The Encyclopedia of Cross-Cultural Psychology, Volume 3, Pages 891–897. Published by Wiley-Blackwell Publishing Ltd., © 2013; Table 7.1 on p. **102** Harry Gardiner, Lives Across Cultures: Cross-Cultural Human Development, 6e, 9780134629445, © 2018; Figure 7.1 on p. **103** Based on material from "Socialization and Cognitive moral Influences on Justice Rule Preferences: The Case of Indian Culture" by L. Krishman in Culture, Socialization and Human Development: Theory, Research, and Applications in India, T. S. Saraswathi (Ed.), 1999. Thousand Oaks, CA: Sage Publications, © Harry Gardiner; Excerpt on p. **103** From Psychological Anthropology: An Introduction to Human Nature and Cultural Differences by Erika Bourguignon. Published by Holt/Rinehart and Winston, © 1979; Excerpt on p. **103** From Village in the Vaucluse, 3e by Laurence William Wylie. Published by Harvard University Press, © 1974; Excerpt on p. **104** From Psychological Anthropology: An Introduction to Human Nature and Cultural Differences by Erika Bourguignon. Published by Holt/Rinehart and Winston, © 1979; Excerpt on p. **104** From "Aggression" by Jennifer Zwolinski in The Encyclopedia of Cross-Cultural Psychology by Kenneth D. Keith. Published by Wiley-Blackwell, © 2013; Excerpt on p. **104** From Yanomamo 5e by Napoleon A. Chagnon. Published by Holt Rinehart and Winston, © 1997; Excerpt on p. **105** From "Peer Relationships" by Brown, J. R.., Greve, K., and DeGuzman, M. R in The Encyclopedia of Cross-Cultural Psychology by Kenneth D. Keith. Published by Wiley-Blackwell, © 2013; Excerpt on p. **106** From "Brother to Brother: African American Modes of Relating Among Men" by George W. Roberts in Journal of Black Studies, Vol. 24, No. 4, pp. 379–390. Published by Sage Publications, © 1994.

**Chapter 8** Excerpt on p. **112** From "Gender" in The Encyclopedia of Cross-cultural Psychology by Kenneth D. Keith. Published by Wiley-Blackwell Publishing, © 2013; Figure 8.1 on p. **114** The thoughts of youth: An international perspective on adolescents' ideal persons by J. L. Gibbons and G. A. Stiles. Copyright © 2004 by Information Age Publishing. Reprinted by permission of Judith L. Gibbons; Table 8.1 on p. **115** World FactBook 2009. Published by CIA; Box 8.1 on p. **118** "Culture and Gender" from unpublished manuscript, St. Louis Community College by Vicki Ritts. Copyright © 2001 by Vicki Ritts. Reprinted by permission of Vicki Ritts; Excerpt on p. **120** From Readings on the Development of Children by Mary Gauvain and Michael Cole. Published by Worth Publishers, © 2005; Excerpt on p. **125** From "Divorce Culture and Marital Gender Equality. A Cross-National Study" by Carrie Yodanis in Gender and Society, Volume No 19, Issue No 5, pp. 644–659. Published by Sage Publications, © 2005.

**Chapter 9** Excerpt on p. **125** From Diagnostic and Statistical Manual of Mental Disorders, 5e. Published by American Psychiatric Association, © 2013; Box 9.1 on p. **130** "Infusing Culture into Parenting Issues: A Supplement for Psychology

Instructors" from unpublished manuscript, St. Louis Community College by Vicki Ritts. Copyright © 2001 by Vicki Ritts. Reprinted by permission of Vicki Ritts; Excerpt on p. **131** From "Medical Diagnosis and Treatment Across Cultures" by W. J. Lonner and R. Malpass in Psychology and Culture by Lisa Beardsley. Published by, © 1994; Excerpt on p. **131** From Applied Cross-Cultural Psychology edited by Richard W. Brislin. Published by SAGE Publications, © 1990; Box 9.2 on p. **132** Harry Gardiner, Lives Across Cultures: Cross-Cultural Human Development, 6e, 9780134629445, © 2018; Excerpt on p. **135** From "Coping and Coping Styles" by R.Chao and C. Wang in The Encyclopedia of Cross-cultural Psychology: E - O, Volume 2 edited by Kenneth D. Keith. Published by Wiley-Blackwell Publishing, © 2013; Excerpt on p. **136** From The Hurried Child: Growing Up Too Fast Too Soon by David Elkind. Published by Pearson Education, © 1988; Excerpt on p. **137** From "Eating Disorders" by R L Miller and R M Broadwell in The Encyclopedia of Cross-cultural Psychology edited by Kenneth D. Keith. Published by Wiley-Blackwell Publishing, © 2013; Excerpt on p. **139** From "Pathological and Clinical Aspects" by J.G Draguns in Cross-Cultural Topics in Psychology by Leonore Loeb Adler and Uwe Peter Gielen. Published by Greenwood Publishing Group Inc, © 1994; Excerpt on p. **140** From "Acculturation" by A,M.T Nguyen in The Encyclopedia of Cross-Cultural Psychology edited by Kenneth D. Keith. Published by Wiley-Blackwell Publishing, © 2013; Excerpt on p. **142** From "Stress and Caring for Elderly Relatives: Interpretations and Coping Strategies in an American Indian and White" by Catherine Strong in The Gerontologist Volume 24, Issue 3, pp. 251–256. Published by The Gerontological Society of America, © 1984.

**Chapter 10** Excerpt on p. **147** From "Relations between value orientation, childrearing goals, and parenting: A comparison of German and South Korean mothers" by B. Schwarz, E.Schafermeier and G.Trommsdorff in Culture and Human Development: The Importance of Cross-Cultural Research for the Social Sciences edited by Wolfgang Friedlmeier, Pradeep Chakkarath and Beate Schwarz. Published by Psychology Press, © 2005; Excerpt on p. **148** From Language and cognition,1e by Aleksandr Romanovich Luria. Published by V.H. Winston & Son, © 1982; Excerpt on p. **150** From "Contributions of cross-cultural psychology to research and interventions in education and health" by Sara Harkness and Constance H. Keefer in Journal of cross-cultural psychology, Volume 31, Issue 1, pp. 92–109. Published by SAGE Publications, © 2000; Excerpt on p. **151** From Parental Socialization and Children's Acquisition of Values by J.E Grusec in Handbook of parenting, Volume 5: Practical Issues in Parenting, 2e edited by Marc H. Bornstein. Published by Psychology Press & Routledge, © 2005; Excerpt on p. **151** From "Parental socialization and children's acquisition of values" by J.E Grusec in Handbook of parenting Volume 5,2e edited by Marc H. Bornstein. Published by Taylor & Francis, © 2002; Excerpt on p. **152** From "Parenting and contemporary reproductive technologies" by Golombok and Susan in Handbook of parenting Volume 3, 2e. Published by Lawrence Erlbaum & Associates, © 2002; Excerpt on p. **153** From Fathers in Cultural Context by David W. Shwalb, Barbara J. Shwalb and Michael E. Lamb. Published by Routledge Ltd, © 2013; Excerpt on p. **153** From "Fatherhood in Brazil, Bangladesh, Russia, Japan, and Australia" by David W. Shwalb and Barbara J. Shwalb in Online Readings in Psychology and Culture, Volume 6, Issue 3. Published by, © 2014; Excerpt on p. **154** From "Child temperament and parenting" by Samuel P.

Putnam, Mary K. Rothbart and Ann V. Sanson in Handbook of parenting, Volume 1,2e.Published by Lawrence Erlbaum & Associates, © 2000; Excerpt on p. **155** From Social psychology across cultures,2e By Peter B. Smith and Michael Harris Bond, Published by Pearson Education, © 1999; Excerpt on p. **155** From "From A secure base from which to explore the environment" by Everett Waters and E. Mark Cummings in Child Development, Volume 71, Issue-1, pp. 164–172, Published by Society for Research in Child Development, © 2000; Excerpt on p. **155** From "From Attachment and Culture: Bridging Relativism and Universalism" by F.Rothbaum and G. Morelli in Culture and Human Development: The Importance of Cross-Cultural Research for the Social Sciences edited by Wolfgang Friedlmeier, Pradeep Chakkarath and Beate Schwarz. Published by Psychology Press & Routledge, © 2005; Excerpt on p. **155** From Different Faces of Attachment: Cultural Variations on a Universal Human Need by Hiltrud Otto and Heidi Keller, Published by Cambridge University Press, © 2014; Excerpt on p. **155** From "How Parents can Maximize Children's Cognitive Abilities" by W.M Williams and R.J Sternberg in Handbook of Parenting: Volume 5: Practical Issues in Parenting, 2e. Published by Psychology Press & Routledge, © 2005; Excerpt on p. **156** From "Cultural influences on health" by R. A. R. Gurung in Cross-Cultural Psychology: Contemporary Themes and Perspectives edited by Kenneth D. Keith, Published by John Wiley & Sons Inc, © 2011; Excerpt on p. **156** From Lives Across Cultures: Cross-cultural Human Development, 5e, by Harry W. Gardiner and Corinne Kosmitzki. Published by Pearson Education, © 2011.

## Photo Credits

**Chapter 1** p. 2 © Harry Gardiner; p. 7 Colaimages/Alamy Stock Photo; p. 8 Alberto Arzoz/Axiom/Design Pics Inc/Alamy Stock Photo.

**Chapter 2** p. 14 © Harry Gardiner.

**Chapter 3** p. 34 World History Archive/Alamy Stock Photo; p. 34 Paylessimages/Fotolia; p. 35 © Harry Gardiner ; p. 37 © Joe Oppedisano.

**Chapter 4** p. 50 © Harry Gardiner; p. 54 Friedrich von Hörsten/Alamy Stock Photo; p. 62 Monkey Business Images/Shutterstock; p. 63 © Harry Gardiner.

**Chapter 5** p. 68 © Harry Gardiner; p. 71 © Harry Gardiner; p. 73 J Marshall - Tribaleye Images/Alamy Stock Photo; p. 74 Sunabesyou/Fotolia; p. 78 Novastock/Stock Connection Blue/Alamy Stock Photo.

**Chapter 6** p. 86 Amble Design/Shutterstock; p. 89 Blue Jean Images/Alamy Stock Photo; p. 90 Creatista/Shutterstock.

**Chapter 7** p. 98 Kovgabor/Shutterstock; p. 109 J. Henning Buchholz/Shutterstock.

**Chapter 8** p. 117 Poznyakov/Shutterstock; p. 117 Westend61 GmbH/Alamy Stock Photo; p. 123 Ian Trower/Alamy Stock Photo.

**Chapter 9** p. 133 Corporation/Alamy Stock Photo; p. 135 Florian Kopp/imageBROKER/Alamy Stock Photo; p. 136 Oote Boe 3/Alamy Stock Photo; p. 138 Kuttig - People/Alamy Stock Photo.

**Chapter 10** p. 147 Tati Nova photo Mexico/953605/Shutterstock.

# Name Index

## A

Abdulcadira, J., 40
Abela, A., 4, 48
Adams, E., 16
Adelson, J., 58
Aerts, E., 148
Ahadi, S. A., 92
Ahuja, N., 130
Ainsworth, M. D. S., 97
Akande, A., 89
Albaum, G., 108
Aldous, J., 56
Ali, A., 137
Allik, J., 92
Almond, D., 116
Anderson, J. A., 125
Andersson, G., 49
Angleitner, A., 92
Anker, M., 5, 139
Anstey, K. J., 78
Antonucci, T. C., 110
Anwo, J., 40
Archer, J., 113
Archetti, E. P., 109
Ardelt, M., 79
Arnett, J. J., 58, 106
Asendorpf, J. B., 93
Ashwin, E., 113
Assmar, E., 7
Atkin, A., 58
Atkinson, P., 26
Atkinson, R., 90
Auyeung, B., 113
Ayachi, S., 48
Azhar, M. Z., 129
Azuma, H., 3

## B

Bailey, R. C., 98
Baiyewu, O., 93
Baltes, P. B., 78, 79, 80
Bandura, A., 89
Banks, C. G., 137
Barbaranelli C., 89
Barlow, K., 56
Barnard, K. E., 55
Baron-Cohen, S., 113
Barrett, D. E., 133
Barry, H., 59
Barry, O., 19
Barton, B. A., 134
Baskin, D., 105
Basseti, B., 67, 68
Bates, J. E., 154
Baumwell, L., 70
Beach, L. R., 26

Beardsley, L. M., 131
Beatty, S. E., 108
Becker. G., 143
Beiser, M., 107
Belsky, J., 53
Ben-Porath, Y. S., 131
Bergen, D., 21
Berry, J. W., 2, 4, 5, 25, 26, 48, 69,
     73, 105, 140, 151
Bertrand, J. T., 121
Best, D. L., 116, 155
Bethon, G., 76
Bharti, B., 35
Bialystok, E., 71
Birdsong, D., 71
Bjarnason, T., 56
Blehar, M., 97
Blinn Pike, L., 106
Bochner, S., 87
Boehnke, K., 102
Bogg, T., 93
Bolton, R., 49
Bond, M. H., 150, 154
Bond, T. G., 76
Bono, J. E., 89
Borgatti, S. P., 27
Bornstein, M. H., 33, 53, 70
Borovoy, A., 137
Boski, P., 150
Bouchard, T. J., 83
Bourguignon, E., 103
Bradley, K., 124
Braine, M. D. S., 73
Brennan, A. L., 58
Breugelmans, S. M., 5
Brislin, R., 131
Broadwell, R. M., 136, 137
Bronfenbrenner, U., 5, 7, 13, 14, 15,
     16, 22, 28, 69
Brooks, P. J., 73
Bross, F., 68
Brouwers, S. A., 76
Brower, A. M., 150
Brown, B. B., 27, 106
Brown, J. R., 105
Buchtel, E. E., 77
Budwig, N., 68
Bulbeck, C., 125
Bushong, L. J., 42
Buss, D. M., 46, 47, 113
Butcher, J. N., 131

## C

Cabrera, N. J., 70
Calabrese, R. L., 107
Caldwell, M. L., 37

Calhoun, D. W., 108
Campbell, J., 52
Cantor, N., 150
Caprara, G. V., 89
Caravolas, M., 74
Carey, G., 9
Carr, E. R., 55, 57
Carraher, D. W., 39
Carter, D. B., 30, 44
Cassidy, J., 155
Cattell, R. B., 77, 80
Chadda, R. K., 130
Chagnon, N. A., 104
Chan, H., 60, 61
Chan, M. C. H., 62
Chao, R., 129, 135
Chapin, B. L., 56
Chapman, B., 9
Charles, M., 124
Chasiotis, A., 5
Chavajay, P., 69, 76
Cheema, A. K., 143
Chen, C., 62, 107
Chen, H.-H., 55, 57
Chen, J.-L., 135
Chen, S., 114
Cheng, S., 99
Chess, S., 86
Cheung, K., 150
Chisholm, J. S., 33
Chiu, M. L., 39
Christensen, K., 9
Chua, A., 56
Chun, K. M., 140
Clark, K. B., 91
Clark, M. P., 91
Coffey-Corina, S., 71
Cohan, M., 56
Cole, M., 25, 39, 41, 76, 103,
     120, 134
Cole, S. R., 39, 41, 76, 103, 134
Coleman, J., 57, 58
Colin, V. L., 36
Collinsworth, P., 61
Comer, J., 60
Conboy, B. T., 71
Connolly, J., 104
Cook, P., 131
Cook, V., 67, 68
Cook-Flannagan, C., 150
Cooley, C. H., 7
Cooper, B. B., 148
Cooper, J. E., 5, 139
Corman, H. H., 69
Correa-Chavez, M., 31
Corsaro, W. A., 99, 100

# Subject Index